Alan Strachan is a theatre director. In London's West End he has directed over thirty productions, and has also worked in regional theatre as well as in Amsterdam, Copenhagen, Dublin and New York often with leading actors and on plays ranging from Shakespeare, Shaw and Tennessee Williams to Alan Ayckbourn and Tom Stoppard. He is the author of *Secret Dreams: A Biography of Michael Redgrave* (2004) and, with Michael Codron, *Putting It On: The West End Theatre of Michael Codron* (2010).

ALAN STRACHAN

DARK STAR

A BIOGRAPHY OF
VIVIEN LEIGH

I.B. TAURIS

LONDON · NEW YORK

Published in 2019 by
I.B.Tauris & Co. Ltd
Reprinted by Bloomsbury Academic 2019
London • New York
www.ibtauris.com

ISBN: 978 1 78831 208 0
eISBN: 978 1 78672 456 4
ePDF: 978 1 78673 456 3

A full CIP record for this book is available from the British Library
A full CIP record is available from the Library of Congress

Library of Congress Catalog Card Number: available

Typeset in Stone Serif by OKS Prepress Services, Chennai, India
Printed and bound by CPI Group (UK) Ltd, Croydon, CR0 4YY

For Jennifer – again

A Dark Star is shadowed, often detectable by its gravitational effect on other bodies. It is often a component of a binary star and can cause the brightness of its visible partner to vary periodically.

Contents

List of Plates

Plate 1 Vivien Leigh as a child with her mother, c.1922 (Courtesy of the Vivien Leigh Circle).

Plate 2 *In the Mask of Virtue's* eighteenth century costume, 1935 (© Hulton-Deutsch Collection/CORBIS/Corbis via Getty Images).

Plate 3 Vivien Leigh and Laurence Olivier in *Fire Over England*, 1937 (© Everett Collection Inc / Alamy Stock Photo).

Plate 4 Angus McBean surrealising Vivien Leigh as Aurora, 1938 (Angus McBean Collection, MS Thr 581 (olvwork662704), Houghton Library, Harvard University).

Plate 5 Vivien Leigh as Aurora, 1938 (Angus McBean Collection, MS Thr 581 (olvwork656184) Houghton Library, Harvard University).

Plate 6 Scarlett O'Hara and Rhett Butler with Victor Fleming on the set of *Gone With the Wind*, 1939 (© Entertainment Pictures / Alamy Stock Photo).

Plate 7 Vivien Leigh at the Oscars with David O. Selznick (© Everett Collection Inc / Alamy Stock Photo).

Plate 8 Vivien Leigh and Laurence Olivier as Romeo and Juliet from *The Sketch*, 1940 (copyright holder unknown).

Plate 9 Sabina in *The Skin of Our Teeth*, 1945 (copyright holder unknown).

Plate 10 Kieron Moore and Vivien Leigh in *Anna Karenina*, 1948 (© Photo 12 / Alamy Stock Photo).

Plate 11 Watercolour of Vivien with cat by Roger Furse (© Estate of Roger Furse).

Plate 12 Laurence Olivier and Vivien Leigh leaving Australia, 1948 (© Alamy Stock Photo).

Plate 13 Vivien Leigh, Peter Finch and Laurence Olivier in Australia (© National Film and Sound Archive, Australia, ID 633614).

Plate 14 Durham Cottage painted by Felix Kelly (© Estate of Felix Kelly).

Plate 15 Notley Abbey painted by John Piper (© The Piper Estate / DACS 2018).

Plate 16 The Library at Notley (copyright holder unknown).

Plate 17 Vivien Leigh and Laurence Olivier relaxing at Notley (© Kendra Bean Collection).

Plate 18 Vivien Leigh, Leigh Holman, Ernest Hartley, Tarquin, Suzanne, and Olivier's legs (from right) at Notley (© Kendra Bean Collection).

Plate 19 Shakespeare's *Antony and Cleopatra*, 1951 (Angus McBean Collection, MS Thr 581 (olvwork545487) Houghton Library, Harvard University).

Plate 20 Kenneth Tynan and Elaine Dundy at their wedding (© Trinity Mirror / Mirrorpix / Alamy Stock Photo).

Plate 21 Vivien Leigh with Tennessee Williams and Elia Kazan in *A Streetcar Named Desire*, 1951 (copyright holder unknown).

Plate 22 Vivien Leigh and Laurence Olivier in *Macbeth*, 1955 (Angus McBean Collection, MS Thr 581 (olvwork553060) Houghton Library, Harvard University).

Plate 23 Vivien Leigh and Keith Michell in *Twelfth Night* (Angus McBean Collection, MS Thr 581 (olvwork567047) Houghton Library, Harvard University).

Plate 24 Yves Saint-Laurent sketch of Dior's design for Vivien Leigh in *Duel of Angels*, 1958 (Image recreated with the kind permission of the Actors' Benevolent Fund (Reg. Charity No. 206524)).

Acknowledgements

I never met Vivien Leigh although I worked with several of her close colleagues in the theatre who, whenever the conversation turned to other actors – during breaks in rehearsal or at other times – often spoke vividly of her. They included Margaret "Percy" Harris, Michael Redgrave, Rachel Kempson, Alec Guinness, Margaret Leighton, David Dodimead, Derek Nimmo and Dame Dorothy Tutin and I remain grateful to all of them.

I owe a great debt to several institutions and their unfailingly helpful staffs: The Victoria and Albert Museum: by far the major source of previously unseen material for this book was the Vivien Leigh Archive held in the Theatre and Performance Collections. Acquired in 2013, this has been meticulously catalogued; it contains an enormous number of letters including Olivier's to Vivien Leigh during *Gone With the Wind* filming, during *Henry V* location work and on the Old Vic's European tour of 1946 as well as a wide range of correspondence with friends, colleagues and fans. It also includes most of Vivien Leigh's diaries for the years 1930 to 1967, the Notley Visitors' Book and a rich collection of photographic and related material.

The Laurence Olivier Archive: held at the British Library, this includes letters from Vivien Leigh and many others, scripts, film treatments and a huge amount of related material including tape recordings of interviews and correspondence.

The British Film Institute (BFI): this houses John Merivale's papers, given to the BFI by his widow Dinah Sheridan. It includes the letters from Vivien Leigh during *Tovarich* rehearsals and try-out and her letters from Nepal and India.

The Noël Coward Archive: includes letters to Coward from Vivien Leigh.

Others who provided assistance, gratefully acknowledged, include:

Mark Amory, Kendra Bean, Alan Brodie, Anton Burge, Sir Michael Codron, Peter Docherty, the late David Dodimead, Kate Dorney, Dr Peter Fraser, Heywood Hill Ltd, Dame Penelope Keith, Keith Lodwick, Miller Lide, the late Alec McCowen, Patricia Macnaughton, Richard Mangan, Bruce Montague, Tarquin Olivier, Sotheby's Ltd, Hugo Vickers, Amanda Waring.

Permission to quote from copyright material is gratefully acknowledged: From Sir Cecil Beaton: (c) The Literary Executors of the late Sir Cecil Beaton, 2018; From Sir Noël Coward: quotation from *The Collected Short Stories*, *The Letters of Noël Coward* (ed. Barry Day) and *The Noël Coward Diaries* (ed. Sheridan Morley and Graham Payn) by permission of N.C.Aventales AG; From Sir John Gielgud: with the kind permission of the Executors of the Sir John Gielgud Charitable Trust; From John Merivale: by kind permission of the British Film Institute.

I am extremely grateful to both Joanna Godfrey and Sophie Campbell of I.B.Tauris, always supportive, and to Michael Alcock and Andrew Hewson of Johnson and Alcock Ltd, my literary agents, without whose efforts this book might not have been written.

Also I owe heartfelt thanks to Sheilagh Dunk, who somehow produced flawlessly typed pages from a manuscript often less than easy to decipher.

Prologue

Shortly before Christmas 1938 the Hollywood mogul David O. Selznick, facing the imminent principal shooting of the greatest gamble of his career – the film of *Gone With the Wind*, Margaret Mitchell's worldwide bestseller of the American Civil War – after a two-year highly publicised search, had still not cast the most sought-after leading role in cinema history, Scarlett O'Hara. Since his early days in silent movies and through more recent adaptations of major classics (Greta Garbo in *Anna Karenina* and Ronald Colman in *A Tale of Two Cities*) Selznick had stressed the importance of casting, especially of female roles. He once wrote to his business partner John ("Jock") Hay Whitney:

> Sometimes you can miscast a part and get away with it: but there are certain stories where miscasting of the girl will mean not simply that the role is badly played but that the whole story doesn't come off.

He had secured the public's choice of Clark Gable as Mitchell's raffish heart-throb Rhett Butler alongside Olivia de Havilland as Scarlett's cousin Melanie, and Leslie Howard as the heroine's more conventional love interest, Ashley Wilkes, but he was uncomfortably aware that a miscast Scarlett could ruin all his ambitions and plans. He had considered and rejected most of the established star actresses suggested – Bette Davis, Tallulah Bankhead, Katharine Hepburn included – and still had in reserve three well-known possibles, of whom Paulette Goddard led the field, but from the outset Selznick had wanted to have "a new girl" as Scarlett; the nationwide search for an unknown – over 1,500 seen, many screen-tested – had of course provided an avalanche of free advance publicity but it had always for Selznick been more than a stunt. Although he was a voracious reader and hired top scriptwriters (the dramatist Sidney Howard for *Gone With the Wind*), Selznick, like many who cut their teeth in silents, thought in images, knowing how potent the initial perception of a character is, especially one originally from a famous book, which could dictate an audience's reaction. From his first reading of the novel, he had his Scarlett vivid in his mind and with the first scenes with his cast scheduled for January 1939 he was frustrated, contemplating what he saw as "the greatest failure of my entire career", expressed in one of his notorious lengthy memos to the film's director, George Cukor:

> I am still hoping against hope … If we finally wind up with any of the stars we are testing we must regard ourselves as absolute failures at digging up talent, as going against the most violently expressed wish for a new personality in an important role in the history of American stage or screen.

One month after this *cri de coeur*, the role was cast in an episode apposite for a film of epic sweep and bold emotions and as colourful as anything in Mitchell's book or out of the earlier Selznick film, *A Star is Born*. Selznick's image of Scarlett was taken directly from the novel's description of this headstrong survivor, the iconic Southern belle with an "arresting face", "pale green eyes without a touch of hazel" and "magnolia-white skin". The chosen Scarlett met these criteria; some described her as intrepid, occasionally wilful like Scarlett, and although she had achieved some success in England on stage and screen, she was certainly "a new girl" in America. However, she was no Southern belle (in her one previous film requiring an accent, *St Martin's Lane*, her cockney barely passes muster). She was not even American, let alone "of French and Irish descent".

Selznick needed to clear the backlot at Culver City for building the principal sets for *Gone With the Wind* – including the plantation house of the O'Hara clan, Tara – and so scheduled for December the incineration of old movie-sets for the filming of the burning of Atlanta by General Sherman's troops. Towards the end of the shoot, late in the evening, Selznick met for the first time the British actress Vivien Leigh, brought to the filming by Selznick's agent-brother Myron along with his client, a more established British actor, Laurence Olivier. Vivien had arrived the previous day, ostensibly to see her lover Olivier. Almost instantly Selznick and Cukor were convinced that she could be their Scarlett.

Vivien was then 25, married with a daughter, and Olivier, seven years her senior, was married with a son. They had been lovers for two years and had been miserable apart recently while Olivier filmed *Wuthering Heights* in Hollywood. Selznick later said of their meeting: "I'll never recover from that first look." He was a producer-*auteur* before the concept of film "authorship" had been invented, a classic control-freak. Cukor too, who had said prior to the long "search for Scarlett" that "The girl I select must be possessed of the devil and charged with electricity", was immediately intrigued by Vivien but in effect the decision would be Selznick's ("Great films are made in their every detail according to the vision of one man").

There was, however, one crucial difference between the actress and Mitchell's heroine, encapsulated in the opening five words of her novel: "Scarlett O'Hara was not beautiful."

Vivien Leigh was very beautiful indeed. She died in 1967, late on a Friday evening and so too late for Saturday's newspaper deadlines. On Sunday the normally sober *Observer* bannered the news on its front page above seven contrasted photographs: "Vivien Leigh, the Greatest Beauty of her Time, Dead at 53." On Monday, newspapers worldwide heavily featured the collapse of her fabled marriage to Olivier in 1960 and her long struggle with manic depression (before Bipolar Disorder was the preferred term) alongside the stress on her looks, often barely mentioning a career of striking range while concentrating essentially on her two Oscar-winning performances – Scarlett and Blanche Du Bois in *A Streetcar Named Desire*.

Other great beauties of her day – society's Lady Diana Cooper, Gladys Cooper (both her friends), Ava Gardner, Greta Garbo – could not match her range and offered no competition on stage. Truly great beauties – Lily Elsie, Maxine Elliott, Lillie Langtry, Elizabeth Taylor – rarely make great stage performers, largely because they do not have to be. One of the great theatre names of the twentieth century, Edith Evans, off stage unremarkable but with an alchemical ability to assume radiance on stage, used to say that beauty was "the primitive passport" to success in the theatre.

Vivien's first major success in England was due, as she acknowledged, to that passport. But no career enduring over three decades, covering work on stage in Shakespeare, Shaw, Chekhov, Tennessee Williams, Jean Giraudoux, Noël Coward, Terence Rattigan and a Broadway musical – a range wider than many actresses of her generation – alongside an outstanding screen career, can be sustained solely on looks. She had luck in her career, as she never denied, but bad luck haunted her too and it seems, always, that she constantly had to attempt to escape various shadows.

Not the least of them was that beauty. The photographer Florence Entwistle ("Vivienne") claimed that she was "the most beautiful woman in Britain, if not the world", echoed by her favourite photographer, Angus McBean – "She was the most beautiful woman I ever photographed and remained so, I believe, up until the haunting last sitting just before her death", while to David Niven she was simply "the most beautiful woman I ever saw outside an art gallery". Appraisals of her beauty were intriguingly varied. The Hungarian-born movie producer Alexander Korda could not categorise her; he liked to contract "types" such as the "exotic", a "beetch" or an "English rose" and turned Vivien down in 1935 accordingly, only becoming interested when she scored a major stage success – she was just not a "type". She could, if required, project a dewy ingénue innocence but had an underlying quality of something more dangerous, less "English rose". It was not difficult for her to suggest a more exotic allure; once, when seeing a McBean photograph of her, strikingly shadowed and with a spray of camellias over one ear, Olivier commented that she could pass for a "Javanese tart". In an era when the ideal of home-grown beauty was an Anglo-Saxon demure delicacy Vivien was not immediately classifiable or fixed in her time, as fellow actress Gladys Cooper noted ("I considered her the most beautiful woman of her age and to me her beauty was not of any period").

In her centenary year (2013), critic Laura Thompson wrote perceptively that behind the crystalline perfection "she was always more interesting than the pretty-girl roles she was given early on ... her smile had a quality of perverse intrigue".

Many people blessed by beauty simply take it for granted, like having red hair or big feet; Vivien always shrugged off compliments and was wearied by critics' constant mentions of her beauty, turning it into Byron's "fatal gift". The "primitive passport" which gave her initial theatre fame led at once to a British screen career and it was her looks which journalists stressed ("the loveliest sight on the British screen so far") and struggled to describe:

> The face a triangle, gleaming palely in the frame of feathery dark hair growing upwards, faun-like. The bone-structure will make artists rush to set it down. But the tilted nose, the tender curve of the mouth, deep eyes lifted at the corners, dark in distance, revealing themselves as grey-green lamps, obviously floodlit, her young, touching smile, will make the public rush to set the face down in their memories.

The art historian and connoisseur of beauty, Kenneth Clark, was another who understood that the bones and planes of her face were the key to her looks but he always felt that her outward appearance was complemented by the inner quality of her style. His friend, international art expert Bernard Berenson knew Vivien in his old age and agreed with Clark, addressing her as "Dearest of beautiful and life-enhancing women". Without that interior quality – "her beauty was somehow both inside and outside" according to theatre producer

Toby Rowland – beauty can be purely passive, rarely a true asset on stage or even on screen. This was the special quality valued by Berenson and so many of her friends. One of them, director Glen Byam Shaw, who knew her for over 30 years, tried to define that essence in a 1953 letter:

> You have the ability to get the best out of life. It is a wonderful gift. Diana has it also – I mean Diana Duff Cooper. When I was on tour with her we used to have such times together – she could make drinking a cup of lukewarm coffee in Donnydoonhead a delightful event in one's life. The answer is, I suppose, that you both have "magic".

Byam Shaw could not have known that his letter, sent to Vivien on location in Ceylon, would arrive just as one of the most explosive episodes triggered by the Bipolar condition from which she suffered (it was as yet unnamed) was beginning.

That gaiety of the heart and her beauty were mixed blessings. She said herself:

> People think that if you look fairly reasonable you can't possibly act … I think beauty can be a great handicap.

Early in her career her friend John Gielgud, seeing her in Max Beerbohm's *The Happy Hypocrite*, found her "ravishing", adding:

> I suppose your beauty will always be more hindrance than help to your acting. Almost incidentally either it blinds the critical faculty or produces a perverse determination to pick holes.

George Cukor felt the same ("a consummate actress, hampered by beauty") while another American friend, the director/dramatist Garson Kanin, described her as:

> a stunner whose ravishing beauty often tended to obscure her staggering achievement as an actress … She was ambitious, persevering, serious, often inspired.

Vivien actually made comparatively few films (19 in a 30-year career) but she had very rapidly assimilated the screen's special demands; her early British films, made at a time when there were few native directors of major talent, still had some inspired, mostly émigré cinematographers from whom she absorbed an unquantifiable amount. Most British actors then tended to patronise the cinema – Ralph Richardson's attitude ("You sell to the cinema what you learned in the theatre") was representative – but while Vivien came to love the theatre more she was too intelligent to short-change film work. Even in some of these less than classic early efforts, many of them low-budget and quickly shot, a latent vitality, a sense of the complexity of a nature both fragile and infused with a tensile strength, is communicated. Monkey-quick, she grasped the essence of screen acting remarkably swiftly (much ahead of Olivier) – that above all the camera photographs thought, that the eyes are the index to interior life. Her eyes were what immediately struck both Selznick and Cukor; the latter had said from the outset on *Gone With the Wind* that he wanted someone "with fire in her eyes". Directors and cameramen mostly loved to photograph Vivien's eyes – many of her films contain memorable close-ups – and virtually all the obituaries and features covering her death mentioned them in their focus on her beauty, masking the question of her talent, a lingering shadow.

An even longer shadow was – and similarly remains – that cast by Olivier. When they met he had made films in Hollywood and England, none markedly successful; in the theatre, apart from supporting Noël Coward in his *Private Lives* and an exuberantly athletic portrayal of a John Barrymore-inspired actor in the American comedy *Theatre Royal* he had had many failures but was now beginning his rise to classical stature alternating Romeo and Mercutio with John Gielgud in the latter's production of *Romeo and Juliet* in London, going on to consolidate his position with a string of major Shakespeare roles, including Hamlet, at the Old Vic. Their affair blazed into a consuming mutual passion in Korda's film *Fire Over England* (1937) before they acted on stage together for the first time when Vivien played Ophelia to his Hamlet at Elsinore, a miserable time for Vivien's husband Leigh and Olivier's wife Jill, neither of whom agreed to immediate divorce.

The couple left separately for America in late 1938, Olivier for Heathcliff in *Wuthering Heights* while Vivien followed later, desperately missing him, but also conscious that Scarlett remained uncast. They were finally able to marry – in California in 1940 – returning to England after filming *Lady Hamilton* together. Over the next two decades, rarely working apart on stage, they built up a joint reputation as "The Oliviers", a spotlit First Couple of the British stage, like Alfred Lunt and Lynn Fontanne ("The Lunts") in America or Jean-Louis Barrault and Madeleine Renaud in France. Both continued film careers; Olivier reinforced his heroic national status in his fanfare of native patriotism, the screen *Henry V* (1945) which he also directed, followed by a film *Hamlet* during which he was knighted. Vivien made further films but also established a formidable record of stage performances ranging from the vaudeville of Thornton Wilder's *The Skin of Our Teeth* to Tennessee Williams's *A Streetcar Named Desire* in London and then on screen as the fading Blanche Du Bois, one of the richest (and most demanding) female roles in the theatre. Befitting their status, as the country began to emerge from postwar austerity they made a quasi-royal pairing for the Festival of Britain in Shaw's *Caesar and Cleopatra* and Shakespeare's *Antony and Cleopatra* and then gave London a contrasting modern regal frivol with Terence Rattigan's *The Sleeping Prince* for Coronation year in 1953.

Their private lives were similarly on the glamorously grand scale at the restored medieval country estate of Notley Abbey which became an English equivalent of William Randolph Hearst's Californian San Simeon (*Citizen Kane*'s Xanadu) with weekend parties of West End and Broadway actors, Hollywood celebrities and writers, designers, politicians and composers. Everything the Oliviers did was news; Vivien's miscarriages in 1944 and 1956 were splashed across the popular press, although Fleet Street in the 1950s was less intrusive than today and so relatively little of the backstage whispers as the marriage began to crumble under its various strains found its way into the newspapers. After rumours and speculation of affairs on both sides they divorced and Olivier remarried – a third actress, the younger Joan Plowright, with whom he had three children. Vivien, although forming a Last Attachment in the 1960s with actor John Merivale, never remarried. Most of her post-divorce work was in a kind of exile – in Australia or America – although she was about to return to the West End at the time of her sudden death.

Olivier had a whole crowded final act left to play, putting the seal on his reputation as the greatest actor of his time. A son of the cloth, he had always regarded the theatre with a quasi-religious zeal. The notion of a National Theatre – of which he became the first Director in 1963 – had been special for him for years and he regarded heading it as a charge amounting to genuine National Service. Based at his beloved Old Vic until moving to the South Bank under Peter Hall, inevitably Olivier's tenure had troughs but its peaks were often awesome including some of his later great performances (as Othello and, in *Long Day's Journey Into Night*, as the old actor James Tyrone, in which Vivien might, had circumstances been otherwise, have played his wife). Rarely latterly free from illnesses, any one of which might have poleaxed lesser men, his National decade was an heroic achievement.

Olivier received the most elaborate Memorial Service accorded any actor, in Westminster Abbey with every possible member of the great and good in attendance, scored by his old colleague William Walton. Vivien's Memorial Service more than 20 years previously was crowded too, but in a smaller venue (St Martin-in-the-Fields) with decidedly less pomp and circumstance. By the time of Olivier's death in 1989 she had become, if not forgotten (remastered and reissued versions of *Gone With the Wind* and *Streetcar* ensured that), definitely less valued. Olivier's reputation had cast a long shadow long before Vivien's death. Garson Kanin noted in the 1940s:

> It must be maddening for her, a young actress at the peak of her powers and popularity, to find herself in the position of a hanger-on who has come along for the ride.

Olivier in his autobiography – rather less revelatory than its title *Confessions of an Actor* (1982) might suggest – wrote of his detestation of this attitude: "Critics should not go on for ever letting their judgments be distorted by her great beauty", a veiled dig at one particular critic.

Critics and performers can be friendly; the Oliviers were close to Alan Dent who reviewed for The *Manchester Guardian* then The *News Chronicle* and assisted Olivier on the texts of his Shakespearean films. The critic/actor relationship can be awkward, however. It is in retrospect ironic that the critic thought by Olivier to "distort" Vivien's work most damagingly should, after the Olivier divorce, work closely alongside him at the National Theatre.

Kenneth Tynan was without question a major figure in postwar British theatre, the finest dramatic critic since Bernard Shaw; an exhortation to inspiration above his desk read: "Rouse tempers, goad and lacerate, raise whirlwinds", all of which he did in prose of firecracker brilliance. He aimed to be a war correspondent, not a necrologist; he wanted to blast what he saw as a fossilised 1950s London theatre of trivial comedies, thrillers and parish-pumpery revue into extinction. Like Shaw's attacks on "Sardoodledom" (the "well-made" plays following the style of Victorien Sardou) in order to champion Ibsen, so Tynan wanted to raze the flim-flam of what he called French-windowed "Loamshire"-set plays to the ground as he encouraged new radical writing and Bertolt Brecht. A lifelong atheist, he relished causes, campaigns and crusades.

In his younger years he was fired by great heroic acting, the work of magnetic figures such as Donald Wolfit or, above all, Laurence Olivier. For Tynan, Olivier was the supreme modern actor and his worship (it was nothing less) remained constant even as he shifted his dramatic preferences to more overtly political drama, inspired by his Brechtian conversion. He changed his views on some Olivier rivals; from the time that The *Daily Telegraph* suggested that Wolfit might be a potential head of a National Theatre – he viewed that position as reserved for Olivier – he switched to a relentless, at times gleefully savage, demolition of Wolfit's performances.

There is no doubt about Tynan's importance in redrawing the map of the British theatre, especially his championship of the New Drama appearing in the wake of *Look Back in Anger* in 1956, but some of his judgements were often wayward, and not a few of his *obiter dicta* were off target, occasionally troublingly so. Often behind his writing on actors there was a signally sadistic streak; actress Eileen Herlie, dismissed with whiplash vitriol, was an early victim. He always lauded Olivier's pantherine vigour above the more poetic Gielgud (Olivier was, in Tynan's view, the Burkean Sublime to Gielgud's harmonious but inferior Beautiful).

Sometimes actors could survive to point up the flaws in Tynan's judgements after he ceased regular theatre criticism. He had always insisted that Gielgud had little gift for modern work and rarely succeeded in comedy. This had never had solid foundations and was spectacularly undermined by later Gielgud performances in new plays, often very funny, by Alan Bennett, Harold Pinter and David Storey.

Vivien had not that luck. She suffered, more than any other actor, from Tynan's lash. He was practically reviewing her even before he was officially a critic; in an introductory piece for the *Daily Sketch* he wrote that he longed to see his idol as Macbeth but preferably "with a more challenging Lady than his charming wife". He reserved his most lethal, exquisitely phrased dismissals for her classical performances, seemingly at his most blistering on those widely praised by other critics and, notably, by fellow actors.

There is no doubt that the cumulative impression conveyed by the most influential critic of his era has affected Vivien's posthumous reputation. She was a different theatrical animal from Olivier but that does not make her a necessarily second-rate one. And she was a star on screen in a way Olivier never quite matched (possibly because he did not want to, ruthlessly competitive though he could be on stage). A true movie star is both actor and embodiment of his or her myth; Olivier's sheer protean quality undercut that, but on film so often Vivien defines screen stardom.

The shadow of Tynan's perspective was impossible for Vivien, who died so young, to break free from. But, 50 years on from her death, a scrutiny of her career should see that and other shadows recede, revealing her in a clearer light.

CHAPTER 1

A Child of the Raj

One of Tynan's weaker puns – admittedly from early in his career – was "We all make our own mystiques". Not so in studio-era Hollywood, where the moguls fully moulded their "properties", as they regarded their indentured talent, supervising every aspect of their image, capping teeth, altering colour and cut of hair, shaping brows, paying special attention to what Selznick called "the breastwork" of their female stars and monitoring their off-screen lives. They grasped that a genuine star is more than an actor; the public fuse what is on the screen with their perception of a star's private life as shaped by their bosses and the media. So, from the outset of Vivien's association with Selznick International Studios, a process of re-creation began. Initially the publicity machine presented her as a discovery, airbrushing from publicity most of her British work on stage and screen. Only when filming on *Gone With the Wind* was under way was mention of her previous experience made, referring only glancingly to a husband or child with not a whisper of her involvement with Olivier. As many similarities as possible between actress and character were stressed, often with scant regard for truth. Selznick wrote personally to Ed Sullivan, an influential columnist prior to his television career, just after Vivien was contracted, pointing out that although she was not American, a large part of the South would prefer that to casting a Yankee and that just as Scarlett's parents were French and Irish, "identically, Miss Leigh's parents are French and Irish".

This was complete invention. Question marks and vague half-truths have continued to hang over Vivien's ancestry however, even in her biographies. Her father, Ernest Hartley, although he spent much of his early life in India where his daughter was born, was and remained a proud Yorkshireman from a family based originally for generations in Pontefract. Ernest's father was an industrious civil service administrator; his wife Elizabeth, a butcher's daughter from York, gave him seven children. The couple, following a peripatetic career taking them across England to Ireland and the Hebrides, retired to the Yorkshire seaside town of Bridlington. Vivien's father was born during the family's Scottish stay on the island of Islay in 1883. The youngest of the family, he grew up an adventurous boy, never especially academic and a popular extrovert. Like many younger sons of his generation he saw fewer opportunities at home than in some of the flourishing outposts of the Empire, still in the early years of the twentieth century a mighty commercial network. He sailed for India in 1905.

Calcutta then was the epicentre of the British Raj with its national administrative significance at its height. The capital moved to Delhi in 1911 but Calcutta remained a clamorous, buoyant city to which Ernest was immediately attracted. Working as an exchange broker for the respected company of Pigott, Chapman & Co, he was highly popular amongst a wide range of friends, mostly fellow expatriates; he was enthusiastically sporty – mad about polo and cricket – and a passionate horseman, a regular at the Tollygunnga racetrack. He took to all the traditional pastimes of the British sahib; years later a contemporary of Ernest sent Vivien photographs of her father and his friends hunting in the Indian jungle, complete with solar topees, rifles and a retinue of native bearers, the epitome of privileged Raj life.

His other consuming interest was the theatre; amateur dramatics were popular in that Maughamesque society and a particularly active group, the Calcutta Dramatic Society, presented a regular series of productions, often with Ernest in central roles, usually in the Grand Opera House, a splendid new building on the site of the old wooden theatre opposite the Hogg New Market. Ernest's friend Geoffrey Martin was also a regular in the productions; his daughter Frances ("Mills") Martin, later a friend of Vivien's, remembered Ernest vividly:

> He was marvellous to have fun with. He had a histrionic ability to relate terrible jokes ... He enjoyed fishing and golfing and spending money in flashy hotels. He was "hail fellow well met" but very much a fair weather friend.

Within a few years Ernest's success at the brokerage firm was making him a rich young man and he began to contemplate taking a wife. Ernest always – before and after marriage – had an eye for a pretty face although there was not an unlimited number of attractive single girls of marriageable age in the circles in which he moved. But Ernest was instantly attracted when he was introduced to Gertrude Yackje, five years his junior, a beauty with thick brown hair, clear blue eyes and the most delicate magnolia-pale skin. Various accounts state that Gertrude had an Irish background, while other biographies claim that, like Ernest, she was Yorkshire born, even with a Bridlington connection. She had actually never left India. The facts are that Vivien's mother was born (1888) in Darjeeling and met Ernest in Calcutta. There have been suggestions of a Parsee or Bengali heritage, although Yackje is not a common Parsee or Bengali name. Her mother Mary (née Robinson) indeed was of Irish Catholic extraction but Gertrude also had Armenian blood, from her father's side. Her Armenian ancestry can be traced back with certainty to Johannes Gabriel ("J.G.") Yackje, who worked for a wealthy Armenian merchant, Jacob Eyoob, and who left Persia (now Iran) with his wife and young family for Calcutta in 1843. Life there proved different and difficult; J.G. became an insolvent debtor only three years later before overcoming his setback to become an indigo merchant by the 1860s. His elder son Michael – Gertrude's father – had been born in Persia and worked in Calcutta as an Assistant Goods Clerk for the East India Railway, but his younger son Gabriel was less fortunate. He is listed in 1867, aged 30, in the Annual Returns for Patients Treated in the Asylum for Europeans in Calcutta, described as suffering from "mania chronic (cause unknown)". It seems likely that Vivien never knew of her great-uncle's condition, a family secret of which Gertrude never spoke. Later, when Vivien's mental problems were surfacing, Olivier asked Gertrude and Ernest if there was any genetic history of such illness in either family and was forcefully told that there was no question of any such problems.

Whatever Gabriel's eventual history, Michael by the time of his death in 1893 – Gertrude was five – was described as "a landed proprietor". Gertrude had an older sister, Mary, who shortly after their father's death married Percy Feilman, a businessman who later changed the family name to Fielding and it seems that Mary and Percy supported her mother and Gertrude. Eight children were born to Mary and Percy, but Mary died in childbirth in 1918 giving birth to Alexander ("Xan") Fielding, later a noted travel writer and Vivien's cousin, although they met rarely. Xan remained always uncertain of his maternal family's true origins; he recalled one of his aunts, Orlene, as notably dark-skinned and came to believe that his grandmother Mary might have been mixed race Parsee Indian, unaware of her Armenian background. The lack of much definite information chimes with the family background; at that time, to both the British in India and pure Indians, mixed-race people were stigmatised, their origins often sanitised or disguised which explains the frequent accenting of the family name to Yackjé and the use of the Robinson maternal name (Gertrude's marriage certificate is in her real name of Yackje).

The circumstances parallel those of another actress, one who acted later with Olivier and married Alexander Korda, Merle Oberon – née Estelle Thompson. She was born in Bombay two years before Vivien to a Eurasian-Maori mother and a British engineer. Later she reinvented herself, claiming Tasmanian origins while her mother during her lifetime passed as Oberon's maid.

How much Ernest knew of Gertrude's background is unclear. He seemed to possess fewer of the prejudices of most of his circle and was determined to marry this self-possessed beauty. The courtship was brief; Gertrude was liked by Ernest's friends including his two closest, Geoffrey Martin and John Thomson ("Tommy"), a drily entertaining Scot of independent means who made a good double act with the exuberant Ernest, often prompting his anecdotes and accounts of sporting triumphs. Calcutta had a lively social scene, sections of which reacted ultra-conventionally when it became known that Ernest and Gertrude planned to marry. Geoffrey Martin's son, Hugh, remembered that Ernest experienced a degree of social ostracism, because of Gertrude's perceived mixed-race status, from the pillars of the Bengal Club and the Saturday Club, from both of which he was obliged to resign, despite the support of Tommy and Geoffrey.

Ernest wanted to marry in England and he sailed with Gertrude and her mother Mary in late 1911 to London where the women settled in Holland Park, occasionally visiting Ernest's Bridlington family, before the wedding the following April at Kensington's Catholic Church of Our Lady of Victories. They then sailed back to India, landing in Bombay before going on to Calcutta to begin their married life on the sub-continent.

They came to make a popular pair in Calcutta's European society. Although Gertrude would never be noted for a strong sense of humour she was always interested in others and a good hostess. The social climate was in flux; Gertrude became a proficient golfer and Ernest continued his game-hunting and sports. Soon the doors of the city's exclusive clubs reopened to him and as Calcutta's mercantile boom went on Ernest's income allowed for a comfortable lifestyle with a large house and extensive garden, fully staffed, in the fashionable suburb of Alipore.

Gertrude was pregnant in the spring of 1913. Traditionally the British left the baking cities for the cooler hill-stations in summer and in May the Hartleys left for Darjeeling, quite an adventurous journey, by train to Siliguri then an eight-hour ride on the packed Darjeeling Himalayan Railway (known as The Toy Train) on a meandering track, often climbing at a steep gradient. Known as

"Queen of the Hills", 7,000 feet up in the mountains, Darjeeling in 1913 was a sleepy hill town, occasionally – with Nepal off limits – the base for Himalayan expeditions, with breathtaking views of Everest and Kanchenjunga.

The Hartleys had rented a comfortable house, Shannon Lodge, a traditional two-storeyed building with a wide sloping roof in a garden of shrubs and tall trees, all occasionally – in an Eastern version of *Brigadoon* when Darjeeling's rapidly shifting weather saw dense mists almost mystically sudden in arrival and dispersal alike – wrapped in a romantic cloud. Ernest returned to work once Gertrude was settled with the house's servants; there was little for her to do except a round of golf with other wives from Calcutta or resting in the garden overlooking the hills. She was happy to sit looking over one of the most beautiful views in the world, more than half-believing the ages-old superstition that if a pregnant woman gazes in silent contemplation of the transcendental majesty of Kanchenjunga she is guaranteed that her child will be graced by beauty.

Gertrude may later have told her daughter of that superstition. She certainly invented another story to surround Vivien's birth. On the evening of 5 November, there were fireworks for Guy Fawkes' Night lighting up the skies, the bangs and crackles punctuating Gertrude's labour pains and her baby's first cries. On subsequent early birthdays, often spent in Darjeeling, when the fireworks began and Vivien asked why people were celebrating, Gertrude would tell her "It's for your birthday, darling."

Ernest had returned for the birth and shortly afterwards the expanded family returned to Calcutta. She was christened Vivian Mary Hartley; the name "Vivien Leigh" resulted from her first London stage success. It was in many ways an idyllic early childhood; Gertrude had supervised the creation of a beautiful garden in Alipore Road, full of jacaranda trees, rhododendrons and lilies, an oasis surely triggering Vivien's passion for flowers, their colours and for gardening. She loved all the activities involved in planting and nurturing shrubs (roses especially) and flowers, becoming a proper "hands-on" gardener, remarkably knowledgeable. She relished arranging flowers in her homes, dressing-rooms and hotel suites and was forever sending them to friends for opening nights or birthdays, like Tennessee Williams's heroine in her penultimate film, *The Roman Spring of Mrs Stone* ("Flora, the goddess of Springtime was not more lavish in a dispersal of flowers").

From the outset, she was a signally alert, active child, rarely sleeping for long; her concerned mother took her to their doctor who diagnosed her as simply "not a sleepy baby". (Olivier, who suffered – at times *in extremis* – from

Vivien's insomnia, used wryly to say that that would be a good title for Vivien's biography). Idolised she may have been by both parents but she was not indulgently spoilt. Many mothers in that society left their children to be more or less wholly raised by their ayahs but Gertrude, raising Vivien to be a devout Catholic, hired an English nanny of the faith while her early education was from Gertrude. She was the one who taught her to read, a remarkably easy process; by the age of five Vivien was an eager reader, especially fond of Kipling (the *Just So Stories* her favourite), Lewis Carroll and Greek legends. Her religious instruction also was mainly her mother's responsibility; the days revolved round the markers of Mass, confession and prayer. To train her powers of observation, Gertrude introduced Vivien to "Kim's Game" – from those mental exercises used to hone the brain-agility of the British Intelligence in Kipling's novel *Kim*. Last thing before lights out at bedtime Gertrude would arrange some objects in a pattern on a tray, remove them and have Vivien recreate the pattern in the morning. Gertrude was determined to give her child every advantage prior to formal education. Above all, she instilled in her a preternaturally structured set of manners – to be a good guest one has to consider one's host, while a good host must give first attention to the guests. And one had to be polite and considerate of others on all occasions.

The summers saw Gertrude and Vivien return to Darjeeling. Vivien said later of India that "I have only confused impressions of its beauty and of the gaiety of life there", but those periods spent cradled in the pine and oak-covered hills looking down to the river, the occasional excursions to beauty-spots like Senchal Lake, ringed by wild orchids and azaleas, fed by a mountain stream, all spurred the child's imagination. Sometimes there were treats in Darjeeling town, with exotic smells from the sweet-vendors – burrakee-ball ("old ladies' hair"), a kind of candyfloss, or armsuth, a toffee made from dried mangoes. There was a memorable journey on ponies in the early dark to Tiger Hill on the edge of town, climbing a tower to its balcony to wait in the starlit dark until slowly dawn rose over the Himalayas like the curtain rising on a play.

Ernest in Calcutta was usually happy too. He and Gertrude had been through the deeply distressing experience two years after Vivien's birth when Gertrude had twins who lived for only a week, but his roving eye soon regained its glint. Casual adulteries were prevalent in that society and, to an often surprising degree, tolerated by many of the wives. The devoutly Catholic Gertrude could not use contraception or countenance divorce but friends grasped that she knew of and accepted Ernest's "flings", often when she was in Darjeeling. If no wit, Gertrude must have had at least a sense of mischief; one well-recollected incident told of how she organised an elaborate formal dinner-party at their home, arranging for Ernest to arrive shortly after the guests were seated, entering to find that every woman present, each escorted by her husband, had been, on one occasion or another, a lover of his. If Gertrude for Vivien was associated with discipline and order, her father carried a nimbus of fun, ebullience and – as children can intuit – subversion.

Ernest liked to involve Vivien in his amateur theatricals, sometimes taking her with him to dress-rehearsals of Theatre Royal or Opera House productions – *The Scarlet Pimpernel* in which he played the villainous Chauvelin, or Gilbert and Sullivan – and teaching her to ride before she was given her own pony.

The Hartleys had planned an English trip in 1914, taking Vivien to meet the Bridlington relations, but the outbreak of war prevented that. Ernest joined the Indian Cavalry, initially training remounts for Allied troops in Mesopotamia before a transfer to Bangalore in southern India. Gertrude and Vivien moved to be closer to him, renting a villa in the hill town of Ootacamund, always full of English military men.

The Ootacamund memsahibs were formidably organised and always had a full calendar of social events, dances, concerts and fetes. An Ootacamund audience witnessed Vivien's first public stage appearance, one marked by the determined will that would stamp her career. In the few photographs of her then her gaze to the camera is open, unafraid, slightly challenging. For the concert at which Vivien was scheduled to sing "Little Bo Peep" Gertrude had carefully coached her, making an effective costume of a muslin frock and bonnet finished off by a shepherdess's crook trimmed with a large silk bow. It was a full house, pride of place occupied by Lady Willingdon, wife of the Governor of Madras. Vivien entered on cue to centre stage as rehearsed. The pianist's hands were poised above the keyboard, as rehearsed, only to freeze as Vivien banged three times with her crook (not rehearsed) to announce in a firm, clear voice "I won't sing. I shall recite." From all accounts the spoken version brought the house down.

The end of the war saw the Hartleys once more in Calcutta with the household's full complement of staff ensuring its smooth running. There were occasional chauffeured trips into the city, sometimes to join Ernest for tiffin or ices, even allowing Vivien to see inside the majestic Bengal Club, rebuilt in 1911 and dominating the city skyline, just one of several magnificent examples of Raj architecture in that bifurcated city ("City of Palaces" and Jain temples cheek by jowl with some of the world's most densely populated slums which Vivien was never allowed near). The city – and Ernest – prospered further

(Ernest was now a full partner in his firm) in the postwar years but with Vivien now six her parents had to settle her education. Gertrude – who would have brooked no opposition even had Ernest offered it – insisted that Vivien must have a Catholic education and although there seemed no suitable Calcutta establishment there were some perfectly good boarding-schools for European children in India, notably the Catholic Convent in the Himalayan foothills at Murree. But it was a long-established custom for sons and daughters of the wealthier Raj to be sent to "the homeland" to be educated; Ernest's money and Gertrude's ambitions for Vivien allowed them to choose from the best possible schools. It possibly seemed an alluring prospect to Vivien at six to be promised a sea voyage to England; whether she was told beforehand that she would then be separated from her parents for the best part of ten years is not known. In early January 1920 the Hartleys sailed on the *City of Baroda*, travelling in considerable style. Vivien did not see India again until nearly half a century later – there was one, ill-fated intervening visit to Sri Lanka – when she travelled with friends to Nepal and India. Back in 1920 she was about to become, in effect, a displaced person.

CHAPTER 2

Hours Nearer Death

India had been vibrant, hot, its skies mostly unclouded; all that Vivien would have seen as their ship moved up a muddy Thames to Tilbury in February was austere, grey and chilly. She was still surrounded by the warmth of family when her parents took her to Bridlington to meet her paternal grandparents and two unmarried aunts, Lilian who energetically pedalled everywhere on an ancient bicycle and the deaf but kindly Hilda. In 1920 Bridlington was quiet in winter but crowded in summer when both beaches ringing the town were packed with holidaymakers. Vivien enjoyed her Bridlington summer, often paddling in the sea – she developed into a surprisingly strong swimmer – going on donkey rides and walking in the early evening along the esplanade, although the Bridlington candyfloss was blander than the delicious Darjeeling burrakee-ball.

Towards the end of that first English summer the Hartleys returned south, to London's deluxe Carlton Hotel where they had stayed on arrival. Also staying there was their Calcutta chum Tommy (John Thompson), who often travelled with the Hartleys until his death shortly before World War II. It has been hinted that Gertrude and he were lovers and indeed Tommy's niece Elizabeth Thompson was told by Gertrude that Tommy was "the love of her life" but – as she stressed to Elizabeth – this was barely voiced at the time and nothing was done, or could be done about it, given Gertrude's profound religious orthodoxy. Tommy and Ernest had Scotland in common; Ernest was born on Islay while Tommy's family was centred round the lochside Campbeltown. They often went golfing together in Scotland or to Ireland to fish, usually at Waterville in County Kerry. Tommy's nephew Ian Thompson remembered his attachment to the Hartleys ("confirmed bachelor" then had none of its modern connotations):

He was a wonderful fellow, in the eyes of a teenage boy. He had enough money, being a bachelor, to do all the things I thought were wonderful like big game fishing ... shooting, sailing etc. he was a charming chap with a 'way' with women. He also had hollow legs.

Elizabeth failed to comprehend why Gertrude could really prefer her steadfast uncle Tommy to the ebullient, spirited Ernest, who entranced adults and children with his zest for life and entertaining stories. There seems no evidence to support the suggestion of any ongoing Tommy/Gertrude affair; the triangular relationship suited all three and certainly Vivien always seemed to regard Tommy as a benevolent uncle with no Maisie-like perceptions out of Henry James.

Her life changed dramatically in September. Vivien had shown a precocious love of the theatre; she was taken by her parents to a West End show as a treat (or sweetener) on 20 September and the next morning was taken with her luggage to the Convent of the Sacred Heart at Roehampton. She was then left in the care of the nuns. Gertrude's diary records a visit to Vivien on 26 September. ("very sad indeed") and on two further occasions, once for a trip to London Zoo, before she and Ernest sailed for India on 10 October. It would be nearly two years before she saw her daughter again. It seems harsh today but such arrangements were far from unusual then (although Vivien was slightly younger than the normal entry-age – in fact, she was the youngest pupil there).

A high, thick-walled building dating from 1850 in Roehampton Lane, the Convent was part of the global network of the Sacred Heart organisation, founded in post-revolutionary France by Saint Madeleine Sophie Barat to re-establish the power of Christian life through the education of girls. Its motto was "Cor unum et anima in corde Jesu" ("One Heart and One Mind in the Heart of Jesus"). The Roehampton Convent achieved fictional fame as the Convent of the Five Wounds in the novel *Frost in May* by Antonia White, a pupil there shortly before Vivien with a lifelong love–hate relationship with Catholicism. Her story of a new girl, Nanda, and her experiences became a bestseller in 1933 (Vivien's diary records that she bought it then); it spares few punches in its portrayal of the pervasive austerity of convent life.

Stories of English school life tend to be better when set in boys' schools than those for girls (which mostly are populated by what another novelist, Elizabeth Bowen, called "the curl-tossing tomboys of St Dithering's") but White recalls the Colette of the *Claudine* stories with a similar unblinking clarity.

She captures the institutional life immediately – the smells of soap, beeswax and incense, the regularity of bells (the Angelus bell for 6.30 rising at Roehampton, bells for early Mass, mealtimes, classes, bells major and minor dividing sacred duties from secular). Beds were in 20-strong unheated dormitories, curtained into cubicles at night behind which girls dressed and undressed, allowing no glimpse of nudity. Soiled undergarments had to be neatly arranged on a stool, covered by specially made silk squares, which became Vivien's lifelong custom. The Convent relentlessly underscored the tenets of Catholic orthodoxy – the constant reminders that life is the path to death – with the regular quotation from St Teresa at the striking of the hours by the bell: "An hour nearer to death. An hour nearer to heaven or hell." Sin – "wasting time in idle dreaming" was a special anathema as was personal vanity – would be owned at Confession and self-abnegation was not discouraged (salt instead of sugar on rhubarb to mortify the sense of taste). Over the omnipresent sense of sin hovered the spectre of the Fires of Hell.

Certainly some aspects of Vivien's school life were grimly forbidding and also, like most "closed-order" establishments, often peculiarly snobbish. At Roehampton many girls were from "landed" old Catholic families with some foreign minor royalty also attending; there was a suggestion about Vivien that she came from a background of 'trade' which could make for some spiteful barbs. However, she had the compensatory hint of glamour from India which stamped her as different and, trained by Gertrude to be always well-mannered to everyone, she was fairly rapidly after her initial sense of loss – even abandonment – popular with fellow pupils and nuns alike. In *Frost in May*, Nanda develops "a hard little protective shell" as a carapace for survival. Vivien had no need to cloak her feelings quite to that extent. Her sheer charm was an advantage, too; there was a strict "No Pets" rule but, partly because she was so young, Reverend Mother allowed her special exemption to keep a stray kitten, the animal which probably sparked her lifelong love of cats.

Roehampton life was not all discipline and mortification. Compared to other such institutions, it was relatively liberal. A small lake at the bottom of the large gardens would often see Vivien alone, simply gazing at the movement of the water – her favourite element – far enough away to avoid charges of "wasting time in idle dreaming". The girls could play tennis in doubles and there were occasional plays – Vivien played Mustardseed in *A Midsummer Night's Dream* and Miranda in *The Tempest*, the latter directed by future playwright Bridget Boland, large and bossy even as a child, who chastised Vivien for tripping over some of her lines with a well-aimed offstage thump with a candlestick. Music was encouraged and she learnt to play the piano, also playing the cello in the school orchestra. She shared early dreams with one of her best friends, a vivacious Irish girl, Maureen O'Sullivan, who had acting ambitions even then too and who recalled Vivien as one of the most popular pupils, decisively announcing to Maureen: "When I leave school, I'm going to be a great actress." Another Irish-born friend, Patsy Quinn, also remembered her vividly as:

> obviously delicate. Her chest was already weak ... A "special child" you'd say. Even her presents from home were special. Vivien was so tiny and delicately made ... with the only complexion I have seen that really was like a peach.

Patsy stressed that, while a sincere Catholic, Vivien was not exactly pious ("she never struck me as a 'believer' in the deeper sense"). There was for her, along with others at the Convent, a sense of identification in 1925 with the romantic story of Thérèse Martin, canonised for her devotional writing as St Thérèse of Lisieux; the identification may have evaporated but the *Notebooks* of St Thérèse would always be on her bookshelves.

The 'special' presents mentioned by Patsy Quinn consisted mostly of bracelets and colourful silks from India but for her first birthday at the Convent, not long after her arrival, a huge wooden box was delivered for Vivien. She and some of the girls including Patsy joined in the excitement as the suspense built during the unwrapping of the many layers of packaging, finally revealing a large, expensively costumed china doll. But in transit the head had been cracked right across – later a television documentary saw this as a fateful metaphor of Vivien's life – which caused tears all around.

Her few surviving letters from Roehampton – always read by the nuns before posting – have no real complaints about the regime, to which she adapted once she realised her circumstances would be unlikely to change. And convent life had its compensations; she was never especially studious, apart from enthusiasms for Egyptian history, her music and dancing classes:

> I can scarcely remember when I first thought of going on the stage, because it was such an accepted fact of my childhood ... I was fortunate to have understanding parents and all my education and early life were shaped to that end ... I was allowed to specialise in history, literature and music.

Writing home, she peppered her letters with phrases out of Angela Brazil's books of girls' school life with some wild stabs at spelling. Caught talking in class, she was punished by missing part of her half-term holiday.

> Don't you call it beastly? I do think it's simply the BUN! Mother Bruce-Hall said she hoped I had tribulation – she said it would do me a lot of good.

She enthused about Egyptian history:

> I wish we could dig all the sand away and that all those marvellous spinxes [sic]
> and tempels [sic] could be seen again.

Even more enjoyable were the occasional outings to plays ("ripping fun") and revues. A school trip to a Christmas perennial of the time, *Where the Rainbow Ends*, had triggered her request to have dancing lessons; Maureen O'Sullivan admired her for taking the classes alone, mainly in basic ballet steps for which Patsy Quinn thought she had "extraordinary poise – she was always a very mature person for her age", sensing also a quality instilled by Gertrude:

> One was always gay and laughing with Vivien ... She was generous to a fault.
> I think what people noticed most was her perfect manners and I think this was
> really more her tremendous consideration of other people.

She was fervent about all the rituals involved in the preparation for her first Communion in 1921, enclosing in her letter home a photograph of herself in her pure white dress, and even more thrilled when Gertrude replied with news that she would be sailing to visit her the following spring. That made for a happy time, with Gertrude satisfying Vivien's theatre mania with a visit to catch a favourite performer, the bowler-hatted, bug-eyed star George Robey (later memorably glimpsed as Falstaff in Olivier's *Henry V* film). She was even more thrilled in the summer when her parents – Ernest joined them – took a Lake District holiday and found Robey resident in the same hotel, ever ready to chat to his stagestruck fan and give her treasured signed photographs. Until the end of Vivien's time at Roehampton, Gertrude now visited every year – Ernest every second – broadening her daughter's horizons with more "improving" plays including a Stratford *Hamlet* throughout which Vivien, at 11, sat spellbound.

Other holidays were spent with family at Bridlington, less frequently now both grandparents were in failing health, or with the daughter of Ernest's Calcutta friend Geoffrey Martin – Vivien was friends with Frances ("Mills") Martin – who had a home in the West Country. On a few occasions when there was nowhere for her to spend a holiday period she would remain at the Convent where the lay nuns could accompany her to art galleries or to suitable serious plays.

Just sometimes the seemingly model pupil revealed another aspect of a more complex personality. Patsy Quinn was one who noticed Vivien's occasional retreats behind a remoteness, a kind of self-communion when she would be found alone by the lake, intently focusing on the movement of the water or the reflection of the trees' movement. Another friend confided in an Olivier biographer, noting that for weeks Vivien would seem untroubled, but:

> Then, suddenly, a complete turnaround. Sometimes it would last only a few hours, other times a day or more. But when it happened we'd see a completely different girl – moody, silent, petulant, rude, often hysterical, disturbed in some way that she had no control over … It was frightening when it happened, almost on the order of a dual personality.

The screenwriter Gavin Lambert later observed that the outward control of Vivien's life – her immaculate grooming, the impeccably arranged houses and gardens – cloaked possibly an amount of inner chaos. These convent 'episodes' prefigure the descriptions of her later mood-swings and perhaps those schoolgirl phases were eruptions out of a desolating loneliness of which both her upbringing and convent discipline forbade expression.

Certainly when away from Roehampton there seemed no such eruptions; Mills Martin, who saw her often on shared Devon holidays, always stressed her gaiety then ("she had this extraordinary star quality and emanated something that other people didn't").

Under normal circumstances Vivien would have remained at the Sacred Heart until she was 16. But – once again abruptly – those circumstances changed. Ernest's financial position was now seemingly so secure that he decided to retire early and enjoy travelling through Europe for a time with Gertrude (Tommy occasionally joined them) and Vivien. The marriage had settled into a mutually comfortable groove; Gertrude, who would seem to have had no great sexual drive, or to repress it, would be happy to enjoy a kind of 1920s Grand Tour while turning a blind eye to Ernest's casual flings. She stipulated that Vivien's education must continue; she wanted her to have as many accomplishments as possible, ideally eventually to make "a good marriage". A period in Europe would give her polish plus the advantage of learning other languages, providing in effect an ideal finishing school.

Vivien, sharply perceptive even then, may well have sensed undercurrents in her parents' relationship but she was perfectly happy to embark on what sounded like a glamorous change of lifestyle.

In fact, most of the next two years were spent back behind convent walls. First she was placed in another Sacred Heart institution at Dinard in Brittany. On the Côte d'Emerande, washed by the Gulf Stream which helped its mild climate, Dinard had since the previous century been popular with the wealthy British who rented its Belle Epoque villas or stayed in its luxury hotels, appreciating its air of quiet respectability and walks along the beautiful

Promenade du Clair de Lune, fringed by tropical plants. Once Vivien was settled in the Dinard Sacré Coeur Convent, Ernest and Gertrude travelled extensively, occasionally returning to Dinard, which Gertrude adored. An old friend of the Hartleys, Henry Musgrave, was now in Europe from India and also joining them at times was a wealthy Liverpool cotton-broker, Maurice Stern (nicknamed by Vivien "Mama's cotton beau"); there was no question of any dalliance but while Ernest was otherwise engaged and if Tommy was not around then both Musgrave and Stern would compete to squire Gertrude to the casino or to a dance.

Vivien liked the town of Dinard whenever allowed outside convent walls, inside which life was less than idyllic. Puberty saw Vivien mature more quickly than was usual then and she was undoubtedly conscious of interest from Dinard's youths. Her French improved so much that she was soon fluent but the nuns were joyless compared with those at Roehampton. Patsy Quinn noticed her altered mood ("I remember unhappy letters from her first very strict convent in France").

There was a welcome break at the end of her first Dinard year when she spent most of the summer of 1928 with Ernest in Biarritz, months of hedonistic fun at the racecourse or swimming in the bay in a daringly low-cut swimsuit, a present from Ernest of which Gertrude, returning from a trip to Paris, deeply disapproved. Seemingly working her way round the Mediterranean coast, Vivien was next installed at another Sacré Coeur convent, much more to her taste, in San Remo on the Italian Riviera, another ritzy 1920s paradise of elaborate villas, streamlined yachts in the harbour and a white wedding cake of a casino. Vivien now was beginning to champ at the bit, bound by the routine of institutional life; she still faithfully attended Mass but the chains were often irksome. She deeply disliked the unsmiling San Remo Reverend Mother; letters were censored there too but she managed to send one to her parents which ended saying "The Reverend Mother is a – – -" followed by a pen-picture of a lavishly be-whiskered cat. What she did respond to was San Remo itself, especially its flora, the exuberant mimosa and roses, above all the peonies, huge and blowsy, growing in abundance in the fields above the town, the petals of which the girls were allowed to scatter before the processions on the Feast of Corpus Christi.

Now 15, and shedding the last of any puppy-fat and growing into a willowy adolescent beauty, Vivien had a contrasting damp and misty Irish summer, fishing in the River Erriff at Ardsleagh. Often pictured as a quintessentially metropolitan sophisticate, she was in fact usually happy in the countryside and with country pursuits. Before returning to France the Hartleys visited Ernest's mother – grandfather Hartley had died the year before – and then Vivien began one of the happiest times of her younger years. In the autumn of 1929 she went to Paris, enrolled for a term in a highly regarded establishment, the Villa Sainte-Monique in the respectable suburban Auteuil district. Not precisely a finishing school, with academic discipline of no great stringency, there was strong emphasis on French language and literature (Vivien's appreciation of Montaigne began there) which she found no great hardship. Even more to her liking was the coaching from Mlle Antoine, reputedly an Artiste of the Comédie Française:

> She was a most inspiring teacher and I owe a great deal to her care in correcting my diction and to her encouragement. "I believe you have a future in the theatre, *mon enfant*" she told me, "but you must go back to England and work, work, work."

Vivien during this period in Paris was emerging into full beauty. She was popular with the other girls, a polyglot mixture including some from Roehampton. A fellow pupil, Betty Harbord, recalled Vivien at nearly 16 as the youngest in the school and especially vivid in her memory was one of the Saturday evenings to which friends of the school's proprietrix were invited for bridge while their sons, mostly from St Cyr University, joined to dance with the girls, all assembled waiting nervously to be joined by the teenage boys. Vivien clearly had already mastered the art of a good entrance:

> Suddenly they all turned round. Vivien had come into the room, in a short simple little dress when all the rest of us had long ones, and no make-up. The rest of us were deserted and all the boys excused themselves to go and ask Vivien to dance. She hadn't said anything … she had that charisma.

Vivien would happily have stayed on in Paris but Gertrude, who had heard disquieting whispers of trips into Paris for films, not to mention experiments with lipstick, had different ideas. To fluency in French and Italian now German would be added to Vivien's accomplishments, completing the blueprint for turning out a polished young woman. Inwardly Vivien may have groaned contemplating, at nearly 17, yet more education; she may also after years of literally having no fixed abode, have sighed after a less peripatetic life, with a room of her own. However, her time at her German school near Salzburg in Bavaria at Bad Reichenhall, turned out to be exhilarating. 1930 is the first year for which any diary of Vivien's survives; for most of the next 37 years she used an annual chic pocket diary, slim and leather-bound, usually with her initials embossed on the cover and generally ordered through Smythson's of Bond Street or from Fortnum and Mason. Gradually the entries tapered off, replaced by notes of the appointments in a hectic life but for the early 1930s she squeezed in, her writing already rather loopy, as much as she could into each day's small space.

Hopefully Gertrude did not sneak a glance at these teenage diaries. Vivien was, in Oscar Hammerstein's words, "Sixteen going on seventeen/Waiting for life to start" and all the longing and frustrations of adolescence were poured into her diary. Initially the entries were innocuous enough – in the spring of 1930 she and usually both parents (Ernest sometimes made brief visits to England) drove through France to the Spanish frontier then through Aix to San Remo ("Oh, what memories!"), stopping for rounds of golf en route. Then ("beastly leaving Mum") she began her final "finishing" at the upmarket Bavarian establishment run by the Baron and Baroness von Roeder at Bad Reichenhall where apart from the early starts ("Getting up at 6.30 is perfectly poisonous!") life was decidedly relaxed with German lessons confined to mornings, afternoons spent in the town at the cinema ("Emil Jannings in *His Last Command* – marvellous!") with informal dances in the evenings or even trips to Salzburg for the opera which became Vivien's latest enduring passion, bowled over first by "a wonderful *Fledermaus*".

Soon, alongside noting dancing at the local Park Café, increasingly there are references galore to letters from and to quite a number of boys – Arthur and Louis (clearly rivals) most frequently. She was also indulging in forbidden fruit ("Lay on the balcony and smoked"), even reading the scandalous novel of a young man's initiation by an older vamp, *Three Weeks* by Elinor Glyn ("Would you like to sin/With Elinor Glyn/On a tiger skin?/Or would you prefer/To err/ With her/On some other fur?").

By contrast the summer holiday that year was another damply tranquil time in Ireland ("Topping being back") when she had a happy reunion with Patsy Quinn, learnt to drive, blackberried, fished and collected from the sleepy local post office treasured letters from Arthur (none, seemingly, from Louis).

Joe is the next young man on the scene, back in Bavaria; after agonising waits ("Again, no letter") finally "A letter – unexpected of course – *so* happy! Four more days." And four days later she travelled to Leipzig with her friend Ebette from school and spent Christmas and New Year there, seeing Joe regularly; all three went to *Die Meistersingers* ("very well done") and climbed the Hasenbourg and then just before returning to school she recorded what would have been a surprise for Gertrude ("Joe decided to tell his family about our engagement. Vicemutter was adorable … she's happy about it"). Vicemutter was clearly a wise woman to leave things to take their course. For the next two months many letters from Joe arrived for her (in late January – "Wild letter from Joe. I wrote a poem in the evening") but in March she had a "dear Vivien" letter ("had the letter from Joe. Maybe it's better as it is"). She may have sobbed in identifying with tragic young love in Salzburg the following evening as she watched *La Bohème* but seems quite equable next day ("All over with Joe – he's a silly ass anyway").

A few days later a new love appears, referred to only as Ruppa or 'R', who turned up at Bad Reichenhall in the spring, taught her gypsy dancing ("a ripping day"), took her for long country walks and then, after leaving, wrote "such dear letters – ... made me fall over with joy". Luckily he had left before Joe was back in the frame just before Vivien left Bavaria for the last time, leaving poor Joe disconsolate but joining her school friends seeing her off from Leipzig "almost buried in flowers, flowers and more flowers".

Ernest met his now "finished" daughter at the Hook and they travelled together to Ireland, back to Aasleagh. On the journey she began to comprehend a change in her father's fortunes. Although far from on his uppers, his finances had been damaged by investments which had suffered during the volatile late 1920s financial climate and before much longer, having thought himself retired for life, he would have to find employment. Gertrude, always more resourceful, would turn her interest in beauty treatment and diet into a solid London business concern with her Academy of Beauty. In the meantime life continued much as before. There was still money available to pay for Vivien's stage training once she had been accepted for London's recently opened RADA (The Royal Academy of Dramatic Art); her decision definitely to pursue an acting career might well have been prompted by the first film she saw after her return, *A Connecticut Yankee*, in which her schoolfriend Maureen O'Sullivan – whisked off to Hollywood after being "talent-spotted" – had starred.

In Ireland, letters from Ruppa arrived with Teutonic regularity while Vivien spent most of her time with the recently reappeared Arthur, driving, riding, playing poker, swimming and fishing with him ("all marvellous fun – we're on the best of terms again"). Later – "After dinner we talked out of our rooms late – a marvellous moonlight night." Further development of any romance was guillotined by yet another rapid change in the Hartleys' circumstances; altering plans to take a London house, Ernest rented a house in Teignmouth – the West Country was familiar from holidays with the Martin family. Vivien saw a good deal of the Martin girls and one morning Mills and Vivien joined the crowd at the gathering of a meet of the Dartmoor Draghounds, one of whom, a fair young man on a chestnut horse, greeted Mills Martin. According to Mills's recollection, when she asked Vivien if she thought the man, Leigh Holman, was handsome, Vivien replied: "I think he looks the perfect Englishman. I'm going to marry him" and when Mills told her that he was practically engaged to her sister Dulcie, Vivien was unfazed: "That doesn't matter. He hasn't seen me yet."

Leigh Holman saw more of her two weeks later when the girls attended the South Devon Hunt Ball held in the hall on Torquay Pier. He was from what would have been considered an "old Devon" landed family, established for generations in the area. After Harrrow and reading Law at Cambridge he was now a leading member of a thriving London legal firm in the Middle Temple. With his lean face, wavy blond hair and shy smile he somewhat resembled a favourite actor of Vivien's, Leslie Howard; he had perfect manners and, although far from a Fred Astaire, clearly enjoyed dancing with Vivien, who had chosen a floaty turquoise dress for the occasion and was at her most captivating. They talked of many things but at that time Vivien made no mention of any acting ambitions; subsequently Holman said she did not seem to have that aspiration "or the qualities that brought her fame".

Arthur followed Joe, Louis and Ruppa into oblivion and Vivien's diary for the next few months repeatedly records Leigh Holman's name. He is first mentioned on 29 December 1931 ("Marvellous Hunt Ball – met Leigh – adored it"); the following day she accompanied him to Exeter to the cinema (Marlene Dietrich and Gary Cooper in *Morocco* – "wonderful film") and soon "drove round and saw Holman Estate. Met Leigh."

How genuinely, deeply attracted Vivien was to Leigh Holman and how much of the appeal was a "crush" underpinned by a latent desire to free herself from dependence on her parents is debatable. She certainly thought she was falling in love with him but for all her surface sophistication she had been very little in the world, mostly cocooned in convents or schools or in her parents' lifestyle, although what she felt for Leigh was very different from ephemeral teenage fancies. There was something steadfast beneath his seemingly diffident, courteous exterior and indeed he would remain, most remarkably, utterly devoted to and in every way possible supportive of her through separation, divorce and her worst emotional crises until her death (he never remarried). This quality in him – he was 11 years older – Vivien may have felt she needed after years of never quite settling anywhere and unpredictable parental circumstances. There was also at least a grain of truth in Patsy Quinn's observation:

Vivien was so young and wanted anything she couldn't get. And she was going to be so lovely. No wonder Leigh wondered about marrying her.

Back in London, where the Hartleys took a flat in Cornwall Gardens, Vivien and Leigh met up again soon ("Dinner and show with Leigh. *The* most marvellous evening"). Things moved fast – several lunches, a tea at Leigh's apartment, then "Dinner with Dad and Leigh at Quaglino's." She tore herself away to visit Bridlington (now "this dreary hole") as promised – a six-week stay during which she received many letters (sometimes two in one day) from Leigh, but much as she loved her aunts it was a dull time alone, too cold to swim, often with only reading and knitting to console her. With an enormous "HURRAY!" she recorded her return to London and at once was in a whirl of lunches, dinners, plays, the Boat Race (cheering for Cambridge, of course) and Henley Regatta with Leigh. He now knew of her RADA plans – he seemed to regard it as another finishing school of sorts (Vivien recorded in May: "RADA first day – love it").

Her courting continued during RADA; Leigh would wait for her in Gower Street at the end of each Academy day and they would go on to dinner, a play or splashy social events such as the Caledonian Ball. Vivien was introduced to Leigh's legal friends and two especially close to him, both of whom introduced her – no snob in the usual sense but drawn to challenging minds – to new worlds. Hamish Hamilton (always known as Jamie) was of Scottish background although American-born and met Leigh at Cambridge where he was a star on the river (he won silver in rowing at the 1928 Olympics). Tall, with a dry wit and attractive to women, he had recently formed his eponymous publishing house. The theatre was a major interest; he had married the striking but troubled actress Jean Forbes-Robertson but by the time he met Vivien the marriage was fraying (they divorced in 1934). Jamie was dazzled by his first meeting with Vivien ("a vision of beauty far lovelier with her eyebrows unplucked before the theatre people got hold of her"). Even stronger a friendship for Leigh was that with Oswald Frewen, also with a legal background. Frewen had previously been a Commander in the Royal Navy; quiet, balding and slim, he was the son of Clara, sister of Jennie Jerome, who married Randolph Churchill (Oswald was close to his cousin Winston), and Morton Frewen (nicknamed Mortal Ruin), the popular but prodigal MP. Leigh had helped Oswald create The Sheephouse at Brede in East Sussex, a house in the grounds of Brede Place which had belonged to the Churchill family; it was converted from an ancient sheepbarn into a delightful home with superb views over the extensive gardens (laid out with Leigh's help) to the Brede Valley.

Vivien came to know and love Brede even after her separation from Leigh. She also took greatly to Clare Sheridan, Oswald's sister, an intrepid, pioneering and multitalented woman; she and Oswald had travelled extensively to Russia and Spain and she had rejected marriage proposals from the wealthy Earl of Wilton to pursue careers as a sculptor and writer, along the way fitting in love affairs, with Trotsky and Lenin (she made busts of both) in Russia and Charlie Chaplin in Hollywood among her conquests. She and Vivien formed an instant bond.

Although Leigh's formidable mother was unsure about their suitability together, Leigh had fallen deeply in love with Vivien; she had beguiled him utterly and he was taken aback by the force of his feelings for her. Vivien's 1932 diary alternates between busy RADA times – she acted in *As You Like It* and Somerset Maugham's drama *Caesar's Wife* – and an ever-busier social life with Leigh at cocktail parties, dinners at the Bath Club or the Berkeley where Jamie Hamilton often joined them; he loved dancing so would often take the floor with Vivien while Leigh looked on benevolently. She wanted Leigh to experience Ireland and they went with "The Victorians" as she referred to her parents and Tommy, who joined the party. Staying in Bridlington – braving the fierce currents to swim in the bay – briefly beforehand, she wrote to Leigh:

> What a heavenly sight that light morning will be in Ireland. Enhanced by the knowledge that the day will be a beautiful one and that one will drive out to the 'silversands' where there's never a soul, a surf ride at a tremendous rate up Killarney Bay to a little scooped-out beach ... I know you'll love it there.

The Irish trip was a signal success; "The Victorians" stayed on for more fishing while the now officially engaged couple ("Great thrilldom" Vivien wrote of this to her friend Jane Glancy) returned to London to prepare for the wedding. It had been agreed with Leigh that Vivien would leave RADA, about which she seemed to have made no objection, although her departure disappointed the Academy's founder Sir Kenneth Barnes, who told her that he had noticed her hard work and that he felt she would have succeeded on the stage, to which she allegedly replied: "Wait and see – I'll be back." The trio of the Hartleys and Tommy were back in London in December, ready for the marriage; Gertrude greatly enjoyed shopping with Vivien for final items of her trousseau. On 20 December 1932 Vivien made a brief diary entry: "Too tired to write, but I got married. *Wonderful* day."

CHAPTER 3

Young Wife and Mother

The wedding of Leigh Holman to Vivien Hartley was a fashionable affair – Gertrude was gratified that a photograph of the couple in *The Daily Sketch* appeared alongside one of King George V and Queen Mary – held at the Catholic church of St James's in Spanish Place. Patsy Quinn was a bridesmaid and remembered Vivien in a simple white satin dress and a Juliet cap of pearls holding a more elaborate veil:

> So young – so slim and a little frail, her heart as a child at school was never robust and I remember her chest was always weak.

Everything was along conventional lines for a comfortably-off couple of the period. The "Holmen", as Oswald Frewen dubbed them, honeymooned ("blest hours") in Paris and then Vivien was able to show her husband some of her favourite places – Salzburg ("very glad to be there again – showed Leigh everything") and Leipzig ("everything the same but different with Leigh"). They began London life together at Eyre Court, Leigh's Finchley Road modern-block apartment. Gertrude was in Biarritz for a course in facial massage, planning the consolidation of her business, initially based in Dover Street, while Ernest was adapting to a new job in the City as a bill-broker and so Vivien alone adapted Leigh's bachelor flat with new soft furnishings more to her taste. That accomplished, there was little for her to do; Leigh already had a maid who cleaned the compact flat and was used to preparing weekday meals. Long hours on the telephone to friends from Roehampton or RADA only increased her sense of isolation.

In marrying so young and determinedly Vivien had imagined she was taking the reins of her life; in fact, she had, not untypically, rather impulsively thrown herself at it. Her diary by contrast with the previous year is often blank,

simply noting a few lunches with friends, including Jamie Hamilton's lively
new girlfriend and later wife, Yvonne Pallavicino, weekends at Brede,
sometimes with Clare Sheridan ("divine person") present who made Vivien's
life seem humdrum, and Devon visits usually coinciding with local hunts or
point-to-points. Much as she liked the country, this was not her ideal scenario,
and it soon changed.

First she persuaded Leigh to allow her to re-enrol at RADA, slightly bending
truth to convince him that mainly this would maintain her French (RADA did
have a French course then), and sometimes he could be coaxed into seeing
a play (she adored *Richard of Bordeaux* which catapulted John Gielgud to
stardom) or to supper at the Embassy, sometimes with Jamie Hamilton, who
recalled that period of his life before his second marriage:

> Kaleidoscopic memories of your first coming to my flat at Knightsbridge Court
> with Leigh, a silk scarf round your neck, of motoring to RADA, of dancing at the
> Embassy ... of your wedding and that weekend in Devon when you knew you were
> pregnant.

Her pregnancy, most likely dating from a visit to Devon in February for the
funeral of Leigh's mother, was unlikely to have been planned; there would
have been little point in arranging to return to RADA in preparation for an
acting career. She loved the atmosphere in Gower Street – the classes, the
rehearsals, the "shop" gossip – and again she would have to leave. At least she
had something to occupy her; Leigh's apartment was too small for a baby (and
the obligatory nanny) and it was Vivien who did most of the house-hunting,
finally finding a stylish small Queen Anne house in Little Stanhope Street in
that village-like Mayfair enclave of Shepherd Market. Even today it still has
some mews houses, narrow side streets, pubs and independent shops with
the affluent jostling the raffish. A bonus – or omen – for Vivien was that the
London-born Broadway star Lynn Fontanne had lodged in the house early in
her career, but Leigh liked its quirky charm too. The rooms were small but they
both had good eyes for furniture (later Vivien said Leigh taught her most of
what she knew of antiques) and together they furnished Little Stanhope Street,
top-floor nursery included, with finds from weekend drives to small Cotswold
towns where the antique shops often had bargains. Her flair for home-making
was helped by a good colour sense and a knack of cleverly adding interest
relatively inexpensively with lamps, cushions and objets d'art. She enhanced
the room dimensions by adroitly placing mirrors or opening up cupboards
beside fireplaces to create open shelving, sometimes backed by mirrors and
backlit to boost the illusion of space. They entertained regularly, with Leigh's

legal friends regular guests and sometimes Vivien's RADA chums whose liveliness and gossip were less to Leigh's taste.

Social life diminished in late summer; although her pregnancy was trouble-free her labour was long and the birth on 10 October (Gertrude was present) painful, as she told Patsy Quinn ("That was a very messy business. I don't think I'll do it again in a hurry"). Later she surprised Olivia de Havilland in Hollywood by describing childbirth as "humiliating", a situation in which a woman has no real control. The event was recorded in her diary, somewhat laconically ("Had a baby – a girl"). She wrote describing her daughter – named Suzanne – to her friend Jane Pauling in similarly ironic vein:

> The spinster Holman is minute, and does not allow anyone to be very proud of her yet, as she only makes rude noises, and shows a tendency to greed and petulance … *Radiant* motherhood (if there really is such a thing) hasn't hit me yet.

Vivien was ambivalent about motherhood, not entirely surprisingly for one barely out of her teens. She said later:

> I loved my baby as every mother does but with the clear-cut sincerity of youth I realised that I could not abandon all thought of a career on the stage. Some force within myself would not be denied.

Partly because of events, not least her separation from Leigh and Suzanne after meeting Olivier and then the outbreak of war when she was in America, the maternal bond never had a proper chance to thrive initially. Brought up mostly by her father and grandmother, Suzanne loved her mother deeply and in later years they were strongly attached. Vivien later was also understanding and considerate with her stepson Tarquin, who had a similarly fractured early life, without ever usurping the role of his mother.

But following the birth, the nanny controlled Stanhope Street's nursery; a cook and a maid were also on the staff. Mills Martin called once on the nanny's day off, to walk into a wall of wails from Suzanne with Vivien paying scant attention (Mills noted: "It is possible to give birth without the maternal glands working"). And actress Fabia Drake, who had met Vivien at a lunch party and often visited the Holmans, thought that while Vivien admired Leigh and appreciated his intelligence and kindness, "she was bored with her marriage to a barrister".

What Vivien really wanted was to work. Not for money primarily but because of what she had described as "some force within myself". She still had a circle of RADA friends, one of whom, Hazel Terry, tipped her off about a film to be made by Gainsborough Pictures starring the musical-comedy star Cicely Courtneidge with scenes set in a top-drawer girls' school. That period, with films still in the early days of sound, was hardly the British movie industry's finest hour, although change was on the horizon. Most studios were mainly involved in turning out "Quota Quickies" to satisfy the percentage of domestic screen footage demanded by the Government in return for permitting the lion's share to Hollywood product. It was then a much less unionised business; small parts and extras were often cast from recent drama school graduates or debutantes for a token daily pound or two as payment. Vivien left some photographs and her forwarding address with the production office before leaving with Leigh for a sailing holiday in Scandinavian waters. Their first stop was Copenhagen, where she found a telegram saying she might be required for filming which was enough (even without a firm offer) for Vivien to leave the sailing party and set out for home. This did not please her husband (he wrote back to her that if they were to be regularly separated in this way he might want her to stop "this film business").

Inevitably the studio schedule changed and Vivien did not make her professional debut until a week after her return. *Things Are Looking Up* is no masterpiece (contrary to some reports it is not a "lost film" and Vivien's single line as one of a group of unusually glamorous sixth-formers – "If you are not made headmistress I shan't come back next term" – was not cut) but for Vivien it was a thrilling experience. The director, Albert de Courville, had worked in the theatre and he created an easy on-set atmosphere, working speedily on the film, the plot of which was loose, to say the least, with "Cis" Courtneidge in a double role as twins Bertha and Cicely Fyffe – one a jolly fairground artiste, her sister a stern schoolmistress. Complications arise when one stands in at the school for the other after a surprise elopement but knows little of geometry or tennis (the latter involves a surprise guest appearance from Wimbledon champion Suzanne Lenglen). De Courville licked the 80-minute film along with some energy although the tight schedule allowed for little finesse and even the most brilliant talent-spotter would have been unlikely to predict a dazzling future from Vivien's brief screen-time. Still it was a start, leaving her hungry for more. Even the waits between set-ups allowed her to take in at least some of the mechanics of filming and during her time on set she watched, absorbing everything she could, even in scenes which did not involve her. She made new friends among the other girls, including Anne Wilding, a fellow crossword-addict, who remembered them leafing through a movie magazine ("We saw a picture of Laurence Olivier and I remarked I didn't like his eyebrows. But Vivien thought he was the tops").

Another aspirant on set was Maud Miller, who wrote 20 years later of meeting Vivien on the Cobham location, noticing how she managed to catch the eye of the assistant director to snaffle her one line ("looks like she'll get some place some day" Maud wrote in her own diary). Maud asked Vivien if she was doing the job just for fun, to be greeted by one haughtily raised eyebrow ("I happen to be an actress. I am *not* playing at the game"). Maud went on perceptively to write of Vivien then:

> a warm-hearted person when you get to know her ... a curious mixture of child and sophisticate, actress and mother with a suspicion of the siren Cleopatra ... there is one streak that only those who know her best are aware of. It's her steely determination.

The one "snaffled" line raised Vivien to the status of a "special" artiste. She became friends with Dora Nirva, who worked in the production office and eased her way into being driven home in a studio car with the "special girls".

The freemasonry of the unemployed among actors continued to help Vivien. Another RADA friend, Beryl Samson, told her of a new young London theatrical agent – few actors can negotiate a career without a good agent – called John Gliddon. Like many agents, Gliddon was an ex-actor, pragmatic enough to realise his limited talent, who had set up with a little money from his father in a tiny Regent Street office (vital to have a good address in such a status-conscious business). He was determined to build up a client list from actors for whom he could help shape careers, somewhat along Hollywood lines. He always liked his independence and although he found some major talent – Deborah Kerr and Stewart Granger included – inevitably (it still happens) clients often moved on once established to larger, multi-agent organisations. Gliddon was discreetly gay, well-dressed and good company. He had stressed to Beryl Samson his intention to foster home-grown talent which he could help groom for the expansion of native cinema which he foresaw; she mentioned Vivien and Gliddon told her to bring her to meet him.

Vivien took great care to present herself well – wearing one of her most flattering dresses, a picture hat and generous sprays of scent – although Gliddon said it was her green-blue eyes which first struck him. He spotted something in her at that first meeting, something of that "force" she mentioned herself:

> For my part I had made up my mind that here was a very beautiful girl who possessed that rare gift – star quality. I wanted her to be quite certain that I meant business. Firstly I needed to get her to sign a contract with me so that I alone would be responsible for her progress to stardom.

Gliddon was at least partly responsible for her stage name. After various suggestions – April Morn was, rightly, sharply vetoed – Vivian Hartley became Vivien Leigh by taking her husband's first name as her second (the Vivien came when her first West End producer said Vivian could be a man's name too). The business side involved Gliddon consulting with Leigh, who seemed none too keen on the turn of events; he was not exactly rude but would not agree to a long-term contract to tie his wife down and Gliddon had to be content to leave Little Stanhope Street with initially only a two-year contract. He remembered how, as Leigh and he talked, Vivien sat quietly "like the Cheshire cat", adding that as he saw her:

> Sitting there with the firelight reflected in those green eyes I looked at Leigh Holman and thought to myself, you'll have a devil of a hard job holding this one.

Vivien was happy enough then to put herself in Gliddon's hands. Although a relatively novice agent, he knew how the business worked. He calculated that Vivien's looks would get her noticed and planned to make sure that she was seen in all the right places where influential theatre and film people congregated. If money needed to be spent on some first nights, lunches at the Ivy, the Savoy Grill or the Moulin d'Or it was worth it to show off what he regarded as an investment for the future; if under his tutelage Vivien became a star then his percentage of her earnings could be substantial. Soon Gliddon was able to find her some film work through his contacts who included John Payne, who ran an agency specialising in casting for "Quota Quickies".

These films were looked down on at the time and indeed many were technically clumsy and poorly scripted. The 1930s are sometimes portrayed as a Dark Age of British film; certainly the industry was still Hollywood's poor relation and not only in competitive terms. The cinema was phenomenally popular in a period of anxiety and depression; by the end of the decade it was by far the most important medium of British popular culture (18 million tickets sold each week) with an average of three new cinemas opening weekly, those "Dream Palaces" or lavish secular temples where stars were worshipped. It was essentially an era of escapism. There was successful local product, mainly the films of music-hall stars like Gracie Fields or George Formby and a few outstanding directors (Alfred Hitchcock or the young Carol Reed) but little of the output held any kind of mirror to British society.

Although Vivien's first films were made against that background, she was in fact entering an industry on the cusp of change. Throughout the 1930s a whole wave of émigré talent arrived in England as the Nazi threat expanded. Alexander Korda, a Hungarian mostly self-invented charmer of a producer/director ('I don't grow on trees' he once said grandly but accurately), arrived with his two brothers, soon establishing London Films, with the effrontery to compete with Hollywood in the international market, producing biopics such as *The Private Life of Henry VIII* and *Rembrandt*, both with one of Britain's few world stars, Charles Laughton.

Korda is recorded as (but not credited with) co-producing *Things Are Looking Up* and he was followed by a remarkable line of émigré talent, from cinematographers to designers, several of whom Vivien would work with throughout the decade. And the scorned "Quota Quickies" nurtured talent, despite limited budgets and tight schedules; Carol Reed, David Lean and Michael Balcon all cut their teeth in that fast turn-around world.

Balcon had produced Vivien's first film and another rising talent, Anthony Havelock-Allan, who later worked closely with David Lean, oversaw her second, *The Village Squire* (1935) which Gliddon found for her through John Payne. Just over an hour long, it was made in one week (six guineas a day for Vivien), directed by one of the theatre directors recruited for the screen by film companies in the early sound days. Reginald Denham, a journeyman writer/director, was in charge of *The Village Squire*, another heavy-handed comedy, set around a production of *Macbeth* by the amateur dramatic society in a sleepy English village with a splenetically moviephobic Squire and a visiting film star drawn into the subsequent quarrels. Made at Elstree, the part of one of the Squire's daughters was at least a significant supporting role and Vivien has a cool aplomb as the rather snooty Rose while the star falls for her sister. Some luck came from this film too; the Squire was played by a splendid English character actor, David Horne, a rubicund figure with the most eloquent jowls on the British stage or screen prior to Michael Hordern. Always encouraging to actors with talent just starting their careers, he also liked crosswords and he and Vivien duelled over the *Times* puzzle during breaks. He was delighted when Havelock-Allan, who had also noticed Vivien, cast her alongside him in another "Quickie", *A Gentleman's Agreement* (1935).

A more serious film, this apparently (no print survives) had a poor script – a switched-identity story of an educated wastrel and a down-and-out – with Horne as an aristocrat and Vivien in a flatly written part as an unemployed typist. It had an interesting director, however. George Pearson, forgotten today, was one of early British film's pioneering figures, an ex-teacher with a passionate belief in the cinema as a cultural and educational force. After many silents, he worked for Gaumont before his experiment of an independent studio bankrupted him, forcing him into whatever work he could find (he directed eight "Quickies" in one year alone). He was as inventive as possible within the restrictions imposed; the camera-work in his films is markedly more fluid than that of many directors then (he pioneered the moving camera-shot) and Vivien, always a quick study, again could absorb priceless hints about the sheer craft of film-making.

It was David Horne, continuing as mentor, who made Vivien's professional stage debut possible. He had just started rehearsals for *The Green Sash*, a period play set in fourteenth-century Italy, when the actress cast as his alluring younger wife was taken ill and had to withdraw. Horne remembered Vivien and the theatre called Gliddon, who sent her out to the "Q" Theatre on Kew Bridge to audition. The "Q", previously a roller-skating rink and then a small film studio, was one of a handful of smaller "off-West End" venues (the Embassy in Swiss Cottage and the Gate in Villiers Street were others) producing sometimes offbeat new work, usually for brief runs. It was controlled by the remarkable pair of Jack and Beatrice de Leon, he an all-round theatre man, Beatie a shrewd negotiator (young actors – Dirk Bogarde, Margaret Lockwood, Irene Worth – often had early breaks there largely because Beatie could get away with low – and on occasion no – pay). Jack, directing *The Green Sash*, was dubious about Vivien's lack of stage experience but Gliddon cleverly coaxed him into rehearsing with her for a day on approval before deciding. Her probation as Giusta, a flighty Florentine young wife, luckily involved scenes with Horne, who could ease any nerves, de Leon was a capable director, and she was contracted at the end of the day.

She loved everything about the "Q" experience, the backstage life, the camaraderie, the smell of size and greasepaint. The "Q", a somewhat quirky enterprise seating just under 500, ideal for Vivien's still underpowered voice, had a regular audience, a cosy backstage ambience (complete with Green Room) and was most efficiently run, with high scenic and casting standards. Vivien's role in an underdeveloped play – the local press complained of its brief running time – was demanding, rarely off stage and with some challenging later emotional scenes but she acquitted herself well. Oswald Frewen drove to Kew to see it ("I liked it and thought it good") and although *The Times* critic judged the play (by T.P. Wood and the wonderfully named Debonnaire Sylvester) flimsy, it boosted Vivien's confidence to read that her performance "had a precision and lightness which should serve her well when her material is of more substance". She said herself later that she was too inexperienced for such a demanding part and was probably not entirely at ease but she had the smell of theatre strongly in her nostrils after "Q".

Leigh was beginning to realise that his wife's acting ambitions might be more than what Oswald at first diagnosed as a transient fancy ("Once she gets it out of her system she'll be alright"); perhaps he took more heed of Jamie's suggestion that it would be unwise to try to stop her ("But it will be the end of your marriage").

Gliddon still squired Vivien around fashionable London watering holes, determined to avoid more "Quickies", now set on moulding her into a star, convinced that she had real talent apart from her astonishing looks. Vivien still saw her girlfriends; perhaps to thank Beryl Samson for her help she took her to lunch in the autumn of 1934, as her diary records, then to a matinee of the successful *Theatre Royal* by George S. Kaufman and Edna Ferber, a fast-moving Broadway satirical comedy based on the Barrymore acting dynasty, directed by Noël Coward with a rising star, Laurence Olivier, as the John Barrymore figure in a performance highly praised for its athletic brio, full of physical agility, swordfights and exuberance. In what sounds like a replay of her first glimpse of Leigh – if the often-repeated story is true – Vivien whispered to Beryl "That's the man I'm going to marry" and when Beryl replied "Don't be silly! You're both married already", her immediate response was "That doesn't matter, I'm going to marry him." She did not meet Olivier on that occasion; their first meeting was some time away.

Using his contacts again, Gliddon persuaded an old schoolfriend, Basil Dean, to see Vivien. Another largely forgotten figure, Dean in his day was one of the most powerful figures in the British theatre, running London's St Martin's Theatre with his business partner Alec Rea, presenting the ReanDean company in work by authors as varied as John Galsworthy, Somerset Maugham and Clemence Dane, with his actors including established names and newcomers, most notably the mesmerising Meggie Albanesi, who died tragically young and by whom Dean remained obsessed. Moving into films he was central to Associated Talking Pictures (ATP) at Ealing Studios but, although in the theatre a superb stager and technical wizard, Dean was inept behind the camera and most of his films are inert with next to no rhythm or comedic flair. He was an appalling bully, given to acid sarcasm – actors called him many things behind his back, the politest being "The Basilisk" or "Bloody Basil" – and was not always astute financially. He fell out with ATP's main backer and never directed another film after 1938, but for a time, exploiting separately the appeal of Gracie Fields and George Formby, his films were popular and lucrative.

Dean was interested enough to secure an option on Vivien's services but after the enjoyable times on her early minor films her experience on Dean's

Look Up and Laugh (1935) – optimistic title given the results – was wretched. The film was, remarkably, scripted by J.B. Priestley, who had written Fields's major hit *Sing As We Go!* but this was wan by comparison. "Our Gracie" played a variation on her usual indomitable working-class heroine, here a successful singer returning to her fictional home town of Plumborough to fight on her ailing father's behalf to keep the town's market-stalls open in defiance of the ruthless capitalist department-store owner plotting to develop the site. Not a subtle film – but then subtlety was never the point of Fields on screen – this has the grace of a Sherman tank, with some dire set pieces (Gracie impersonating an operatic diva, an over-extended chase through the store). Although made on a decent budget, the technical work looks cheap – the opening sequence, with Gracie trilling the title number as she drives along, has the crudest back-projection – as do the costumes. Vivien had little to go on; cast as the daughter of the store's manager (the bullfrog-faced farceur Alfred Drayton, well over the top), unaccountably engaged to the star's gormless brother Tommy Fields whose stutter vanishes whenever he sings (too often), her material is poor and she had scant help from her director. Still, she manages to squeeze some independence of spirit into her character, defying her bellowing father by taking the stallholders' side. Dean wrote in his memoirs:

> She was so uncontrollably nervous that for a while she seemed unable to take direction, a circumstance for which I made insufficient allowance. I became impatient.

Irascibility rarely gets the best out of actors. Dean seemed even crosser on set than in the theatre, probably because he was insecure, aware of his limitations, in the film studio. Gracie Fields was in effect carrying the film but she found time to console Vivien after another Dean tongue-lashing: "Don't worry, lass. You've got something."

Dean thought otherwise and did not take up his option on Vivien despite the advice of his shrewd casting director Aubrey Blackburn (later a leading agent) who urged his boss to reconsider. Gliddon quickly arranged an interview with Korda, a major force in British cinema now and working out of Isleworth Studios shortly before creating his own studios at Denham. Vivien had high hopes of this, again dressing in her best, but again was disappointed. Korda, as was his habit, kept Vivien and Gliddon waiting, but then it was a brief, non-committal interview from behind his cigar-smoke screen with only the vague suggestion of a screen test at some future stage.

Luck, once more, played a key part in the pattern of Vivien's career, just after she had seemingly failed to make much impression on Korda. One of the West

End's great characters then was Sydney Carroll, ex-critic, producer, entrepreneur (recently he had helped establish the Open Air Theatre in Regent's Park), talent-spotter (Greer Garson, Jack Hawkins) and journalist, with a regular *Daily Telegraph* column, one of those Fleet Street/West End jacks-of-all-trades of the era, like the critic James Agate who similarly wore different hats using various pseudonyms. Carroll was preparing a West End production of *The Mask of Virtue* by the exiled German writer Carl Sternheim. A period play set in 1745 France (inspired by Diderot's *Jacques Le Fataliste*), it was a small-scale piece with one role especially difficult to cast, that of a young girl of good family whose widowed mother has fallen on times so hard that her beautiful daughter has to take to prostitution; they become pawns in a revenge plot by the powerful Mme de Pommeraye, spurned mistress of the Marquis d'Arcy, a libertine who has tired of his lover who now uses the young, innocent-seeming Henriette Duquesnoy as bait, not bargaining for real love to develop between her victims. Written in 1918 as *Die Marquise von Arcis*, the play was unusual for Sternheim, best known for satirical comedies (*Die Hose – The Knickers –* probably the most performed). He had left Germany in 1935 and was present at some rehearsals with his translator Ashley Dukes, himself a dramatist. For West End audiences then it was unusual fare, an acrid-toned comedy of mostly bad manners with a challenging last-act confrontation.

Henriette was a crucial role. Her looks, stressed in the text, had to be special and a quality of innocence was essential, with a suggestion of wordliness underneath. Carroll had had a tough time already on casting; George Grossmith was originally to have played the Marquis but fell ill and two others fell through before Carroll cast Frank Cellier, a popular Shakespearean actor. Lady Tree was cast as Henriette's mother and Jeanne de Casalis, acerbic and stylish, was to play the avenger. With this strong trio it was vital that Henriette be more than a passenger. Carroll had tried Peggy Ashcroft and Anna Neagle besides others but no suitable candidate seemed available. With time running out, Carroll called his friend Aubrey Blackburn for suggestions, emphasising the necessity of finding an actress of genuine beauty. Blackburn at once suggested Vivien (subsequently everyone from Carroll to Gliddon claimed credit). Vivien never lost touch with Blackburn; when he wrote to her when she was going through a difficult time in 1960, he quoted her as "sweetly saying you would always regard me as your Godfather in the theatre".

Carroll arranged for Vivien and four other candidates – he now decided to cast an unknown actress, a wiser move in fact – to read in his office with the director Maxwell Wray who looked at the assembled possibles in the outer office and then said to Carroll: "If Vivien Leigh is the girl at the end, then as far as I'm concerned the part is cast." When she read, Carroll sat gazing at Vivien, at her most exquisite, and Gliddon, accompanying her, watched Carroll:

> He was smitten, and Vivien knew it. She did her spell-binding act and in what seemed an amazingly short time Sydney had hired her at £10 a week subject to a satisfactory audition on stage.

Carroll liked fostering new talent, especially female – his casting couch reputedly had considerable wear (although not with Vivien) – but, still unsure about this particular casting in light of her youth, he asked his friend, the sophisticated actress Dame Lillian Braithwaite, to sit in on the audition and talk to Vivien. The Dame was able to reassure the producer: "Sydney, put your mind at rest. Miss Leigh is married and already has a child."

With rehearsals under way, Vivien realised that much of the evening rested on her shoulders but again she was lucky – she was surrounded by actors both strongly cast and genuinely helpful and had a sympathetic director. Maxwell Wray had a good eye – recently he had directed a well-received elegantly-designed *Twelfth Night* at Regent's Park – and also a good ear, later directing many West End musicals. On Sternheim's chamber-piece, with Jeanne de Casalis and Lady Tree perfectly cast, he was able to take special care with Frank Cellier, toning down his natural ebullience, and with the inexperienced Vivien. He quickly grasped that she had genuine grace in movement and repose, arranging as many passages of the latter as possible for her beauty to register the more strongly; he also kept her downstage much of the time so that her voice, still low on resonance, would not be strained, even in the intimate Ambassador's Theatre (it seats around 500). Vivien's bonus was the consideration from her fellow actors, something with which they would not have bothered had they thought her inadequate, giving her practical tips (Lady Tree passed on an exercise – to take three deep breaths before each entrance to control the breathing muscles – which Vivien practised throughout her career) and rehearsing out of hours to mine the supposedly virginal qualities of earlier scenes and the contrastedly emotional final confrontation when the ruse is exposed and Henriette pleads for redemption.

Carroll deliberately kept press interest at a minimum prior to opening (no out-of-town try-out and, in those days, no London previews) and while Vivien had gone through rehearsals with growing confidence she was still extremely nervous on 15 May 1935 with Leigh, Ernest and Gertrude, John Gliddon and Beryl Samson out front.

Her first entrance in *The Mask of Virtue* was, nerve-shreddingly, only after a long, barbed scene between the Marquis and his discarded lover; when Vivien appeared, there was an audible gasp from the house (whispers of "Who is she?") and then pin-drop attentive silence throughout. The play, a sexual spider's web somewhat akin to *Les Liaisons Dangereuses*, held throughout, even through the perilous later scenes of high-wattage emotional tension, and at the curtain the applause was thunderous, described by the *Daily Mail* critic as "one of the biggest ovations a newcomer has had for quite a long time". That critic, Harold Conway, went backstage to report:

> a new British star arose on the stage last night with spectacular suddenness ... In a difficult leading costume role her exceptional beauty and assured acting set the experienced first-nighters excitedly asking who this unknown actress was.

Fleet Street then seized on such theatre stories. Like Basil Dean's tragic discovery Meggie Albanesi in Clemence Dane's *A Bill of Divorcement*, Vivien became a star overnight. She knew that much of this was press-hype; she may have had star quality but she was aware that James Agate in the *Sunday Times* was right when, although generally praising her performance, he suggested she needed to work on her voice. Sydney Carroll admired her pragmatism.

> Her personality is charming in the extreme, but its possessor realises that something more than personality is called for in the struggle up the ladder.

There was still the savouring of success to enjoy; Vivien and her party celebrated at the Florida, a chic Berkeley Square nightspot, and she and Leigh went down to Fleet Street for the morning-paper rave reviews. There was little sleep before the press descended on Little Stanhope Street. Photographers and reporters packed the small sitting room while she posed in various outfits for different papers (rather unconvincingly strumming a ukulele in one). Much of what appeared was blatant invention – Vivien had "won RADA's Gold Medal", had "an Indian Cavalry father", was "just nineteen" (she was 22) and had actually "acted at the Comédie Française". She told the respected journalist and early feminist Margaret Lane that she thought it possible to combine marriage and a child with a career. Leigh may have been less sure as Gliddon went into action to maximise his client's sensational success. Accounts vary as to Korda's sudden interest in Vivien – she had heard no word about the vaguely promised screen test but he had tickets for her opening night and definitely saw some of it, possibly only the second act, but was obviously keen enough, glossed by her reviews, to call Gliddon the morning after to discuss a possible contract. Gliddon, cheekily, kept Korda waiting, saying he could only meet the following day. He was in a strong position, with other studios nibbling (Basil Dean came back with a revised offer which Gliddon enjoyed rejecting) and Korda, who liked to boast "I never bargain", was forced to up a paltry initial offer to a five-year contact which, should it go to plan, would pay Vivien £18,000 for two films in its final year, handsome money in the 1930s.

Leigh Holman had a thing or two to say about this, bringing his own solicitor to argue with Gliddon that he would be making too much personal profit if Vivien's contract ran its full term, even if Gliddon had her written consent to represent her. Leigh was clearly worried that Vivien's career could hole their marriage below the water-line; a reticent man, the ballyhoo of showbusiness somewhat alarmed him. In trying to assert his authority he compromised, with Gliddon to receive 10 per cent of Vivien's earnings (a standard rate) but for three years, not five.

In the immediate term some momentum – it often happens – went out of the rocket-like trajectory of Vivien's career. Carroll, unwisely, tried to capitalise on *The Mask of Virtue*'s success by transferring it to the larger St James's Theatre but the move was announced late and business there never built sufficiently over the next two months, after which Vivien was both out of work and deflated. If Leigh imagined she might now settle to a more domestic lifestyle he was mistaken. If there was no film or stage work she was happy to keep her face before the public with personal appearances or by following other actresses in advertising skin cream or new publications. She also occasionally modelled for a young South African-born couturier, Victor Stiebel, who became a close friend, together with his partner, composer Richard Adinsell. She was also photographed for *Vogue*, in a Stiebel outfit, by Cecil Beaton, his first session with her, for which the caption described her "like a Persian gazelle in the dark studio forest".

Leigh, suited to a peaceful domestic life in London with occasional weekends in Devon or at Brede, felt it better not to rock the boat and seemed happy enough for Vivien to be out "being seen" in the evenings when not working, understanding her youth and love of dancing and comfortable enough with her spending time with other escorts. One personable squire was the good-looking American John (Jack) Wilson, lover and soon business partner of Noël Coward, who shared her love of dancing:

> We became fast friends – we would start off at London's more routine places – the Ritz, Claridge's or the Savoy – until they closed at one a.m. which was the law. But London had a nest of places called "bottle clubs" and we would continue whirling about until four or five in the morning. I would then take her home in a taxi, chastely kiss her on her forehead and send her into her husband who was

presumably sound asleep. I never saw him and, what's more, I never met anyone who had.

Leigh had no worries about Wilson, nor about Robert Helpmann, the actor-dancer who had admired Vivien in *The Mask of Virtue* and swept her into his coterie, often squiring her to the same "bottle clubs" as Wilson, although Leigh was less taken by his outrageously camp jokes. More dangerous a companion was John Buckmaster, a figure who crops up at several points in Vivien's life, usually balefully. The good-looking son of actress Gladys Cooper by her first husband Herbert Buckmaster, actor and founder of Buck's, the St James's men's club, "Bucky" had a whiff of sulphur about him, a nervous edge which could lead to severely depressed spells (his mother described them as "the 'flu"); he was doing passably well as an actor and had a profitable sideline in a nightclub act performing his own material. Clever as a box of ferrets, good company and an experienced ladies' man, he would seem, from the evidence, to have been Vivien's first extramarital affair. In August 1935 there are nine diary notes of meetings with "Bucky", and more into the following year. She also lunched several times with Clare Sheridan ("wild, divine creature"), never one to counsel caution in affairs of the heart. Again, Vivien was flinging herself at life, with no guilt – sex was appetite and pleasure – and it is likely from what she suggested to friends that Leigh no longer satisfied her in bed. The circles in which she was moving, among actors and writers in nightclubs and Soho bars, a world of alcohol-fuelled casual promiscuity, together with her insomnia, kept her in a kind of permanent "high", a state of euphoria, at that time.

After opening in *The Mask of Virtue*, Vivien and Leigh had spent the next weekend after her success at Brede where Oswald Frewen, worried that such a triumph might change her, scrutinised her carefully before pronouncing "Well, I don't *see* any change" to which she insisted "There isn't any change and there never *will* be, Oswald." But soon he could tell that there was some shift; she was still delightful and a loyal friend, but he now understood that her work had never been just an enjoyable diversion. She was pressing Gliddon to pursue Korda who as usual was juggling too many projects. There was some excitement when it seemed she would play Roxanne in *Cyrano de Bergerac* opposite Charles Laughton but plans were jinxed by script problems and Laughton's usual havering while he worried about Vivien's hair, the screenplay and the length of Cyrano's nose, before it joined the long list of Korda's abandoned projects. The social whirl continued, including her first meeting with Olivier. According to the French actor Jean-Pierre Aumont, he intuited some sexual magnetism between Vivien and Olivier possibly even before they had properly met. He was dining in Soho with the actor Anthony Bushell in 1936 and became aware of "the most ravishing creature that can be imagined" eating with an older man. She seemed abstracted, pursuing some interior dream, glancing now and then towards another table where a blonde woman sat with a darkly handsome man whose looks were marked by something intense:

> I said to Tony: "That young woman and that young man at the other table are madly in love with each other." Tony laughed: "That's a Frenchman for you! I know them both – she's Vivien Leigh, he's Laurence Olivier. I don't even know if they've ever met!"

Whatever the precise chronology, they were formally introduced by Buckmaster (Vivien, knowing he knew Olivier, may well have engineered the meeting) at the Savoy after a late supper. Since *Theatre Royal*, Olivier's star had risen further when he alternated Romeo and Mercutio with Gielgud in the latter's production of *Romeo and Juliet*, with Olivier's Romeo, played as a testosterone-fuelled hot youth proving highly controversial although many, Vivien included, thrilled to its virile athleticism. Olivier and his actress wife Jill Esmond dined often at the Savoy Grill after performances. After first being rebuked by Vivien for criticising Olivier's looks after shaving off his Ronald Colman-ish moustache, Buckmaster introduced the Oliviers to Vivien in the Savoy foyer as all four headed for taxis. The Oliviers invited Vivien and her husband to the house near Maidenhead which they were renting for weekends (Vivien's diary prominently recorded "Larry Olivier's for weekend").

In his memoirs Olivier recalled a visit shortly afterwards to the New Theatre:

> I was making up for a matinee when she popped into my dressing-room; it was ostensibly to invite us to something or other; she only stayed a couple of minutes and then she gave me a soft little kiss on the shoulder and was gone.

He had seen her on stage, writing of her in *The Mask of Virtue*:

> Apart from her looks, which were magical, she possessed beautiful poise ... She had something else: an attraction of the most perturbing nature I had ever encountered.

The words "ostensibly" and "perturbing" reinforce the impression of echoes of Evelyn Waugh's just-audible "batsqueaks of sexuality" in these early encounters.

Work separated them for a time; Vivien made her Shakespearean debut in *Richard II* under Gielgud's direction, playing the supporting role of Richard's sad Queen for the Oxford University Dramatic Society (OUDS) which had a tradition of productions with professional directors and actresses in the female roles. Both Gielgud and his associate director Glen Byam Shaw (Gielgud's acting commitments in London reduced his available directing time) had admired Vivien in *The Mask of Virtue*. Byam Shaw had acted with Gielgud's company and was now turning to directing although it was Gielgud who had suggested her:

> She had a lifelong devotion to the theatre and determined to work there diligently through the years ... she was modest and shrewd enough to face the challenge of developing herself so as to find the widest possible range of which she was capable.

Such professional insights rather give the lie to suggestions that it was only when Olivier became a kind of Svengali to her passive Trilby that Vivien began to take the stage seriously. Byam Shaw found her so terribly nervous when she auditioned – on stage at the New where she had so often watched *Romeo and Juliet* – that he initially questioned Gielgud's judgement, but any doubts soon evaporated:

> She was wonderful to work with. She was tremendously serious, sensitive, eager for direction, punctual and professional ... it was the start of a friendship always very precious to me.

Motley's design, a simple but effectively variable triptych of arches, with costumes of the period in strong colours, enhanced a very striking OUDS production. Max Beerbohm, whose actress-wife Florence Kahn played the Duchess of Gloucester, saw the production, pronounced it first-rate and stayed on to reply to the toast of "The Guests" at a celebration dinner after the final performance. Gielgud caught a matinee and said of Vivien's performance:

> She managed to endow it with every possible grace of speech and movement and wore her medieval costumes with consummate charm.

The Oxford experience was like a working holiday for Vivien. Gielgud had predicted that all the undergraduates would be captivated by her and they were; for the fortnight of the Oxford run she must have felt like Beerbohm's Zuleika Dobson reincarnated, gracing parties, sometimes driving a group of cast members for picnics in the country in her little car.

Beerbohm figures in her next stage appearance too. Ivor Novello offered the role of the captivating dancer Jenny Mere in Clemence Dane's version of Beerbohm's story *The Happy Hypocrite*, an enterprise, as usual with Novello's productions, infused with fun. There was an air of *fin de siècle* and *The Yellow Book* in Beerbohm's tale (subtitled "A Fairy Tale for Tired Men") although it is set in the Regency era, a teasing variation on Oscar Wilde's themes of masks and deception in *The Picture of Dorian Grey*. Dane's adaptation preserved its quality of fantasy, enhanced by Richard Adinsell's pastiche score and a witty design by the Motley team once more – sisters Margaret (Percy) and Sophia Harris and Elizabeth Montgomery – who had done such superb work for Gielgud. All the ingredients were ideally in place for the story of Lord George Hell (Novello), a metropolitan rake ("I have not seen a buttercup for twenty years") who quits London society after falling in love with the dancer Jenny, who has been alarmed by the dissipation etched on his features. Disguised by a mask, Lord George takes to an Arcadian cottage in the woods (surprisingly close to Kensington) but the idyll between him and Jenny is shattered by his discarded mistress La Gambogi, who, at the climax, tears off the mask to reveal his face – now transformed by Jenny's love to its original beauty. This was the only moment when Novello's adoring public could glimpse the Great Profile, one reason perhaps why the production, mostly hailed by critics, failed at the box-office.

Novello was impressed by Vivien's "painstaking application to her work". The role required some ballet dancing, some *en pointe*, so:

> Each morning for an hour before rehearsals she religiously took herself off to ballet lessons so she would not disgrace us in the eyes of any balletomanes.

This application was also noticed by Angus McBean, who made the mask for Lord George; Novello also offered his fellow Welshman the chance to take the production photographs and was delighted with the results, very different from the stiff, posed style of theatre photography then, and launching the career of the leading twentieth-century theatrical photographer. Vivien became an instant fan and he, although gay like Novello, admitted "I was more than a little bit in love with her."

The pre-London tour of *The Happy Hypocrite* consolidated these friendships and Vivien also had a good relationship with another great beauty of the English stage, Isabel Jeans, who played La Gambogi with stylish aplomb and shared Vivien's passions for crosswords and card games. Work on the play continued on the road as Vivien, in mock rage, reported to Leigh:

> I have told Clemence Dane that if Gambogi is written up any more I shall insist on *two* more scenes, *another* dance and *another* song!

Also in the cast was Peter Graves, who recalled endless backstage card games while another actor, Carl Harbord, told others that he had a brief fling with Vivien ("It doesn't count if it's on tour" remains the usual excuse), later telling Jack Merivale: "Even when she was sleeping with *me* she was talking of Laurence Olivier."

The production was well received in London; Vivien was gratified by Beerbohm's praise ("exquisite sensibility – a foreshadowing of how much to come") but it managed only a two-month run. First-nighters had included Olivier and a pregnant Jill Esmond. Vivien and Olivier had met on only a few occasions in recent months – a couple of lunches and, always recalled by Olivier, a first dinner for just two at "The 400" – and Vivien dropped a brick, touching on private information including his child's possible name, when she asked, looking at Jill's belly: "How's little Tarquin coming along?"

Unexpectedly available when *The Happy Hypocrite* closed, Vivien was glad of the chance to appear in another Shakespeare production, even in the small role of Anne Boleyn in *Henry VIII* at Regent's Park, opposite the tall, imposing Lyn Harding's King. Like many early mentors, Harding was extremely generous to her, coaching her in how to deal with the space's difficult acoustics. The part is no great challenge – basically Anne has to allow an audience to see why Henry would want to exchange Katharine of Aragon for her, no real stretch for Vivien. She enjoyed the experience, even in a dank summer with the stage's grass often sodden underfoot.

Korda had watched her theatrical progress with interest and now made his move. First Gliddon was told she would co-star with Conrad Veidt in a version of *Under the Red Robe* but that collapsed when Korda quixotically decided that a French-financed film should have a Gallic actress and cast the French star Annabella instead. Another film mooted – which to Vivien sounded more appealing – was a production by Erich Pommer, now working for Korda after leaving Germany, where he had produced many UFA films (including *M* and *The Cabinet of Dr Caligari*), a film based on a novel by A.E.W. Mason in which, as Korda's lawyer told Gliddon, "Larry Olivier and Ralph Richardson are playing."

As it transpired, Richardson did not appear in *Fire Over England*, in which Vivien and Olivier acted together for the first time. Both later related how they bumped into each other on their first day at Korda's new Denham Studios. Vivien politely said how much she looked forward to their working together. Olivier replied: "We'll probably end up fighting. People always get sick of each other making a film."

CHAPTER 4

Enter Olivier

L aurence Olivier loved music from boyhood, beginning when a choirboy at one of his prep schools. His education at All Saints, the beautiful High Church with its own choir school near Oxford Circus, was to a background score of Bach, Schubert, Palestrina and his beloved Handel. It was only later – making his first film, in Berlin – that he came to respond to Wagner. Like Vivien in Salzburg, it was initially to *Die Meistersingers* and during the rapture of their early times together he would often compare their pairing to that of the composer's Tristan and Isolde or Sigmund and Sieglinde. A born self-mythist, he was given to such dramatisation, his life divided into a series of self-created acts.

Vivien and he met when each was at a kind of crossroads, artistic and personal, she beginning to feel constrained in her marriage and increasingly ambitious personally and he, married to Jill since 1930, likewise troubled by professional uncertainties and personal doubts. And guilt – guilt stalked Olivier like the Hound of Heaven. Not for nothing was his autobiography titled *Confessions of an Actor* ("Bless me, Reader, for I have sinned"). His make-up was as complex as Vivien's and, from hints in what each said about the other about their early time together when they were friends only, it would seem that they were both aware of the dangers involved (each had a "perturbing" attraction) and so when finally the subterranean tremors under that initial period exploded into their tempestuous affair, the fall-out was seismic.

When they met, Olivier at 28 was the bigger name although not quite yet a copper-bottomed star. Most of his London stage appearances had been flops and his films unsuccessful but even then his ambition, crystallised early as an aim to be the best living actor, was unquenchable. He seemed destined to act in the theatre (he remained aloof about films until *Wuthering Heights*), encouraged by his clergyman father, who was a remote figure but had himself once harboured adolescent operatic dreams; he delivered colourful sermons and the boy's education only encouraged his sense of drama. The All Saints' atmosphere – heady with ritual, music, acolytes' robes, candles, incense swung in the thurifer – made a potent form of theatre for an impressionable child. He was also an inveterate and inventive liar ("What is acting but lying?" he asked later), something the mother he adored tried to dispel.

His sister Sybille (six years his senior) briefly caught the acting bug while his elder brother Gerald ("Dickie" to family), after Radley became a rubber planter in India. The family, from Huguenot stock in Catholic Pyrenean France, had settled in Holland and then England. His father, Gerard ("Fahv") allowed his wife Agnes to hold the family together; she was a loyal wife to a somewhat irascible husband and had a peripatetic existence for most of the children's childhoods while Gerrard had different livings in or near London. For the boy Laurence at 12, his mother's early death (at 48), from a brain tumour, was devastating ("I don't think I've ever got over it. I've been looking for her ever since" he told Tynan in an interview). Never close to his austere father, he channelled his emotions into All Saints where, under an inspired teacher-priest, Father Geoffrey Heald, the school's reputation for drama was extremely high. He played Brutus and Katharina there, seen by eminent actors including Sybil Thorndike and her husband Lewis Casson, Ellen Terry and Johnston Forbes-Robertson, all of whom marked him down as an actor of great promise even then. With no solid career plan on leaving school at 17, it was Fahv who suggested the stage, possibly more impressed by the boy's performances than he had revealed.

With fellow students including Peggy Ashcroft, he trained at the Central School under the great teacher and voice coach Elsie Fogerty, one of his early mentors. His early career was undistinguished until the Cassons, also his mentors and almost surrogate parents, took him on for their production of *Henry VIII*; it was Sybil who then recommended he contact Sir Barry Jackson, whose private wealth subsidised the Birmingham Repertory, then the most prestigious British regional theatre. There he began to take his profession seriously although often a bad "corpser" (giggler) while over nearly two years with the company he played an enormous range of parts including the title role (at 19) in *Uncle Vanya*. He took to the camaraderie of company life at the Rep – developing crushes on both Peggy Ashcroft and Angela Baddeley (both married) and an enduring friendship with Ralph Richardson.

The Rep company occasionally toured and played in London; in the summer of 1928 Olivier played the upper-crust young squire in the London company's production of John Drinkwater's comedy *Bird in Hand* in which he had acted opposite Peggy in Birmingham. As Peggy was unavailable, she was replaced as the pub landlord's daughter by an established actress, Jill Esmond. Uncannily like Vivien's reaction on first seeing Leigh (and then Olivier), Jill thought when she first saw him "I knew he was the man I was going to marry." Olivier had scrubbed up from Birmingham days as a snaggle-toothed, near monobrowed and shaggy-haired juvenile. Now, as his friend Denys Blakelock commented:

> He had had the gaps between his teeth filled in, his eyebrows trimmed and straightened and he was beautifully and rather gaily dressed.

Some of this improvement was due to Jill, by whose pedigree Olivier was deeply impressed. Her father, H.V. Esmond, had been a noted actor-dramatist who took to drink and died in 1922 – and her redoubtable mother, Eva Moore, was a prominent leading actress and women's rights campaigner. Jill had something of her mother's briskness ("The Colonel" was one nickname), living with Eva in Chelsea or at weekends in Berkshire. When Eva realised Olivier's interest in Jill she fostered the relationship and invited him often to stay, becoming another mentor, introducing him to her famous colleagues (he called her "Mum") while Jill devotedly helped improve his appearance further, plucking his low hairline and guiding his dress sense. Although slightly younger, she had been on the stage for six years and in many ways was the more mature. Not conventionally beautiful, she had an open, candid face, a sharply intelligent comedic instinct and excellent timing (Noël Coward had approved of her in his *Hay Fever*). She, too, was complex, partly because of fluctuating professional confidence, but also with some sexual ambivalence. Olivier, who in later life and in his memoirs could be unfeeling (and inaccurate) about her, would say that she had always been essentially lesbian. She did share most of her post-divorce life with close women friends, but both admitted to scruples and doubts to the other before and after their engagement.

Jill left for New York to appear in *Bird in Hand* there. Olivier followed later after another London flop in *Beau Geste*, directed by Basil Dean, crosser than usual, and although his Broadway whodunit was unsuccessful his salary was enough for a Tiffany's engagement ring before he had to sail home. He wrote a long, adoring letter to her on board, stressing his love but hinting also at the melancholy often underlying feelings of happiness. Jill in America made it clear in her letters that she adored him, despite her doubts. She wrote lively, funny letters from Chicago when on tour, mixing with mobsters, bootleggers in speakeasies and the outrageous nightclub owner Texas Guinan. Both touched on what they called "our particular pet devil"; some interpret this as her latent lesbianism and his suggested bisexuality but it is more likely that sex itself was that "devil", as it was for many young people then, when contraception was neither a simple nor absolutely reliable matter to organise even for emancipated women, while Olivier had his firm Anglo-Catholic religious convictions still. He once said he had been "alarmingly loose" before marriage – this probably refers to his many crushes, usually on married women – but in *Confessions* he implies that he and Jill were virgins on marriage. When later he downplayed the debt he owed Jill and Eva he implied that the primary reason for his marriage was finally to have sanctioned sex, glossing this by saying of Jill that although not ravishingly beautiful "she would do tolerably well for a wife" (which sounds like a line from a bad Restoration Comedy). But as their letters make plain they had many happy times together and their marriage was far from the arctic relationship suggested in his memoirs or by some biographers. They married in July 1930 at All Saints (the following day he wrote a joyful letter to "Mum" Eva, carolling "Oh Shenandoah, I love your daughter!").

Olivier had been in the solid-gold hit of Coward's *Private Lives* in London in the supporting role of Victor and when the stars (Coward and Gertrude Lawrence) agreed to a three-month Broadway run Olivier went too, with Jill replacing the pregnant Adrianne Allen and giving a glintingly funny performance (as Sybil, surely named in order to be told not to quibble). Despite Coward's disdain for "Haaahllywood", Jill and Olivier were tempted by wooing from the studios and both finally agreed to RKO contracts (David O. Selznick then worked for that studio). It seems perhaps, from what Olivier said and wrote, that their sex life had not yet been especially satisfactory but in New York a doctor established that Jill must have an operation to remove an ovarian cyst which may well have made sex difficult for her. This was done before leaving for California. Olivier had a lifelong and slightly macabre fascination for medical procedures – part of his actor's forensic, detached observation – and watched the operation, writing a detailed description to "Mum" describing Jill's blood-soaked intestinal tubing, perhaps infelicitously in the circumstances describing her as having "more guts than anybody I've ever met".

This may well have helped matters. Certainly for most of the next six years leading up to Tarquin's birth, their lives seemed happy. Financially they were doing well, they lived in Los Angeles in a house on Appian Way with spectacular views and had many English friends (Ivor Novello, Clive Brook, Ronald Colman) and new American ones (Joan Crawford and her then husband Douglas Fairbanks, Jr) as well as a young British actor, Anthony Bushell who would later work regularly for Olivier. Jill had one big chance, possibly to star in George Cukor's film of Clemence Dane's play *A Bill of Divorcement* but Olivier, whose films of this period were all box-office disappointments, wanted to go home and Jill, rather than risk her marriage (and believing Olivier who told her that Katharine Hepburn would be cast in the film – she eventually was but the decision had not then been made) decided to accompany him.

Back home they leased an imposing house on Cheyne Walk, once Whistler's studio, fashionably designed with a huge baronial fireplace and much bleached furniture à la Syrie Maugham. They made a film together – the tepid *No Funny Business* – before Olivier was lured back to Hollywood by the possibility of co-starring with MGM's reigning superstar Greta Garbo, only to suffer the humiliation, after a brief period on the set of *Queen Christina*, of the sack. Retreating to Broadway he appeared with Jill in a strangely perfumed drama of gay domination, Mordaunt Shairp's *The Green Bay Tree* which had lavish praise but neither could properly enjoy the success. Both – especially Olivier – suffered at the tongue of its producer/director, Broadway's *wunderkind* self-destructive genius Jed Harris, loathed so much that Olivier later based most of his *Richard III* sinister make-up on Harris's saturnine features.

His London reputation increased when replacing a miscast Ralph Richardson as Bothwell in *Queen of Scots*, directed by Gielgud and bringing him together with colleagues – the Motleys, George Devine, Glen Byam Shaw (now married to Angela Baddeley), the outstanding character actor George Relph and his wife Mercia Swinburne – who became lifelong friends. The self-dramatising Barrymore figure in *Theatre Royal* saw him established as a West End leading man of unusual versatility.

He could have continued in such work but instead chose to alternate Romeo and Mercutio in Gielgud's *Romeo and Juliet*, designed by Motley, knowing that his Romeo was likely to be very controversial. Which it was, with many accusations of his "butchery" of Shakespeare's verse and of excessive physicality. This Romeo seemed to be on a high as if with a permanent erection, an impassioned Italianate sexual dynamism which shocked the purists. But he was trying, he said, to "sell realism in Shakespeare"; he always said that acting was fundamentally sexual, "like coming for a living". He was still insisting on this in his later career, telling a young Michael Gambon at the National Theatre: "Every woman and man in the audience should want to fuck you." For many, this magnetism was novel and thrilling, as it was for Jill and Eva. As it was, too, for Vivien.

With Jill pregnant when filming on *Fire Over England* began, Olivier's feelings of guilt – rarely absent for long – must have lain heavy. He knew that there were tremors in the air, as yet unarticulated, between him and Vivien. The Holmans and the Oliviers had had occasional dinners, although at this stage Olivier found the reserved Leigh somewhat dull. He had had at least two lunches (the first with Gielgud also present) with Vivien and that dinner at "The 400". It also seems that he had already been unfaithful to Jill; his diary shows that he was meeting Ann Todd quite regularly at this time (there was no professional connection then); David Niven recalled first meeting Olivier when Todd took him backstage to his dressing-room. Helen Spencer, who had acted with Olivier in the West End, wrote to him in terms which suggest a relationship, as did another actress, Annie Rooney ("If a mistress can send love to a wife, give yours my love!"). Later in life Jill confided to Tarquin that she was sure that Olivier and Peggy Ashcroft had briefly been lovers during *Romeo and Juliet* (possible – a letter survives from Ashcroft when Olivier was working on *Confessions* suggesting that, although nothing is included in the published book). She also said that Mercia Relph had told her Olivier had a brief fling with the newcomer Greer Garson when he cast her in *Golden Arrow*, a short-lived directorial effort.

These had been brief encounters. What Olivier began to feel for Vivien was utterly different, soul-shattering, shaking the roots of his religious and moral being. Just as Vivien retreated from Catholicism after marriage, so Olivier, profoundly Anglo-Catholic till then, abandoned conventional religion on marriage (more guilt, of course). Both – he, in particular – retained a strong consciousness of sin. Also divorce then carried a distinct stigma.

Fire Over England was another of Korda's historical projects. For some time he had planned a film centred on Elizabeth I (the original title was *Gloriana*) against a background of an England imperilled with a foreign enemy set on invasion, in this case Philip II and the Spanish Armada. It was for the time a big-budget (£75,000) project and Korda took unusual care in assembling the right personnel, bringing over Erich Pommer to produce and also importing American director William K. Howard, who had a major career in silents before turning to sound, including a superb film anticipating *Citizen Kane* with Spencer Tracy as a railroad tycoon in *Power and Glory*. That had been innovatively photographed by James Wong Howe relatively early in his career as one of the great Hollywood cinematographers, also brought to England for Korda. The script was mainly the work of Clemence Dane, a large and jolly character (the model for Coward's *Blithe Spirit* psychic Madam Arcati), who became friends with both Vivien and Olivier, both of whom – like others – were tickled by her unconscious verbal brick-dropping ("Larry – it's well-known that Shakespeare sucked Bacon dry!"). It was adapted from A.E.W. Mason's novel, a stirring tale of a fictional English pirate's son, Michael Ingoldby (Olivier) who vows to avenge his father's death at the hands of the Inquisition. Michael, in love with the beautiful Cynthia (Vivien), a lady-in-waiting to the Queen, escapes to the English court and after a welcome return to Cynthia's arms is sent as a spy to the Escurial of Philip of Spain (a brooding Raymond Massey). There is derring-do galore, sea-fights, leaps from burning boats and rooftops, duels and betrayals before the film – finally – links up with history at Tilbury with Elizabeth's call to arms, underlining Dane's anti-appeasement subtext. With no Drake around, it is the newly knighted Michael who leads the fleet to defeat the Armada to Richard Addinsell's brass-heavy score.

This lively canter over G.A. Henty territory is splendid escapist adventure. Olivier matches Errol Flynn's virile athleticism – one later critic described him as "a 1930s Henry Cavill, only slightly less inflated and wearing more guyliner" – and Flora Robson is an outstanding Virgin Queen (she and Vivien have a delicately played scene as the ageing monarch removes her elaborate wig). Vivien looks luscious throughout, clearly besotted by Ingoldby and ready to take any risk for him, finding a spirit and fire to the character only touched on in the script. She was greatly helped by James Wong Howe, who taught her (and Olivier, always intrigued by the technical) a good deal about cinema lighting and camera angles. Known as "Low Key Howe" for his trademark contrasted interior lighting – he often shot Vivien in shafts of light through mullioned windows in vast Tudor rooms or in chiaroscuro – he was even then exploiting deep-focus photography (before Greg Toland and *Citizen Kane*) which kept foreground and background in balanced focus. Some scenes are shot in silhouette, some by torchlight, all of inestimable help to Howard, who steered a rousing movie, fused with romance and action, one Vivien had truly enjoyed making. The elation of a developing love affair comes through the screen; the many close embraces and lingering kisses allowed her and Olivier practically to make love on set, their closeness certainly noticed by the crew (who called them "The Lovers") and by Korda, who had possibly considered the likelihood of the on-screen chemistry when he cast them together. He simply smiled when Vivien told him they were in love and said "Of course, my dear. Everybody knows."

It was for both a giddily intoxicating time, freeing in them a fierce sexuality probably new and certainly exciting to Olivier especially. And surprising – a fellow actor mentioned to him how tired the physical demands of the part must have made him and he confessed "It's not the stunts. It's Vivien. It's every day, two, three times." Later the difference in their sexual drives would become a problem in the marriage but at Denham in *Fire Over England* they inhabited Yeats's "country of the young", as Vivien later told her journalist friend Godfrey Winn:

> I wonder whether – if the film was shown again – you would see it in our faces, the confrontation with our destiny. I don't think I've ever lived quite as intensely since. I don't remember sleeping, ever; only every precious moment that we spent together ... I trusted everyone and I imagined, like the very young always do, that everything lasts for ever.

Vivien had one day between the last take on *Fire Over England* and her first on *Dark Journey* – Korda was working her hard. Long studio hours could be used as an excuse to encourage Leigh not to come home in a hurry (he was sailing again), writing to him regularly with no hint of the emotional roller-coaster on which she was travelling, offhandedly mentioning, *en passant*, that Olivier had taken her to the ballet. Oswald Frewen was becoming aware of Olivier's presence; one evening he arrived at Little Stanhope Street to find Vivien in bed with a cold and Olivier ministering to her. Oswald went to the nearby pub for a tot of rum for her and near-farce developed as Olivier was visibly put out when Oswald did not accompany him when he finally left (Oswald occasionally spent a night in London on the Holman sofa) and called the next day to ask who he was. When next she wrote to Leigh, Vivien mentioned her cold and Oswald's visit but made no mention of Olivier.

The filming of *Dark Journey*, which began in late 1936 – again at Denham – also proved an enjoyable time, even if the script was at times hard to follow (more so in the released version which cut some 15 minutes, increasing the plot-confusion). It was directed by Victor Saville, a Birmingham art dealer's son who had a prolific and varied career – including popular 1930s musicals such as *Evergreen* with Jessie Matthews. Ambitiously he set up his own company to produce films for Korda (*Dark Journey* was the first).

Saville's sets were known for their relaxed ease although he had a reputation also for sticking to budgets and schedules, and Vivien also had some friends in the cast, including Anthony Bushell, now back in England after an American divorce. Korda aimed for classy production values again; set towards the end of World War I (confusingly, the costumes suggest a more contemporary film), mostly in neutral Sweden, *Dark Journey* had some costly settings including nightclubs with chorus-lines and a luxury Grand Hotel plus lavish costumes by the Swiss-born René Hubert who had worked on *Fire Over England*. Top-billed was the lean, dark-eyed (often monocled) Conrad Veidt (star of *The Cabinet of Dr Caligari*) as Baron von Marwitz, a German officer who is actually head of his country's secret service, opposite Vivien as Madeleine, a dress-shop owner able to travel unrestrictedly between Stockholm and Paris. She in fact is a double agent, working for the Allies; details of vital naval and troop locations are worked into the patterns of her imported fashions. Most of the cat-and-mouse plot is taken up with Madeleine's latest assignment as a counter-agent for French intelligence to identify the head of Germany's secret service. The convolutions as the Baron and Madeleine become drawn to each other include Bushell as a smoothy-chops British agent who devises a complex scheme for von Marwitz's capture, although the final reel, set as the war is soon to end, suggests that the lovers will be reunited.

Saville made this into relishable hokum, using wipes and montage inventively to get across a good deal of expository material and the film is atmospherically shot by Georges Périnal, who gave Jean Cocteau's *Sang d'un Poète* its hallucinatory quality and Harry Stradling, Sr, who worked in Europe in the 1930s. Their collaboration gives the studio Stockholm a shadowy, slightly sinister atmosphere. Vivien looks stunning in her many close-ups and she and Veidt, with his air of world-weary disenchantment, have an intriguing, offbeat chemistry, negotiating lines like "Why are you trying to resist? You won't succeed" with ease and sharing an erotic first, extremely lengthy kiss after revealing their respective roles in espionage. Vivien never felt she had given her best in *Dark Journey*; she dubbed it, her first real leading film role, a personal failure. But she actually more than holds her own opposite the far more seasoned Veidt. Now, after five films, she had absorbed how much discipline was involved in the sheer technical details of film-making – hitting one's marks, remembering the pace and rhythm of the previous scene, especially when shooting out of sequence – and with that confidence she could concentrate on her performance. She felt that in *Dark Journey* she was still somewhat tense, but actually the underlying, enigmatic nervous apprehension to her Madeleine is absolutely right for a character who has spent three years in increasingly dangerous work as a double agent.

Korda was delighted with the film and publicised it heavily, pushing the romantic element of star-crossed lovers – the advertising slogan was "Their Lips Kissed – But Never Told!". It had excellent notices on both sides of the Atlantic – "a tingling drama of lovers' battle of wits" with Vivien described as "England's most charming screen actress" – and Korda was highly pleased by its box-office returns, convinced that he had backed a winner in Vivien.

The shooting was against a background of personal turmoil. Towards the end of filming on *Fire Over England*, in the middle of a love scene with Vivien, Olivier had been telephoned with news of his child's imminent birth and at once rushed home for Tarquin's arrival. Jill was grateful but for one detail – "the smell of Vivien" (Vivien had begun to wear Patou's "Joy" – her signature scent). The following day he took Vivien back to Cheyne Walk after filming, as she described to Leigh with news of Tarquin:

> It really is very attractive, very big but not fat. Larry says it is like Edward G Robinson which is a little cruel. He has already started reciting Shakespeare to it.

Tarquin later posited that bringing Vivien to Jill's bedside was a kind of double-bluff, acting the innocent bringing a fellow actor from work to offer congratulations.

As if in recompense for her pains, Olivier soon took Jill – a Norland nanny took care of Tarquin – on a Mediterranean holiday on Capri. The following weeks really require a novelist – Henry James or Ford Madox Ford, some specialist in the deceptions and self-deceptions of the human heart – to scrutinise events. Vivien – as if just by chance – turned up in Capri with the innocent Oswald as chaperon – "beard" in today's parlance – while Leigh was, once again, on a sailing trip – and the undercurrents must have been more turbulent than Capri's blue waters although superficially the setting and the situation (three of the quartet were actors) resembled those of any formula 1930s comedy. Frewen's diary noted his arrival with Vivien at the Hotel Quisiana:

> Larry, the other side of the Hall, cried loudly "Darling!" and Jill uttered further love-cries as all three met in the middle of what I could only describe as a joint passionate embrace.

The newcomers were found a room each on either side of the Oliviers:

> So we were there in line and all on a communal basis – nobody ever knocked to enter and we all three used all three rooms at will.

A photograph, presumably taken by Frewen, was taken of Olivier by the pool with Jill and Vivien on either side; his right arm is around Jill at whom he is gazing but the left is much more closely round Vivien's waist.

Of this time he said "Guilt was a dark fiend." Conscience-riven he tried to persuade himself, a new father, to give Vivien up, only to be haunted like Macbeth ("Then comes my fit again"). He was also about to take a major professional gamble, adding to his uneasy mind; director Tyrone (Tony) Guthrie, an inspiring, iconoclastic director, was inviting him to move further into the classical field for a season at the Old Vic which Guthrie then ran for its formidable boss, Lilian Baylis, beginning with the challenge of an uncut *Hamlet* (actors call it The Eternity Version). Vivien and Jill separately urged him to go to the Waterloo Road (for £20 p.w.) – Guthrie had cast Jill as Olivia in *Twelfth Night* too.

By now Jill surely had at least an inkling of what was being played out – she must have noticed, as others had, that Vivien had picked up Olivier's liberal use of four-letter words – but gave little away. On Capri she had behaved with preternatural *sangfroid*, enjoying meals on the terrace as if on any other carefree holiday. For the time being, in trying to hold on to her husband she further befriended Vivien back in London. Her son wrote later of Jill's visits to Vivien's exquisite house:

> She was making it happen, she would sit unbelieving: she had gone there to fight for her family ... She was astonished to find herself passing on all she could to Vivien, as though they were the closest of friends.

The penny had dropped for Frewen too on Capri and he had been glad to leave for Rome with Vivien en route for home while the Oliviers had remained. He recorded that she had a "crise de nerfs" in Rome after receiving a telephone call from Olivier ("I begged her to give herself time, not to do anything impetuous"). Later he disclosed that Olivier had said in that call that he had decided to end his marriage but on this occasion Vivien listened to Oswald and returned to London. Olivier's Capri break during which he also had to analyse the morass of torn conscience and guilt in *Hamlet* could hardly have been a rest-cure.

On her return Vivien was plunged into work on another film, *Storm in a Teacup*, also directed by Victor Saville. One of the more beguiling 1930s British film comedies, this was based on a German satirical comedy, Bruno Frank's *Storm in Wasserglass*, adapted by James Bridie for both stage and screen, relocated to a favourite setting of Baikie, a small Scottish coastal town. It revolves round the rumpus caused by the stern Lord Provost (Cecil Parker) leading the local council's refusal to allow an old woman amnesty for non-payment of her dog-licence. Fomented by *The Baikie Advertiser*'s crusading new journalist from London (a suavely lean Rex Harrison) the town revolts, inconveniently for the Provost, planning to stand for Parliament representing a new Nationalist Party with the slogan "Scotland for the Scottish" ("Oh, does somebody else want it?" asks Harrison). Feather-light, the comedy is niftily whipped up by astute casting, not least the great Irish actress (O'Casey's original Juno) Sara Allgood as the malapropistic Honoria Hegarty. Saville cleverly just touches in the anti-autocracy theme; the Baikie Town Hall is a clever pastiche of Teutonic architecture while Harrison defends himself when grilled by the Provost's cronies: "Where are we, Berlin? Or Moscow? I'm Nordic, if that's what's worrying you." He and Vivien took to each other at once and their on-screen rapport has a snappy raillery reminiscent of Nick and Nora in *The Thin Man* films. Vivien plays Victoria, the Provost's daughter, returning from finishing school in Paris; she and Harrison, initially antagonistic, find themselves attracted to each other as she becomes aware of his sense of justice. Their comedic rhythms complement each other especially well in a games-arcade scene in which Victoria begins to thaw towards the newcomer.

Harrison found Vivien tantalisingly alluring but "All she wanted to do was to talk about Larry so I went along with that, gazing on that beautiful face with unhopeful ardour." He also witnessed a sudden, brief eruption of distress towards the end of filming, one of Vivien's "episodes". She had told him of her classical ambitions and of the possibility she might take over Ophelia opposite Olivier when *Hamlet* played at Elsinore the following spring but when she was told it might not happen "she broke down in the dressing-room in wild hysteria, anger and anguish".

Storm in a Teacup is no forgotten masterpiece – Cecil Parker looks deeply uncomfortable in the kilt and his Scottish accent is the screen's worst before Mel Gibson's in *Braveheart* – but while its anti-fascist stance may have lost resonance it remains, with its anticipation of the Ealing Comedies, a pleasing reminder that not all British comedy's output in the 1930s featured Fields and Formby.

Korda was pleased with the film and wanted to put Vivien into another as soon as possible, preferably again with Olivier. He had to wait; the Old Vic occupied him and with no immediate project from London Films, after a ski-ing break with Leigh, Vivien went into a West End play, *Because We Must* at the Ambassador's in February 1937. The only noteworthy feature of this short-lived piece was that its author Ingaret Giffard had studied under Carl Jung, whose influence pervaded her earnest psychological drama. Vivien's was a main role – a young wife tempted by London's fleshpots – but the play was dim. Better but similarly offering little to challenge her, was Sydney Carroll's production of *Bats in the Belfry* by the husband and wife team of Diana Morgan and Robert

MacDermot (billed as "A Very Light Comedy" – a kind of *Hay Fever* involving a clerical rather than a theatrical family with an enjoyable cast of characters). Vivien's role as a daughter of the cloth was very much in support although she liked the cast which included her old champion Lilian Braithwaite, who had all the best lines as an outspoken Bohemian aunt. During this rather fallow period she was taking regular voice lessons with Elsie Fogerty and also with Beatrice Wilson, another excellent coach, recommended by Bobby Helpmann. Her work seemed in her eyes pedestrian compared with the excitement across the river where Olivier's Hamlet was drawing capacity Old Vic houses. The Freudian subtext – Hamlet's suppressed Oedipus Complex – keenly pursued by Olivier and Guthrie had barely been noticed and some critics found his performance over-physical (to Agate this Hamlet was "the best performance of Hotspur the recent stage has seen") but audiences were wildly enthusiastic. Vivien saw it many times, once taking Oswald and Leigh. The outwardly impeccable behaviour of the marital quartet remained preserved although the underlying strains must have now been extra taut. There were still regular foursomes for dinner, often at Soho's Moulin d'Or where once they were joined by an ebullient Michael Redgrave after *Hamlet* (he played Laertes) on the night his wife Rachel Kempson gave birth to Vanessa – adding to a skein of theatrical betrayals, for at this time, even during Rachel's pregnancy, Redgrave had been having an affair with Edith Evans. Also at this time, under the pretext of late meetings, Olivier and Vivien snatched time together ("sporadic little hops" he called them), registering at hotels using Fahv's middle name as "Mr and Mrs Andrew Kerr", one memorable hop being to Stamford, Lincs, when he shared a bath for the first time with Vivien, an erotic memory which remained sharp in his mind.

At that stage of heady intoxication in the heat of the affair the element of risk added extra spice. As the Old Vic moved on to *Twelfth Night* with Jill in the cast (Olivier, elaborately made-up and padded, played a sozzled Toby Belch) there were fewer chances to meet but the Olivier/Holman quartet still dined often and spent a weekend at Rye, going over to Frewen at The Sheephouse on the Sunday. Frewen's son has said that it was then, in the oak-panelled drawing-room, that Olivier finally decided to leave Jill and that, alone with Vivien, he formally proposed marriage.

He did not act on that immediately, however. As if the Old Vic workload combined with the offstage drama needed additional pressure, he was filming with Vivien during the daytime and preparing to take *Hamlet* to Elsinore for a week of performances in the castle courtyard. Korda had paired them in a rum affair directed by Basil Dean adapted from a John Galsworthy story, *Twenty-One*

Days. In the theatre Dean had directed several Galsworthy plays, including a stage version of this story, titled *The First and the Last*, in which the leading female role had been played by the darkly intense Meggie Albanesi with whom Dean, an unlikely but regular Lothario, had had an affair and by whom he remained, *Vertigo*-like, obsessed; he called Wanda, the girl at the centre of the story, "the Albanesi part".

The title was changed for the film, which remains a simple enough tale; a rakish Larry Darrent (Olivier), returned to London from Kenya, accidentally kills his girlfriend Wanda's blackmailing ex-husband. When a down-and-out is arrested for the murder Larry and Wanda are conscience-stricken but he opts to do nothing for 21 days and then turn himself in. The whole business is complicated by Larry's brother (Leslie Banks), about to be appointed to the Bench and appalled at possible scandal. After three weeks of happiness for the lovers, the tramp is found guilty, Larry goes to confess only for Wanda to spot a headline with news of the condemned man's death in custody and to run after Larry, catching up just as he is about to enter the police station.

The script is workaday, a collaboration between Dean and Graham Greene (probably responsible for the best scene – a lively legal dinner with Vivien's old mentor, David Horne, as a rotund bigwig) while Dean's direction, apart from the long final sequence as Wanda pursues Larry, is static despite some brooding shots of foggy London back streets (the cinematographer was another émigré, Jan Stallich). Olivier is still not entirely comfortable before the lens; his voice is overpitched as if to an invisible dress circle and his body language fussily indicative (a long scene with Leslie Banks, agonising over his dilemma, has so many hand gestures it borders on semaphore). Vivien's Wanda has a quiet resignation – a character who suggests life has offered her very little and who snatches even a brief chance of happiness. Probably Dean wanted something of Albanesi's low-key intensity; if so it was on-screen from Vivien.

Neither thought much of the script or of Dean's work. He could be maddeningly pedantic, on one occasion wasting a day waiting for the "right kind" of sugar for a café scene (he never understood why he was called "Sugar" for the rest of the shoot). Dean is decidedly sniffy about them in his memoirs, recalling huffily the laughter on set because their "joyous awareness of each other" prevented them from taking the script (which he had co-written) seriously. But undeniably they could be naughty; Stuart Freebon, the make-up supervisor, had to ban Olivier from Vivien's dressing-room after one occasion, just after her make-up was completed, when Olivier came in and kissed her so passionately that the whole job had to be done again. Dean was not amused.

Korda was less pleased with this Hitchcock-lite effort and shelved release for a time. Surprisingly, when it did appear, the reviews were fairly kind in America; released after both *Wuthering Heights* and *Gone With the Wind*, it was more circumspectly received ("will chiefly thrill devotees of the Leigh–Olivier Liebestraum").

When not called on *Twenty-One Days* Olivier fitted in a lightning trip to Denmark to finalise *Hamlet* arrangements. Some of the Old Vic cast were unavailable (Anthony Quayle replaced Michael Redgrave). Whether Cherry Cottrell was unavailable to repeat her Ophelia is not known but she too was replaced. By Vivien. The general opinion was that Olivier insisted on her casting (he always denied this and certainly Guthrie was not usually a pushover in such matters), and it was agreed they would rehearse their scenes together as much as possible during filming.

The benevolent Korda granted time off for his two artists – potential golden geese – to play Elsinore, an excursion with more than a few time bombs ticking away amongst the company. Jill was there as a spectator; Alec Guinness, playing Osric, had the duty of escorting her, steering her as much away from Olivier and Vivien as possible. Vivien wrote blithely to "darling Leigh" that they were working hard but that the Danes loved late hours ("Funny that a whole nation should feel like me!"). Olivier recorded later the pressure of the situation as they rehearsed ("We could not keep from touching each other, making love almost within Jill's vision"). He was alarmed too by a sudden "episode" after one rehearsal when Vivien turned on him, briefly breaking down in a flash of hysterical rage; it passed quickly although he realised she had no real memory of it, putting it down to nervous strain before opening.

They now planned to inform Jill and Leigh of their joint decision to end the marriages and to marry after their divorces. In Olivier's diary for 7 May 1937 – three weeks prior to Elsinore – he noted simply "Durham Ready". This referred to Durham Cottage, in Christchurch Street, Chelsea on which he had now signed and sealed the lease. Jill knew nothing of these plans. Leigh had no inkling of what Vivien intended. Against that background, *Hamlet* had its problems. Guthrie had only limited time with his new actors; he could be a daunting figure, impressively tall in flannels and gym-shoes with a bristling Auchinleck moustache, barking out rapid-fire instructions which sometimes sounded disconcertingly camp ("Oh, fucky-poo!" was his reaction to crises), and he was quite tough on Vivien, ruthlessly stripping away any suggestion of the Dresden shepherdess in Ophelia. She actually welcomed clear, strong direction and the performance rather surprised those who saw her as a film star over-reaching herself. She and Olivier certainly provided high-octane, sensual performances – this Hamlet and Ophelia both knew what he meant by "country matters". Vivien was perhaps lucky that the first performance coincided with torrential rain so heavy that a theatre had to be improvised indoors in a ballroom of the nearby Marienlyst Hotel with Guthrie and Olivier feverishly altering the staging while Lilian Baylis in heavy tweeds clucked around her brood dispensing coffee.

That performance, famously, became a kind of thrust-stage production with exits and entrances through the audience, undoubtedly planting the seeds for Guthrie's later theatre-pioneering at the Edinburgh Festival, then in Canada, and influencing Olivier with the Chichester and National Theatre stages. In the indoor intimacy Vivien's voice had no problems with projection and those critics visiting from London were extremely impressed. J.C. Trewin, writing for *Plays and Players* 30 years later and a *Hamlet* connoisseur, still vividly recalled his Elsinore experience: "Few people mention her Ophelia, yet the mad scenes endure... the tragedy was there, and unprettified." Among the guests were friends Diana Cooper and Juliet Duff, the latter later writing to Olivier recalling "the loveliest performance of *Hamlet* I have ever seen".

The company returned on 8 June with the lovers facing crunch time doubtless with mixed dread and exhilaration. For Olivier the affair was as fatefully irresistible "as for any couple from Sigmund and Sieglinde to Windsor and Wallis" – "It sometimes almost felt like an illness but the remedy was unthinkable; only a Christian martyr could have faced it."

He faced Jill two days later and after that Vivien told Leigh of her decision as their diaries record (Vivien's states only: "Told Leigh" on 10 June 1937). Jill moved out of Cheyne Walk with Tarquin to go to her mother's in the country (Eva's comments can only be imagined). On the Monday of the following week Jill went to see Vivien; she must have had some premonition of events but the blunt facts would have been a sickening shock, especially as she still loved her husband. But as she said to Tarquin later: "Real passion – I've only seen it that once. If you are ever hit by it, God help you. There's nothing you can do."

Vivien moved out of Little Stanhope Street ("Left with Larry" she wrote on 16 June) leaving Suzanne with Leigh. After a few nights staying with Tony Bushell and his girlfriend Consuelo Langton-Lockton in Iver, with the necessary work on the house finished, they moved into their first home together.

CHAPTER 5

Altered States

D urham Cottage was like a retreat, a *rus in urbe* house in the oasis of a walled garden entered through a door in the street wall, surrounded by larger buildings and flats. It would be a London home for Vivien and Olivier for nearly 20 years. The marital splits, common knowledge in the theatre world, had not been reported widely; Tony Bushell told them "The press boys have been uncommon forbearing, I cannot understand it but am none the less relieved." They were not perhaps big enough fish then for the tabloids; it would be a very different picture within a few years.

Inevitably the period following had some awkwardnesses. People took sides. Gertrude was deeply distressed, divorce being anathema to her profound faith. Sybil Thorndike, nearly a surrogate mother to Olivier (and Tarquin's godmother), was shocked as were many of an older generation:

> I gave him hell. I was furious. I was brought up in the Church as he was and I hate divorce. Once you've given yourself to someone, if things go wrong you've just got to lump it.

Olivier was deeply sensitive to status and such attitudes stung. Some of Leigh's friends, Jamie Hamilton included, cold-shouldered Vivien while some of Jill's ostracised Olivier. It was difficult for friends of both. Glen Byam Shaw wrote to Olivier shortly after the break-up:

> Jill came to see me on Monday night at the theatre ... I tried to find the right words to say to help. But it is so terribly difficult as you and Vivien must know well enough. Anyhow, be happy, Larry – that is the important thing. And I feel sure there is something pretty good waiting for Jilly if one can induce her to have a look.

The sympathy of friends was difficult for Leigh and Jill – both had their pride – although they remained similarly dignified. Leigh, understandably, had been poleaxed and Frewen, who had found it impossible to "sneak" to him about two people of whom he was also fond, had tried to prevent Olivier from behaving rashly, as he had done with Vivien:

> Larry discussed it with me – he was deceiving himself that it was to V's benefit that she should live with one who shared her artistry and her life and not with Leigh.

Frewen, like others, thought that the affair was a matter of physical passion only, writing after the splits:

> They have fought against themselves, *each* of them, *hard* ... But the disaster is none the less there and I'm terribly afraid that he is inconstant and unbalanced and that it won't last ten years – perhaps not five.

Vivien continued to try to reassure Oswald:

> I am sure this is the right thing and better in the long run for all four – it wasn't a hurried or callous decision.

Lives had to be restructured. Jill moved with Tarquin and a nanny to a St John's Wood house; Leigh hired a nanny for Suzanne, while Gertrude often helped with her granddaughter although Vivien called regularly when Leigh was at Chambers. She had also arranged for her maid, Daisy Goguel, to remain at Little Stanhope Street (she looked after Leigh until he died but took time to accept Olivier: "We were such a happy house until he came along").

The lovers also had to introduce each other to their respective families. Ernest and Olivier got on at once although it took Gertrude some time to thaw (she remained always in touch with Leigh). After *Twenty-One Days* Olivier took Vivien to meet Fahv, now remarried (his new wife, warm and friendly, was called Isobel – "Ibo" to family) and his sister Sybille, who remembered the occasion in an unpublished memoir of her brother:

> This lovely young thing, with big green eyes and dark curls to her shoulders in a figured biscuit-coloured cotton frock with no hat and stockings, holding Larry's hand as she came shyly up the path in the sun.

Vivien remained outside with Sybille and her husband Gerald for tea – discussing among other things, *Gone With the Wind*, which all three had read – while inside Olivier talked to Fahv and Ibo, knowing that Fahv was desperately upset; Sybille had one divorce behind her and now here was his son, not yet divorced but living with Vivien. Sybille, romantic like her brother, responded to "the delicious vitality and happiness that at this time glowed through Vivien" adding "Anyone who understood Laurence at all realised that here to him had come at last the fairy-tale princess of childhood dreams." Even Fahv, although shocked by the whole affair, "slowly melted under her fascination".

The future remained unclear, however. Quietly but firmly Leigh remained opposed to any immediate divorce ("he still hopes to get her back, so powerfully that you begin to believe he may" wrote Frewen) and Jill, still in what she referred to as "the Bad Time", agreed with him. Trying to put the loose ends behind them for a while, Olivier and Vivien escaped the pressure-cooker of London on the Orient Express to Venice (briefly flush, they put up at the Danieli) and to Salzburg where, as she had done with Leigh, Vivien could show Olivier landmarks of her youthful past). They returned for separate films – he in *The Divorce of Lady X* for Korda, Vivien "lent out" by the producer for MGM's first British-made film, *A Yank at Oxford* opposite Robert Taylor.

Taylor then was a valuable MGM property. The studio wanted to beef up his "pretty boy" image, casting him as Lee Sheridan, a bumptious college track and field star arriving in a class-conscious Oxford which takes less than favourably to his gung-ho American confidence. Romantic involvements and misunderstandings come thick and fast before Sheridan is accepted, helping Oxford win the Boat Race. MGM gave the project the works with luxury casting (Lionel Barrymore as Sheridan's doting pa and Maureen O'Sullivan as his love interest). An American director was assigned to the project, Jack Conway, who had a reputation as an "action director" although he had also directed literary adaptations including *A Tale of Two Cities* with Ronald Colman. The script is credited to American writer George Oppenheimer but in Hollywood studio-system style it had been worked on by others including F. Scott Fitzgerald, who had little luck in movies. On *A Yank at Oxford* he aimed to bring "significance" by elevating the script to a scrutiny of Anglo-American tensions but most of his work ended in the bin.

Vivien is excellent – and slyly funny – but she was far from happy making it, unable totally to shrug off the recent *Sturm und Drang*, with Olivier at a different studio and the indulgent Korda rarely around either. More than anything she longed for the equation of relationships to be solved; although she cared little for any prejudice against "living in sin", she desperately wanted marriage to Olivier.

The part of Elsa Craddock was something of a departure for Vivien, the vivacious younger wife of an Oxford bookseller with a cougar-like interest in the male student population ("I love to help the undergraduates. Especially the new ones"). She had a teasing candour, flattering any man she is with by standing very close, coquettish, troubling and altogether a handful. René Hubert gave Vivien another striking wardrobe – outfits trimmed with ocelot, a chic plaid three-piece and witty little hats over an insouciant curled hairdo. Elsa in fact is a much better role than the formula girlfriend played by O'Sullivan and there was an intriguing duality in Vivien's playing, an outward conventionality covering the suggestion of a wilder interior.

Whatever the reason for her dissatisfaction on the film, her behaviour worried John Gliddon, who had to cope with some uncharacteristic diva conduct as Vivien became fixated on a ridiculously vexed issue of special shoes needed when she injured her foot; her demands that MGM pay seemed excessive enough for Gliddon to be summoned to Denham for a warning that his client's behaviour, if continued, might force London Films to re-examine her contract. When he visited Durham Cottage to discuss this, Vivien's wild over-reaction alarmed him. After yelling at him in fury she suddenly turned on a sixpence to become chillingly quiet:

> It was far more frightening. Her voice turned suddenly hard. But the worst thing was her eyes … They had completely changed from the smiling eyes I was accustomed to. They were the eyes of a stranger.

As was to happen with others in the future following such eruptions, she called Gliddon to apologise, admitting that these "states" frightened her too. Clearly at that time she was aware of some problem, a mental disturbance, even if it remained unnamed. To her parents and to Olivier then, the "episodes" were displays of an actress's "artistic temperament".

The uncertainty of their situation affected Olivier differently. Periods of personal upheaval often coincided with professional forward leaps and a return to the Old Vic for a series of great roles – Macbeth, Iago, Coriolanus – saw one such advance. Vivien saw to the transformation of Durham Cottage, helped by Sibyl Colefax and the outstanding interior decorator John Fowler, who had recently formed their Colefax and Fowler business, initially in the King's Road. Fowler's aesthetic coincided with Vivien's – unostentatious good taste, seductive patterns for materials (chintzes, often floral, were a speciality) and comfort (such as fitted carpets) before fashion – and the Colefax suggestion of subtly scenting a room by burning dried herbs in bowls rather than pot-pourri was rapidly adopted in Durham Cottage. While Olivier studied his next roles Vivien appeared at the Old Vic when cast by Guthrie as Titania in *A Midsummer Night's Dream* for a 1937/8 Christmas season. Everyone assumed the formidable and devout Miss Baylis would disapprove of Vivien; she liked married couples in the company and had taken to Jill. But she was nothing if not pragmatic, appreciating the box-office value of occasional star-casting, and was decidedly more liberal-minded than many assumed from her frumpy old-maid exterior ("Well, dear" she had said to an over-virginal Isabella after a turgid *Measure for Measure* dress-rehearsal, "all we can do now is get on our knees and pray for lust"). She and Vivien got on very well; Baylis always appreciated a strong work ethic. On this production Guthrie collaborated with the *grand maître* of English decorative design, Oliver Messel. He came up with a ravishing Victorian-style setting incorporating a *corps* of flying fairies choreographed by Ninette de Valois on little more than the usual skimpy Old Vic budget, designs that were talked of for years, creating an entrancing vision of Athens framed in an elaborately decorated proscenium with the forest scenes a romantic world of gauzes painted with oversized calyxes of orchidaceous blooms and exotic giant bell flowers. Vivien was a vision of white tarlatan studded with seed pearls like dewdrops and Robert Helpmann's Oberon a glittering green scarab beetle, both seemingly from another world, savage and tender by turn.

This was not exactly in the Old Vic's style of minimalist design, based on Harley Granville-Barker's notions of simple Shakespearean staging – Guthrie even had an orchestra playing Mendelssohn's score instead of the usual simple Cecil Sharp-arranged folk songs – but, produced at a time of increasing international tension, it was perfect entertainment then, packing the theatre to the rafters.

Vivien had been jittery; Titania's first scene, erupting instantly into a quarrel with Oberon, has an especially demanding long speech describing the disasters in the natural realm caused by the fairy-world's dissension and Guthrie wanted it delivered standing stock-still stage-centre throughout. Her physical poise and the work she had put in on her voice paid off; the Oberon/Titania episodes were infused by an unusually forceful passion before their final reconciliatory dance, a favourite moment for Vivien and Helpmann. With Ralph Richardson's beamish-boy Bottom also cast, it was a happy Christmas time backstage – Helpmann's sharp tongue entertaining the adults with outrageous stories and West End tittle-tattle. So successful was it that Guthrie made plans at once for a revival the following Christmas.

Olivier followed *The Dream* into the theatre – a season which included Michel St Denis's production of *Macbeth*, a strikingly modern and controversial approach with Darius Milhaud music and an abstract design, coinciding with the shock of the news of Lilian Baylis's death. Nevertheless that season progressed Olivier's establishment as the supreme modern classical actor.

Korda had reunited with Erich Pommer and the unpredictable genius of Charles Laughton for Vivien's next film, *St Martin's Lane* (*The Sidewalks of*

London in America). The actor and Pommer had formed Mayflower Pictures; for the new outfit Pommer had directed Laughton in *The Beachcomber*, featuring Tyrone Guthrie, still occasionally acting to supplement his Old Vic salary. The story for *St Martin's Lane*, scripted by Clemence Dane, was suggested by Laughton, providing him with one of his masochistic loser-in-love roles as Charlie, a London busker (street entertainer) who takes into his troupe and falls for a young Cockney girl, Libby (Vivien), living on her wits and by pickpocketing. She in turn is taken up by a silky-smooth showbiz composer (Rex Harrison once more) who grooms her for stardom; when successful, she tries to help Charlie but he chooses to stay in his old life outside rather than in London's theatres.

The film is patchy to say the least, largely because of a script with too many cooks, with Laughton, Pommer and the film's American director, Tim Whelan, all chipping in to Dane's original which had set out to make a classic of London street life. It becomes broken-backed, partly reminiscent of *A Star is Born*, partly anticipating *Limelight*. The opening is wonderful, with a bravura post-credits sequence – a montage of neon-lit theatre facades segueing into St Martin's Lane and the surrounding alleys, with Laughton at impressive lung-power declaiming "The Green Eye of the Little Yellow God" to the gallery queues before realising that his takings have been stolen. Despite the authentic setting, this sequence looks like nothing out of a British film of that time. The lighting suggests something from a UFA Expressionist film; the other buskers, including Guthrie, impossibly tall and gangly, seem lit from below, looking almost surreal. This was the work of another outstanding émigré cinematographer, Jules Kruger, an artist of smoky, suggestive lighting (he had shot Abel Gance's *Napoleon*). His contribution to the film is immense, as Vivien realised, most hauntingly in an early scene in which Charlie follows Libby to a dilapidated empty mansion, full of crepuscular shadows and silvered, dusty mirrors. In a vast empty ballroom lit only by shafts of moonlight through shuttered windows, she dances – improvised, free, increasingly defiant – watched by Charlie, spellbound.

These arresting scenes are sadly followed by other limper sequences, especially those set backstage as Libby rises to stardom in musicals with titles such as "Big Time Girl" featuring sub-Busby Berkeley routines. The film needed a tougher director than the genial Whelan, a veteran of Harold Lloyd comedies; although Laughton gives one of his more restrained performances, touched often by genuine pathos. He did not especially care for Vivien; Korda had cast her instead of Laughton's wife Elsa Lanchester and Laughton was uneasy with

Vivien's Olivier-derived liberality with the 'F' word, as he had been in Hollywood with Carole Lombard.

Vivien is a revelation. Like the film, she can be all over the place (her Cockney certainly is, moving from Docklands to Dublin within the same sentence). But as Simon Callow says in his perceptive study of Laughton: "She is phenomenal: which is always better than being competent or solid." Just as Kruger's photography often suggests European cinema so her Libby (short for Liberty, a free spirit) has something of the same loose-cannon independence as Louise Brooks in Pabst's *Lulu* films:

> She combines within her a spirit of anarchy, a real danger and unpredictability ... a daemon, a siren, a pussycat with the sharpest of claws and a tongue that spits like a lynx.

Of Vivien's early films, *St Martin's Lane* best illustrates her quality, unusual in British acting then, of objectivity, of playing the character from the character's viewpoint with here a refusal to soften Libby's hard-edged ambition without ignoring the underlying vulnerability. There is a remarkable shot when Harrison is seeing her home at night and she is caught in the light of a streetlamp looking up at him. Her sleepy smile evaporates, her eyes widen, even the shape of her mouth seems to alter; for an instant she seems utterly, hungrily carnal and needy. There is an incandescence about her in much of this film, not least when she dances with the buskers, dressed in striped trousers, sleeveless shirt and tie, seeming almost to glow as she struts her stuff. Undoubtedly this sheer animal vitality came from the consuming physical passion at the height of her affair with Olivier.

This was certainly evident during filming. Harrison had to pine in vain still while Larry Adler, appearing later in the story, noticed that Olivier seemed to appear on set whenever Vivien had scenes with Harrison:

> They would disappear into her dressing-room and it was quite a business to get her back to work.

The film's schedule was tight and tiring but during it Vivien tried to visit Suzanne regularly. Although by her own admission not markedly maternal – she liked children after they were babies – she was acutely aware that Gertrude to a degree was becoming a surrogate mother to Suzanne. Some said that Vivien acted callously, even wickedly, by walking away from husband and daughter (Jill did not agree with Frewen that she had wrestled with her conscience) but both her words and the time she took before finally acting on her feelings go some way to contradict that.

With some time free for both in that long warm summer of 1938, Vivien and Olivier had one of their happiest (and longest) holidays. Work to Olivier was sacred, holidays an indulgence but most of July was an idyll, driving through France in Vivien's battered Ford V8. They had intended to follow a gastronomic map provided by Laughton but money was tight (Durham Cottage's refurbishment, Jill's alimony, meagre Old Vic salaries) and many meals were impromptu picnics rather than gourmet restaurant luxury. They enjoyed one period of social activity at Saint-Paul-de-Vence, meeting up with John Gielgud, holidaying with producer Hugh ("Binkie") Beaumont, then just beginning his rise to overlord of London's commercial theatre heading the firm of H.M. Tennent. When Vivien mentioned *Gone With the Wind*, which she had read on publication, and said that she would love to play Scarlett, it was Beaumont who advised her that if she wanted to work in Hollywood she should acquire an American agent. Vivien basked while there; she always liked the company of homosexuals, responding to that penchant for the telling phrase, the sense of style and, often, the substrain of drama among the gay London theatrical set – Gielgud, Coward, Novello, Rattigan, Beaumont and his partner-lover John Perry, the bisexual Emlyn Williams, with Bobby Helpmann a kind of court-jester figure.

During their holiday a significant telegram had arrived from Hollywood; Samuel Goldwyn Studios dangled a tantalising possibility – a film of Emily Bronte's *Wuthering Heights*, directed by William Wyler, with Merle Oberon as Cathy, Olivier as Heathcliff and Vivien as Isabella. Since the Garbo debacle Olivier had remained sniffy about Hollywood but this could not be rejected summarily. Vivien was not even mildly drawn to Isabella but after reading the script by Ben Hecht and Charles MacArthur she realised that even with major cuts from the novel, which she knew well (Olivier had never read it), it offered him a unique chance. There were also financial considerations; the Inland Revenue, the actor's perennial headache, was pressing both for back taxes – he had only an Old Vic salary for *Coriolanus* to look forward to while her next engagement, *Serena Blandish* at the tiny Gate Theatre would pay only a pittance. Goldwyn was offering $50,000.

William Wyler, tipped off about Olivier by Ben Hecht, came to London to meet them both. Only 36, Wyler had major movies such as *Dodsworth* and *Jezebel* with Bette Davis as a Scarlett forerunner to his credit, a charming, erudite and persuasive man. Olivier liked him but stressed how vital it was for him then not to be parted from Vivien, and took him to see *St Martin's Lane* still trying to convince him that Vivien could play Cathy. But while Wyler admired her Libby, he had to repeat that Goldwyn was set on casting Merle Oberon, suggesting when they dined at Durham Cottage the next evening that Vivien, unknown in Hollywood, "would never do better than Isabella for a first American movie." She sweetly but firmly declined. However, she did not want Olivier to lose his chance, worried that if he rejected this offer because of her and then another actor scored a big success in the part, he might then come to resent her. The wily Wyler had made sure that Olivier knew he had already tested another British actor (Robert Newton). She convinced Olivier that during his absence she would be busy first at the Gate and then back with the fairies at the Old Vic for Christmas. Olivier still needed final persuasion; he telephoned Ralph Richardson in America to ask his advice and his colleague, always more aware of costly things like transatlantic telephone calls, crisply answered "Yes. Bit of fame. Good." and replaced his receiver. The contract was signed.

John Gliddon was aware that Vivien now listened more to Olivier than to him. He was only marginally involved in *Wuthering Heights* discussions. Olivier could be oddly snobbish about such things as agents, rather looking down on Gliddon's operation as small-time. He was represented by a power-broking outfit, the Myron Selznick office, the London branch of which was run by Cecil Tennant, a commanding (6'5") figure (Eton and the Guards) only interested in "A-listers" and conscious of his power. At Olivier's instigation Vivien asked Gliddon to arrange for the Myron Selznick office to look after any business affairs in America for his agency. Only belatedly did he realise that while Tennant of course was keen to handle major players like Vivien and Olivier he was unlikely to be burning to handle John Gliddon.

Prior to Olivier sailing for America Vivien went into rehearsal for an unusual play which she sensed would probably not be hugely commercial but which she simply liked. The novel *Serena Blandish, or the Difficulty of Getting Married*, by Enid Bagnold, had been a minor sensation in 1924. The author's name appeared nowhere on it; her conventional military father had been so shocked by its contents that he insisted it be published anonymously (it was – as "By a Lady of Quality" – which only slightly appeased the parent while providing much press speculation and publicity). At the time there was a racy flavour to the story of the alluring but impecunious heroine's attempts to find a husband, ending in her snaring an aristocrat, but one who is mixed-race, decidedly shocking in 1924. Bagnold was an intrepid character herself, very much a "New Woman" who had some early success but nothing on the scale she sought so avidly until her later novel *National Velvet*. She did not tackle the adaptation herself; this was the work of the urbane Broadway dramatist S.N. Behrman, an Anglophile enchanted by Bagnold's exquisitely filigree prose and intrigued by what he called her "tough awareness of the metallic facts of life." With an episodic structure adopted from Voltaire's *Candide* it made for problems moving to the stage with scenes shifting from the interior of a luxury limousine to Monte Carlo, from an elaborate Ritz luncheon to the top of a London bus. It was first produced on Broadway by the *monstre sacré* Jed Harris as a vehicle for his then-mistress Ruth Gordon, but although Harris practically threw dollars at the Morosco Theatre stage, hiring Robert Edmond Jones for lavish sets and demanding a hidden orchestra, *Serena Blandish's* appeal was limited (described by one critic as "for audiences of well-decorated people") and the run unexpectedly short.

The little Gate Theatre near Charing Cross had no Harris budget but an ingenious design answered all the staging demands. Nominally directed by Esmé Church, more often Olivier took over – he would leave for New York just before the opening – and he went through Vivien's scenes in her lunch-breaks too. Stewart Granger, a recent Gliddon client, was cast as Lord Ivor Cream, a rakish plutocrat, and noticed that when Olivier left rehearsals "Vivien spoke so you could hear Larry" and only really settled into Serena, a tricky fusion of gossamer and granite, when he sailed for America. Also in the cast, to Vivien's delight, was Jeanne de Casalis as the stylish, manipulative Countess Flor di Folio. In a piece reminiscent of Ronald Firbank, the yawning trap was one of archness, not least for the character of Serena of whose qualities an admirer praises – "your sparkle, your charm, your health" – a mix of innocent and minx not unlike the heroine of *Zuleika Dobson*. As in New York the evening proved caviar to the general and its air of brittle 1920s hedonism was less resonant in an atmosphere of impending war, but Vivien seemed to delight everyone, with many critical mentions of her "wistful charm" or "her genuinely witty nonsense of the luncheon-party scene."

The opening coincided with great Gliddon excitement when Vivien was offered a lucrative movie for Cecil B. De Mille, *Union Pacific*, which would film in Hollywood while Olivier was there. He was left poleaxed when she insisted on consulting Tennant and then when she made impossible demands of more money and an option for only one further film instead of four. De Mille's cable had stressed "big studio interest in Leigh" but of course that interest vanished when Gliddon conveyed the terms. At the time he could not comprehend why, almost unknown in America, she would pass on the offer. From the outset of their association he had wanted to be part of the moulding of Vivien into an international star but he sensed that with Olivier's hold on her: "She had found another adviser and he was one with whom I simply couldn't compete."

Still in *Serena Blandish*, Vivien went with Olivier to Waterloo to see him off on the boat train to Southampton. They parted gloomily; she could not accompany him to Southampton, with a performance that evening. It was 5 November, her birthday. She had wanted to see Leigh to discuss divorce once more but it was still too painful for him to meet, although he allowed her to have Suzanne for a few days. Vivien took her to a child's birthday party and also to tea with Olivier's old flame, also a friend of hers, Helen Spencer, who promptly wrote to him in Hollywood saying that Vivien seemed preoccupied with possibly getting to America to see him, even if briefly (rehearsals for the Old Vic *Dream* were looming), and that she fretted that he might be tempted by the Hollywood beauties ("You! ... I suppose when a girl has fucked a bit herself she finds it difficult to understand constancy").

Vivien never joined the company of the *Dream* revival. When precisely after *Serena Blandish* closed she decided to go to Hollywood is not totally clear. Gertrude had been in Scotland, where Tommy was dying of cancer at Campbeltown. Vivien had written to Leigh mentioning a "possibility of my having to go to Hollywood for one film sometime soon" and Gliddon also recalled a call from her saying she might go over on a lightning trip but would return just before Old Vic rehearsals. On 27 November she told Leigh that she would sail on the *Majestic* to New York and fly on to Los Angeles.

Olivier was having a miserable time; although prodigal with money he had regular spells of acute parsimony (a legacy from Fahv), switching off lights and ranting about telephone bills, but he made three expensive calls during his *Normandie* crossing, "blind with misery" without her. With her photograph at his side in his cabin he poured out his unhappiness in a long letter of longing:

> There are certain things I dare not let enter my mind – it's such torment and would be worse if I let it go. Oh, I love, love, love, love my lambkin.

Also on board was congenial company – Noël Coward, Leslie Howard and producer Stephen Mitchell – with whom he had several meals. Never politically hugely engaged, even after the Munich agreement with Hitler, he was rather taken aback by the turn of conversation ("I never realised that everyone was so het-up against Chamberlain"), but insisted that despite the socialising (one dinner was accompanied by "3 vodkas, 4 champagne cocktails and champagne with dinner. Then backgammon") he was "really completely black with missing you". His letters from the Beverly Hills Hotel were similarly passionate, wondering in Biblical terms if the separation might be a "task" for them ("Poor Jacob had fourteen years before he got his Rachel"). There was a surge of optimism when Goldwyn had a contractual dispute with Merle Oberon; it seemed as if Vivien might after all play Cathy but the hope died when the matter was settled. Wyler refused to give Olivier time off from fittings to fly to New York to spend just a few days with Vivien if she sailed over ("I really am in Hell, my love – the valley of the shadow ... I keep crying"). When he received a cable from her with her arrival date he went from deepest despair to instant euphoria ("I am so gloriously happy – should die without you any longer").

Obviously his longing for her and hers for him spurred Vivien's decision. But Olivier's authorised biographer is wrong to state that *Gone With the Wind* "was not in her mind or his. She went to Hollywood for love and lust of Larry." A scrutiny of the facts suggests otherwise. Vivien had read and instantly adored Mitchell's novel on its British publication (1936). Her opening-night present to each cast member of *Because We Must* was a copy of the book. The company manager on that play was future dramatist Gerald Savory, who remembered her asking everyone if they agreed she would be well cast as Scarlett – they all did although the film was two years away.

The following year, aware of Selznick's casting problems, she urged both Gliddon and Korda to do whatever they could for her bid to be at least considered for the part. Korda told her he thought her chances of such a quintessential American role were slim but did assure her he would talk to Kay Brown, who handled Selznick's East Coast affairs (she had urged him to buy the book). The shrewd Brown, after watching *Fire Over England* (arranged by Korda) responded to something in Vivien and suggested her boss consider her but Selznick temporised. He had screened *A Yank at Oxford* and liked Vivien's "excellent performance" but he still was not convinced she was a contender.

There was a day of location-filming on a Thames riverboat to Southend during *Twenty-One Days* with some showbusiness journalists on board, including the *Observer* film critic C.A. Lejeune. Heavy rain postponed work, which led to conversation about the much-publicised casting of *Gone With the Wind*, about which Lejeune wrote twice. In a 1939 article she mentioned that Vivien suggested she could play Scarlett, a notion not taken seriously by the others. In her autobiography the story is more detailed, with one journalist suggesting Olivier as a possible Rhett Butler before Vivien spoke:

> She drew herself up on the rainswept deck ... pulled a coat snug around her shoulders and stunned us all with the sybilline utterance "Larry won't play Rhett but I shall play Scarlett O'Hara. Wait and see."

When Stewart Granger worked with Vivien on *Serena Blandish*:

> She impressed me as very hard working and certainly very ambitious. She had two passions, her love for Larry and her determination to play Scarlett O'Hara.

Also, Vivien had called her friend Angus McBean to arrange to visit his studio for some publicity shots "for her own requirements". McBean asked her to bring the wide-brimmed black hat she wore in *Serena Blandish* and she happily posed while he snapped away, taking eight pictures (six guineas) some with the hat, some with a spray of blossom. When they were ready she asked him to bring them to Durham Cottage in the evening, pronouncing herself thrilled by the results – "They're wonderful, Angus dear. Just what I wanted. Have you read the book?" – explaining that *Gone With the Wind* was "her Bible" and "I am going to play Scarlett if it's the last thing I do", presenting him with a copy inscribed "With love from Scarlett O'Hara". At that point Olivier arrived home, also admired the pictures but after hearing how she planned to send them to Hollywood, briskly told her to "forget the silly dream" because it was in the evening paper that Norma Shearer was cast ("Too old!" responded Vivien and, indeed, Miss Shearer soon was out of the running). According to McBean, Vivien told him subsequently that it had been the photograph in the black hat (50 years later immortalised on a Royal Mail stamp) which had especially drawn the eye of Myron Selznick.

Fabia Drake was another taken aback by Vivien's will power, that sense of wishing for something so intensely it may be made to happen, when she spoke of her determination to try for the part:

> "But Vivien, you could never play Scarlett! She's too ruthless." Vivien looked back, her eyes glinting mischievously and she smiled a secret smile – the smile of Scarlett.

Irene Mayer Selznick was fully aware of progress on her husband's most ambitious project:

> It seems far-fetched that a dark horse could show up at the last moment but occasional tales still surface to challenge the fact. Vivien Leigh, a relatively minor actress under contract to Alexander Korda in England, came to town apparently to see her sweetheart, Laurence Olivier.

Ten years later, after divorce from Selznick, she learnt from Hugh Beaumont, by then a colleague and close friend, that:

> Her timing was not coincidental. Vivien was as determined as she was beautiful. What she desperately wanted was Larry and Scarlett, in that order; they were both in California and each made the other more possible. Moreover Larry's agent was Myron.

This is glossed by Jamie Hamilton, who coincidentally sailed on the same *Majestic* as Vivien on the last November Saturday of 1938. He had disapproved of her separation from Leigh and was somewhat aloof, but:

> When I reached the dining-room that irresistible laughing face popped up and we danced the whole way over. *Inter alia* she said "You will love Larry!" I replied "No, I hate him for robbing my best friend of his wife." Vivien said "You won't." And of course she was right.

Inevitably he asked her why she was going to Hollywood and was told "Partly because Larry's there and partly because I intend to get the part of Scarlett O'Hara." Hamilton, like others, laughed this off, even betting her £10 that her mission would fail, although later he added wryly "I fear it was left unpaid!"

John Gliddon would soon realise why Vivien had refused De Mille and why the question of American representation had been raised. Vivien knew that Selznick had to begin filming soon and that Scarlett remained uncast. She had always felt – without realising the depth of Selznick's own conviction – that the part would be best played by a new face, to which audiences could bring no preconceptions. And she had nothing to lose – she would still see Olivier. When she stepped on board the *Majestic* the possibility of Scarlett – of course along with her longing for her lover – was indeed very much in her mind.

 CHAPTER 6

Printing a Legend

As Shakespeare's Cleopatra, one of Vivien's favourite speeches was from the great threnodies of loss after Antony's death:

> I am fire, and air; my other elements I give to baser life ...

Fire was the element which marked her final progress to Tara and Scarlett O'Hara. She had arrived in New York, promptly putting her foot in it by answering a reporter questioning the reason for her visit with "To see Laurence Olivier." The Goldwyn office was aghast; no studio risked offending American mores by seeming to condone adultery, whatever went on in private, with vulture-columnists like Hedda Hopper or Louella Parsons hovering for titbits. She flew on to Los Angeles where Olivier was waiting at Clover Field airport, blanketed in the back of a limousine as instructed by the studio. Ensconced in the Beverly Hills Hotel, crucially discreet, their reunion was joyous. Olivier had been in a state ("My emotions were in a bit of a whirl. I was most deeply in love with Vivien and I could think of little else") and had initially found *Wuthering Heights* and Wyler difficult, only now beginning to find his feet, helped, as he would later acknowledge, by Wyler, taciturn but patient. Olivier had called his director "sour Willie" to begin with and had still not stopped brooding of Vivien as Cathy until Wyler told him "Well you'll just have to *think* of her and act with Merle." (When Olivier asked what Oberon would do, Wyler replied: "She'll just have to think of Alex Korda!"). Vivien's lightning trip turned into an American stay of almost a year.

The story of her casting as Scarlett has even more versions than the Japanese legend *Rashomon*. Director John Ford said that if, for a movie, you had the facts and the legend, then "Print the legend!" In this case legend would seem to be fact.

The master-manipulator behind the events of the next few days was Myron Selznick, the uber-agent for whom the phrase "The art of the deal" might have been coined. Like his brother he was a gambler but had a cooler head; he had scant respect for Hollywood's power-elite and many felt he was driven less by money than by a steely resolve to avenge the manner in which a previous era's moguls had conspired to bankrupt his producer-father, Lewis J. Selznick. He liked his client Olivier, would have heard about Vivien and had seen her photographs including McBean's photograph of her in the black hat. It is evident, too, that Olivier had mentioned her ambitions to his agent: "I had a few quiet words with Myron Selznick, indicating to him that there was someone coming to visit me who might possibly be of extraordinary interest to him" he wrote in *Confessions*.

Myron met Vivien the day after her arrival in Hollywood and although she was not yet formally a client it would seem from the evidence that he then planned an extremely canny strategy. With Olivier filming, he took Vivien first to United Artists studio to make her known for likely future casting and then on to a favourite haunt, the Santa Anita racetrack where he had a number of informants who kept him abreast of the affairs, financial and otherwise, of executives, information often useful leverage in contract bargaining. He introduced Vivien to a key Selznick Studios employee, Daniel O'Shea, with whom he organised a provisional screen test for the near future.

All of Hollywood knew about Selznick's plan formally to launch his film with a night-shoot of the burning of Atlanta, a logistically complex sequence involving destroying old sets (from *King Kong* and other films), special effects, doubles (for the stars in long-shot), extras, horses, wagons, gallons of kerosene and the larger quotient of Los Angeles's fire department. That night Myron's plans involved a supper with Vivien and Olivier at the Brown Derby restaurant (telephones primed for calls on progress from the Culver City lot, about to be cleared to create the exteriors of *Gone With the Wind* after the burning). Vivien, surely guided by Myron, had dressed with care – a simple silk dress, belted to show off her tiny waist, under a thin coat, worn unbuttoned, and her hair loose under the black hat. She wore no jewellery and simple make-up using a touch of eyeshadow to highlight her blue-green eyes.

The trio arrived at the lot shortly after the fire had reached its height. Myron bided his time until Selznick and Cukor had descended from the tower used to supervise filming, led his guests forward and said, using the ironic greeting often used to his brother: "Hey, genius – meet your Scarlett O'Hara!" Just as Vivien stepped forward, the dying flames suddenly sparked again into life as a burning beam crashed down, illuminating her face, highlighting her eyes as strikingly as the most gifted cameraman could have devised. Irene Selznick always thought that detail was pure synchronicity but Cukor felt that it was appropriate for "an inspired bit of agentry" from Myron. Ironically the director had seen *A Yank at Oxford* and although he had enjoyed her performance had felt she was "not quite sufficiently fiery" enough for Scarlett. But now, hooked by her firelit appearance – and those eyes – both Selznick and Cukor forgot any previous preconceptions.

If luck played some part in that meeting there was nothing fortuitous about the immediate sequence of events. Looks alone would not land Vivien the part. Now after midnight – Selznick appreciated Vivien's insistence that she never tired, like him – the group moved to Selznick's office whilst a test was discussed (O'Shea, also present, kept quiet – best to let Selznick think everything was his idea) and, without attempting a Southern accent, Vivien ran a few scenes with Cukor. An experienced theatre director and dialogue coach earlier in his career, he was someone to whom Vivien responded immediately as he fed her the lines. Even without a Southern lilt (although he giggled at her "pissy English accent"), his ear told him that Vivien's line-readings, above all her sense of the rhythms of Mitchell's dialogue (the script was then very faithful to the book and of course Vivien knew it practically by heart) had the necessary vitality and intelligence. And fire. Selznick was intrigued further too; the gambler in him, already on a high with the launch of his epic, was elated by the thought that this eleventh-hour throw of the dice could deliver "the unknown girl" he had always imagined. Vivien had gambled too, against what most had said were ridiculous odds, by coming thousands of miles on not much more than a chance. The two intuited this trait, this relish of risk and even danger, in each other and both seemed inexhaustible, even if Selznick was fuelled by the Benzedrine he swallowed like candy. He wrote to Irene in New York of the "frightening but exciting knowledge that GWTW is finally in work" and that the new dark horse "looks damn good".

His shortlist was expanded to four, with Vivien joining Jean Arthur, Joan Bennett and Paulette Goddard (the latter at that stage still the favourite despite Selznick's qualms about the legality of her "marriage" to Charlie Chaplin). She had one week to prepare for her test, going through her scenes with Olivier in the evenings after his filming – most crucially the episode in which Scarlett fails to tempt Ashley Wilkes away from Melanie and the early scene with Mammy, the O'Hara's housekeeper (and slave), lacing Scarlett into her stays.

Vivien had contacted Guthrie warning him that there was a chance that she might be unable to return for Old Vic rehearsals. She also wrote, slightly *fausse-naïve*, to Leigh enclosing Christmas presents for him and Suzanne, and explaining there was just a possibility she might not be in England for Christmas after all because of the film chance:

> No-one is more surprised than me ... I am working frantically hard and studying a Southern accent ... I don't know what to think or what I hope.

She hoped, of course, to land Scarlett O'Hara. The tests – in a costume which she swore was still warm from the previous wearer's body – were all directed by Cukor, who was becoming enchanted by her, especially the contradiction between the delicate exterior and her occasionally Rabelaisian tongue. She in turn responded to the good-natured ribbing which could accompany direction which was unfailingly purposeful and succinct.

The tests survive; her "Missie" is spirited and full of rebel, wincing as Hattie McDaniel's Mammy tightens the laces, but the real challenge came with the Ashley scene. She plays this with a glinting edge, no tearful pleading here but a woman initially confident that she can get what she wants, shocked and desperate when it seems she cannot. The suggestion of an imperious will charges her Scarlett with a frightening intensity, utterly different from the competent but bland portrayals from the other candidates, Paulette Goddard in particular emerging as almost vapid. Leslie Howard played Ashley (rather better than he does in the actual film) with all four contenders but was unavailable for the final test scene later, a demanding extract set in the post-bellum days when Scarlett again tries her wiles on Ashley. This time Douglass Montgomery stood in; even with his stolid delivery Vivien again makes the most interesting choices, finding a rapidly shifting, opaline range of emotions, still exciting to watch. It was perhaps this quality which so clearly struck Margaret Mitchell. She did not want close involvement with the film or its casting but Selznick sent her stills of the tests and of Vivien she wrote to him:

> I am impressed by the remarkable number of different faces she has. In the stills ... she looks like a different person every time she is shown in a different mood.

All the tests were flown to New York for viewing by Jock Whitney and Kay Brown, who agreed with all the personnel at Selznick Pictures, including Selznick's executive assistant, Marcella Rabwin:

> And of course she was a brilliant actress. They tested her, silent tests, wardrobe tests, she was just the ideal. She was the most glowing, vibrant, dynamic woman I had ever met.

Vivien finally learnt of the decision on Christmas Day, 1938. Invited to brunch at Cukor's exquisite house on Cordell Drive, surrounded by its cypress-planted Italian garden and with Impressionists on the walls, he teased her by keeping her in suspense for a moment after telling her the part was cast before adding "I guess we're stuck with you." She was sworn to secrecy; possibly it was as well the news was not out by New Year, some of which Vivien and Olivier spent at Myron's Lake Arrowhead house where guests included her rivals Paulette Goddard and Joan Bennett. When it became known, there was some predictable press indignation, notably from a shrill Hedda Hopper, that Scarlett would not be played by an American ("Well, you've won again!" was her message for England).

While still in suspense and with Old Vic rehearsals imminent, Vivien had gambled and told Guthrie she would not be returning. There were no hard feelings; he had Dorothy Hyson standing by and wrote back: "purely out of loyalty I bet a pound (£1.0.0) that you *would* come back" – later congratulating her on "your great choice".

Moving quickly, Selznick tied up legal formalities with Korda, to whom Vivien remained contracted, Tennant and Gliddon, who was beginning to feel excluded. As, in the ruthless ways of show business, he was. Vivien had to accept Selznick's offer of $25,000 and a seven-year contract; the fee was low (Gable was paid $120,000) but the contract had yearly options which Myron would be able to renegotiate, although Vivien held out for a clause permitting her to take on stage work – a vital issue for her – the granting of which "would not be unreasonably withheld", words which would reverberate some years later. Gliddon received compensation (a less than princely £2,700) for losing his client while "Uncle Cecil", as Olivier and Vivien called Tennant, and Myron took over her affairs. Gliddon seemed to harbour no rancour towards Vivien, writing to her on occasion into the 1960s. It was then generally assumed that her film career would continue predominantly in America where Gliddon had no experience or bargaining power. Vivien prudently did not broadcast her private feelings about Hollywood; she wrote to Leigh "All their standards are financial ones" and to her mother "I know I could not stay here without Larry ... I should go mad."

Olivier was actually less than helpful over her contract, feeling she was being exploited. He barged into Selznick's office to insist he would not allow Vivien to fulfil her contract unless it included terms more advantageous to her. Never Olivier's biggest admirer, quietly Selznick reminded him that at RKO he had scuppered Jill's chances on *A Bill of Divorcement*, adding "Larry, don't be a shit twice."

Ten days before main shooting on *Gone With the Wind* at the end of January 1939 the studio held a press ceremony to announce the signing of Vivien's contract, presided over by Selznick at his most avuncular. This was her first meeting with Olivia de Havilland, who remembered Vivien dressed simply in black, her hair centre-parted:

> She came forward to shake hands with her special air of cool, contained and delicately assured good manners ... she had quicksilver elegance and composure, like a small Siamese cat.

The friendship which developed between them through the long, sometimes chaotic filming of *Gone With the Wind* undoubtedly helped enrich the Scarlett–Melanie bond in the film, which finally saw actors face the cameras in late January.

No film in history has been so extensively analysed, deconstructed, lauded and excoriated, not even the *Star Wars* or *Harry Potter* phenomena. The statistics have been recycled countless times, books scrutinising its history, racial and sexual politics, its place in the South's history, myth and sociology still appear by the shelfload. There have been sequels, parodies, a television series and two musicals – one premiered in Japan where *Gone With the Wind*'s popularity is phenomenal, one the brainchild of theatre director Trevor Nunn which sank beneath its grandiose sentimentality. The novel continues to sell strongly – it has never been out of print – but the essential questions for the film remain: does it still stand up as a classic movie and does Vivien's Scarlett stand the test of time?

Its starting advantage, as Selznick (and Vivien) always stressed, was Mitchell's novel. It may not be great literature – the prose is no more than serviceable, some of its characterisation is pasteboard at best and at times the dialogue teeters on the very edge of bathos but – a huge but – she tells an enthralling story and, perhaps owing something to her journalist's background, has an uncannily good sense of how to pace her narrative, a plus which Sidney Howard carried into his screenplay (although extensively reworked, by Ben Hecht and F. Scott Fitzgerald among others, much of it finally remained Howard's work). Apart from its epic evocation of the seismic schism in American history it struck a resonant chord with the public just as the likelihood of an even more cataclysmic war began to loom, and it had the central figure of a strong, free-spirited woman of the nineteenth century seemingly in tune with a 1930s post-Depression generation which saw countless women begin to work outside the home.

Inevitably, as sexual, racial and political values shifted, perspectives on book and film alike altered. For many twenty-first-century feminists and critics

Gone With the Wind is anathema; the writer Angela Carter produced a particularly provocative piece describing the film as meretricious, "*The Taming of the Shrew* in hooped skirts", portraying only the feudal darkness of the South with an "anorexic, overdressed Scarlett". Some go further; critic Lou Lumenick in 2015 denounced the book and film as "undeniably racist", essentially romanticism of the South and of slavery which "should be rejected along with the Confederate flag" not least because they imply a denial that the Civil War was fought over slavery.

The film is more vulnerable to some of these charges than the book, certainly in the context of the racism charges (Selznick watered down the portrayal of slavery, even cutting a Ku Klux Klan episode, fearing it would offend Klan officials). But the book at crucial points has a context impossible to reproduce or suggest on screen. The famous climax to the first half with swelling music underscoring Scarlett's vow "As God is my witness, I'll never go hungry again" is a powerful movie moment but Vivien has to suggest a romantic kind of defiance whereas on the page Mitchell can set it within one of the novel's most memorably unsentimental passages recalling a post-bellum generation of "bitter-eyed women who looked backward, to dead times, to dead men" while her heroine on screen never would ~~look~~ be allowed to look back.

Others argue that much of the adverse criticism is unfair and that we should simply enjoy a woman-centric book and film, which rather overlooks that it is possible to enjoy something while accepting that it may be imperfect (which Angela Carter implies by a throwaway line in her demolition job – "Goodness me, how enjoyable it all is!"). The argument that Scarlett is no true feminist but someone guilefully presenting herself as a distressed damsel who plots and schemes to get her own way must be countered by recalling that she survives a brutal national conflict in which she sees many die (and kills a man herself), loses two husbands, has three children, suffers a miscarriage and goes from a stereotypical delicate, fluttering Southern belle to survive as a successful businesswoman. Scarlett lies, double-deals and exploits to do so but – and this is reinforced by Vivien's performance – she is a three-dimensional character. And is so because she is imperfect, flawed.

Artistically, too, the film is flawed. Olivier's sharpest biographer, Roger Lewis, no admirer of the film or of Vivien, wrote as divertingly as Angela Carter:

> The Civil War rages; Atlanta is a cliff of flame; Tara is despoiled, and Scarlett weeps in the vegetable plot ... The Cyclorama goes yellow, apricot and crimson ... and all

the while Scarlett and Rhett are meant to be cut out for each other, making love among the ruins. With Vivien flaring her nostrils like a filly however, we can have no interest in their plight.

Yes, the colour (more so in the remastered version) is at times garish (Technicolour cameras – the film used all seven then available – were still in their cumbersome infancy), Max Steiner's lush music is overused, Leslie Howard's Ashley has all the sexual charisma of a damp dishcloth and poor Butterfly McQueen has to simper and quiver in a one-note role but – and again it is a big but – this war film without one battle scene has a sweep which few epics have, moving through the nearly 15 years of its action with a controlled unity of tone the more remarkable in light of its going through three directors, its countless script revisions, a crazy schedule (unions today would forbid it) of six-day weeks, long hours and Selznick's control-freakery. Many sequences – the burning of Atlanta, the panoramic revelation of a seemingly unending vista of Confederate dead, the scenes of intense sexual chemistry between Vivien and Gable – retain their forceful impact.

Vivien was worked hard, even prior to filming, with wardrobe fittings for Walter Plunkett's costumes (some of which Selznick ordered to be padded to enhance the "breastwork"), make-up and hair tests and coaching in the Southern accent (Maureen O'Sullivan's first husband, Will Price, was one of her teachers). Then the filming – six months of long days, usually shooting out of sequence in uncomfortably hot costumes ("like working in Death Valley" said de Havilland) – was often draining. The other stars had sections of the story which did not involve them but Vivien was on call virtually throughout (she was granted a couple of days off whenever she was menstruating). Worst of all she had to adjust to life in California without Olivier. Already signed by Selznick to play Maxim de Winter in the film of Daphne du Maurier's *Rebecca* later in the year for Alfred Hitchcock, he had no desire to hang around Hollywood while Vivien starred in the biggest film of the year and also the studio was anxious to see him off, fearful as the moguls were of any whisper of scandal. As it was, Olivier had been ostensibly resident at the Beverly Hills Hotel and had to be smuggled, with minders and military precision, into and out of Vivien's rented house on North Crescent Drive.

In the house Vivien had Sunny Alexander (later Lash), a bright Texan who had worked in Myron's office, as her secretary/housekeeper. She was "an angel of kindness and goodness" to Vivien and would work for her on future occasions in America, becoming a confidante as well as friend; she could identify with Vivien's mercurial nature and the occasional mood-swings

(Sunny herself had a nervous breakdown in the 1950s). Without her understanding of Vivien's underlying tensions, the experience of making *Gone With the Wind* would have been even more taxing.

Olivier left for New York in March to rehearse opposite Katherine Cornell (automatically dubbed "The First Lady of the American Theatre") directed by her husband Guthrie McClintic in S.N. Behrman's *No Time for Comedy* on Broadway. He was good casting as Cornell's dramatist-husband, diverted from his usual light-comedy style by an attractive rich woman who urges "significance" from him in a darkening world.

Vivien had been remarkably nerve-free when filming began; the apprehensive one was Gable, who had never been desperate to play Rhett Butler (he needed the money for a divorce settlement in order to marry Carole Lombard) and he moaned constantly about his costumes, his hair and his dialogue. Vivien and de Havilland adored working with Cukor but Gable seemed still out of sorts as work progressed – slowly – and they were unprepared for the director's abrupt dismissal after just two weeks for reasons still not totally clear. The suggestions that Selznick caved in to Gable's demand that Cukor go, to be replaced by his chum Victor Fleming, because he felt that Cukor, unfairly typed as "a woman's director", was favouring the women or, as Hollywood scuttlebutt hinted (and still, without foundation, hints) that Gable was uncomfortably aware that Cukor knew something about some supposedly gay episode in the actor's early career, are rubbish. The reasons were professional, the decision made with the Hollywood ruthlessness which over-rides friendship or past loyalties; Cukor was going over schedule, although it was suggested by cinematographer Lee Garmes that this was mainly because he was finding it difficult to handle the screenplay's dialogue and the scenes for early filming had been heavily revised by Selznick himself ("no one wanted to tell the Czar he was wrong" said Garmes) and also Selznick began to fret that, good as he was at intimate scenes, Cukor perhaps was less suited to the grand sweep demanded by the material. His sacking distressed Vivien and de Havilland but their appeals were firmly rejected (although both continued to work on scenes privately – separately – with Cukor on Sundays). Vivien wrote to Leigh: "George Cukor was my last hope of ever enjoying the film."

After finishing *The Wizard of Oz* on one set, Victor Fleming walked on to another to begin work on *Gone With the Wind* (another film in which the heroine, like Dorothy after Oz, returns to native soil). Macho, laconic, hard-drinking and a crony of Gable's, Fleming never has been a fashionable director. With no particular defining specialist genre, the *Cahiers du Cinema* boys never included him among the American *auteur*-directors (Douglas Sirk, John Ford) but he was responsible for some of the outstanding films of the "Golden Age of Hollywood", working mostly for MGM for many years (*Captains Courageous, Red Dust*). As Cukor was stuck with the "woman's director" label, so Fleming was associated with gung-ho male-centric material, although he drew excellent work from actresses including Judy Garland and Jean Harlow. Stories abound that he and Vivien detested each other, that he mocked her Britishness and found her difficult to handle but the evidence seems to contradict this. In a letter to Gertrude Vivien said how much she sympathised with Fleming ("I like Victor Fleming well enough") who was obviously tired after *The Wizard of Oz* (the Munchkins' behaviour alone would have challenged the toughest director). He was never especially subtle ("Ham it up!" was one piece of direction Vivien recalled) and occasionally needled her – probably deliberately – when he wanted extra spirit in a scene, but he could create some order on-set amid the Selznick-created chaos and relaxed the cast ("Only another six scenes before we're through for the day, boys and girls"). Differences which did arise tended to concern the script. Vivien had been troubled often by its departures from Mitchell and had her dog-eared copy of the novel always with her. Fleming had not even had time to read the book before he began work (he did find time – Leslie Howard never bothered) and occasionally found Vivien's fervent championship of it tiresome. Selznick too could at times be irritated by Vivien's criticisms of the script but he did understand her grasp of the story's background and of Scarlett's complex drives. Gavin Lambert, who later wrote a book on the film's making, said of this: "She became a creative influence on the picture, far beyond the limits of an actress."

Selznick's script discussions with Vivien gave him a glimpse of these sudden flashes of an underlying hysteria that could be deeply disconcerting. An especial bone of contention focused on a passage in the novel after the funeral of Scarlett's second husband when she drinks to forget her guilt at stealing him from her sister and admits to Rhett that she is happy her mother died before witnessing this ("She brought me up to be kind and thoughtful and ladylike just like her and I've been such a disappointment"). Vivien fought with unusual vehemence, once almost uncontrollably intense, to retain the lines while Selznick was afraid that they would alienate the audience and lose sympathy for Scarlett. It is possible, of course, that Scarlett's self-laceration reflected the complex feelings Vivien had for her own mother whose religion she had abandoned along with her own daughter to "live in sin" but of course the lines over which she fought with Selznick only add to the layers of Scarlett's inner life. She understood the character better and less conventionally than Selznick ("She is *my* Scarlett" said Margaret Mitchell on finally seeing the film).

Considering the fevered atmosphere of the film's making, Vivien's performance is the more remarkable. The spine of the performance and of the film is her suggestion of Scarlett's sheer indomitable will power, another illustration of her refusal to sentimentalise her performances. This Scarlett, often mean, earns the sympathy Selznick was so fearful of losing by never once asking for it. This quality rivets the film's two halves – the ante-bellum Old South, all white-colonnaded mansions and wisteria blossom leading to the national tragedy of the Civil War and the later sequences of a family saga, deaths and desolation. She also finds in Scarlett a valuable vein of humour – never overplayed – and is unafraid to suggest that there are occasions when she takes herself altogether too seriously. As a perceptive writer on the American South and on *Gone With the Wind*, Helen Taylor, has written: "A steel magnolia becomes a transgressive, epic feminist heroine." As the film progressed, it was increasingly voiced by those working on it that Vivien's performance was astonishing given her British background and inexperience. This overlooks the sheer hard work which went into perfecting her accent and the amount of background reading she did in addition. Also the Selznick publicity machine had played down her work in British films, none of them much known in America. But the amount she had absorbed from those she had worked with had imbued her with the readiness to be able to handle the demands of *Gone With the Wind*. She had by now an uncanny instinct for movie acting, a true camera sense. Gavin Lambert wrote of her:

> She knew exactly how to minimize her effects for a close-up, how to enlarge them for a longer shot, as if the camera for her were now some kind of magic mirror in which she could always obtain the desired reflection.

Alexander Walker's biography of Vivien quotes a Selznick apparatchik saying that his boss would have paid her a percentage of profits on the film "if she hadn't behaved so badly while making it". He gives no source for this. Olivier's authorised biographer claims that "she was not easy to direct" on *Gone With the Wind* but provides no evidence. Of course during an exhausting and often chaotic shoot there were occasional flare-ups but the major participants would seem to contradict Walker and Coleman. Cukor always wanted to work with Vivien again and Selznick offered Vivien countless scripts. Olivia de Havilland had nothing but admiration for Vivien's behaviour on a set with predominantly male personnel (reflecting a patriarchal movie industry), not all of whom approved of any actress speaking her mind:

She was perfectly prepared, precise, adept, she never lost her poise despite the immense strain she was under. She had a self-discipline which was not harsh but of an exquisite order.

The self-control of which de Havilland spoke was especially necessary when Olivier took off for New York. She literally ached for him and he for her; both missed the sex as is clear from his many letters surviving from this time (Vivien's do not exist – possibly destroyed by Olivier although he kept some later ones), nearly a hundred, often written in instalments during rehearsal breaks, in dressing-rooms on his pre-Broadway tour or, in New York, backstage at the Ethel Barrymore Theatre, in his hotel, even in the wings during performances, some of them with his quirky little drawings. They tried to speak regularly on the telephone but this was often unsatisfactory – coast-to-coast calls had to be booked for specific times and Vivien was regularly kept late at the studio, Olivier worried about being overheard and, as for many lovers, a crackling connection could quickly dampen ardour. Olivier's letters explicitly map out his feverish thoughts of Vivien – lustful, ardent, tormented, exhilarated and melancholy with all the confused feelings of a passionate and consuming love affair. She is addressed variously as "Pussy", "Poosey", "Puss", "My Darling Mistress", "My Little Rhapsody", occasionally as "Mummy", with envelopes addressed (to throw off the press), using her middle name, to "Mrs Mary Holman" or their old hotel-weekend subterfuge-name of "Mrs Andrew Kerr". In some letters she is addressed as "My Darling Carnation", a sly nod to their attempts to sublimate erotic longings; he would wear a carnation from the bouquets Vivien sent regularly in his undershorts, enclosing the crushed flower in his next letter while she regularly mailed him a pair of her panties, the latter forming part of a kind of shrine in his hotel room ("Your letter under my pillow, your picture beside me, your drawers inside my pyjamas").

Yet it is plain that temptation – phone sex, self-pleasure – was sometimes impossible to resist, especially in his case on waking ("We've never been able to resist in the mornings hardly, have we?"), for all Olivier's determination to see the separation as a test to be overcome. He quoted from the illuminated text above his bed hung by his mother ("He that overcometh shall inherit all things"). Often he veered from the quasi-sacred (when he heard Kirsten Flagstad sing their favourite *Tristan and Isolde* "tears simply *gushed* from my eyes and 18 tigers had me by the throat" and he reminded Vivien that they "must just think of what Heloise and Abelard went through") to the profane in the same letter ("My pants are now in the air flying to you").

Vivien was working exacting hours in Hollywood while after opening on Broadway Olivier's life was hardly arduous, able to include immersion in New York's theatrical world (fascinated by The Group Theatre's work and friendly with members such as Harold Clurman and Luther Adler), drinks with actor chums, not always wisely ("I'm never going to drink another mint-julep!") reporting (possibly tactlessly) meeting Vivien's old flame John Buckmaster ("it wasn't a sour look he gave me so much as a bitter smile, but I couldn't help thinking – well!") and altogether enjoying what he described as "one dizzy kaleidoscopic sweep".

This led to some awkward telephone calls, some accusations and counter-accusations, as he wrote:

> You bite and scratch and spend a family's food bill for a week telling me I don't love you … Darling, please forgive me if ever I'm not sweet on the 'phone – it's only nerves.

Sunny wrote at times to Olivier, urging him to try to arrange some kind of flying visit and Olivier had been alarmed by Vivien's weight loss in a recent photograph and then by a call from Selznick pressing him to come to Los Angeles, however briefly. He was allowed to take two days off before the out-of-town dress-rehearsal of *No Time for Comedy* in Indianapolis although he was terrified of publicity, and avoided cables if possible, having been told by actress Ruth Chatterton that "she had been warned by Louella Parsons in a drunken moment that the papers had access to them", so he used his old *nom d'amour* of Andrew Kerr once more to cable travel plans. He and Vivien met in a hotel not far from Burbank and later once again, briefly, near Kansas City for which Vivien, granted two days off, was grateful to Selznick ("Larry met me in the hotel lobby and we went upstairs and we fucked and we fucked and we fucked the whole weekend").

No Time for Comedy was a New York success but Vivien's worries increased when Victor Fleming buckled under Selznick's relentless pressure and collapsed under the stress, for a time replaced by the experienced Sam Wood (just off *Goodbye, Mr Chips*), a quick worker which suited Vivien, eager to finish the film and get to New York. Sunny felt that the continuing separation "put so much fire and anger into her and it was projected out through Scarlett". She had virtually no social life apart from occasional visits to friends, director Anatol Litvak and his actress-wife Miriam Hopkins ("one does not feel one is in Hollywood in their company"), a few Sundays by Cukor's pool and sometimes a small dinner-party for friends among the English colony including David Niven or Ronald and Benita Colman. As time drew close to the end of filming, she and Olivier began to think about the future, private and professional. Olivier pondered the possibility of Vivien being cast opposite him in *Rebecca* as the second, never-named Mrs de Winter, a notion on which she now became extremely keen, persuading Selznick to allow her to test for it immediately after she had finished with Scarlett. Olivier agreed that if needed he would be ready to play opposite her in a test in New York but before long he began to back-pedal slightly, insisting that while of course he would love to film with her "even in Hollywood" now he was thinking "because I am so *very* inclined to it, it takes the form of a temptation and needs therefore double consideration".

The professional future was complicated by the international situation. Tony Bushell had written to Vivien in April to say that he felt war was now inevitable ("Grab all you can while the going is good") echoed by George Relph ("The feeling is one of complete inevitability – and doom, fixed and decided") and Olivier was concerned to hear of some actor-friends leaving to join the Territorials. He was evading Korda's attempts to lure him into a film of *Manon Lescaut* with Oberon, more interested to discuss a possible London season with Vivien under Michel St Denis or an American theatre production of *Romeo and Juliet* for them together. He was clearly contemplating the latter with some seriousness, outlining his plans for the possible staging in a letter to Vivien, complete with a detailed ground-plan, while sharing his longing to be united with her professionally and physically. He wrote to Gertrude at this time of "this self-imposed separation":

> We are both very ambitious and I think we both probably have futures – therefore the important thing is to finish up together, for which we will gladly suffer now.

On the personal level they had tried to urge Leigh and Jill to reconsider divorce. What he regarded as recalcitrance on Leigh's part began to irk Olivier:

> I can't help resenting his attitude a bit ... if there is no part of you or rather no wish or *will* in you to be held by him – then he has released you – maybe against his will but he *has* released you ... I don't say this is *right*, I simply say it is so.

Jill, more pragmatic, seemed to be thawing, referring to "our jolly little divorce" although her letters, sometimes with photographs of Tarquin, inevitably aroused old guilt feelings, to the extent that he prayed for the first time in years – undoubtedly sparked too by Fahv's death while he was on tour – and wrote to his former confessor Karl Treadamanay. When Vivien gathered that Jill might consider divorcing Olivier, naming her as correspondent, she approached Leigh once more:

If only, Leigh, you would divorce me from your *mind*. I am so sure that it would be easier for you instead of clinging to a hope.

Before their marital dilemmas could be further resolved Olivier had a major panic when Sunny called him late one night from Los Angeles, terrified that Vivien had taken an overdose of sleeping tablets. He was left in an agony of uncertainty until Sunny called again later to reassure him that Vivien finally had revived under a cold shower. Sunny lied to the studio, saying that Vivien was unwell and unable to film the next day, writing to New York.

So sorry I had to alarm you ... but I was so alarmed myself I had to tell somebody ... Vivien had no idea that the pills were such strong sedatives.

The extent of Olivier's panic comes through in his next letter to her, assuming the role of a cross paternal figure scolding her for causing such panic at five in the morning:

I'm afraid you lead your loving ones one hell of a dance and that's *terribly* naughty.

Sunny's letter had said "I get so upset when things aren't right and Vivien is impossible – or need I tell you?" There had been enough "impossible" incidents for him to wonder if not everything might be symptomatic of the immense stress of her working conditions.

On 27 June Vivien finally finished on the Selznick set and could leave Scarlett behind. After her lunch she walked over to another sound-stage on the Selznick lot to test for *Rebecca*. Dressed down as the subservient, mild Mrs De Winter in nondescript blouse and cardigan opposite Alan Marshall as Max, she shows clearly that six months of Scarlett could not be thrown off with her crinoline; in the test scene in which she confesses that it was she who broke one of Max's dead first wife Rebecca's china pieces, she is edgy and fussy, quite wrong for du Maurier's heroine of latter-day Gothic romance. She knew herself it was not good work but she would still be able to try again in New York with Olivier.

The next day she flew – Sunny accompanied her as "beard" – to New York in time to catch Olivier's final matinee of *No Time for Comedy* with her friend Radie Harris, the always sympathetic columnist, before a delirious reunion backstage ("They clung to each other as if they were never going to see each other again" Harris wrote later). Then she saw the play all over again in the evening. Olivier was practically paranoid about press pursuit; *Wuthering Heights* had opened during his Broadway success, combining to boost him to star status in a city which followed celebrity, all of which he treated with disdain, offhand to stage-door fans and churlish with journalists in interviews. He had fretted over where he and Vivien should stay ("in this country living in hotels with ladies one is not married to" presented problems and "it's so *v* bad for girls to be thought badly of"). Finally he had abandoned the idea of a hotel and they had their short break together at Sneden's Landing in upstate New York where Katherine Cornell lent her house; he had sketched the pre-Revolutionary building for Vivien in a letter along with a sketch of a boat, named "Fiddle-dee-dee" after Scarlett's catch-phrase, in which they could potter about on the Hudson.

An idyllic time ended with a return to New York where Vivien was introduced to the many friends Olivier had made – Alfred Lunt and Lynn Fontanne, Cornell and McClintic, Garson Kanin and Ruth Gordon (who would soon marry), George S. Kaufman and S.N. Behrman (who bonded with her over their shared love of Montaigne, his favourite author) – and to make that vital second *Rebecca* test. Some books say this did not survive but it does exist, fascinating to compare with the first. In a darker cardigan, her hair slightly untidy, Vivien is decidedly better, even carrying off such lines as "You're my father, my brother, my son, all of these things", and the love which this anonymous young woman harbours for Maxim comes burning through. Which is part of the problem; her character is just too emphatic for a role requiring the very absence of intensity which Max longs for after the volatility of Rebecca. Also, although Olivier clearly allows the camera to favour Vivien, his performance is muted, somewhat uncommitted. That hint of doubt in his letters seeps into his playing. Much later he did admit: "The worst part of it was I really did not want her to get the part." He claimed that with the strain of their divorce worries and the European situation it was perhaps better "to have a little vacation from constant togetherness" which seems special pleading considering that they had been apart for most of the past few months. Very possibly – and given his on-set coolness to Joan Fontaine, finally cast – he wanted *Rebecca* to be primarily his film; he was now a major star, with his brooding Heathcliff image dominating posters all over America, and might well have been reluctant to co-star with someone whose star-power after *Gone With the Wind* was released might match – or eclipse – his own. If Vivien sensed any of this, she kept quiet. She did not yet know that Selznick did not consider her suitable casting, while Hitchcock put it best, saying later that Vivien was a terrific actress and ideal casting but not for the part she wanted. She would, he said to Henri Langlois, have made the perfect Rebecca with her perturbing sexuality, flaunting a strong identity with her initials and monogram everywhere (there is a photograph of the Oliviers, as they then were, about to sail from Australia in 1948 which could be Max and Rebecca, with Vivien clutching her boldly monogrammed handbag). "She and Rebecca were both uniquely strong women who knew what they wanted and how to get it" said Hitchcock. But of course, Rebecca never appears in the novel or the film.

Arriving in London after sailing on the *Majestic* was sobering. Gas masks were being distributed against an increasingly febrile sense of imminent crisis. Olivier met with Jill, remarkably free of rancour, who now agreed to divorce him, accepting that he, she and Tarquin no longer constituted a family ("Without us being together or you loving me I can't feel I'm your wife"), while Tarquin of course could barely recognise him (his son said later "A three year-old cannot pretend love"). Leigh remained seemingly unswerving in his resolve to take no action and refused to permit Vivien to take Suzanne back to America with her. This was not a happy visit for Vivien, which is perhaps why she seemed to need Gertrude more than usual, even asking her to accompany her and Olivier back to America.

Returning on the *Majestic*, cables from Selznick arrived for both. Vivien's was one of his lengthy ones, giving various reasons why she would not be in *Rebecca*, with fulsome assurances of exciting future plans, while Olivier's was briefer, pointing out (accurately) that Vivien had shown no interest in the part until he was cast as Max. Vivien was not used to rejection and was not best pleased.

Settled in a different Beverly Hills house – where Gertrude took to California life instantly – Vivien had to forget her disappointment by preparing for some retakes on *Gone With the Wind* against a background of increasingly grim news from home. The trio enjoyed a weekend on Colman's yacht anchored at Catalina Island with David Niven joining the party and it was while there that they heard, on a crackly ship's radio, Neville Chamberlain's announcement that Britain was now at war with Germany. "It was one of the few times I saw her cry" said Niven.

Decisions suddenly seemed paramount and difficult. Gertrude arranged to return to England at the end of September while Vivien and Olivier contacted their friend Duff Cooper at the Ministry of Information in London. Friends were leaving America – Niven included – while Ralph Richardson at home had joined the Fleet Air Arm (FAA), Leigh was in the Royal Naval Volunteer Reserve (RNVR), stationed in Ramsgate, and Oswald Frewen was based in Gibraltar with the Navy. Cooper informed them that for the time being British people in their position should stay in America to do as much as possible for the war effort, not advice easy to accept with newspaper articles on both sides of the Atlantic sniping at British show business stars enjoying themselves in the Californian sun. Olivier was actually not much enjoying *Rebecca* and Vivien was somewhat in limbo. At one stage Selznick seemed set to unite the pair in *Pride and Prejudice* directed by Cukor which for everyone was a delightful prospect but Greer Garson, Olivier's old flame, was cast as Elizabeth Bennett. Then the plan to remake the weepie of *Waterloo Bridge* in which both would star looked all ready to go before Robert Taylor was cast opposite Vivien, robbing her – as she saw it – of another chance to co-star with Olivier. They both suspected – rightly – that money was at the root of Selznick's decisions; he earned more by lending out both of them to MGM rather than producing one film himself starring them together. Olivier was able to console Vivien by promising that at least they would be together in his stage production of *Romeo and Juliet*; Cukor had convinced him that their pairing would make for sensational American box-office returns.

After the retakes, editing and scoring Selznick at last was ready to launch his masterwork. Vivien had to be included in the hoopla surrounding *Gone With the Wind*'s world premiere in Atlanta, an extravaganza into which Selznick poured almost as much attention as into the film itself, an epic celebration with a State holiday declared as the population of Atlanta swelled to many times its normal size, with Klieg-lights blazing, brass bands playing, sirens wailing, balls, receptions and dinners, all giving Selznick even more publicity. Vivien gave the organisers a headache by insisting Olivier accompany her, which was eventually arranged under the flimsy pretext that he was there as Selznick's guest in a kind of trailer for *Rebecca*. Flying into Atlanta, Vivien nearly put her foot in it again; hearing the band strike up "Dixie" she exclaimed "They're playing the tune from our picture!", not quite how Atlantans would wish to hear their state anthem described. The quick-witted Howard Dietz, MGM's publicist, explained it away as just a joke commenting on the jubilant welcome. As it transpired, *Gone With the Wind* topped even everything Selznick could have hoped for. The critical reaction was virtually unanimously positive; even Hedda Hopper ate her words, if not one of her alarming hats. The surviving photographs and newsreel footage show Olivier near – never quite next to – Vivien and looking decidedly pinched and unsmiling. He would have realised that Vivien too was now a major star (when he had seen *Gone With the Wind* at a private screening during *Rebecca* filming he had been astonished, quietly saying "I didn't realise she had it in her").

Everything seemed to have happened very quickly. She would from now on be associated with the cinema's most successful film and with one of its greatest female roles, giving her an iconic fame on a scale which could dwarf Olivier's.

Waterloo Bridge and *Pride and Prejudice* both filmed at MGM, so work often overlapped, a consolation for Vivien. Cast as Myra, a ballet dancer in 1918 wartime London, she trained as hard as she had done for *The Happy Hypocrite*, taking lessons from choreographer Ernest Matay, requesting only that "two strong girls who can prop me up" be cast beside her for the dance sequences. She had not looked forward to the film – it was not her choice, it was a remake and Olivier was not opposite her – but it turned out both a pleasure to make and eventually one of her own favourites.

Waterloo Bridge may be corn – a film for a wet winter afternoon beside a fire – but it is corn supremely well handled within the limits of the Hollywood Production Code, the censorship of the era then run by Joe Breen. Based on a 1930 play by Robert E. Sherwood it had been filmed in 1931 with Mae Clarke as Myra, in that version (pre-Code) a London chorus-girl moonlighting with some light prostitution while in S.N. Behrman's new screenplay, told in flashback, she is a ballerina who meets Roy, an army colonel about to leave for France in 1918. They are about to marry when a chain of bad luck and misunderstandings parts the lovers; Roy is (erroneously) reported as killed in action, Myra is fired from the ballet company and, destitute, follows a friend onto the streets. Outside Waterloo Station one night Roy miraculously returns (from prison camp), but although he still loves her and takes her to meet his aristocratic family in Scotland, Myra realises she cannot marry him, obeying the Production Code's law that A Fallen Woman Cannot Rise Again. Back on Myra's beat the film's ending anticipates *Anna Karenina* and her train with her going under an army truck.

Summary underlines the hokum and the coincidences, but the film often surmounts its *Peg's Paper* overtones. It manages to evoke that sense of time suspended in wartime ("No one who has been in this war is young" says Roy) and a period when women with no income or prospects become caught between the pressures of survival and the social values which damn their conduct. The ballet scenes, the screen filled with a shimmering *corps* show Myra, in tulle and virgin-white swansdown, ineffably delicate, seemingly ethereal and utterly captivating Roy and then after their separation she morphs into something to be seen as blotted and sullied, isolated at the close against a void of night sky while the camera moves in for a close-up of her eyes:

> The empty space, the unsaid, anticipates her death. For prostitution is absolutely irrecuperable. Roy can cross class demarcations to marry her but once she slips into prostitution she is lost ... she is, literally, unpresentable and must die.

An example of Hollywood Studio expertise, *Waterloo Bridge* was well cast (the hatchet-faced Maria Ouspenskaya as the ballet-mistress, C. Aubrey Smith as Roy's crusty old uncle) and given deluxe personnel including art direction by Cedric Gibbons, directed by Mervyn Le Roy. Something of a Horatio Alger figure, Le Roy had worked for Cecil B. De Mille and was extraordinarily versatile as producer (*The Wizard of Oz*) and director of gangster films, romantic comedy and musicals. He was friendly and approachable; he and Vivien had a warm working relationship. Selznick, set on moulding Vivien into megastardom, was especially proprietorial on this loan-out to MGM; Vivien was his "property" and he wanted the best possible attention given to her "to capture her very strange beauty", demanding from Bernie Thau at MGM that he be consulted on the choice of cinematographer, pressing MGM to present her "just as though she were your own star under contract".

If the choice of Joseph Ruttenberg was Selznick's, it was inspired. Russian-born, he emigrated with his family and began as a photojournalist before moving into films, making his first silent in 1917, then worked for D.W. Griffith and Fritz Lang. He was a master of black-and-white photography, balancing inky blacks with sharply contrasted luminous "silver screen" close-ups, and of sensitive lighting. He and Le Roy solved a major problem on the film's most striking scene, set in a nightclub in which Roy and Myra dance before his departure, originally with tender dialogue of which Behrman and producer Sidney Franklin were especially proud, a demanding sequence with an orchestra, extras and choreography to integrate. As Le Roy recalled, on set the scene, despite excellent performances by Vivien and Taylor, remained inert, refusing to come to life. Finally he broke for the day, sitting alone on the set, reading the scene over many times before realising "what silent directors had ever known and what I should have remembered".

This was, he realised, a scene in which music (a haunting "New Year Waltz"), movement and expressions were infinitely more potent than words, a scene of "basic human behaviour". Next day he began with a long shot of Myra and Roy dancing:

> Then I cut to the orchestra; each musician had a candle on his music-stand; one by one, they snuffed them out. Cut to a close-up of them dancing, looking deep into each other's eyes. Back to the orchestra and more candles being put out. Before all the candles were extinguished the message was clear – they had fallen deeply, completely in love. Not a word had been uttered.

Ruttenberg's close-ups throughout are a vital part of this sequence and of the film's entire fabric – early ones of Myra and Roy confined in an air-raid shelter,

Myra in a foamy sea of white in her *Swan Lake* costume looking up to see Roy in the audience, a startling shot of Myra suddenly seeing Roy again through the fog at Waterloo, her face reflecting in a few fleeting moments a range of conflicting emotions, and the final sequence closing in on her face and then her eyes as relentlessly as the camera does with Garbo to end *Queen Christina*, and as potently.

It is a delicate, finely tuned performance from Vivien while Robert Taylor has a breezy optimism which is ideal opposite Vivien's suggestion of a melancholy back-story for Myra, an awareness that happiness rarely lasts ("You're so young and lovely but you don't seem to expect much from life" says one character). Selznick was pleased when *Waterloo Bridge*, a definite contrast to *Gone With the Wind*, proved a box-office winner and a personal success for Vivien, with *The New York Times* judging her "as fine an actress as we have on the screen today. Maybe even the finest." With *Pride and Prejudice* also successful and Leigh now agreeing to divorce Vivien at the same time as Jill divorced Olivier, with Jill and Leigh given custody of the children, it was now only a question of a six-month wait for the decrees to become absolute after which they would be free to marry. Everything seemed brighter as they prepared for possibly the most romantic of Shakespeare's plays, their first joint American appearance coinciding with their screen fame. As on so many occasions Olivier sought advice beforehand; the only caveat had come from Ralph Richardson, who had appeared in *Romeo and Juliet* on Broadway a few years before with Cornell and was characteristically terse. "Bit too luxurious for wartime" he advised, but Olivier on this occasion paid no attention to a lone cautionary voice.

CHAPTER 7

Star-Crossed

Olivier had previously directed a couple of plays, neither successful, but with the confidence of inexperience he advertised *Romeo and Juliet* as "Produced and Directed by Laurence Olivier". Laurence Olivier was also responsible for the "scenic concept". And the music (composed with Alexander Steiner). And Laurence Olivier played Romeo. He never budged significantly from the complicated set he had sketched for Vivien in a letter from New York – a huge wall bisecting a revolving stage which swung round to reveal various locations including the Capulet house, Juliet's bedroom, its balcony, the tomb and the Verona streets. Two of the Motleys, "Percy" Harris for the set, Elizabeth Montgomery for costumes (Renaissance-period, similar to those for Gielgud's 1935 production), were brought over to Los Angeles while *Pride and Prejudice* was filming. Percy Harris had to interpret Olivier's sketches, a difficult adjustment to make after her simple, virtually permanent setting for Gielgud. A reluctant convert to the screen, Olivier now planned to bring film's ability to cut from scene to scene to the stage; Percy tried to dissuade him but he insisted on his revolve-concept which had mostly to be shaped in consultation with the assistant director, Robert Ross, while Olivier was filming, after which he would arrive and tinker with everything. The programme note announced that his design-concept "will move the scenes in perfect sequence" which was fine when the revolve worked satisfactorily but it was far from reliable, often jamming as it turned. Worse was that the production had booked its pre-New York tour and its Broadway destination into theatres of large capacities to make (at a $3.30 top – unusually high then) as much money as possible ("Larry and I were too greedy" Vivien told John Merivale) which meant that on the enormous stages the revolve had to be placed well upstage, sabotaging any question of intimacy.

Further, it pushed the various locations into small, wedge-shaped spaces ("Juliet's bedroom was two feet, six inches across" remembered Percy Harris).

A great actor, Olivier was rarely a great director and few of his stage Shakespeare productions were much more than competent (the National Theatre's opening *Hamlet* was especially disappointing – and also had a recalcitrant revolve). He could be somewhat literal-minded; for *Romeo and Juliet* he designed an elaborate background sound-score of bells, dogs barking, choirs and clocks, the whole caboodle essentially inimical to the cumulatively fleet arc of the play (The Chorus's "two hours' traffic" stretched to three).

The production had been planned with military precision; using a model-box and pipe-cleaner figures every move had been plotted in advance, every musical phrase composed to the last note to synchronise with exits, using Palestrina chants for the church scenes. It was as strongly cast as possible, using several Hollywood-based British actors (Dame May Whitty, an old friend of Eva Moore, as the Nurse) and some promising younger talent including Cornel Wilde as Paris and the Canadian-born John Merivale (Gladys Cooper's stepson) as Balthasar. He had auditioned for Paris but knew he was wrong for the part and suggested his half-brother John Buckmaster, to be rather surprised by Olivier's dismissive reaction.

Rehearsals began in Los Angeles; Vivien and Olivier led the company well, as they would do with all their subsequent companies, treating them as surrogate family. Before the tour began there were mixed delights at the Academy Awards ceremony (29 February 1940); Olivier lost to Robert Donat's Mr Chips but Vivien's Best Actress Award for *Gone With the Wind*, presented by Spencer Tracy, was no major surprise. She looked radiant; most women present were in couture finery, whaleboned and stiffly coiffed, while Vivien with her love of flowers chose an elegantly understated chiffon dress by Irene Gibbons, patterned in enormous red poppies, her hair loose. She made only a brief speech, becomingly grateful as a first-time winner and a Brit, paying what sounded genuinely sincere tribute to Selznick's vision. In the post-ceremony photographs she looked equally radiant with Selznick (and Oscar) although Oscar is signally absent from those taken with Olivier, who told Tarquin later that when their studio-arranged separate limousines had secretly returned them to their own car: "It was all I could do to restrain myself from hitting her with it. I was insane with jealousy!" Characteristic Olivier exaggeration but, like so many similar pronouncements, carrying at least a kernel of truth.

After supervising frustratingly slow technical rehearsals at the Geary Theatre in San Francisco, its overtaxed Romeo had a miserable opening night, the nadir coming at the close of the balcony scene for which he had devised an athletic farewell to Juliet ending with a daring leap over his famous wall. Physically and vocally flagging, he ran towards the wall on his final couplet:

> Hence will I to my Ghostly Friar's close cell,
> His help to crave and my dear hap to tell

but his final "tell" emerged as an extended wail ("teeeell!") as he failed to make the leap, left hanging by his fingers until a merciful electrician faded the lights.

In Chicago they played in the echoing barn of the Auditorium Theatre (seating over 3,500) where the receptions and reviews were rather better than those in San Francisco (Vivien wrote to Gertrude: "I have come out of it better than I expected"). She rather took to Chicago, impressed by the wonderful Van Goghs in its art gallery and having a merry post-show dinner with Gene Kelly.

Somewhat arrogantly Olivier anticipated success on Broadway, convinced that more sophisticated audiences would respond to his vision and in interviews airily laying out plans for him and Vivien to rotate some classics in repertoire in New York the following Spring. It would be more than a decade before Broadway saw them together again. The notices for *Romeo and Juliet* were stinging. There possibly was an element of "Tall Poppy Syndrome" in this, with critics seeing a chance to cut two film stars down to size after their floods of publicity, and Olivier's patronising attitude to the press during *No Time for Comedy* had not been forgotten. The production was savaged ("not merely weak but calamitous" and "The whole production was strictly from Hollywood"). Olivier's performance was not controversial as it had been in London; it was unanimously reviled ("he talked as though he was brushing his teeth" or "Olivier was far worse than Miss Leigh"). Olivier had stressed Juliet's youthful innocence; she bounced a ball in rhythm to the verse as she awaited the Nurse, and Vivien did look remarkably fresh. But in the vast 51st Street Theatre (formerly a cinema, as several reviews sarcastically mentioned) and upstaged by the set, she was not always totally audible although some critics found her impressive:

> She not only looks the part that Shakespeare had in mind but she plays it with grace and eloquence.

There was little prospect of a decent, let alone a profitable, run. After the second night, at a Charity Ball they were greeted by Noël Coward with "My dears, how *brave* of you to come!" which made them feel no better, but both remembered their invitation to an elegant dinner by the Lunts, who behaved with immense tact and never once mentioned *Romeo and Juliet*. They moved out of their expensive hotel and retreated to Sneden's Landing while at the theatre keeping up a front of cheerfulness to maintain company morale. But playing out a flop is always a difficult time – damp weather made Vivien feel often unwell, which may have contributed to one of her sudden, disconcerting mood-swings. Jack Merivale had been invited for a weekend at Sneden's Landing and on the Sunday evening, while Olivier read, he and Vivien played Chinese Checkers when suddenly Vivien turned on him – as she had on John Gliddon – to accuse him shrilly of cheating, then, when he protested innocence, of trying to come between her and Olivier. Merivale stole away early next morning. This instance may also have been due to her pent-up feelings of disappointment on Olivier's behalf – he had taken the fiasco of *Romeo and Juliet* very badly – even to an intuition of a smothered attraction (she and Merivale would be a couple for the last years of Vivien's life) or to a warning signal to herself (years later she reflected to Merivale "Perhaps I saw you as a danger") but it was still a perplexing shock to Merivale. Olivier had simply continued with his book, explaining it away to Merivale as just an example of highly strung behaviour.

Flying lessons at a nearby airport occupied Olivier following *Romeo and Juliet's* closure after just over a month's run – he hoped on his eventual return to England to join Richardson in the FAA – but the couple had some serious problems then, not least financially. It is estimated that their Shakespearean venture lost $96,000 (a huge sum then), the combined savings from their American films. Jill said to Tarquin that "Vivien did *not* put one penny of her money into it. She has more sense" but this remains unclear, while at various stages Olivier claimed that Warner Brothers had invested in the production. In any event, money was tight. Also Olivier had had an unpleasant scare when Jill, living with Tarquin in a snowbound remote country cottage, had to cope alone with, for a time, a seriously ill Tarquin and he now desperately wanted to evacuate his son away from the war just as Vivien fretted about Suzanne's safety. Duff Cooper continued to advise them to remain in America and soon the British Embassy in Washington reinforced that by insisting that all British subjects over 31 (Olivier was 32) should stay. Professional possibilities seemed nebulous; Vivien was attracted by the leading role in a Theatre Guild offer of *Marie Adelaide*, centred round the Grand Duchess of Luxembourg who abdicated after 1918 to become a Carmelite nun, but Selznick refused to allow her to take on another play after *Romeo and Juliet* which she took badly. Increasingly disenchanted by Hollywood's venality, she was now genuinely more focused on her stage career.

Alexander Korda rescued them providentially with a film (originally titled *The Enchantress*) for them both in Hollywood – the romance of Admiral Nelson and Emma Hamilton for which he advanced them each half their fee, which would allow them to clear their debts and arrange passage to Canada for Tarquin and Suzanne. Negotiations – helped by Leigh and Jill – were complex but finally it was arranged for Suzanne to travel to stay with Ernest's sister in Vancouver while Tarquin travelled with Jill, also to Canada coincidentally on the same *Scythia* as Suzanne, who travelled with Gertrude. In Toronto Olivier finally met again the wife and son he had not seen for over a year, combining a visit to the city with a film gala along with Vivien. Jill went to the hotel where they were staying ("We were *so* charming to each other and *so* sincere") but according to her when she wrote to Eva:

> He got on well with Tarquin but didn't seem really interested and never asked about his illness. He wanted me to go out with him and Vivien but I said "No".

Vivien met Tarquin with Olivier; Tarquin was in bed but although he had seen photographs of her as Scarlett, when he saw her "I was amazed. Larry introduced her to me as Bibs" and later he asked her to kiss him goodnight ("She leant down, kissed my forehead and I was enveloped in her perfume").

Jill moved on to New York, sharing an apartment for a while with Jessica Tandy (who had played Viola in the Old Vic *Twelfth Night*) before going on to Hollywood where Robert Donat and his wife Ella (with whom Jill later spent part of her life when back in London) were extremely kind to her and Tarquin. She worked occasionally but it remained a sadness that Olivier seemed so remote from his son ("I think he is a nice person. He was just *very* weak and still is. Maybe the war will make him grow up").

Vivien was able to see Suzanne and Gertrude too, taking Selznick's extravagant gifts of clothes and Scarlett dolls for Suzanne. After the long separation she was delighted by Suzanne's progress, telling Leigh: "She looks beautiful and completely enchanting, she seems to have grown even sweeter." Then she had to leave for work, moving into a house which Sunny had arranged in Cedarwood Drive, still in Beverly Hills. Sunny had recently married Harry Lash, an ex-actor, but she was not present – hardly anyone was – when Vivien married Olivier just a few weeks later.

Having waited until the midnight of the final day of the six-month mandatory period for both divorce decrees to become absolute, they were set on as unostentatious a ceremony as possible. Witnesses would be required, so they dragooned their house-guest, the extrovert, gossipy writer-director Garson Kanin as best man and he immediately enlisted his friend Katharine

Hepburn as maid of honour, a role she was pleased to accept even though she had met the happy couple on only a few occasions. Ronald Colman had advised them to avoid Los Angeles and the press, arranging for them to hold the ceremony at the Ysidro Ranch, a deluxe country hotel which he co-owned at Montecito, Santa Barbara. Kanin wrote of the occasion subsequently but, something of a self-mythist, possibly somewhat embroidered his recollections (Hepburn certainly did not recall a tipsy judge declaring the marriage legal with "All right. That's it. Bingo!"). The couple did, however, insist on standing side by side facing eastward – towards England – during the brief ceremony. The honeymoon was short – the Colmans arranged champagne and flowers on board their schooner moored at San Pedro – and they continued to evade the press although at sea the following day Olivier was discernibly peeved that not a single announcement appeared on any radio news bulletin or in any newspaper for quite a while.

Korda was delighted at news of the wedding. Now he could exploit the film's scandalous story-line of Nelson's affair with Emma, paralleling the Leigh/Olivier relationship, bathed in what Olivier had called "the limelight of adultery", without snide press speculation on his stars' personal status. There was still no final screenplay for *Lady Hamilton* (*That Hamilton Woman* in America) as it had been titled, which rather reflected the haste surrounding the project from conception through to its shooting. Much has been made of Winston Churchill's involvement; he had got to know Korda, one of those maverick figures like Max Beaverbrook or Brendan Bracken to whom he was drawn, during his 1930s "wilderness years" and was shrewdly aware of the cinema's propaganda value. He was most likely responsible for using Korda's presence in America, which involved some undercover work, to set up a film centred on Nelson, a national hero he revered and whose resistance to Napoleon would parallel even more urgently than *Fire Over England* Britain's struggle against tyranny. Certainly he encouraged Korda's US set-up to act as a covert monitor of the extent of American isolationism and to do anything possible (*Lady Hamilton* included) to advance the British cause, now perilous after the fall of France and the retreat from Dunkirk. Whether, as is often claimed, Churchill actually wrote any of the script, including much-quoted lines in a scene in which Nelson exhorts the Admiralty ("You cannot make peace with dictators. You have to destroy them – wipe them out!") remains open to question, although it became by far his favourite film.

The need to stress the propaganda element was something which Korda took on board, but – romantic as he was – he wanted the film also to celebrate what he regarded as a supreme love affair. When he saw his art-director brother Vincent's design for the main set, the vast library of Sir William Hamilton's British Embassy at Naples, he instantly commanded: "I can't set a love-story in a bloody library – change it to a bedroom!" Vincent's work is one of the film's strong points, especially in light of the budget (Korda was, not unusually, ducking and diving financially) and tight schedule (six weeks) and wisely he kept those scenes outside the Embassy to a minimum, using simple, suggested sets requiring only astute dressing and inventive lighting, with the Trafalgar scenes executed in the studio tanks using models. Yet the film at times suggests the extravagant opulence of a Max Ophuls – Sir William Hamilton's villa with its view of Vesuvius across the bay is stuffed with statuary (all papier-maché but convincingly marbled), vast draperies and a gigantic bed with an elaborate headboard, while the costumes from René Hubert (now in California), if more "Hollywood Historical Glamour" than authentically period, also look sumptuous, giving Vivien a wardrobe heavy on flowing fabrics, embroidered silks, spangled gauzes and glittering lamé, all geared to Korda's ideal of Emma, not the blowsy tippler she became but perennially the beauty of the Romney portrait. Similarly Nelson, first appearing sailing into Naples to "Rule, Britannia", is presented as a fearless hero literally without warts, the embodiment of British patriotism and a riven romantic lover. The script was written piecemeal by R.C. Sherriff (*Journey's End*) and Korda's Austrian-born colleague Walter Reisch (*Ninotchka*) with only the early sequences completed before filming began at the cheap and cheerful General Service Studio. Sherriff recalled that there was no time for the usual in-depth script discussions he was used to:

> From then on it was a desperate race to keep up with them … It was like writing a serial story with only a week between your pen and the next instalment.

The urgency of the war situation and the schedule-dictated script actually helped the film. Korda as director could be heavy-handed but *Lady Hamilton* has a pace and energy infusing every reel. Also the sense in the studio that the film was in part designed to boost the cause of the country from which most involved were temporarily exiled enhanced the high-octane level of everyone's work. No other Korda-directed movie has the flair of sequences such as Emma's exhilarated, swooping run from her room along the gallery, out on to the balcony and into Nelson's embrace for a long, long kiss as Miklos Rozsa's strings crescendo. There are moments of kitsch and lines pulsing with cliché ("Why do we always meet only to say goodbye?") most memorably in a scene set as midnight strikes to mark a new millennium (1800) when Nelson kisses

Emma as the chimes begin, finishing as they end with: "Now I have kissed you across two centuries", but both leads commit totally to their roles and, helped by a supporting cast of real depth (Gladys Cooper a pillar of icy rectitude as Lady Nelson, Henry Wilcoxon creating a Hardy of genuine gravitas and Sara Allgood – still broad Dublin – as Emma's voluble mother), they carry the film home. Vivien in the two brief glimpses of the imprisoned, raddled older Emma, bookending the film, is surprisingly effective, using a deeper, brandy-soaked voice, baggy-eyed in tattered finery (in one late close-up startlingly and briefly anticipating an older Blanche Du Bois, out of luck and lost). Her vitality charges many scenes – coping with the chaos of the Naples court, all yapping dogs and bawling infants, with unfazed aplomb – contrasting with the later scenes of Emma settled in the English countryside waiting for news from Trafalgar and then listening stock-still, eyes unblinking, her needle frozen above her tapestry-work throughout a long scene, to Hardy's account of Nelson's death. Olivier had less to explore, given this airbrushed version of the character, with nothing like the emotional landscape of Terence Rattigan's Nelson in *A Bequest to the Nation* in which he tries to explain why the rector's son, taught to abominate sexual passion, should find with Emma that carnal love can concern the soul as well as the body. His performance is vocally low-pitched except for the anti-Bonaparte rhetoric when the Olivier brass can resonate at its most spine-tingling. Still Vivien tends to be the one who stands out in their scenes; she had mastered screen acting in a way which Olivier still had fully to achieve.

The pair look superbly right together in this film, however ("at their most heart-stoppingly beautiful and mutually enraptured" said critic Molly Haskell), helped by Korda's clever choice of Rudolf Maté as cinematographer. In Europe before the war, the Polish-born Maté had collaborated with Carl Dreyer on films including *The Passion of Joan of Arc* with its unflinching close-ups of the great Falconetti, and in America with Hitchcock. Here he worked magic with some breathtaking close-ups, often using shadows, realising how well the planes of Vivien's face took to bold shading, notably in a scene with Emma in Nelson's cabin, lit only by a flickering ceiling-lamp low in oil, when after an absence of some time she first sees his damaged eye and lost arm.

Lady Hamilton performed strongly at the box-office in England and America, to reviews more mixed in America, with *Time* finding the parallels with current events had "all the subtlety of a sock on the jaw" while *The New York Times* noted the "surprising frankness" of the story and finding Vivien "a delight ... All of the charm and grace which Miss Leigh contains is beautifully put to use to capture the spell which Emma assuredly must have weaved". Recently a new generation of film critics have reappraised the film, including Ian Christie and Tim Robey, the latter intriguingly suggesting that Korda's style here recalls the crisp elegance of William Wyler's early work, centred round strong female roles, and saying of Vivien that "she never looked so perilously lovely ... this might just be her most under-regarded performance." And in America Molly Haskell wrote of the couple: "You feel their love as divinely ordered, inevitable – that if they'd lived at opposite ends of the earth they'd somehow have found each other." For her it ranks as one of the most romantic movies ever made, adding of its stars: "However brief and self-mythologising their love, let us celebrate *Lady Hamilton* as its definitive memorial."

The closing lines of the film are Emma's in answering her cellmate's plea to know what happened after Nelson's death ("What then? What happened after?") with: "There is no 'then'. There is no 'after'." Tenses for Vivien and Olivier then seemed similarly in limbo. Duff Cooper still counselled caution. They were offered *Caesar and Cleopatra* by the Theatre Guild, still keen to find vehicles for either or both, but Olivier was pressing to return home while Vivien knew she still had some years in which to play Shaw's Egyptian queen. Vivien flew to Vancouver to see Suzanne who had settled in well but the visit caused problems when the strict Reverend Mother of Suzanne's convent school, fearing that the offspring of such a famous star might make her vulnerable to kidnap, insisted she be removed. Gertrude, who had planned to return to England and was doubtless eager to find out how Ernest had been behaving (or misbehaving) in her absence, stayed on to see Suzanne settled into another school. Vivien had questioned whether under such circumstances it was the better course to return home but Olivier had had enough of America and an enormous amount for both of them had been crammed into two momentous years – film stardom, Broadway disaster, financial straits, marriage, family problems and the feeling of impotence living thousands of miles from home. Vivien, with Sunny's help, packed up Cedarwood Drive and then they said goodbye to all their Hollywood friends. Irene Selznick originally somewhat admired Vivien for being "courageous and romantic" in returning to London and the Blitz with Olivier, but when it transpired that Vivien would never work for Selznick again, contract notwithstanding, she added "It turned out that I was the romantic one." They stopped briefly in New York where it was also a time of goodbyes – to the Lunts, Cornell and McClintic, Garson Kanin, Sam Behrman and all their friends. The voyage home was an experience neither ever forgot. They had booked on an American liner, the *S.S. Excambion*, leaving just after Christmas, 1940, bound for Lisbon. It flew under the American flag and was technically neutral, but its atmosphere was uncomfortable, even sinister. The captain was an American citizen but German-born and at dinner on New Year's Eve proposed the toast "Deutschland Uber Alles" and Vivien's German was good enough to pick up some remarks which suggested that at least some of the crew were Nazi sympathisers. There were only 20-odd passengers on board but everyone seemed on edge, fearing a possible U-boat surfacing alongside. Arrival in Lisbon soothed no nerves; the city seemed in a chaos of transience with spies seemingly lurking in every hotel lobby, black-market dealings and con-men everywhere. Bagging the last two seats on a plane for England, landing at Bristol, took time and string-pulling and the flight itself was as fraught as their sailing. Panic erupted well before landing when a crew-member appeared in the passenger-cabin with a fire extinguisher; a window had been left closed in the cockpit when the pilot fired a recognition-signal and the cockpit was now on fire. Eventually it was extinguished and the journey continued only for arrival to coincide with a heavy air-raid on Bristol, a return which plunged them immediately into the realities of wartime Britain. It was below zero in Bristol and the only hotel in which rooms were available could offer only a room with both windows blown out and covered in sacking. They left next morning for London where now all the parks had been dug up and stripped of railings and with only too vivid evidence of Blitz damage; Little Stanhope Street had been utterly destroyed.

In their absence, Tony Bushell and Consuelo (still his girlfriend) had sometimes stayed at Durham Cottage when Bushell was on leave from the Welsh Guards; apart from some serious damp issues it had survived fairly well but would need some renovation. They had to re-establish themselves in London – ration-books and all sorts of registration to see to – while they caught up with friends including Ralph and Mu Richardson (actress Meriel Forbes), staying briefly with Jamie Hamilton in Sussex, attending the wedding of John Mills and Mary Hayley Bell. Mu Richardson recalled them then:

> They were enchanting, so much in love. It was one of their best times. They liked to be seen. It was not a secret love affair.

And Leigh, seeing her for the first time since their divorce, told Gertrude that he found her "a dream of beauty ... I have never seen her so lovely."

Both had worried that their absence since 1938 might give rise to some press sniping but in fact there seemed much more interest in their possible professional futures. Which concerned them deeply. They were home, their children were safely away from immediate danger. It was bitterly cold that winter, the fog often made the Chelsea streets impenetrable in the black-out and rationing could make for skimpy meals far removed from the plenty of Hollywood or New York but Vivien found that she did not at all miss even California's sunshine. The one thing she – and Olivier – wanted was some work, some purpose.

CHAPTER 8

Wartime Dramas

L ondon initially seemed an uncertain home for both Oliviers. Friends were scattered, family similarly – Dickie Olivier in the RNVR, David Niven joining the Rifle Brigade and Tony Bushell in the Welsh Guards while Olivier failed at first to join Ralph Richardson in the FAA (rejected because of a damaged nerve in one ear), having to be content with a cameo role as a French-Canadian trapper in a propaganda film, *49th Parallel*, directed by Michael Powell alongside Leslie Howard. Vivien had a good deal to occupy her domestically – Durham Cottage had to be put back into shape, not easy with wartime restrictions although John Fowler found time to help her find materials and paint. It was back to its previous jewel-box comfortable charm remarkably quickly (Leigh told Vivien "if you ever get tired of the stage you would make a wonderful universal aunt"). She was an even busier correspondent than usual then, once she had established the whereabouts of friends, especially those actors at various fronts. George Devine and Glen Byam Shaw were both serving in India, widely apart – "we chase each other round India like two mad dogs in a maze" Devine replied to her – but were glad to have letters and news, as was Alan Webb who was amazed to receive letters and Fortnums' goodies in the middle of the Eastern desert ("I can't imagine how she knew where I was stationed"). Friendship for Vivien was vital, a key element in her life, and she always made every effort to keep her friendships in good repair. Constant activity also helped keep demons at bay, although there were some "down" periods then, often when she found familiar areas of London (some of Shepherd Market included) under the Blitz's rubble.

An early thought was to find work. The Old Vic was based at Burnley during the war but Guthrie had no place for her; he thought that a star of the magnitude Vivien had become would unbalance what was something of a scratch company, with so many actors in the services. It was not, as has been alleged, because Guthrie did not rate her work, as several surviving letters (up to her final film) attest.

When Olivier eventually was seconded to the Royal Navy's training school for gunners near Winchester he moved nearer the air station into a house nearby (called "Forakers", which required careful pronunciation on the telephone), commuting to work on a thunderous motorcycle. Vivien moved to be with him and, for both, the period there, although relatively uneventful, became one of their happiest times (Olivier wrote to Douglas Fairbanks Jr: "by and large I can't remember ever feeling such contentment – it sounds an odd thing to say but life feels more peaceful than it ever did before"). Vivien brought some things from Durham Cottage – their Aubusson carpet, some paintings (including a Boudin she had snapped up for a bargain £200 – one of the earliest in what became a small but choice collection including Renoir, Sickert and Bonnard) and favourite books. Carefully monitoring the petrol allowance she would tootle about in their battered little Invicta car to shop, and she tackled the house's overgrown garden with vigour. Evenings were usually spent together listening to the radio or playing records after supper (the country isolation had the plus of eggs from local farms). Occasionally, weekends were spent as part of a concert party started by their Chelsea friends, actress Constance Cummings and her playwright-husband Benn Levy along with acting couple John Clements and Kay Hammond, performing mainly at air bases with various programmes of songs, sketches and extracts from plays including the wooing scene from *Henry V* between Hal and the Princess of France for which Vivien's French proved an asset. Clements thought that she was very funny in some Herbert Farjeon revue sketches – cheerfully making herself up to look gruesome as a horrid schoolgirl in one – and said "It was then in those odd scratch rushed-up affairs that I became conscious that Vivien was a real professional."

Olivier sensed that Vivien's energies would be more fully charged by a good part but there was no great range of choice when both stage and film production was restricted. It was Hugh "Binkie" Beaumont of H.M. Tennent, now established as London's leading commercial theatrical management, who came up with the answer. In any serious study of British postwar theatre or any biography of its leading performers, Beaumont inevitably occurs, often misleadingly presented as a dictator concealing his iron fist in a glove of exquisitely tooled leather, a somewhat malicious homosexual who ran his empire like a fiefdom, surveying Shaftesbury Avenue from his office high up in the Globe Theatre, dispensing or withdrawing favours at his caprice (the diminutive "Binkie" compounds this). He was more interesting than that. One of his closest friends was the Irish writer Molly Keane (whose earlier novels and plays – produced by Tennent's – were published under the pseudonym M.J. Farrell) to whom he had been introduced by his lover of some years (and business partner) John Perry, who grew up near Keane in Ireland's Ascendancy world and who collaborated on her plays. In Keane's biography by her daughter Sally Phipps she agreed with director Peter Brook that Beaumont wanted the theatre to be a home for style and beauty, but saw further:

> He had a look of Proust, a purring sort of voice, a feline grace and hooded eyes … The stars were attracted to him because he was one of their kind. He understood the masque of glamour and the darkness and vulnerability that it concealed.

A group of H.M. Tennent's regular stars would confide their doubts and inner fears to him, confident that he would not gossip while he treasured their uniqueness and their foibles, finding in turn he could reveal to them his own emotional hurts, often inflicted by the acid-tongued Perry. This was especially so with those women – sharply intelligent all – who made up a small intimate circle (Keane, Peggy Ashcroft – "The Red Dame" to him later – Irene Selznick and, especially, Vivien) who became, to widespread surprise, his closest confidantes. He saw Vivien as not only a supreme beauty but also an actress of wit and range who had yet to reach her full powers. And of course it was a bonus that she was a copper-bottomed star at the box-office. Beaumont knew everything that went on in the theatre in London, New York and Paris and had noted the success of Bernard Shaw's *The Doctor's Dilemma* revived on Broadway by Katherine Cornell in 1941.

Now he proposed it for Vivien as a wartime contribution to tour for six months throughout a theatre-starved UK prior to a West End season. Her role would be that of Jennifer Dubedat, wife of a brilliant but amoral artist at the centre of the title's problem; Louis Dubedat is dying of tuberculosis, as is a poor but worthy colleague of Shaw's anti-hero, newly knighted Sir Colenso Ridgeon who has produced a cure, but with enough to treat only one patient, and has become attracted to the bewitching Jennifer. Which patient does he save? Vivien at first found the part what Edith Evans called "a white role" – one with little variety or shade – and would have preferred to tackle the more challenging Shavian Cleopatra. Producer Gabriel Pascal, who had charmed the dramatist into granting him the rights, was planning a screen version but had no interest in presenting it on stage first and so, with the longer-term plan of landing Cleopatra if her Jennifer won Shaw's approval, she signed with Beaumont.

The producer had calculated shrewdly. *The Doctor's Dilemma* had had no major London revival since 1906 – it has four sets and a sizeable cast – and while he understood Vivien's scruples, he pointed out one major advantage; throughout most of the first act a succession of eminent physicians call on Ridgeon to offer congratulations on his knighthood, each pontificating on his lucrative speciality and each asking about the beautiful young woman waiting in his reception-room, gradually building up expectations until the audience is agog to see her. Vivien could then sail into the play "looking like a Sargent canvas come to life" as one critic wrote, especially fetching in the costumes by Motley's Sophia Harris (now George Devine's wife), notably her defiantly dazzling last-act outfit of deep purple velvet following Dubedat's death. Shaw had told Lillah MacCarthy, the original Jennifer, that she would have her work cut out to make the character interesting and on the page it may seem that Jennifer's function is merely to look beautiful and radiate adoration of her husband, no great difficulty for Vivien. She saw that, as Shaw said, she had to try to find aspects of Jennifer to make her more interesting than a walking mannequin, which she did by subtly suggesting first that it was something of the rebel in Louis that had attracted her and then that possibly she was at some level aware of if not complicit in his chicanery.

Despite her reluctance to be away from Olivier during such a lengthy tour there was another reason for Vivien's agreement to take on Shaw's play. It is generally assumed from what has been written that Vivien suffered two miscarriages during her marriage to Olivier; one in 1944 and the other in 1957. But a *Photoplay* article from 1941 touches on a plan for them to film together in *This Above All*, shelved "because of Vivien's impending motherhood", with "her baby due in January 1942". This tallies with Alan Dent's recollections of a wartime dinner at Claridge's (where the Oliviers occasionally stayed at that time) given for Duff and Diana Cooper by the couple. Dent was also a guest; this must have been prior to her miscarriage of 1944, which occurred at a time when Dent was not in London. He recalled:

> the fragile beauty of Vivien waving goodbye to me along the corridor – fragile because she had had one of her miscarriages not many days before and was wearing an invalid's shawl of the purest and whitest and softest wool.

The letters from Olivier from New York to Vivien while she made *Gone With the Wind* refer to their desire to have children and her miscarriage must have been a miserable experience. As so often, work might be a kind of salvation; certainly *The Doctor's Dilemma* was a major success on tour, playing everywhere to packed houses. Olivier visited and had his "notes" for her, stressing his feeling that Vivien should be more sympathetic – "more affected by the picture of her dying husband – more catch in the voice with a genuine self-pity" – but Vivien never was one to play overtly for sympathy, never a sentimental actress, and it would seem she tactfully did little to act on this advice.

The tour was hard work, with eight performances a week, journeys every weekend, often on unreliable and unheated trains with blackout-restriction dimmed lights by which Vivien read all of Dickens (favourites were *Dombey and Son* and *David Copperfield*), trying to snatch whatever time might be possible with Olivier. Whitehall constantly emphasised the vital role of the arts in sustaining wartime morale and with capacity houses and strong receptions the company felt their work was valuable and worthwhile. George Relph played the deserving Dr Blenkinsop, sometimes joined by Mercia – they were among those who managed to remain friends with Jill as well as Vivien and Olivier – and was a valuable support, helping to organise company outings whenever possible. Some dates seemed oddly detached from the conflict; their week in Edinburgh, looking at its best then, was especially tranquil and there Vivien met up again with Cecil Beaton. His career since their first encounter a decade previously was now established on both sides of the Atlantic, although he remained avid for social and theatrical A-list advancement. He thought little of Irene Hentschel's production of *The Doctor's Dilemma* (which was content to focus on the more romantic strain, neglecting the socio-ethical scrutiny of private and state medicine which in the immediate postwar years became such a burning issue) but was fascinated by Vivien's personality and her descriptions of the rituals of backstage life, arriving early in her dressing-room, chatting, reading her mail, slowly dressing and making-up before a quiet final half-hour gathering her concentration for the play. The discipline of the theatre mattered greatly to her – the call-boy's knocks, the bells rung front-of-house to announce the minutes before curtain-up, or the stage manager's show-calls over the tannoy were the equivalent of the convent's constant bells, a way of announcing the set elements of ritual, of keeping disorder at bay. Beaton dined with her after the show and back at Vivien's hotel they sat talking until the night porter began vacuuming the lobby. Later in his diary Beaton wrote:

> Vivien is almost indescribably lovely. Hollywood is at her feet. She knows if all else fails she has merely to go out there to make a fortune ... she is madly in love with her husband ... and is convinced he is a much greater person than herself. She is unspoiled, has many loyal friends and only ambition to succeed as an actress. The adulation of her beauty leaves her cold.

This chimes with Beaumont's perspective; he knew that praise of her looks meant nothing to her, astutely noting that she had "a man's mind" in that she always honed in on the essentials of any subject. In turn this is echoed by the observation of Kenneth Clark's younger son Colin, who worked for Olivier for a time:

> She had a mind which left most people behind. Most of us simply don't keep our minds in diamond-cutting gear all the time. We get lazy ... Vivien didn't do that. Vivien's mind was just like a diamond drill.

Beaumont grew closer to Vivien during the tour, often visiting the production; they had similar tastes in books, gardening and paintings in a relationship which tended to exclude Olivier, always polite but never really warming to Beaumont although he appreciated the care he took of his star. *The Doctor's Dilemma* was booked into the Theatre Royal, Haymarket, the West End's most prestigious theatre, impeccably maintained with just the right capacity and acoustics for Shaw's play and a star dressing-room envied by all actors, complete with working fireplace and private bathroom, a suite which would be Vivien's second home for over a year. The production photographs could not be taken by Angus McBean, imprisoned for homosexual offences, but Vivien insisted that a McBean portrait of her illustrate the programme and be used front-of-house, prominently credited to his name.

The production was greeted enthusiastically as a welcome addition to an escapism-heavy West End and Beaumont was confident that the "House Full" boards would be outside the Haymarket for some time. However, the early part of the run became unexpectedly fraught when Cyril Cusack (Dubedat) was sacked for alleged drunkenness, replaced first by actor-director Peter Glenville, a Tennent's protégé and then briefly, to Vivien's delight, by Gielgud (no Shavian but drawn to the part's poetry and by the chance to act with Vivien).

Vivien's Haymarket dressing-room was rarely without visitors, especially on matinee days when between shows her dresser would make tea and toast crumpets, if available, over the fire. At this time Kenneth Clark popped in regularly from the National Gallery nearby; even after a performance, with a towelling-turban round her head and removing cream slathering her face Clark realised that her beauty was "based on structure and proportion, irrespective of artifice", and that her beauty was informed by her personality and style. He pinpointed that style through her conversation which for him possessed:

> an ear for the rhythm of words, a personal voice, and an occasional sacrifice of the whole truth in the interests of economy. These seem to me the chief characteristics of style, and Vivien had them all.

Possibly inspired by seeing Vivien's Jennifer on stage in Dubedat's studio, Olivier commissioned Augustus John to paint Vivien who sat for the artist in 1942. A red-chalk sketch survives – with a candid, wide gaze, her hair worn loose, it captures that fusion of the serene and a suggestion of the untamed in Jennifer (and Vivien) – but it was never realised in a finished portrait. Vivien was hard to draw or paint – Don Bachardy, partner of Christopher Isherwood in California, noted when he drew her in the 1960s that she could not keep still for long – but when the John sketch came up for auction at Sotheby's in 2017 it was widely reported, quoting family members, that in 1942 Olivier had become decidedly jealous, worried that John, notoriously randy well into old age, might make a pass at Vivien. Only one sitting (in February 1942) is noted in Vivien's diary.

Beaumont understood the hazard of boredom setting in over a long run and cannily arranged a charity matinee as a Benefit for the veteran Cyril Maude, once a notable Sir Peter Teazle in *The School for Scandal* at the Haymarket, with Vivien partnering him as Lady Teazle in the screen scene, described in *The Observer* as "fresh as a rosebud with Mr. Maude as mellow as an old pear-tree in the sun". During the run Olivier continued with his flying work and Vivien commuted nightly (before-matinee days excepted) to Hampshire, a period of which he said: "In these limpid conditions life pursued its uncertain way with quite a lot of happiness in its uncertainty". When he was given a brief leave in the late summer of 1942 Beaumont closed the Haymarket for a week so that Vivien could join him on a holiday spent in Wales, at Aberdavon where the weather had been atrocious but suddenly brightened as they arrived. Olivier wrote to Trudy Flockhart, who would be a loyal friend to Vivien as her maid (and occasional dresser) over many years, that their break "was like paradise", adding:

> We went to the furthermost corner of Wales – just to get away from every kind of association ... we needed it as our nerves were in quite a bad way and we really felt a change was essential. We just forgot everything for 8 whole days! Walks, picnics, picking blackberries ... Nobody has ever been made so happy as Vivien makes me – she's my whole life.

For the first time since their respective separations there was a reunion between Leigh, Oswald Frewen, Vivien and Olivier over dinner back in London. Leigh had previously struck his cuckolder as "a bit peculiar – at least to me. Not *barmy* but eccentric in a funny little bookish way" – but now, describing the occasion to Trudy as "a good evening", he found him "greatly grown in stature and personality" (which might also have applied to himself). Jill was still in

California with Tarquin – she sent Olivier regular updates and photographs although he was less than conscientious in replying – while in Canada Gertrude and Suzanne had moved to Banff. Selznick was still pursuing his "property" with offers, recently trying to lure Vivien into the title role in *Jane Eyre* opposite Orson Welles with the unsubtle bait of suggesting Suzanne as the young Jane, a notion at once vetoed by Vivien and Leigh.

When *The Doctor's Dilemma* finally closed in April 1943 Vivien had no immediate professional plans, while Olivier made another propaganda film, *Demi-Paradise*, for Anthony Asquith, also making regular heroic recruiting speeches including an Albert Hall occasion delivering his rousing version of Henry V's "St Crispin's Day" speech, good preparation for a major project which would change his career and in which he planned to involve Vivien. In 1939 in New York he had met Jack Wilk of Warner Brothers who "was interested in backing a film of *Henry V*". Nothing came of that early possibility but now, speedily, dreams of the first of his Shakespearean films as director/star became reality. It was produced by the maverick émigré Filippo del Giudice (whose English seemed permanently more fractured than broken) backed by the flour tycoon J. Arthur Rank, with Alan Dent's assistance on editing the text and his favourite designer Roger Furse also on board. During filming the Oliviers lived at Fulmer in Buckinghamshire, near many friends – John and Mary Mills, David and Primmie Niven, Rex Harrison and Lilli Palmer included. Niven remembered glorious times both there and at Durham Cottage with many evenings finishing as dawn broke, with Vivien on the piano and Olivier singing *The Messiah*.

The plan to have Vivien in the *Henry V* film as Katharine, the French princess, was frustrated by Selznick, who refused to allow her to appear in what he regarded as an "insignificant" role, a sharp reminder that she remained his contracted "property". Olivier was furious, describing Selznick as "a bastard" and writing to Vivien:

> I am so heartbroken about *Henry*, my dear dear Baba, but I never would have felt quite guiltless about your doing it as it would only have been for me that you had done it – so *sweetly* though, Pussy. Oh my God, you would have been marvellous.

Renée Asherson was cast instead. Vivien, while remaining always friendly, never felt quite the same about Selznick thereafter. While early location filming for the battle scenes took place at Powerscourt in neutral Ireland, Beaumont placed Vivien in a concert-party revue to tour North Africa for ENSA (the Entertainment National Services Association, known inevitably throughout the profession as Every Night Something Awful, controlled by Basil Dean, as choleric as ever). She was in excellent company, alongside musical stars

Leslie Henson and Dorothy Dickson and the unique revue artist Beatrice Lillie. Their journey was broken at Lisbon, last visited when the Oliviers returned from America and from where Leslie Howard's plane had been shot down just two weeks earlier. Vivien wrote to Olivier describing the enormously fat peonies in bloom but added: "I could hardly bear seeing those lovely high houses in Lisbon without you, my darling." While she toured with *Spring Party* and *Henry V* was at Powerscourt, they wrote or cabled regularly but with often frustrating waits or with mail just missing them. Vivien's schedule was gruelling – ENSA's organisation left something to be desired – often staying in old hotels with little or no running water, performing (often three shows a day) in whatever theatres were viable or in improvised outdoor spaces, sometimes in blistering heat which at least worked wonders on a persistent cough which Vivien had been unable to shake off since *The Doctor's Dilemma*. The material, which John Gielgud had supervised in London, was varied with Vivien's contributions including Clemence Dane's patriotic poem "Plymouth Hoe" and Lewis Carroll's "Father William" plus a wicked send-up of her *Gone With the Wind* persona ("I'm Scarlett O'Hara/The Terror of Tara") by the *New Statesman*'s anonymous parodist "Sagittarius" and also helping Leslie Henson out in sketches. Gibraltar was unbearably hot ("I find I cannot eat or sleep here") but Tony Quayle was serving there as aide-de-camp to the Governor and on a day off drove Vivien and Bea Lillie into Spain: "where we lunched – it was extraordinary to be driving along through a country at peace", marvelling at the profusion of huge lemons and strawberries. She lived for Olivier's letters and cables – "I look into my pigeon-hole at least 20 times a day. Oh, love, I miss you so." He was frantically busy with only a limited Powerscourt schedule, constantly frustrated by rain, recalcitrant extras and an outbreak of lice ("charming"). But his letters are long, packed with detail vividly communicating to Vivien his delight in the work, illustrating them often with drawings and plans of how he intended to film battles using tracking shots or of the caravan which he used as a dressing-room:

> Oh, come back to me and share my caravan with me my own true love. We would be *so* happy, you could just ride around this lovely country all day and rest and get strong ... I'm like a sort of Abelard. I don't even let my *thoughts* of you get too intimate.

Spring Party moved to Tunis, where the female company stayed in a palatial villa which had been General Von Armin's quarters prior to the Africa Korps's defeat. Vivien wrote to Gertrude:

I slept in his room which felt very odd when one considered what a short time before he had actually been there, also of all the unpleasant last hours he must have spent in that room.

In nearby Hammamet they performed on the terrace of Air Marshall Sir Arthur Coningham's villa with George VI in the audience; afterwards he talked to Vivien for some time, recommending she include Alice Duer Miller's "White Cliffs of Dover" in her repertoire (she did later sometimes perform it). At Tripoli, where one performance was attended by General Montgomery, who told her ENSA's work was "a battle-winning factor", their setting in the desert moonlight was the restored Roman amphitheatre at Leptis Magna. Some years later an ex-serviceman (J.R. Bradshaw of the 7th Armoured Division) recalled in *The Times* the highlight of the evening:

> To some of us present the most astonishing part of the performance was when Miss Leigh stood alone on the stage, picked out in the darkness by a spotlight, and recited "You are old, Father William" to a crowd of hundreds of hardened desert soldiers who listened in spellbound silence before breaking into applause.

Olivier's letters sometimes went astray but he was able to warn her of his radical pudding-basin haircut (dyed hair too) for Henry ("you will laugh at your poor Ginger Rogers boy"), at the same time reminding her of his physical longing for her:

> Do you remember when you came to NY after *GWTW*? Blimey, we shall both be like that this time, won't we? How wonderful it will be to laugh with you again.

She missed letters in Cairo and Alexandria, dates involving performances and socialising in heat which she found "terribly exhausting" and where the company felt somewhat discombobulated:

> The war is non-existent and to see huge tables spread with every sort of deliciousness and bowls of cream was extraordinary ... altogether it was the sort of life one had quite forgotten about.

The final date was a return to Gibraltar, where Noël Coward, giving concerts aboard troopships, was staying at Government House along with Tony Quayle and John Perry, who was also stationed there. Partly because of his lover's presence Beaumont had flown to rejoin the company which in its time off had a high old time, the mood as they swam in Rose Bay or enjoyed a final Government House ball possibly heightened by a sense that the tide of the war seemed to be turning.

Vivien returned as Olivier began studio filming on *Henry V* at Denham and they moved into a house at Old Prestwick, Gerrards Cross. She performed in various concert parties, the companies sometimes including colleagues from *Spring Party* or old friends such as Gielgud or Jeanne de Casalis. The Old Prestwick house crystallised Olivier's notion of having a country home as well as Durham Cottage. He and Vivien had both admired photographs of Leigh's new home, a beautiful house (Woodlands) at Mere on the Somerset/Wiltshire border and they were drawn to a handsome church conversion nearby but lost it to another buyer. They continued to scour the pages of *Country Life's* property section in the meantime.

Often at this time Vivien took guests over from Prestwick Green to Denham, including French actors Claude Dauphin and Jean-Pierre Aumont (who remembered Prestwick Green as possessing "a certain damp charm"), both with the Free French in London. Aumont recalled vividly his departure for London from Prestwick Green, late at night with the city ablaze under heavy bombardment:

> All my life I will remember the frail silhouette of Vivien as she accompanied us under the porch, looking serious and serene, nestled in her husband's arms and illuminated by the reddish flashes which signalled that a "V-1" had just destroyed another district in London.

Major projects now demanded time from both Vivien and Olivier. The *Henry V* film had been perfectly timed, its bravura patriotism, underscored by William Walton's rousing score, boosting Olivier's profile more than any Hollywood blockbuster. He chose to cap this by nailing his colours to the classical theatre mast once more, rejoining the Old Vic to help launch a glorious period alongside Richardson and Guthrie and to play a series of roles establishing him as the greatest actor of his era. Vivien had finally been given Shaw's approval to play Cleopatra for Pascal – he had not seen her Jennifer, refusing to visit productions of his plays – after she met him with Pascal at his Ayot St Lawrence home and then, escorted by Beaumont, at his Whitehall Court apartment where the impresario looked on with admiration as she beguiled the old dramatist, chatting away merrily about every subject possible except *Caesar and Cleopatra*, until he told her, after pinching her bottom, that she should play his Egyptian ("the part is fool-proof"). He added the compliment – a dubious one considering what the redoubtable actress put him through on *Pygmalion* – that Vivien was "the Mrs. Patrick Campbell of the age".

Shaw had allowed Pascal to produce successful screen versions of *Pygmalion* and *Major Barbara* (directed by Anthony Asquith), entranced by the Hungarian's huckster personality, claiming that he was doing for the cinema what Diaghilev did for ballet, while in turn Pascal was in thrall to Shaw as the greatest writer in English since Shakespeare. The potential for film as a higher form of popular art was something in which Shaw had long had faith; seeing the Denham set of the mighty Sphinx against a starlit sky he had gasped "What scope! What limitless possibilities!"

Sadly those possibilities were only fitfully realised in Pascal's hands when he misguidedly opted to direct himself. Begun with the highest hopes, *Caesar and Cleopatra* – backed by J. Arthur Rank – emerged as a major disappointment in Vivien's career and finally a miserable experience. Some of the choices of personnel were excellent, not least that of Oliver Messel (Vivien had written to him in 1943 saying she would urge Pascal to employ him and "nobody else in the world must do the costumes") and, with difficult wartime conditions and shortages, his evocation of a diaphanous Egyptian world, suggesting a languorous Alma Tadema-ish sensuality, using sari materials or muslin dyed and stencilled and creating barbaric jewellery and headdresses (often made out of wire, plastic or glass), emerged as one of the film's strengths. It was cast strongly; unable to attract Robert Donat for Caesar, Pascal settled for Claud Rains, a silver-voiced British veteran long resident in America, supported by Flora Robson as Ftatateeta, Cleopatra's fiercely devoted servant, Cecil Parker, the epitome of sublime Anglo-Saxon pomposity as Brittanus and Stewart Granger flexing his biceps as Apollodorus.

Some early problems on what seemed a progressively jinxed project were nobody's fault; London had now to face German flying bombs, one exploding close to the Pharos set just several days into the shoot, adding to even slower transport and postal facilities and consequent long delays for ordered materials to arrive, and then 1944's summer became one of the worst in memory with the cast shivering in flimsy costumes while trying to evoke desert heat.

Still, a halfway decent film might have emerged with a stronger directorial hand but Pascal was hopeless behind the camera, taking ages to map out his scenes and then often changing his mind, indifferent to spiralling costs ("Let him sell more bags of flour!" was his attitude to Rank). Some scenes were salvaged by his cinematographers (he had no less than four – all won Oscars for later work) and it was Jack Cardiff who masterminded the effective episode of Pothinus's murder against a setting sun and the memorable extended shot over the slumbering Cleopatra in her vast curved bed, slowly tracking beyond her out to the ink-black sky and the sea beautifully underscored by the most seductive of musical passages (by Georges Auric, one of "Les Six", another excellent choice). Pascal had demanded lavish sets, designed by Gainsborough Pictures' art director John Bryan in the style of Victorian realist artists – the ancient Memphis Palace is especially awesome – but they seem at odds with the more subtle style of the costumes and also with Shaw's text.

A variation on the *Pygmalion* story, set at the height of the Roman Civil War, Shaw traces the lessons in majesty which the young Cleopatra absorbs from Julius Caesar, a wily and seasoned dictator tired of warfare. There is no sex, and violence is virtually all off-screen. Essentially it is a discussion piece, urbane, paradoxical and often playful; in the theatre it can work (if taken at a swift pace), handling its ironies with a light touch, but Pascal's hand is heavy throughout. He was also not greatly gifted at dealing with actors. Rains detested him and simply went his own way and while his Caesar is lucid and beautifully spoken it is somewhat dull. Vivien is often very fine, especially in those challenging scenes of the young Cleopatra in which, subtly, she marries teenage timidity to a bolder underlying aggression suggesting a crucially near-savage nature. Even in this inadequate film her work is never less than interesting; Messel's creations and accessories help her both when vulnerably innocent and at her most imperiously regal, tracing the character's potential for greatness. A more recent critic felt that the beauty of her performance lay in its elevation of girlishness to a form of latent power:

> Her monarch of the Nile is no royal cipher, no myth and no parody but a flesh-and-blood girl – a creature more tantalising and paradoxical than a sphinx.

It was sad that her ambitions for the part were undermined by a white elephant of a film which, when finally completed, had become the most vaingloriously costly (over £1,300,000) British film to date. Made while the country continued to suffer sustained onslaught, it was released just after the Allied victory when Caesar's perspective on conquest had potent resonance for 1945 audiences, but an initially strong box-office dwindled quickly. The reviews tended to be more positive in America where it was seen as an elegant spectacle, with Vivien highly praised, but British critics were tepid at best and tended to treat it as an early and unsuccessful swords-and-sandals epic. *Caesar and Cleopatra* lost Rank a fortune and found little public favour.

Vivien did not see the film until six years later when she prepared for a stage production with Olivier, anxious to have a second chance, having failed to satisfy herself on screen. And there was another reason for her reluctance to watch it, reminding her as it did of a period during its making stamped by distressing memories. She had begun filming knowing that she had just become pregnant; thrilled by the news, she and Olivier initially told only immediate family and a few close friends before informing Pascal and others involved in early August. She wrote to Leigh:

Everyone is *very, very* cross and keep asking me how I suppose they are going to make me look like the sixteen-year old Cleopatra and I keep saying I can't help it, it's an act of God!

Her diary has few entries for this period. She was socialising only rarely, just occasional weekend lunches with friends – the Lunts (then appearing in London), the Relphs, Victor Stiebel and Richard Addinsell or the Nivens – and noted in her diary Olivier's departure for Manchester to open the Old Vic's pre-London tour of *Arms and the Man* in early August. On 21 August she noted "Cot – Harrods". Ten days later, with the Old Vic bomb-damage unrepaired, Olivier opened in *Peer Gynt* at the New and she noted in her diary in three faintly pencilled words, underlined: "Lost the baby."

She had filmed the scene in which an angry Cleopatra whips her slave before running up to her throne exulting that she is "a Queen at last – Cleopatra the Queen!" but after it was in the can Pascal demanded more takes the next day. The first frames were in long-shot for which he could easily have used a double but Vivien was called for them and when turning to pursue the slave she slipped on the polished marble floor, falling heavily. A doctor was called and pronounced no bones broken; she was driven home and went to bed but her miscarriage began that night. Olivier was distraught; with his acute observation of detail he insisted on examining the foetus, noting (as he told Tarquin later) that it was a boy, already with a tiny penis. Two days later Vivien's continued bleeding took her into the London Clinic ("first time in an ambulance" she noted) for an operation. Her room was quickly like a branch of Constance Spry's florist's shop and visitors called regularly – Beaumont, Sybil Thorndike and Sibyl Colefax, Rachel Kempson and many more – while Olivier came whenever his New Theatre schedule permitted.

After a week she was back at work, seemingly recovered, although fellow actors noticed that, unusually, she seemed to tire quickly. Then there was one sudden and frightening flare-up of her occasional hysteria. During the complicated scene of the banquet held in Caesar's honour Vivien broke out of leading the Roman guests towards the dining-area and began a furious tirade against her dresser for some oversight with her costume, transformed into a spitting fury, her voice shrill and her eyes narrowed just as John Gliddon had seen ten years earlier. The entire set froze until finally Pascal called a break; Vivien was taken to her dressing-room where her hysteria mounted until it evaporated as unsettlingly quickly as it had erupted. She was driven home, where she wrote notes of apology to all involved in the incident, of which she seemed to have virtually no memory. This time she did not return to Denham for five weeks.

Her diary is blank for that period. Most people, Olivier included, thought that this episode was due solely to a belated reaction to the misery of her miscarriage but there were signs of something more troubling, notably the unpredictable mood-swings between elevation, relative equilibrium and a sullen, even sometimes abusive, attitude – to Olivier in particular but also at times to Gertrude, who was now back from Canada (Suzanne was staying with her father at Woodlands) and who could receive similar treatment. Vivien insisted she had no need of hospitalisation and then the question vanished when she seemed to make a complete recovery, returning to Denham where the later filming saw no recurrence of her unpredictable behaviour.

Olivier had come to grasp that Vivien seemed happiest in the theatre and preferably alongside him. He was contracted to the Old Vic for some time but had come across a play which offered her a hopefully happy contrast to the rigours of *Caesar and Cleopatra*. Although it increased his already tough workload he willingly set up with Beaumont a co-production (which he would direct) of the British premiere of Thornton Wilder's Broadway success *The Skin of Our Teeth* in which Vivien would play another siren figure but one at several removes from the Queen of the Nile.

CHAPTER 9

From Sabina to Anna

Legal matters caused by resentment in California from a brooding David O. Selznick came to take up an annoying amount of time in the run-up to Wilder's play. Vivien and Olivier were also busy with legal affairs of another kind at the same time, involving surveys, title deeds and building permits, before finally they were able to purchase the home of Olivier's dreams.

They had first seen over Notley Abbey near the village of Long Crendon in Buckinghamshire on an icy winter's day in 1943 and Olivier loved it at first sight, convinced when he inserted the rusty old key into an even older lock in the oak door that he had found what he had been looking for, a piece of England – the house, at the end of a long drive, stood in over 60 acres with the River Thame running close by – rich in history. Founded by Walter Gifford, Earl of Buckingham, in the reign of Henry II for the Augustinian order and endowed further by Henry V (this clinched it for Olivier), Cardinal Wolsey had stayed during the building of Christ Church, Oxford. The Abbey had been destroyed – not even bare ruined choirs remained – with the Dissolution of the Monasteries, leaving the house with its tower and mullioned windows, built of grey stone (it looks gloomily Gothic in John Piper's painting but seems warmer in sunlight) with over 20 rooms in the main house plus a cottage – into which Tony Bushell, now with a glamorous second wife, Anne Serocold, moved during early renovations – farm buildings and greenhouses. It was in considerable disrepair with the house riddled with dry rot, dangerously unsafe ceilings, the gardens overgrown with blackberry bushes and ground elder like the Sleeping Beauty's castle, the greenhouses glassless and the river sluggish with weeds and mud. Vivien was more circumspect, concerned about renovation costs at a time when money was tight (her £25,000 fee for *Caesar and Cleopatra* covered a period twice as long as originally scheduled and Olivier's Old Vic salary barely covered living expenses). They made several return visits with friends – Niven and Helpmann advised strongly against a purchase which would devour their capital (the price was £18,000) while the Relphs considered it a brave adventure – but Olivier saw Notley with a theatrical eye. He would be its impresario, its director and its star. His personae altered through his life like the different acts of a play. He had been matinee idol in the West End, film star and classical leading man. Now at the pinnacle of his profession and with a charismatic consort, what he called his "baronial period" would begin as "The Oliviers" came to dominate postwar British theatre. The home was bought.

The battle over *The Skin of Our Teeth* began when Selznick invoked his contractual right to prevent Vivien's appearance, becoming deadly serious when he instructed Daniel O'Shea (now a loyal vice-president of David O. Selznick Inc.) to review his dealings with her, arguing that he had permitted her to appear in *Romeo and Juliet*, which he claimed had "seriously damaged her career" (hard to make this stick when films such as *Waterloo Bridge* and *Lady Hamilton* had subsequently succeeded) and that a 12-week leave of absence to return to England stretched to three years. He then engaged big legal guns, using Sir Walter Monckton to represent him to take out an injunction to prevent her appearance, betraying his animus against Olivier by stressing in the injunction that the *Romeo and Juliet* precedent justified the studio being "fearful that another theatrical engagement prompted and participated in by Olivier" would potentially "cause damage to our property".

The High Court case was gleefully splashed across the front pages of the press with Selznick cast as a predatory American ogre-mogul victimising a frail British heroine ("Hands off our Viv!") while Vivien's counsel in the Chancery Division hearing, Sir Valentine Holmes, practically had violins tremulously underscoring his submissions to the judge that were she not allowed to be in the play then under National Service regulations she might have to take employment in a munitions factory or as a cleaner ("Vivien Might be a Char" – *Daily Mail*). The judge decided swiftly that Selznick would suffer "no appreciable damage" if Vivien acted in a play and the injunction was denied.

Wily Alexander Korda had watched proceedings with interest. Still under contract to him, Vivien had been supposed to star in a screen version of Enid Bagnold's *Lottie Dundas* as a mentally troubled actress and Korda had regularly suggested Thomas Hardy's Bathsheba in *Far from the Madding Crowd* as an ideal role but neither had materialised. Vivien wanted to be in Wilder's play with

Olivier directing, so Korda smartly sold what remained of Vivien's contract to MGM in return for two films with Deborah Kerr. He would not stay cross with Vivien for long.

London was familiar with little of Thornton Wilder's work. Beaumont had presented his Broadway success *Our Town*, which flopped in the West End largely because of the unsurprisingly appalling behaviour of its director Jed Harris, who left rehearsals largely to Wilder's adoring sister Isabel, but the producer was very keen indeed on this new play. *The Skin of Our Teeth* had been a Broadway success directed by the *wunderkind* Elia Kazan with the high-maintenance diva Tallulah Bankhead as Sabina, the Eternal Feminine Lilith-figure at the centre of the play. Even Beaumont baulked at the notion of coping with Bankhead and moreover on reading it had immediately thought of Vivien. She responded positively at once, realising what a marvellous part Sabina was and only slightly reluctantly – he accepted that if he wanted Vivien then Olivier came with it – Beaumont agreed a co-production deal with him.

Olivier directed it well. He greatly admired the retiring, ineffably courteous Wilder and at a time of towering achievement in classical work he had responded to the kaleidoscopic style of this modern play, written as an apocalyptic turmoil threatened to engulf civilisation's attempt to survive. Normally Olivier was happier with predominantly naturalistic pieces as director but on *The Skin of Our Teeth* he for once let his hair down, even if he never quite brought to it the electrically kinetic energy of a Kazan or a Guthrie.

When it opened in New York in 1942 one critic, recalling comedians Olsen and Johnson in *Hellzapoppin'*, a freewheeling grab-bag of sketches, sight gags and vaudeville *schtick*, called *The Skin of Our Teeth* "*Hellzapoppin'* with brains", an apt description of Wilder's three-act "comic-strip picture of mankind involving wars, the black pox, fire, flood and seven-year locusts". Olivier had seen *Hellzapoppin'* in London and found Wilder's challenges (the large cast included dinosaurs, a fortune-teller, Moses and Plato, and a woolly mammoth) irresistible. Set in the suburban household of Mr and Mrs Antrobus (the Greek Anthropos = Man as Everyman) and their children Henry and Gladys with their resourceful and irreverent maid Sabina, it soon transpires that the Antrobuses are about to celebrate 5,000 years of marriage (George Antrobus has invented, among other things, the wheel and the alphabet). The first act is set as an Ice Age approaches, flood threatens the second, set on the boardwalk at Atlantic City where Sabina is the reigning beauty queen, and the last act reunites the family after a war during which they have lived in a cave. Throughout, characters step in and out of the action – Sabina, a kind of Chorus figure, most frequently – to complain about their material ("The author hasn't made up his silly little mind whether we're living in caves or today in New Jersey"), while the set increasingly teeters on the verge of disintegration, all rather like Michael Frayn's *Noises Off* crossed with *The Symposium*.

Yesterday's avant-garde often emerges later as stale routine; Wilder's reduction of characters to archetypes of allegory may seem slightly portentous now but he is far from a theatrical Norman Rockwell as he is sometimes presented. *The Skin of Our Teeth* seems freshest in periods of crisis. Revisited in 1975 it was widely described as "simplistic" but at times when a country struggles with its sense of identity it can seem vibrant again; a New York 2017 production, at a time of fierce national and climate-change debate, was highly successful, with one review headlined "Why Thornton Wilder Matters In The Trump Era".

Vivien led a strong London cast – Cecil Parker the stoic Antrobus, the versatile and comedically adept Ena Burrill as Gladys – but all were aware that the play might prove a shock of the new too far on a then staid Shaftesbury Avenue. She had written to Oswald Frewen, who had recently married: "I don't think I have ever been more excited on the eve of any venture – or more nervous." Audiences packed theatres on the pre-London tour but most were distinctly baffled and sometimes hostile (regular walk-outs during the action as well as at intermission), although the company kept its nerve, buoyed by Beaumont's repeated reassurances; he wrote to Olivier after a Liverpool performance: "Vivien has quite definitely, beyond all doubt, established herself as a seriously considered actress from every point of view." Wilder was able to catch a final London rehearsal and wrote to Olivier, delighted with Vivien's performance:

> I saw and felt the menace hanging over the house … Vivien unrolls a continuous stream of fascinating art, clear and yet subtle, unforgettable – and I dream with joy about the Sabina of Act III.

When *Skin* reached the Piccadilly Theatre in April 1945 London was *en fête* still after VE Day. There seemed to be – for a time – promise as well as relief in the air, a buoyant optimism chiming with Wilder's basic belief in humanity's survival. As if in tune with that feeling, the first night was the most glamorous London had seen for years, a splash of long-mothballed evening gowns and black ties, a West End launch for "The Oliviers" joint reign. And London audiences seemed delighted rather than shocked by the new and equally so by the revelation of Vivien's vitality and mercurial comedic touch. James Agate, near the end of his lengthy critical career, was reminded of the *gamine* French star Yvonne Printemps, describing her Sabina as "half dabchick, half dragonfly". Wilder had suggested the style required should owe something to such vaudevillians as Fanny Brice or Ed Wynn, like a giant Punch and Judy with comic-strip balloon-speeches emerging from their mouths, and Vivien caught the precise pitch of slightly exaggerated playing, slipping in and out of her "break-throughs" of the fourth wall with nimble spontaneity. Far from a display of "unfelt coquetterie" as the young Tynan, not yet a professional critic, described it, this Sabina was undoubtedly indebted to and informed by the brilliant drollery, that askance scepticism when faced with an unpredictable world, which stamped the work of the great revue performer Beatrice Lillie which of course Vivien had observed at close range in *Spring Party*. (Later, at the National Theatre, the play was suggested for Maggie Smith, also experienced in revue, but plans were never realised.)

Vivien was happy in the play; she too had come to treasure "Thorny" Wilder and she had the same response as Olivier to the play's underlying themes. She kept a Commonplace Book in which she wrote favourite passages or phrases, including a passage from Plato in the play which clearly struck a chord:

> Then tell me, O Critas, how will a man choose the ruler that shall rule over him?
> Will he not choose a man who first has established order in himself?

Headed by Olivier, Richardson, Sybil Thorndike, Lewis Casson and George Relph the Old Vic Company took off on its European tour shortly after *Skin*'s Piccadilly opening. During their first separation for some time Olivier wrote constantly, addressing an early letter with "Greetings to the wondrously beautiful, Dearest Beloved, Most Adorable MISTRESS OF NOTLEY", and those letters gave Vivien a fascinating account of an encounter with the realities of war's aftermath, including a visit to Belsen:

> The old camp was all burnt out but still very oppressive with its burial mounds and occasional whiffs of nasty smell – one could just see and feel it all.

Flying over the Rhine revealed dreadful devastation:

> Its bridges are all blown – all the country fantastically seared with bombs ... it looks like the ruins of an entirely bygone civilisation.

He moaned about upset stomachs, hardly surprising given the mostly awful food ("last night for supper I had two potatoes and a *bone!*") but sighed over his misery at this "terrible" separation, especially on his birthday.

> I'm miserable my darling, darling love and nearly burst into tears all the time,
> I think of you ceaselessly with a sort of *hopeless* longing!

He told Vivien that "My genital life has made no manifestation <u>whatsoever</u> – it knows who it belongs to doesn't it – hey?" Letters often went astray, including a number in which he poured out his vexation over the ongoing saga of Notley's water supply and he often fretted when he had no word from her, worrying more when he heard from an RAF friend, Tony Bartley, that Vivien might be seriously ill, becoming even more anxious when Bartley seemed evasive. Finally he received a letter but it seemingly had no specific details:

> inferences can be so much more frightening than facts, my darling ... you say "Now you know". My darling heart, write about this – you know that whatever this dark thing is that the slightest shadow across your life troubles me so much more than any harm to myself.

Only when the Old Vic troupe reached Paris was he able to establish more about the shadow of "this dark thing". The Lunts, then performing in Paris, had seen Vivien in London; initially reluctant to break a promise to her not to tell Olivier, when they lunched with him they informed him that she had been diagnosed with tuberculosis. After three months at the Piccadilly a persistent cough had worsened and she had become so alarmingly thin that Beaumont insisted she see a doctor. An X-ray revealed a tubercular patch on her lung which demanded six weeks of intensive treatment in University College Hospital during which Beaumont closed *Skin*.

It developed into a long absence; after that initial hospitalisation, a further nine months' rest was ordered. She refused with frightening intensity to agree to any suggestion of going to a sanatorium, possibly worried that her recurrent periods of instability might come under institutional scrutiny. Finally it was settled that she could recuperate, with nursing attendance, at Notley where she stayed until the summer of 1946. Having at first been cool about the Notley restoration project, now, in her enforced form of hibernation she slowly came to love the place. Never with quite the same possessive – self-confessedly "obsessive" – love which Olivier felt but at this period, especially as she watched the gardens gradually take shape, it became a haven which slowly revived her.

That first Notley winter was often harsh and bitterly cold but Vivien was a good patient even confined to the L-shaped first-floor room which was their first bedroom, with a capacious fireplace and large windows, pink walls and a primrose carpet. Other early work on the interior, advised by Sibyl Colefax with practical help in John Fowler's hands, included the Blue Room, always given to George and Mercia Relph when they stayed. As the weather warmed and Vivien could see the leaves and blossom begin to appear on trees new and old, she developed her ideas for the garden further. An immense amount of clearance, felling dead or diseased trees and ruthless pruning, slowly revealed the outlines of what would become a remarkable garden. An ambitious avenue of lime trees was planted leading from the river past the mead reserved for old Blanche Kynge, Olivier's Agincourt horse brought back from Ireland, then down each side of the long entrance drive.

Visitors were kept to a minimum. Ena Burrill had a house near Notley and would regularly come over while Beaumont visited with new books, Charbonnel et Walker chocolates and theatre news. A new friend, who became one of her closest, was Beatrice ("Bumble") Dawson, an ample, outgoing, bespectacled woman, once a Sacred Heart girl, now a busy costume designer who sometimes came with Bobby Helpmann, as mischievously gossipy as always. Flowers arrived daily along with letters including one from Beaton hoping for a summons:

> I shall come and Vivien – watch by your bedside (if I am permitted) and we must link up the threads left hanging idly since Edinburgh.

She was slightly surprised by the concern of her recent legal adversary when Selznick – who clearly still had regard for her despite their business differences – wrote to her with details of the latest developments in tuberculosis treatment. Sunny Lash, occasionally working for Selznick, suggested that this may have been a sweetener for yet another effort to lure Vivien to work for him again. ("David would jump at *Vanity Fair* for you"). Yet he remained generous to her; aware she did not want her illness publicised, he urged her in a long cable to visit the air of Palm Springs or Arizona (as his guest), telling his secretary Jenia Reissar: "I have an enormous affection for her and am eager to do everything possible."

While Vivien recovered, Olivier was busier than ever in the theatre. Now one of a triumvirate (Richardson and director John Burrell joined him) in charge of the Old Vic their 1946 New Theatre season became genuinely legendary, seeing Richardson's unmatchable Falstaff (with Olivier doubling a roaring-boy Hotspur with a papery he-ancient of Justice Shallow in *Henry IV*), and the extraordinary bravura Olivier double of Sophocles' *Oedipus* and the outrageously foppish Mr Puff in Sheridan's *The Critic*. Crowds besieged the alley outside the New Stage Door in an early example of mass adulation like Frank Sinatra's bobby-soxers or Beatlemania. He returned each night to Notley except before matinee days – where Vivien and he carried on with their plans for house and garden (a rose garden – of predominantly white roses – was a special project for her). For the most part life was calm but – only occasionally but for Olivier mind-paralysingly – there were instances of Vivien's relapses into a sullen, withdrawn torpor, seemingly unreachable, mood-swings which he could never fully convince himself were nothing to do with him.

The Old Vic had been booked to take a season to New York and Vivien, more concerned for him (he was deeply tired), than for herself, decided to join him "for the ride". Olivier worried that she might have a relapse while in America but in fact the trip was a very happy one. Vivien seemed totally unconcerned that there were no parts for her – she became enduring friends with Margaret Leighton, who played roles including Ilyena in *Uncle Vanya* which might have been hers in other circumstances – acting rather like Den Mother, regularly helping mend costumes or making tea backstage. Also, after a long period of war years and illness, she treated herself to an orgy of theatregoing and reunions with old friends, catching Katherine Cornell in Jean Anouilh's version of *Antigone*, Gertrude Lawrence in *Pygmalion*, and *The Glass Menagerie* by a new writer, Tennessee Williams, which she found deeply affecting, while meeting up with the Lunts, Robert and Madeleine Sherwood, Radie Harris, Helen Hayes and the Kanins (Garson Kanin as producer was wooing them to film *Cyrano de Bergerac*). There were visits to museums, galleries (including her favourite Frick Collection) and to Bloomingdale's for an enormous amount of nylon stockings to take back for friends. The only blot on an exhilarating visit was a frightening journey home; Olivier was suffering physically, in pain from onstage accidents, so they decided to fly home, but their Pan Am Clipper had only been airborne for a few minutes when Vivien screamed and got up from her window seat. Olivier feared an "episode" but a wing of the plane was ablaze, forcing the pilot into a nerve-shredding crash landing, which somehow he negotiated safely in a small field in Connecticut. There were, astonishingly, no injuries; passengers were driven to Hartford and that evening boarded another Constellation Clipper for England.

There was time for a brief period of rest before Vivien had to re-rehearse *The Skin of Our Teeth* to resume its run back at the Piccadilly – this time, to her delight, with George Devine as Mr Antrobus – and before Olivier began rehearsals for his own production of *King Lear* at the New. That made for a peaceful Notley interlude during their first summer since their renovations; house and gardens were still works in progress – the Notley glory years were still some time off – and so initially only close friends such as the Richardsons (Mu Richardson and Vivien exchanged details of tuberculosis, from which Mu had also suffered), Relphs or Nivens came as weekend guests, occasionally joined by Parisian friends Ginette Spanier (*directrice* at Balmain) and her doctor-husband Paul-Emile Seidmann. Family also visited. There had been a distinctly arctic period between Vivien's parents when Gertrude returned with Suzanne from Canada; Ernest had been up to his old tricks, unfortunately with Gertrude's assistant in her Beauty Academy business, Delia Collins, who then compounded her behaviour by leaving to set up her own rival business. Although a chastened Ernest was eventually forgiven it was only after some time in the doghouse. Inevitably there was some awkwardness between Vivien and Suzanne after such an absence although Vivien had written and sent regular presents. It helped that Suzanne had inherited much of Leigh's balanced temperament – she settled happily into school life at Sherborne – and that she adored her mother, which eased the way to eventual mutual understanding. Similarly, Olivier and Tarquin were initially uneasy together after Jill's return from California to a London which must have seemed austerely grey by comparison. Tarquin recalled being taken to the Piccadilly Theatre during *Skin* rehearsals; the auditorium was dark as the theatre manager led him down to the front stalls where his father kissed him and then sat with him watching rehearsals, telling him that the beautiful woman skimpily dressed as Miss Atlantic City was Bibs (one of his pet names, along with Puss, Baba or Vivling – she sometimes called him Puss and Baba as well as Larry-boy), whom Tarquin had not seen since Canada.

When he told her of his interests and hobbies:

> She made me feel that they were precisely the things which interested her too. I felt discovered, understood and cherished. She was master of that art, but in all the years that have passed since that first conversation I have never personally had any occasion to doubt her truthfulness. She, whose passion had deprived me of my father, did all she could to bring us together.

Tarquin spent the following weekend – the first of many – at Notley. He too came to understand how his father could love the place "more than people", appreciating its special quality of peace when lying in the bath on a Sunday morning while the local village church bells united in pealing in Long Crendon, Chearsley and Haddenham.

The Skin of Our Teeth had a happy second run. There had been anxieties over Vivien's health; the Lunts disapproved of her return to the stage in a tiring role, having tried to help her recovery with food parcels from America and butter sent via Denmark but now writing:

> We feel that if you will not continue to be quiet and rest then the next best thing is to come here with Larry and get all the nourishment and good air you can in a dry atmosphere.

Schedules forbade such a visit to the idyllic Lunt retreat in Wisconsin and Vivien was also determined to resume her unfinished business with Sabina. The second run of *Skin* was as commercially successful as the first and her health, physical and mental, remained happily sound throughout. After its extended run and the limited *King Lear* season the Oliviers had to consider their fortunes once more. Notley simply devoured money and even with Vivien on a box-office percentage from Beaumont, Olivier's Old Vic salary (covering administrative duties as well as performances) was meagre, forcing them to consider cinema possibilities. Garson Kanin was still pressing them to co-star in the Ben Hecht-scripted *Cyrano de Bergerac* which he was ambitious to produce but Olivier was increasingly absorbed by plans for another Shakespeare film, convinced that, touching 40, he could still play Hamlet which del Giudice was eager to produce with Rank backing.

It has been widely claimed that Vivien was deeply distressed not to be cast in the *Hamlet* film, desperately wanting to recapture the experience of Ophelia at Elsinore ten years before, and that she was furious with Olivier's refusal to cast her. It is true that Beaton's diary records Vivien in early 1947 in Paris as saying she thought she might be able to balance filming both *Hamlet* and a film of *Anna Karenina* (schedules would not have accommodated this and also Rank wanted a new face as Ophelia) but there is little evidence for supposed fury; she was clear-eyed enough to appreciate that Olivier's own age (about which he had doubts himself – one of the reasons he dyed his hair blond) would dictate the Ophelia choice of a 16-year old Jean Simmons (who looked remarkably like a young Vivien). She was certainly happy enough to join the *Hamlet* planning discussions which del Giudice, ace manipulator, financed with scarce lira coaxed from the Treasury to pay for ten luxurious days at the Hotel Miramar on the Gulf of Rapallo, a welcome mimosa-blossomed contrast to chilly austerity London. It was at this time that Vivien first met the internationally known art critic Bernard Berenson, their meeting arranged by Kenneth Clark. Both Oliviers were entranced by him and by his villa, I Tatti. The reaction was mutual; Berenson invited them again for the following day. Alan ("Jock") Dent had joined the group as Olivier's script collaborator again, now a valued friend; Dent idolised Vivien, with whom he competed to finish *The Times* crossword the quicker and compared notes on their favourite Dickens. It was Vivien, however, who advised a policy of major clean cuts in the screenplay – excision of Fortinbras as well as Rosencrantz and Guildenstern – rather than many minor editings. But now she too had a job for which to return, a reunion with her always-benevolent mentor Korda.

The master-showman, always lucky with his supporters in government – especially after his wartime activities for his adopted country – was as busy as ever but rather lost his touch in the immediate postwar period. Aiming for the international market he set up a series of costly costume films, none markedly successful and one – the dreadful *Bonnie Prince Charlie* with a spectacularly miscast David Niven – a monumental disaster. In 1948 he put two ambitious projects into production more or less simultaneously, both with lavish production values including Cecil Beaton costumes – Wilde's *An Ideal Husband* with Paulette Goddard which he also directed and a new version of *Anna Karenina* with Vivien. Well aware that she would be challenging memories of Garbo in Cukor's 1938 film, Vivien loved Tolstoy's novel and was also attracted to the idea of working with Ralph Richardson as Karenin. There had been early mentions of Olivier possibly playing Vronsky, Anna's lover, but *Hamlet* prevented that, although Korda promised her strong casting in the role.

Beaton was thrilled by the chance to create the costumes for the film and for Vivien. He visited Notley for a preliminary discussion, fascinated, as a connoisseur of both houses and gardens, to see the progress, later writing to Greta Garbo:

> It is very romantic in a medieval way and it is lovely to see something that has been neglected for so long taking on new life. They have planted avenues of trees, 500 roses and are making great improvements both in and outside the house.

Then Vivien and Beaton travelled to Paris for fittings, staying with Duff (now British Ambassador to France) and Diana Cooper at what became known as "The British Embassy Hotel", such generous hospitality was offered by the Coopers to friends. This was a lively time; Vivien and Diana shopped energetically together and there was an especially fascinating dinner with guests including Cocteau and the elderly Colette in bare feet, draped in shawls, "everyone flat on their stomachs *en homage*". Olivier joined for a time, enthusing about *Hamlet* ideas, and Vivien too was in high good spirits, also enjoying a visit to the Coopers' enchanting Chantilly country house before returning for Denham filming on *Anna Karenina*.

Vivien's old friend "Mills" Martin recalled early laughter-filled dressing-room episodes with David Niven, at Denham for tests, being outrageously irreverent in his wayward Scottish brogue from *Bonnie Prince Charlie* but before long the on-set atmosphere altered. Usually astute when assembling the talent on his ventures, Korda made some unfortunate crucial choices on *Anna Karenina*. He had a "pay or play" deal with Julian Duvivier, distinguished director of *Pépé le Moko*, who had directed Merle Oberon in *Lydia* for him and so assigned him to *Anna Karenina* and, unwisely, to adapt the novel with French dramatist Jean Anouilh. Their script, delivered late, was an experiment in angst-ridden existentialism, then in vogue in France, heavily underlining Anna's journey to suicide as the inevitable route to a free life (Anna is saddled with un-Tolstoyan lines such as "You can't escape from yourself")and while Korda may not have been expecting, in a 90-minute script, a faithful rendering of Tolstoy's panorama of an entire social world, he was alarmed by this relentlessly downbeat version which originally was transplanted to a French setting. A British writer, Guy Morgan, was brought on board but he was left with little time prior to shooting and the result was a patchwork job with some jolting narrative lurches (the Kitty/Levin subplot, vital as counterpoint to Anna's story, begins prominently but then more or less completely disappears). The script still suffered from the hasty revisions and the lingering focus on Anna's romantic life at the expense of the crucial carnal element in the Anna/Vronsky affair which Vivien had hoped would be highlighted.

The role of Vronsky had been offered to Michael Redgrave but he chose two films in Hollywood, creating another problem which had to be resolved quickly. Who was responsible for casting Kieron Moore is not certain – Korda and Duvivier must have had some say – but the result to a large degree effectively sabotaged the film. The Irish-born Moore – dubbed "The Boy from Skibbereen" in the tabloids – had recently made a success as (of all roles) Heathcliff in a stage version of *Wuthering Heights* and the precedent of Olivier's success in 1939 perhaps influenced the decision. Moore was not untalented but he was hopelessly miscast and out of his depth which comes through in a performance which at no point comes close to suggesting Vronsky's sexual magnetism. He seems to have sensed this himself and asked Korda after two weeks to be released (Korda refused), saying later, prior to the film's gala premiere, that he felt he was attending his own hanging. Duvivier was disliked by cast and crew, irked by his autocratic inflexibility on set, and uncommunicative with actors. In the midst of this, canny Ralph Richardson as Karenin, a man who puts his emotions into a safe-deposit box, saw which way the wind was blowing, pretended to listen attentively to anything Duvivier had to say to him and then proceeded to go his own way. He is perfect in the film's first half but somewhat overdoes damp-eyed playing for sympathy as the betrayed husband, although still walking off with the film.

Vivien was left adrift with nothing to play off from a blank-faced Moore and an off-kilter screen relationship with Richardson plus a taciturn director and an absent producer. Korda had gone to California on completing *An Ideal Husband*

and although he did return to attempt to smooth over the on-set dissensions, the damage was done. The performances remained unanchored and a masterpiece reduced to a mostly uninvolving love story. At some key points Duvivier's work demonstrates his talent; the trains in the film seemed especially to animate him, from Anna's first glimpse of Vronsky through a train's frosted window, her eyes for an instant carrying a hint of her destiny in a memorable close-up, through the grim scene of a workman's death in a Moscow station, to the inexorably oncoming engines through the fog at the close for Anna's death, and these episodes are handled with real cinematic flair as is the elaborate polonaise sequence at a Moscow ball, while far too much of the rest is a leaden-paced trudge. Vivien has some genuinely moving scenes but, significantly, is often most striking when alone – fleeing down a massive marble staircase at the opera and, sadly too late to redeem the film, in the long final sequence of her suicide, helped immeasurably by the contribution of cinematographer Henri Alekan, an authentic genius who had worked on such UFA classics as *Metropolis* and on Marcel Carné's masterpiece *Quai des Brumes*. His autobiography was aptly titled *Des Lumière et des Ombres* (*Light and Shadows*); in *Anna Karenina* he contributed the widest range of tones – silvers, whites, greys and deep blacks – possible in monochrome, unforgettably in the closing suicide scene, filmed at dusk in the station exterior and exploiting all the evocative power of lights piercing through mist, fog and the billows of steam from the locomotives. It might have been a different film had all involved had the artistry of an Alekan; Beaton's costumes are undeniably sumptuous, as Korda wanted, swathing Vivien in sables, rich velvets and jewels but, as in *Kipps* and *An Ideal Husband*, they tend to smother the characters.

The British reviews were rather better than Vivien anticipated although the American critics were merciless to Kieron Moore, and the film did no better business than *An Ideal Husband*. Korda had misjudged public taste with this expensively designed but unrelievedly sombre piece. The era of technicolour escapism in costume drama, the dashing English romances from Gainsborough Pictures, had arrived (as *Picture Post* remarked of native cinema in 1947: "The old values were going to the devil"). Margaret Lockwood's horsebacked highway woman in *The Wicked Lady* was much more popular than *Anna Karenina*.

There had been, undeniably, some troubling on-set behaviour from Vivien as filming proceeded. Beaton waspishly noted her complaints about the tightness of her gloves, acidly retorting it was because her hands were too big (she was sensitive about her "paws" as she called them) and her seemingly less than ecstatic response when he offered congratulations on Olivier's knighthood. The real cause of her lower spirits was the deeply disappointing, crushing sense that another film with a coveted role (and she felt she had Anna in what some actors call her "soul case") was slipping away and out of her power to steer back on course. Her perfectionism and loyalty to Tolstoy were offended by Duvivier's intransigence and Korda's unusually cavalier attitude to a vital piece of central casting. For all her wariness of Selznick she would have welcomed some of his obsessive attention to every element of a film on *Anna Karenina*.

With Olivier still absorbed in *Hamlet*, Vivien joined Leigh and Suzanne at Woodlands, the tranquillity and atmosphere of which she found almost as welcome as Notley. If she was still depressed it was far more likely to be because of the disappointment of *Anna Karenina* rather than jealousy of Olivier's knighthood or resentment over *Hamlet*, the filming of which had gone extremely well (and during which Vivien visited the set to be part of the celebrations at the news of that knighthood, also accompanying Olivier later to the recording of Walton's score, lending her coat to muffle a dominant drum). Olivier and Vivien were both certainly fiercely competitive but at this time, despite Vivien's screen disappointments, both were riding high. She accompanied him to Buckingham Palace for his investiture; subsequently her outfit, a restrained black suit and hat, has been much commented on, suggesting that somehow she was signalling a sense of the funereal rather than any celebration, although it is far more likely that she opted to "dress down" to avoid taking Olivier's limelight and he of course was formally and similarly soberly dressed for the occasion. Also she liked black, often wearing it for significant occasions such as the publicity sessions to publicise her *Gone With the Wind* casting. One biographer suggested "Had she been made a Dame that would have been another matter" but, seven years Olivier's junior (and he was then the youngest ever theatrical Knight), Vivien was pragmatic enough to have no such expectations, although she took to the title of "Lady Olivier" from the start.

Celebrating the end of *Hamlet* and the knighthood and taking Suzanne and Tarquin (who became friends), they escaped freezing London for a Riviera holiday spent at a comfortable villa perched on a hillside near Cannes belonging to Leigh's sister and her French husband. Tarquin later wrote that despite the household consisting of a "curious pot-pourri of past betrayals, divided loyalties and present laughter" it was a joyous time, with picnics and fishing trips around the coast and nearby islands. This break was much needed; when the Oliviers returned to London they plunged into preparations and rehearsals for what would prove one of the most exhausting periods of their careers. The Old Vic, under the aegis of the British Council, was booked for a long tour of Australia and New Zealand as a prologue to the royal visit of George VI and Queen Elizabeth the following year, with the Oliviers as leaders of the Company in a repertoire designed to give them equal opportunities. Vivien as Lady Teazle would co-star with Olivier as Sir Peter in his new production of *The School for Scandal* (with designs by Beaton), he would take on Antrobus to her Sabina in *The Skin of Our Teeth* and she would play Lady Anne in a revival of the *Richard III* production in which he had made such an astounding London impact as Shakespeare's most villainous monarch. Both the Sheridan and the Shakespeare would then play in a New Theatre season back in London; the Australian tour would keep them away for nearly a year.

CHAPTER 10

Down Under

Discipline and duty were concepts familiar to both Oliviers. They accepted that the Old Vic tour would involve considerably more than performing in three plays and leading a company for a lengthy period in unfamiliar theatres in countries new to virtually everyone involved. There was no huge financial reward (standard Old Vic salaries plus a modest touring allowance with, for them, a small percentage of any profits). They would be expected to carry out a wide range of extra-curricular activities – attending civic and mayoral receptions, making speeches and broadcasts, all that was demanded of visiting ambassadors or royalty (as which they were virtually regarded). As the Old Vic touring programme put it, they would be heading a company making up "a national expression of the British spirit".

Although deeply involved in World War II, postwar Australia experienced little of the privations, even grimness, of Britain after 1945 and, just as the British appreciated the Australian contribution to the conflict, so there was a marked feeling of gratitude to "the old country", to the Old Vic for making the journey and to the Oliviers – who could have made many times more money in films – for giving up almost a year of their careers.

The Australian writer Alan Seymour was a young man in Perth in 1948 and remembered the visit's enormous cultural impact. In the days when it took weeks to travel from the UK, Australian cities seemed infinitely remote, few more than Perth which saw virtually no professional theatre apart from the occasional musical or old West End hit sent out by one of the few commercial companies based in Sydney or Melbourne, 2,000 miles away. The excitement was huge when the tour's schedule was announced with Perth as its first date:

> This was glamour, this was excitement. Famous stars were far more inaccessible then than they are in these over-exposed days ... hundreds slept out all night on the pavement outside the booking agency so as to be first in the queue.

The company had little idea of what to expect. Sponsored by the British Council to express official thanks for the Antipodean war effort, in truth it was more of an actor-manager's company than the traditional Waterloo Road ensemble although including some fine actors (George Relph, Mercia Swinburne, Peter Cushing). Preliminary rehearsals were held – appropriately for a visit to a continent with a large percentage of its population descended from arrivals in transportation days – in the chilly rehearsal rooms used by Donald Wolfit's company opposite Holloway Prison. Vivien and Olivier threw an extravagant Durham Cottage party the night before leaving, guests including Danny Kaye (a friend from Hollywood days whose early London appearances, less than triumphant, the Oliviers had supported, now starring at the Palladium), the Richardsons, Cecil Tennant and the Bushells. After a snatched brief sleep and fulsome farewells to their Siamese cat New (named after the theatre) they travelled from Euston to Liverpool, welcomed by the Australian High Commissioner before joining the company on board the *Corinthic*, their home and work-space for the next six weeks. They rehearsed in a large dining-room, concentrating more on the one totally new production, *The School for Scandal*, which would play alone in Perth, with the other two plays scheduled for rehearsals later on board and then in Perth.

Elsie Beyer, the formidable general manager, wrote regularly from the ship to both Tennant and Stephen Thomas of the British Council's drama department, an early letter reporting to the latter:

> Larry and Vivien are very, very happy and wonderfully fit. Rehearsals take place morning and afternoon but there is time for swimming, deck games and every other possible relaxation. I don't think actors have ever got up so early in their lives.

An inducement for early rising may have been meals which were distinctly tastier than the powdered-egg omelettes or whale-steak of rationing back home. As was the food on a brief stop-over in Cape Town, where they had a foretaste of their Australian reception. The Oliviers and the Relphs attended a performance of *Perchance to Dream* in which its author/composer Ivor Novello starred. Elsie Beyer wrote to Tennant:

> There was a terrific crowd waiting for them. The moment they entered the theatre the whole audience stood up and clapped and cheered. It was like being with royalty. Vivien looked lovelier than ever and they were both in cracking form.

Fremantle, where they landed in Australia, saw similar scenes with crowds and press thronging the quayside. There were even more press and newsreel cameras in Perth and while it was gratifying to learn that the run there was completely sold out it was less thrilling to face the cavernous Capitol Theatre (an ex-cinema) with over 2,000 seats, poor acoustics and only two practicable dressing-rooms; Vivien and Olivier made themselves even more popular with the company – who nicknamed them "God and the Angel" – when they handed them over to the rest of the company while they changed and made up behind small screened-off areas in the wings. The heat was sweltering – under the lights their eighteenth-century costumes and wigs for Sheridan's comedy were sweat-soaked by intermission – and what seemed armies of large mosquitoes (Elsie described them as "flying elephants") made many look as if they had smallpox.

The new production of *The School for Scandal* was a labour of love for Olivier, who rated the play "the finest pure English comedy since Shakespeare", relishing its fusion of the Old Comedy of Manners with the sentimental decorum of George III's era. Vivien had thoroughly enjoyed her trial run with Cyril Maude and was thrilled now to be playing the capriciously spendthrift Lady Teazle opposite her husband's choleric but fundamentally warm-hearted Sir Peter, giving a clever reading of a tricky role – easy to make her seem merely foolish rather than inexperienced initially – reminiscent of Meredith's "dainty rogue in porcelain". Anticipating the idea of David Hockney designing in monochrome for Stravinsky's *The Rake's Progress* at Glyndebourne by 40 years, Olivier invited Cecil Beaton to design sets mostly in black and white using elements of Hogarth and of Pollock's Toy Theatres, with contrastedly colourful costumes. It was rarely easy working with Beaton, always quick to bridle at even slight criticism and, despite his somewhat sycophantic early attitude ("Darling Larry and Vivien" in letters), there would be tears before curtain-up on this production, although mostly over the London showing the following year. Today it would look possibly over-refined but it was decidedly novel in 1947 and immediately popular with audiences. Alan Seymour, like others, found the evening a revelation, even years later recalling details such as the meticulously staged opening, all timed to Thomas Beecham's arrangements of Handel's "Great Elopement" as Sir Peter and Rowley strolled along a street parallel to the footlights before a painted front-cloth of white terraced houses with black iron railings, stopped outside a central front door and knocked, at which point the cloth rose to reveal his household's interior. In a cultural context which tended to value gritty naturalism, this glimpse of style and elegance was a delightful surprise. Alan Seymour also sensed in the Perth audience a great bond between Australia and the UK; the men and women of both had fought alongside each other and Australia knew about Britain's wartime ordeal and the courage it inspired when "King and Country" carried great meaning. An instinctive patriot, Olivier was delighted that the National Anthem was played at all performances.

Perth was exhausting; the Oliviers had to squeeze in daytime rehearsals of *Richard III* and *The Skin of Our Teeth* with receptions and speeches in uncomfortable heat and Olivier was in pain from an ankle injury suffered during the closing dance in the Sheridan. The press reactions were ecstatic but still Olivier fussed about his own performance and felt that Vivien, while delightfully fresh, "must bubble with delicious laughter both inner and audible". He continued to refine the production throughout the tour, anxious to have it in tip-top form before it was seen in London.

Vivien was surprisingly nervous before opening *The Skin of Our Teeth* in Adelaide, despite having played it in London; some had questioned its choice, rather patronisingly assuming it could be too offbeat for colonial audiences and one newspaper had dubbed it "the Picasso" of the repertoire. It was a riotous success – Sabina's beauty queen persona was especially well received (one review called Vivien "Miss Vitamin B") – and although Olivier on paper was too young for Mr Antrobus, his make-up (of which he was a master) was one of his most convincing and he, too, made a big success in Wilder's razzmatazz evening. Also in Adelaide *Richard III* joined the repertoire, now with Vivien in the supporting but key role of Lady Anne; the macabre black comedy of the wooing scene over her husband's coffin was even more striking in its darkly erotic intensity than in London, with Vivien like some mesmerised creature facing a slithering, venomous snake.

Vivien and Olivier drove on their own to Melbourne, a journey of which she wrote to Beaumont, urging him to visit "this very exciting and wonderful country", describing part of the drive:

> through the most wonderful scenery imaginable, the first bit so Dali-esque as to be incredible – great shallow blue lakes surrounded by glistening white sand – black and white branches of trees sticking out of the water and birds of every kind everywhere.

To Beaumont she also touched on an exciting possible future London play, saying that no final decision could be made until their return to London in November.

In addition to the constant "on-call" touring life the Oliviers had to focus on affairs at Notley where a vast amount of work indoors and in the grounds was going on. Both Tennant and Tony Bushell went there most weekends to check on progress, often joined by John Fowler, and sent regular reports to Australia. Bushell, an ebullient figure with all the public-school speech mannerisms of the era, almost a parody of a P.G. Wodehouse character at times – he addressed them as "Darling Poppypots", sending them clippings from the British newspapers which he called "bladders" – kept them informed of extensive watering during hot spells to save the lime trees and Vivien's treasured catalpa, generally reassuring them that "all at Nottles is jolly ripping". Dorothy Welford, their London secretary, kept them in touch about Durham Cottage, the mousing activities of New and London theatre news. Vivien was industrious in remembering friends coping with food shortages at home; no fewer than 31 large hams found their way to England.

Vivien and Olivier did all they could to keep the company happy, organising barbecues and drinks parties whenever anyone celebrated a birthday (they described themselves as "Mum and Dad in loco"). Vivien seemed to thrive even with the workload of daytime duties, smiling through flower-shows or hospital visits, always immaculately dressed – there was enormous press interest in her outfits, some of them examples of the latest Paris fashions of "The New Look" – while Olivier found the "Food for Britain" speeches which he was deputed to deliver somewhat burdensome, rather resenting what he saw as an implication that "the Old Country" was on its uppers. Like all lengthy tours, after the initial euphoria of travelling to new places and opening the productions had worn off, tiredness and even a certain amount of boredom inevitably set in. By the time the company reached Melbourne, the strain was beginning to tell; Vivien developed bronchitis and missed five performances and then Olivier had to drop out of a *Richard III* performance because of acute pain in his leg. Some tetchiness crept in; Elsie Beyer, something of a headmistress and not greatly blessed with humour, became rather a trial to some of the company, many of whom were by now slightly homesick.

A hop over to Tasmania gave them at least a delightful and intimate theatre (built by convicts, the oldest in Australasia) in which to play. The local volunteer staff had done everything possible to clean and renovate the theatre, unused for some time, but the cold was perishing, the dressing-rooms and backstage areas so icy that Vivien, waiting for her exposure in the screen scene of *School for Scandal*, sat with a mink coat over her costume until the last possible moment.

Most members of that company are dead and few left recollections of the Oliviers then. Michael Redington, later a successful producer, remembered Vivien's Lady Teazle ("a brilliant performance") as a highlight while Mercia Relph felt that Vivien "had a great struggle theatrically against the overpowering thing of Larry ... Yet she was always trying to build up her own abilities." Most believed that she succeeded – in all three plays. But Garry O'Connor, who wrote a book on this tour, suggests that a substrain of marital tension was growing as the venture progressed, instancing a fierce backstage row between the couple over a pair of Lady Teazle's red shoes and portraying the Oliviers as now unsure of their love for each other, putting on a united front like parents hiding uncomfortable truths from the children. Georgina Jumel, understudying Vivien as Sabina, stressed how "very, very tiring" the tour proved, adding "They were very much in love on the tour but it did cool a bit during the last month", although her husband Terence Morgan recalled that to him the pair seemed throughout very much in love, adding that Vivien, aware that Olivier was easily jealous, sometimes teasingly flirted with some of the impressionable younger males in the company ("he used to sit there watching her rehearse and he would embarrass everyone by getting an erection"). And Olivier became deeply concerned whenever Vivien seemed below par, insisting that their Australian secretarial assistant, Floy Bell, make doctors' appointments for check-ups to monitor her tuberculosis. An objective observer, Bell noted: "I know Larry says things started to go wrong there, but in retrospect – I was not aware of anything wrong with them and I was in the same hotel or house."

The kind of spat over a pair of shoes as described by O'Connor is far from unusual backstage behaviour and often rows between theatrical married couples or lovers are the sharpest (the Lunts' regular furious backstage arguments were, after all, the inspiration for *Kiss Me, Kate*). Nevertheless, it seems undeniable, given subsequent developments, that some shift, some readjustment of the Tectonic plates of the deepest levels of their relationship, was developing in Australia.

But when they moved on to Brisbane – a date which gave them a longed-for short break – spirits seemed to lift again. Cecil Tennant flew out to see his clients, bringing a copy of the *Hamlet* film which had opened to mainly warm reviews at home – a company screening was organised – and he joined Vivien and Olivier on a restorative trip to the haven of Surfers' Paradise near Brisbane (the Barrier Reef was a trip too far). While Tennant was with them Olivier confided in him his worries about the Old Vic (struggling in his absence and with Richardson filming in Hollywood), a concern of which Vivien was well aware.

Without that holiday, the longest stint of the tour – eight weeks in Sydney, opening on the coldest night of the Australian winter – would have been even more arduous. The number of civic events organised for them was onerous, although Vivien took greatly to Sydney, finding it a stimulating city ("And the little beaches and bays all round the harbour are *quite* exquisite" she told Leigh) although even with her unquenchable enthusiasm for new places and people a degree of homesickness was setting in. She still organised regular company outings to beaches outside the city but Olivier was in lower spirits. He had continued to fret about the Old Vic, frustrated by being so far away – he had written to Tennant: "I cannot help thinking there is the tiniest bit of hanky-panky going on" – but still was left shattered when in Sydney he received a curt letter from Lord Esher, Chairman of the Old Vic Board, informing him that the triumvirate's contracts would not be renewed after the London season in the spring of 1949 (which would include both *Richard III* and *The School for Scandal*), devastating his dream of nursing the Old Vic into a National Theatre. The reasons for this extraordinary decision remain murky but at the time many detected the hand of Guthrie, the quintessential ensemble-man, always sniffy about "stars", whose relationship with Olivier had become wary with the actor's rise to superstardom (Guthrie was put out when Olivier removed him from directing *Oedipus* when he disagreed with its pairing with *The Critic*, while Olivier had been wounded by Guthrie's terse verdict on the *Henry V* film – "Thought it vulgar"). Vivien did her best to reassure him that the future held untold possibilities for him and for them together after the New season early the following year but his distress seemed so deep that she could not reach him. The company noted a certain remoteness from him in the final stages of the tour following this shock, compounding the physical pain he suffered from the various accidents he sustained.

As a result of what he saw as both rejection and betrayal by the Old Vic, rather echoing Coriolanus's boast of "a world elsewhere", Olivier began to consider a company – LOP (Laurence Olivier Productions) – with its directors including Vivien and an inner circle of confidants (Tennant, Bushell, Roger Furse – joined later by friends or colleagues with names impressive for Company notepaper, including Korda, Kenneth Clark and conductor Malcolm Sargent, all unlikely to oppose him). This would be a commercial organisation, designed as competition for established producers and Old Vic alike. And in Sydney he met a charmingly efficient Old Etonian (always impressive for

Olivier – before long Tarquin would be a pupil there) then working in Australia for the British Council, Peter Hiley. As Secretary to LOP he would work for the Oliviers for nearly 20 years, intensely loyal to both, with a special fondness for Vivien and her gift for and delight in giving pleasure:

> I always felt that in whatever age or class she had been born, she would have found prominence in one role or another – that bright star would have come to the fore.

Another encounter with later consequences was the Oliviers' meeting the leading Australian stage and radio actor Peter Finch. Throughout the tour they had taken an interest in local drama, professional and amateur, and in Sydney they were taken to a glass factory to see one of the condensed "Laughter at Lunchtime" plays performed for workers by the Mercury Mobile Players which Finch had co-founded. Usually Olivier found Molière boring ("as funny as a baby's open grave") but he and Vivien were most impressed by the performances, particularly that of Finch as the sly Argan in *The Imaginary Invalid*. The outgoing, hard-drinking Finch, married to a ballet dancer, Tamara Tchinarova, became a crony of several of the Old Vic Company and met the Oliviers on a few more Sydney occasions. Initially Olivier seemed the more impressed, writing to Tennant about "this exceptionally, I repeat exceptionally clever young actor", suggesting Tennant advise him should he come to London as planned. The same letter worried about "Darling Puss" ("I cannot find a drug to waft away her cough") and also about the now pressing need to find a third play for the New season (*Skin* had already had two London runs), mentioning *Hedda Gabler*, *'Tis Pity She's a Whore* and Shelley's *The Cenci* (which Alan Dent was constantly urging them to do). There was no mention then of the eventual choice of Anouilh's version of *Antigone*, seen by Vivien on Broadway. Possibly he thought then that it might be too much of a challenge. His mood worsened towards the close of their Sydney run when his knee, injured when he slipped and fell heavily during the fierce final fight scene in *Richard III*, was playing up so badly that he had to use a crutch (anticipating Anthony Sher's "bottled spider" Richard on crutches years later).

Five weeks of New Zealand performances remained, with the schedule rearranged to add extra matinees, allowing the company to sail home slightly earlier than planned, leaving little time for relaxation and with Olivier in debilitating pain (the ruptured cartilage was finally operated on in Wellington) he left the final post-show speech to an exhausted Vivien. He then developed lumbago; to board the *Corinthic* for the return voyage he had to be hoisted up the side of the ship on an improvised stretcher (it was hardly surprising that he told a reporter: "You may not know it but you are talking to two walking corpses").

It was down to work again on the voyage home, with rehearsals for *Antigone* finally chosen for the New season, less complex a physical production than other possible choices but one demanding laser-beam precision of concentration. There have been suggestions that Vivien, buoyant again after a few days at sea and with a husband disinclined towards post-rehearsal junkets, behaved flirtatiously with some of the younger male company members and possibly even had a fling with one, Dan Cunningham, cast as her lover in *Antigone*, a suggestion in O'Connor's book which was strongly countered by surviving cast members when it was published in 1984. Olivier's memoirs describe her as seemingly especially close to one actor but state that she ceased the "flirting" when he spoke to her about it. Olivier employed Cunningham subsequently and recommended him to Glen Byam Shaw for the Stratford season of 1955; it seems unlikely that he would do this for a junior actor who had cuckolded him.

Directing *Antigone*, Olivier chose not to take on the leading male role of Creon, Antigone's uncle (George Relph played it with commandingly persuasive authority) but instead cast himself as the urbane Chorus, introducing the play and its characters and steering it to its prescribed end after which the heroine will die; in effect he literally "presented" Vivien in the play, to which she committed herself totally, working even harder than usual on her voice. She felt that Antigone's dilemma in a play muted in its inexorable movement towards its tragic end needed a voice lower than her normal pitch and timbre; she adopted a testing series of vocal exercises to achieve this, to a degree agreeing with Olivier that many acting challenges are essentially technical ones. At Notley once, Orson Welles (playing Othello for LOP) mischievously told Olivier he could never play the role because he was a baritone, not a bass; ten years later Olivier made sure he had lowered his voice by a whole octave before tackling it, following exercises similar to those Vivien used before *Antigone*.

Jean Anouilh was receiving his first mainstream London exposure with *Antigone*, his recasting of Sophocles often close to his source but charged with subtly different moral and political meaning, often related to "metatheatre" in its reminders to audiences that they are watching a play. In a Paris still occupied when the play opened in 1944, Antigone's stubborn defiance of authority and progress to self-sacrifice were seen as barely cloaked encouragement to the Resistance while, ironically, many of the occupying Germans admired the play's portrait of Creon as a just and patriotic leader, only one of Anouilh's deliberate ambiguities. That moral ambivalence spoke eloquently to a postwar public and Vivien's portrayal of Anouilh's grave heroine, unflinchingly determined to bury her beloved brother against Athenian law, gradually releasing the "tensed spring" described by the Chorus to put the tragedy in motion and then moving to her predetermined doom, had a revelatory slow-burn power. In Paris the modernisation of the myth was emphasised by the monochrome simple design with the actors in dinner jackets or Grecian-style dresses. Guthrie McClintic, never the most subtle director, on Broadway with his wife Katherine Cornell showcased, used a setting of rostra against enormous draped curtains, unfortunately resembling a row of outsize directoire knickers on a washing-line, with the male actors in white tie. Vivien had been impressed by the play but not this production, agreeing with Jamie Hamilton, who described Cornell as "Antigone's auntie" and the Creon of Sir Cedric Hardwicke as "a dyspeptic camel". Cornell at 50 was too old for the part and matronly costumed and although Olivier had been initially dubious about the project he realised that Vivien had seen through the distortions of Broadway to a play resonant for London audiences.

She was costumed very simply in a Grecian-style dark green tunic (once more photographed by Angus McBean, released from prison) against Roger Furse's set, spare but practical, with a mostly bare stage against a cyclorama in front of which was a low wall and a classical portico which allowed for powerful entrances and exits. During the Chorus's introductory speech Vivien sat apart, hunched and mute, her hair cropped short and intensely pale before the action involved her and when she spoke, in a voice vibrant with pent-up emotion but fused always with conviction, it surprised both audiences and critics. Reviews for both the play and Vivien's Antigone were predominantly extremely positive and what had seemed possibly a dubious commercial proposition, even with the Oliviers, became a capacity-audience success. Obviously Vivien was gratified by the press reaction but the response of those within the profession meant even more. Sydney Carroll thought it "the finest thing" she had ever done ("It combined the chiselled, clear classicism of the Greeks with the passionately moving impulses of the modern") while Clemence Dane, hard to please, found it "a moving, startling and original performance; it had a curious archaic strength rarely seen in modern feminine acting".

Both *The School for Scandal* and *Richard III*, completing a season marking the couple's first joint appearances on the British stage, were also part of a *succès fou*; it saw queues down to Trafalgar Square waiting for returns and nightly huge crowds of autograph-hunters at the stage door, all carrying an air of intoxicating glamour. The season had opened with the London showing of *The School for Scandal*, unrevived in London since a somewhat perverse Guthrie staging for Gielgud's company (also at the New) in 1937. The Old Vic opening at the New was gala, with newsreel-cameras and press galore outside as a ritzy audience (the Richardsons, the Nivens, Margot Fonteyn and Bobby Helpmann, Margaret Leighton and Terence Rattigan *et al.*) arrived in their finery; this was a time when West End opening nights still saw evening dress in stalls and circle. *The School for Scandal* was a triumph, with Vivien's performance particularly highly praised ("a baggage of the sweetest, impishness" and "beautifully modulating devilment into contrition") although not every critic was wild about Olivier's unusually melancholy undertone to Sir Peter.

Following the opening, Olivier and Vivien jointly cabled Cecil Beaton at the Plaza Hotel in New York, assuring him of success for his contribution to the evening, a gesture intended as a Band-Aid on wounds still open after quite a backstage saga over the design, resulting in an arctic *froideur* between the Oliviers and the designer, now in the throes of one of his fits of affronted *amour-propre*. Everything had begun promisingly, with Beaton's set designs pronounced "wonderful" (still the production staff, not unusually on a Beaton project, had to solve most of the practical technical problems) but with cavils over some costumes. When the production was in preparation for Australia, Beaton's availability was restricted; he had, as always, many projects to juggle simultaneously and a good deal of the work was deputed to his assistant, Martin Battersby. There was little Battersby did not know about the decorative arts but his temperament was as brittle as Beaton's (later they had a spectacular falling-out) and he antagonised the wardrobe staff with his imperious manner. Beaton flattered both stars (still "Darling Larry and Vivien"), buttering up Vivien with references to American advance interest in *Anna Karenina* and unable to resist mentioning showing his photographs of her as Anna to his goddess Garbo ("your predecessor in the part"), who seemingly found them "unbelievably charming".

Anxious in advance about his production for London, Olivier had told Beaton: "This production is my baby of all time and I desperately want it to be yours too." He wrote to the designer before the company left Australia, detailing at length his dissatisfaction with many of the costumes ("made to look like a telephone cover, dear boy" was his verdict on Vivien's first party-dress). All his protestations of affection did little to smooth the designer's ruffled feathers. Relations with Battersby had deteriorated; the wardrobe-mistress, Emma Selby-Walker, found him arrogant and had little more time for Beaton ("He was never there except when the photographers were there"). The upshot was that Battersby was sidelined (Beaton called him "my stooge" in letters to the Oliviers). Costumes (and wigs) always seem to cause more fits of temperament than anything else in the theatre although the atmosphere might have calmed had Beaton been more available prior to the London opening when he remained cocooned in the Plaza's luxury – he was anxious to restore his fortunes and status in New York after his ostracism from American *Vogue* for perceived anti-semitism in pre-war illustrations – although he pleaded poverty ("I am bone poor here") as a reason for not flying home. There was not much to be done at the New except to accept the situation (most of the faulty costumes were remade or improved) but the general feeling was that Beaton had behaved somewhat unprofessionally. Once home he took himself off smartly to the New, to be highly delighted by his own work although he wrote of the Oliviers: "they were both out of my life forever". He had not been pleased on going backstage, as he told Garbo: "The Oliviers rather grudging in their generosity and I fear they are not good friends behind my back".

Beaton's fatal flaw was less vanity than a gnawing, self-destructive jealousy. So hungry was he for theatrical success that his anxieties could lead to considerable umbrage and sundered friendships (with Cukor on the *My Fair Lady* film, with Enid Bagnold and Gielgud on *The Chalk Garden*). Vivien liked and admired him (although some of his *School for Scandal* work she found substandard) and tried twice to repair their friendship with offered olive branches but although polite in reply (only "Dearest Vivien" and "Blessings" rather than "Darling" and "Love" now in letters) he could not bring himself fully to grasp them. He was scathing about Olivier when he was appointed the National Theatre's Director and at his bitchiest when asked to contribute to Alan Dent's posthumous collection of pieces on Vivien; after their Edinburgh meeting he had described her as "almost indescribably lovely" but for Dent, after conceding the appeal of her eyes and the turn of her nose he could not resist sliding in the stiletto ("But did it add up to beauty?").

The *Sturm und Drang* backstage was surprisingly not matched by lingering recriminations over the affair of the dismissal of the Old Vic directorial triumvirate. The Australian tour had been a financial success – its income came at a providential time to make up recent London losses – and the New season with the Oliviers even more so. Olivier, Richardson and Burrell met with Lord Esher; they could have kicked up an almighty fuss but chose not to. Olivier always disliked confrontations (Vivien agreed that dignified silence was the best revenge) and, moreover, he had moved on already, putting – as he so often did – distance between himself and any contention. There was indeed a world elsewhere; he aimed to take LOP to heights outstripping any Old Vic achievements. And LOP had early success with James Bridie's *Daphne Laureola* starring Edith Evans opposite the recently arrived (and rapidly contracted to LOP) Peter Finch, whose London stage debut as an impressionably romantic young Pole made an impact similar to Vivien's in *The Mask of Virtue*. It ran at Wyndham's, with its stage door directly opposite that of the New; "The Oliviers" really were the undisputed reigning West End monarchs.

It was during this heady time when something happened between the couple, according to Olivier's account (the only one we have, written in his old age), something which hit him like a lightning-bolt. Vivien, wrote Olivier in his *Confessions*, said to him "I don't love you any more." He described this as occurring at Durham Cottage in a small vestibule-area where they were lunching on a day of spring sunshine. It should be noted that his sister-in-law Hester later said that she heard Olivier, always a ready story-teller, give an account of this incident on several occasions, placing it variously at different times and in different locations – in a cab, after a performance one night, in the garden; also the *Confessions* are, to say the least, muddled in chronology and on occasion contradictory. He elaborated on the impact of Vivien's words:

> I must have looked as stricken as I felt, for she went on "There's no one else or anything like that, I mean I still love you but in a different way, sort of, well, like a brother" ... It felt as if I had been told I had been condemned to death. The central force of my life, my heart in fact, as if by the world's most skilful surgeon, had been removed.

Olivier was prone to dramatisation but there is no reason to disbelieve the essentials of what he wrote. Much of his remoteness towards the end of the Australian tour can be attributed to physical pain and the anguish of his removal from the Old Vic directorate, but he often said to Vivien – self-mockingly, acting the part of an upper-crust squire (actors often resort to jokey role-playing to mask life's deeper emotions) – "I *lorst* you in Australia." He was not referring to any affair; more possibly to the subtle alteration in the equipoise of their relationship, almost inevitable after over a decade which had begun with such consuming passion. Few love affairs begun at such white heat do not experience some cooling down. His love for Vivien, as evidenced in those letters written from New York in 1939 particularly, was something he considered sacred ("It had been inconceivable that this great, this glorious passion could ever not exist"). Could he accept "humiliation" apparently for the sake of appearances? Slightly bathetically he added in *Confessions* that his knighthood was "sacred" to him too and that he found it impossible to offer the public "crude disillusionment". They should surely remain versions of romantic lovers, like Tristan and Isolde or Siegmund and Sieglinde. So, he argued, they would carry on as if nothing had happened, like brother and sister ("occasional acts of incest were not discouraged") even if that was "so long as I never looked to be happy again".

This is rather contradicted by later letters – to Vivien and others – when his happiness in the marriage was clearly still rhapsodic. Characteristically his memoirs blend acutely observed detail and over-arching self-dramatisation ("He acts writing!" said one critic) and, bearing in mind Hester's comments, it has to be asked: how accurate is his account? Obviously Vivien did not simply say "I don't love you any more" as if playing an ace; the suggestion is that it was said in the context of a longer conversation reflecting on their position, as couples who have been together for over ten years might well do. The centre of gravity in the Vivien/Olivier relationship had subtly shifted, certainly. It may not have seemed so to Vivien ten years earlier in their first flush of careless rapture but much as Olivier loved Vivien he loved acting more. As he took on more and more great classic roles, generally to massive acclaim, this almost erotic emotion swelled with the love he began to feel for his characters, even what he called the "great predators" like *Richard III*. He always agreed with Elia Kazan that acting at root was essentially sexual (it was Kazan who said that Olivier was, above anything else, "a cocotte", that he craved an audience's love). The ambition to be – and remain – the stage's greatest actor still blazed, if anything more fiercely. For their joint appearances, chivalry dictated that Vivien be billed first but in his mind Olivier took second billing to nobody. No wonder his friend George Devine, who understood him well, told his third wife, Joan Plowright: "Marry him if you must. But don't act with him too often or he will destroy you."

Vivien too was ambitious but she loved Olivier more than any role. What had changed was the feeling that she was not – and perhaps never could be – equal in his eyes. LOP bore his name alone; she may have been on its board of directors (and her earnings vitally helped underwrite the venture) but she was there, as she totally understood with no objection, as something beautiful for Korda, Clark, Sargent and the others to appreciate during their meetings, all of which would rubber-stamp whatever Olivier wanted to do.

The likely scenario on that spring day lunchtime at Durham Cottage – if indeed that was the right place and time – was that Vivien, always fundamentally unsentimental, was redefining the equation of their marriage rather than delivering any *fait accompli*, something which Olivier could not help himself from dramatising (three decades later). She had certainly not ceased to love him – she never would – but for a variety of reasons (not least the difference in their sexual drives – Olivier acknowledged that he could find it difficult to be an athlete in the bedroom as well as on stage) she had come to love him in a different way but certainly more – much more – than fraternally.

Different varieties of love stamped their next joint venture. The play which Beaumont had referred to and on which Vivien in Australia had deferred making a decision had now solidified its production plans. Beaumont and LOP would co-present, with Olivier directing and Vivien starring as Blanche Du Bois in *A Streetcar Named Desire*, Tennessee Williams's Broadway success.

CHAPTER 11

The Kindness of Strangers

A Streetcar Named Desire opened in London as the 1940s ended. In *Confessions* Olivier wrote of the subsequent ten years: "I had not the faintest inkling of how life would have taken me and shaken me like a rat before the decade closed." The production of *Streetcar* proved a turbulent overture to that period.

Before rehearsals the Oliviers could enjoy, at last, an uninterrupted long rest, most of it at Notley. Progress there delighted Vivien; her pet projects, the rose garden and "The Folly" – an allée of cypresses leading to a fountain – were taking shape while Fowler's work on the interior delighted them both. The library became a favourite room, with a corner fireplace, the walls hung with an eclectic range of paintings from the work of "bushmen" painters encountered in Australia to flower studies by Matthew Smith, with every possible recent British or American magazine on the long oak table, filled with big jugs and vases holding lavish displays of branches and flowers. The main drawing-room was now a comfortable oasis of deep sofas and armchairs, trademark Colefax and Fowler chintzes and more flowers; it was scented by the trick Vivien now used of burning a Guerlain fragrance (often jasmine) in the fireplace or using it as a spray. Olivier became quite the country squire in this "baronial" era; in tweeds and Norfolk jacket he would go over his acres, inspecting the cows grazing in the fields (they were given names of Vivien's stage and film characters – Sabina, Ophelia, Antigone – but there never was a Scarlett), although the farm and market garden business would come under the supervision of his brother Dickie who had never properly settled down until Olivier paid for him to attend agricultural college. He thrived at Notley, becoming highly efficient at farm business, helped by his younger second wife, Hester.

The staff at Notley – one bibulous butler excepted – both in the house and the gardens proved mostly lastingly loyal (Vivien's Archive contains many affectionate letters from Ethel Helmsing and Trudy Flockhart, both of whom worked with her at home and in the theatre, and from other staff). Mr and Mrs Cook were especially treasured; he was a find of a gardener, always reporting to Vivien any changes or surprises when she was away, while Mrs Cook worked in the house. This all underpinned the great days of Notley from the later 1940s. If the hosts were acting in London, weekend guests would congregate in their dressing-rooms backstage after the Saturday evening performance and then drive (just over an hour) to the Abbey where drinks and later a full formal dinner awaited them, followed by parties with word-games or songs round the piano until dawn. Leisurely Sunday breakfasts – Vivien, usually up before anyone else, supervised all the breakfast trays with the Sunday newspapers provided – were followed by gardening for those inclined (Marlene Dietrich adored weeding, Michael Redgrave dead-headed the roses), time on the river or on walks, with drinks, meals and snacks on tap throughout the day. Notley was a haven for regular guests, mostly family or old friends – Relphs, Richardsons, Byam Shaws, Millses, Duff Coopers, Redgraves, Waltons, George Devine and Sophie Harris, Korda, Dent, Rex Harrison and Lilli Palmer – and colleagues from home and abroad such as Gielgud, Helpmann and his partner Michael Benthall, Beaumont and John Perry, Wyler, Behrman, Welles, Lunts, Wilder, Cukor, Helen Hayes, Katharine Hepburn, Peter and Tamara Finch, Graham Greene, Anthony Eden, Terence Rattigan, altogether making up a Visitors' Book outdoing even William Randolph Hearst's San Simeon. During *Streetcar's* preparatory period Tennessee Williams visited, adding "Ciao!" to his signature in the Visitors' Book, with his partner Frank Merlo to whom Vivien took a special liking. She relished his independent irreverence at an exclusive Hollywood shindig when studio boss Jack Warner condescendingly asked him: "And what do you do?", deadpanned by Merlo with: "I sleep with Mr Williams." Like Coward's partner Graham Payn, Merlo appreciated that Vivien saw him for himself, not merely the accessory to a famous name. Payn was regularly invited on his own when Coward was away, although the dramatist never lost an opportunity to tease Vivien with his bread-and-butter letters after a weekend, often signing them "Lenin" or "Mary Baker Eddy":

> It was so agreeable of you to invite me to your fucking old Abbey. It was most interesting historically and although I found my bedroom on the stuffy side the coldness of the rest of the house offset this minor defect very successfully.

Family were regularly there too – Ernest and Gertrude, Tarquin and Suzanne on weekends away from Eton and Sherborne. In 1949 Suzanne went to a Swiss finishing school – initially rather disconsolate, mainly because of a shortage of horses about which she had been passionate at Sherborne. She was, she wrote from Switzerland, "simply aching" to see her mother again, poignantly adding that she had arrived abroad "only just as we were getting to know each other". They had spent a happy holiday together, prior to Suzanne's departure, in the south of France near Grasse, where Olivier (whom Suzanne had come to like very much) and Vivien enthusiastically painted, usually *en plein air*, relying for guidance on the practical hints from another amateur artist in Winston Churchill's book *Painting as a Pastime*. While Suzanne returned to Switzerland Vivien, seemingly bloomingly healthy, back in London began work with Olivier on *Streetcar*.

She knew the play intimately having had over a year in which to study it and the complex role of Blanche Du Bois, unquestionably the most taxing she had tackled to date. It is generally assumed that Beaumont engineered the British production but that was not quite the whole story. He was thrilled to be involved, writing to Vivien that "it's my dream come true. From the first moment of reading the script I could only see you" and of course, with his theatrical antennae always alert he had heard of the sensational impact of Williams's play and of Marlon Brando's performance on Broadway when it opened at the end of 1947.

These were exciting years for the American theatre. Pre-war stars, many of them with no or little interest in the screen – Cornell, the Lunts, Helen Hayes, Bankhead, Maurice Evans – still retained their Broadway box-office appeal but a rich new generation of dramatists, directors and actors – Williams, Arthur Miller, William Inge, Kazan, Brando, Geraldine Page, Kim Stanley, many of them linked to the Actors Studio (Kazan was one of its founders), opening in the same year as *Streetcar* and itself an offshoot of the Group Theatre – were changing the face of American theatre. Now a new kind of acting, often raw and much less polite, hit the stage, soon reaching Hollywood too as actors such as Brando, James Dean, Julie Harris, Paul Newman, Shelley Winters and Warren Beatty moved speedily west from Broadway (after *Streetcar*, Brando appeared only once more, briefly, on stage), often in films scripted by Williams or Inge. This kind of acting, shorthanded as "The Method" to describe its way of translating Konstantin Stanislavsky's theories into American practice, was urgent, charged with an emotional rawness unusual on the politer British stage in new plays, as directors approached their work, in Kazan's words, as a process of "translating psychology into behaviour". To many of an older guard – in both America and Britain – this approach carried dangers of self-indulgence or of using acting as therapy. Indeed, extreme examples of Method acting could be unfocused or technically unrefined (Olivier was suspicious and Coward, whose approach was its antithesis, described it as "The Scratch and Mumble School") but the British stage at that time with Anouilh, Fry, Eliot, Coward and Rattigan dominating a costive West End, had virtually no plays reflecting contemporary society, its acting undeniably technically superb but threatening to ossify into a glossy imitation of life rather than being rooted in it.

Brando's *Streetcar* performance as Blanche's brother-in-law and destroyer, Stanley Kowalski, had been a revelation. He was not totally unknown after a few Broadway supporting performances; he had appeared, mesmerisingly, as an anguished ex-GI in a small but key role in Maxwell Anderson's flop *Truckline Café*, directed by the ex-Group Theatre's Harold Clurman, produced by Kazan who remembered him when the original choice for Stanley, John Garfield (another Group Theatre alumnus), fell through. Brando's impact on the Ethel Barrymore stage was so powerful that many thought it tilted the balance of the play away from Blanche (played by British-born Jessica Tandy, former Olivier colleague from the Old Vic), although this may well have owed something to Kazan, from an Anatolian immigrant background, identifying with Stanley's Polish-immigrant origins (he directed the scene in which Blanche calls Stanley a "Polack" to electric effect, her words seeming like a racial slur).

Olivier had agreed to direct mainly because Vivien was so passionate about both play and part, and to a degree because he realised that Blanche was a wonderful role, an opportunity for Vivien to further the steps she had taken in *Antigone* towards establishing herself as an actress of depth as well as range. But he never properly understood the play.

Williams's first Broadway success, *The Glass Menagerie*, had had a misbegotten London production. His "memory play" had seen a legendary Broadway comeback from the great Laurette Taylor after years of alcohol-related troubles but she died not long after the run. For London, the role of the Southern mother, Amanda Wingfield, was taken by the gentler Helen Hayes, directed by Gielgud, who further hampered a play more robust than often presented by bathing it in lambent soft focus throughout. Williams deeply disliked the production, making him wary of *Streetcar*'s London plans. He had written to Hayes, prior to *The Glass Menagerie*, that he felt the British had an inherent incapacity to interpret a play soaked in an atmosphere particularly American such as *Menagerie*'s St Louis claustrophobia or the sweaty French

Quarter Kowalski apartment in New Orleans, adding: "The body would be there but some indefinite but immensely important thing would be missing."

Coincidentally Hayes was one of the first of several to alert Vivien to the suggestion of playing Blanche, writing to her soon after the Broadway opening:

> Please get hold of *A Streetcar Named Desire* quickly ... it is one of the great plays of our time and you certainly would act it superbly.

But Vivien had already read the play. Margalo Gilmore, who had played "the other woman" in *No Time for Comedy* with Olivier, had obtained a script pre-publication just after its opening and sent it to Vivien. Olivier had smartly cabled its Broadway producer, Irene Mayer Selznick (it was only the second production of her post-divorce career) to bid for the London rights:

> Would you be interested for us (LOP) to present *Streetcar* in London, me to direct, Vivien to star? We would like to work out some way of associating with Old Vic in the venture.

Selznick cabled back that a Vivien/Olivier package answered "my fondest hopes" adding that "perfection is primary consideration". She did not in the event find perfection in the London *Streetcar* although she fought with the tenacity of a tigress to correct what she saw as its imbalances and flaws.

LOP was only one of 13 London bidders for the rights. Encouraged by Audrey Wood, Williams's equally redoubtable agent, Selznick decided not simply to follow custom and grant the rights in return for a slice of profits but properly to co-produce with an established West End management. Some close New York associates gave Beaumont a strong recommendation. He had been first in line after LOP and now, when Selznick came to London to arrange the production, he outwitted the opposition by meeting her at Southampton with a Bentley then charming and disarming her in the style to which this chic, dynamic woman was accustomed (they became lifelong friends). Beaumont assured her that he knew Vivien was burning to play Blanche, stressing their friendship and adding that Olivier as director might be arranged ("I detected less enthusiasm and no intimacy" Selznick noticed). The Old Vic notion was abandoned and a co-production deal between H.M. Tennent, LOP and Selznick was arranged, with Selznick prepared to wait until late 1949 for Vivien and Olivier to be available. She was confident, based on her opinion of Vivien's Scarlett and her performances at the New (especially impressed by *Antigone*), that Blanche was within Vivien's grasp. Williams, never a passionate playgoer, was initially less sure but realised that "the prestige of an Olivier/Leigh production would be enormous".

Over a dinner at Beaumont's elegant Westminster house Selznick began to understand the friendship between Vivien and Beaumont and also heard alarm bells ringing, if only faintly then, when Olivier asked Williams for freedom to cut the play, a request gently but firmly refused by the dramatist, explaining that it had been already cut "to the bone" for Broadway and that some plays (he cited Eugene O'Neill) were necessarily longer, given their canvas. A Notley weekend followed; this "would be Tennessee's only visit in connection with the production" (hard at work on *Cat on a Hot Tin Roof*, Williams wanted to finish it at home with no distractions). It was a pleasant enough visit although Olivier seemed reluctant to discuss the play with the author; Selznick had the impression that "Olivier scarcely knew *Streetcar* in May". She would not have expected the level of textual involvement originally given by Kazan, practically a co-creator of some of the play in the way in which he worked on it with Williams, but she was concerned enough to remind Olivier that no cuts could be made without Williams's permission, to which he airily responded "Oh, the old boy won't mind", and she also fretted that Beaumont and Olivier did not seem natural collaborators ("their cordiality was only surface"). Back in New York Selznick was told by the dramatist that he was placing the London *Streetcar*, "like Pilate, in your hands."

From rehearsals in London through the Manchester try-out to the opening at the Aldwych Theatre, the London *Streetcar* was "a bruising experience for one and all" in Selznick's opinion. An unflinching scrutiny of disintegration as a fading Southern belle takes refuge in the shabby New Orleans apartment of her sister Stella, recently married to blue-collar Polish immigrant Kowalski, resentful of Blanche's intrusion into his life and her eventual destroyer (her rape by Stanley on the night of his first child's birth is the final trigger leading to Blanche's removal to an asylum in the final, harrowing scene), *Streetcar* was unlike anything seen on a West End stage. The Lord Chamberlain's office, still (and for nearly 20 more years) responsible for theatre censorship, demanded several crucial changes; a long, moving speech in which Blanche describes to her suitor Mitch, Stanley's workmate, her discovery of her young husband Allan's homosexuality and then his suicide following the realisation of Blanche's reaction was cut and altered to leave the reason for his death ambiguous. The Lord Chamberlain had decreed that if the lines were altered from Blanche describing Allan discovered with "an older man" to having her finding him in bed with "a negress", that would be acceptable (it was not – Vivien immediately refused the change, saying she could suggest the real reason in a pause).

In London Selznick was in for some surprises. Renée Asherson had been cast as Stella and a young Canadian, Bernard Braden, as Mitch. Stanley was difficult to cast; even had Brando been available it is unlikely that Olivier would have wanted to redirect him and while Beaumont's shrewd casting director Daphne Rye had suggested a then-unknown Stanley Baker, he chose a young American resident in London who had made some British films. Bonar Colleano was very different from Brando, wiry and whippet-lean (he was from a family of Italian acrobats) and certainly not physically threatening. As for the other roles Selznick had not anticipated Olivier's sense of *droit de seigneur* theatrical power:

> There were no auditions, even for accents. Larry summoned whom he chose and interviewed them in Binkie's own office while Binkie and I sat in the next room.

There were no production meetings in advance. Olivier had opted to use the Broadway set design by Jo Mielziner, an inspired fusion of realism and the abstract, incorporating some beautifully painted gauzes, all tuned to what Kazan called "a poetic tragedy", but he unaccountably rejected the costume designs of Lucinda Ballard, choosing Bumble Dawson instead. This was a cardinal error; Dawson was certainly gifted but knew little of American fashions of the play's background and Vivien's costumes were mostly misconceived, crucially missing that vital sense of Blanche dressing to fit her image of herself as an aristocratic Southerner. The tailored look provided by Dawson, using inferior materials, made Blanche look cheap; some reviews even suggested she had turned to prostitution back in Mississippi when the Du Bois plantation, Belle Reve, had to be sold, overlooking the desolating loneliness which drove her to promiscuity (but not prostitution). Vivien was in a difficult position; Dawson was a friend but she tended then to defer to her director/husband in such areas.

She was mostly obedient under his direction in early rehearsals. Olivier devoted oddly little space to *Streetcar* in *Confessions*, stressing only that his help to Vivien was essentially technical, pushing her to the lower vocal register which they both felt was right for Blanche. He had originally gone into more detail when working with Mark Amory, the writer with whom he initially collaborated on his memoirs. On tape with Amory he made the vainglorious claim:

> If it hadn't been for me Vivien would have been no good in *Streetcar* ... You sometimes need a guy who knows what the fuck he's talking about and can tell you how to get it, and whatever else I am, I know a hell of a lot about the business. I'm very, very good at giving people the right advice.

This material was not included in the published *Confessions*. And before long Vivien was not always biddable. Bernard Braden had been instantly struck by

PLATE 1 Vivien Leigh as a child with her mother, c.1922.

PLATE 2 *In the Mask of Virtue's* eighteenth century costume, 1935.

PLATE 3   Vivien Leigh and Laurence Olivier in *Fire Over England*, 1937.

PLATE 4 Angus McBean surrealising Vivien Leigh as Aurora, 1938.

PLATE 5 Vivien Leigh as Aurora, 1938.

PLATE 6   Scarlett O'Hara and Rhett Butler with Victor Fleming on the set of *Gone With the Wind*, 1939.

PLATE 7   Vivien Leigh at the Oscars with David O. Selznick.

PLATE 8 Vivien Leigh and Laurence Olivier as Romeo and Juliet from *The Sketch*, 1940.

PLATE 9   Sabina in *The Skin of Our Teeth*, 1945.

PLATE 10   Kieron Moore and Vivien Leigh in *Anna Karenina*, 1948.

PLATE 11   Watercolour of Vivien with cat by Roger Furse.

PLATE 12 Laurence Olivier and Vivien Leigh leaving Australia, 1948.

PLATE 13 Vivien Leigh, Peter Finch and Laurence Olivier in Australia.

PLATE 14   Durham Cottage painted by Felix Kelly.

PLATE 15   Notley Abbey painted by John Piper.

PLATE 16   The Library at Notley.

PLATE 17   Vivien Leigh and Laurence Olivier relaxing at Notley.

PLATE 18   Vivien Leigh, Leigh Holman, Ernest Hartley, Tarquin, Suzanne, and Olivier's legs (from right) at Notley.

PLATE 19   Shakespeare's *Antony and Cleopatra*, 1951.

PLATE 20   Kenneth Tynan and Elaine Dundy at their wedding.

PLATE 21   Vivien Leigh with Tennessee Williams and Elia Kazan in *A Streetcar Named Desire*, 1951.

PLATE 22 Vivien Leigh and Laurence Olivier in *Macbeth*, 1955.

PLATE 23 Vivien Leigh and Keith Michell in *Twelfth Night*.

PLATE 24   Yves Saint-Laurent sketch of Dior's design for Vivien Leigh in *Duel of Angels*, 1958.

PLATE 25   Vivien Leigh with Claire Bloom in *Duel of Angels*, 1958.

PLATE 26   Vivien Leigh and Jack Merivale, 1960.

PLATE 27   Vivien Leigh and Warren Beatty in *The Roman Spring of Mrs Stone*, 1961.

PLATE 28   As Marguerite Gautier
in *The Lady of the Camellias*, 1961.

PLATE 29   Vivien Leigh and Laurence Olivier greeting Marilyn Monroe, 1955.

PLATE 30　John Gielgud and Vivien Leigh in *Ivanov*, 1966.

PLATE 31　Vivien Leigh double portrait by Angus McBean.

her ("I'd thought her beautiful on screen but was totally unprepared for the personal impact") and by her no-nonsense approach to long and often arduous rehearsals. She wore a simple black jersey dress each day (when Renée Asherson complimented her on it on the first day she replied "I'm glad you like it because you'll be seeing a lot of it"), not wanting to waste time choosing clothes each day, the more to focus on rehearsals only (her diary records few social engagements for that period). Soon Braden, as much in awe of Olivier as the other actors, realised that something was wrong: "Our distinguished director was systematically altering the script and, on occasions, cutting it." The one person who argued, said Braden, was Vivien and not exclusively about her own part; she fought hard ("They went at it hammer and tongs") to make him retain Stella's lines articulating her feelings for Stanley ("There are things that happen between a man and a woman – in the dark – that make everything else seem unimportant") which Olivier wanted to cut (for some reason he feared they might get a laugh) while Vivien insisted they were crucial lines. She liked Asherson and realised that she was creating a strong Stella, which could only help her own performance. Braden, who had seen the Broadway production, came to grasp that although he knew Olivier to be "a brilliant man of the theatre" there was a problem on *Streetcar* – "he didn't understand the play and Vivien did".

There were various aspects of *Streetcar* with which Olivier was uneasy. Possibly his *pudeur*, for all his liberal use of every possible four-letter word, had something to do with his seeming inability fully to engage with the play. Having accepted the Broadway design he now felt straitjacketed by it, as if he were climbing into Kazan's wet bathing-suit (in the end he acknowledged this with the credit "After the Broadway production" in the programme). Most crucially he could never find the dimensions mined by Kazan, who had from the outset perceived that beyond the personal clashes in the play Williams was dramatising a wider conflict; Blanche, trapped in her inherited notion of what an "ideal" Southern woman should be, something not possible to be accommodated in postwar American society, resorts increasingly to fantasy to become the emblem of a decaying civilisation and inevitably is destroyed by the more brutish elements of modern urban America as she makes what Kazan called "her last curlicued and romantic exit". Olivier could not accommodate this whereas Vivien, who had read extensively (as she did on *Gone With the Wind*), including W.J. Cash's *Mind of the South*, saw past the bones of Williams's plot.

The vein of comedy in *Streetcar* also baffled Olivier. Williams rightly stressed that Blanche should inspire a catharsis of pity and terror in the sense of classical tragedy, but he mined (as in much of his work) a valuable seam of comedy running through much of the play, allowing an audience to comprehend Stanley's viewpoint as well as Blanche's ("Blanche is not an angel without a flaw and Stanley's not evil" he had told Kazan) until, after her past has gradually leaked into the play and Stanley's plan for payback is plain, that audience begins to realise that it is "sitting in at the death of something extraordinary". Directors not infrequently, treating Williams over-reverently, miss this fusion – the critic Michael Billington has written especially perceptively of the dramatist's special interweaving of even his most tragic themes with a comedic strain; Williams would have loved *The Simpsons'* hilarious version with Marge's Blanche.

A scene which Olivier begged Williams to allow him to cut heavily (Vivien did not agree), a scene with a delicate equipoise of pathos and comedy, as Blanche and Mitch return to the Kowalski apartment after an evening out (he boasts of his "lightweight alpaca" jacket, she teases the uncomprehending Mitch in French), leading to her admission of her husband's death and the guilt she feels, was an instance of Olivier's inability to accept this aspect of the play. Walter Matthau, just beginning his career in 1947, noted of *Streetcar*:

> There were half a dozen men in Broadway comedies that season and Brando got more hoots and chortles than all of them.

Blanche, who is also not without irony, likewise becomes a richer character because of Williams's ability to fuse comedy with his serious theme.

That much of *Streetcar*'s density of texture had gone missing was immediately clear to Selznick when she and Beaumont – who had been allowed to attend the first reading but no subsequent rehearsals – were finally admitted to a late run-through. What upset Selznick even more was that much of the play itself was missing; Olivier had made some major cuts, despite Vivien's frequent objections (the other actors, of course, dared not contradict their director and part-employer). Selznick's reaction made Beaumont realise at once that this was a major crisis, not an incidental issue, and he called a summit meeting at his Lord North Street house for that evening, attended by both Vivien (which Selznick naturally found awkward – what she had to say would criticise Vivien's performance under her husband's direction) and Olivier. It was not an easy evening; Olivier did not greatly appreciate criticism of his work and he felt that "Dame Irene" as he called her (behind her back – in person it was "Darling") was far too protective of her author (although Williams, learning of the cuts, had cabled his distress). According to Selznick she "talked for two hours, scarcely drawing breath", outlining not just her concern at the cuts but her fear that Williams's play was in real jeopardy, that Olivier's misconceptions had "left the piece merely lurid". Vivien said very little but listened intently and Olivier realised that he too would have to listen; Selznick was a forceful figure, used as Louis B. Mayer's child to command (allegedly when Beaumont reminded her that the Oliviers were King and Queen of the theatre she shot back "I am the daughter of an Emperor!"), and her passion for Williams's work was palpable.

The meeting did clear the air to some extent although Selznick was later told by Vivien that she and Olivier had been up until six in the morning, arguing. It has to be assumed that Vivien agreed more with Selznick than Olivier; more lines were restored in Manchester and Selznick was happier with what she saw. However Olivier did not give up attempts to have more cuts – in a long letter to Williams from Manchester he implored to be allowed to lose a big part of Blanche's speech to Stella urging her not to "fall back with the apes" while Stanley, unnoticed, overhears; again he fretted about possible audience laughter, although the episode is deliberately on a knife-edge, catching an audience between wind and water, exactly as Williams had intended. Terry Coleman betrayed a surprising lack of understanding of the theatre in describing Olivier's pleading Manchester letter as demonstrating an example of his theatre-knowledge and craft "which themselves amount to genius," not a view shared by Tennessee Williams.

For Selznick "*Streetcar* in London wasn't what it might have been, either artistically or critically", although it was an immediate box-office success. Many London critics treated one of the great plays of the twentieth century as a sordid shocker although Vivien's personal notices were mostly excellent; Tynan, who suggested that in light of Olivier's poor production (a rare criticism of his idol) the play should be retitled *A Streetcar Named Vivien*, described Blanche as "a bored nymphomaniac". He never quite "got" Williams's work and in the Aldwych *Streetcar* felt that the comedy was misplaced, falling into the same trap as Olivier. Others described *Streetcar* as merely "flyblown melodrama" or "a tedious and squalid anecdote". Few saw past the inadequacies of production or casting; although the Stella/Blanche relationship was strong – Vivien and Asherson, who had an intriguingly enigmatic quality, worked well together – Vivien had little to play off against Colleano's diminished figure or the bland Mitch from Braden.

Vivien's Blanche impressed – and surprised – many friends and colleagues with the sheer emotional punch of the performance. Diana Cooper saw it early in the run; afterwards it took her, she said, "half an hour to un-freeze":

All due to your heart and body-shaking performance. I'd heard of course that it was extraordinary but I didn't know how dreadfully magnificent it was until now.

Coward, seeing it with a "beastly audience" thought her "magnificent", her novelist-friend Rosamond Lehmann was fascinated by Vivien's "increasingly pre-occupied" Blanche retreating into herself as disaster begins to crowd in on her and Vivien especially valued the opinion of Athene Seyler, an esteemed actress who also wrote a perceptive book on acting:

You gave the character such dignity, such a sense of fastidiousness, such pathos of weakness and a kind of hidden purity that I am still thinking of the play as if it were a glowering dark long sunset when one sometimes sees a streak of pale light across the clouds.

There had been voices advising Vivien against tackling the play, less for artistic reasons than for fear that such a searing study of a mind slipping into madness might have a baleful effect. The most vocal in opposition was Alan Dent, whose Scottish Presbyterian conscience never adjusted to Williams's gallery of lost souls ("*Streetcar* is NOT a play for Vivien" he insisted, calling it variously tawdry, cheaply scented and "lickorish"). He chose not to review it but saw it later in the run with a Scottish friend, finding it harrowing ("It was like looking on at some beautiful town being destroyed by an earthquake") although he was no more reconciled to the play. Afterwards, as agreed, he was ushered through the pass door to find Vivien still on stage:

She was shaking like an autumn leaf and her lips were trembling. She clutched me and put her head on my shoulder and said in no more than a whisper "Was I all right? Am I mad to be doing it?"

Self-confessedly inept at conventional backstage banalities, Dent told her that he had sat with "a sterling man from the Outer Hebrides" who had told him he was quite wrong about Blanche because "she has – as he phrased it – the truth in her heart" (echoing Blanche – "I never lied in my heart"):

Eagerly and indeed almost frenziedly Vivien at once replied "But why didn't you bring your friend round with you? He's obviously a better drama critic than you are!"

After eight months at the Aldwych both physical and mental exhaustion were setting in. Cecil Tennant's wife, the ex-ballerina Irina Baranova (Vivien was godmother to the Tennants' daughter, Victoria)used regularly to sit with Vivien in her dressing-room between shows on matinee days during the later part of the run. She often then seemed in low spirits although Irene Selznick, back in London towards the close and aware that Vivien was eager to have her opinion, was able to cheer her: "I was moved by her reaction and could honestly tell her she was wonderful."

The London *Streetcar* had triggered some worrying "episodes". During the later part of the run Vivien would often dismiss her car outside the Aldwych stage door and walk home to Chelsea through Soho, sometimes talking to prostitutes, several of whom had been to see the play. Rumours began to circulate in the gossipy West End world that she at times sought sex with strangers or taxi drivers. Certainly one of the symptoms affecting many with Bipolar can be an extremely heightened libido and there is later evidence of such behaviour from Vivien in random encounters from, among others, her friend Joan Cunliffe, who noted that the condition can make Bipolar sufferers "fiendish about sex" – recalling once being kept waiting for an appointment at Vivien's before she appeared, wet through and "bedraggled, covered in mud... she had been in the square with someone". The pressures of the London production certainly exacerbated aspects of her illness (then still to be diagnosed). It was loneliness and the isolation after Belle Reve's loss, the awareness that "the opposite of death is desire", which saw Blanche drift towards many "little deaths" and "the kindness of strangers"; with Vivien, outwardly far from lonely, it would seem there was some inner desolation, possibly born out of some long-buried trauma or guilt which no doctor or psychiatrist could pinpoint, which drove her to such behaviour, the impulse toward self-degradation erupting through her "normal" control. Of all her roles Blanche was the one which stretched the fragile protective shell of her psyche to the most extreme, twisting it out of shape at times. As with the disconcerting flashes of fury or such outbursts as erupted on *Caesar and Cleopatra* little or no memory of her behaviour would remain.

Still tired, her nerves jangling, after *Streetcar* the first play Vivien wanted to see was T.S. Eliot's *The Cocktail Party*, by which she had been deeply impressed when reading it. Rex Harrison, who played Harcourt Reilly, the confessor-psychiatrist figure of the Uninvited Guest, in London, recalled how markedly struck, comforted even, Vivien had been by the notion, outlined in the play, of having what Eliot called "guardians" in one's life. It remained always a favourite play.

Olivier must have wished for similar successes to Eliot's play to come his way as a producer. LOP had taken a lease on the St James's Theatre, just off the beaten theatrical track, once the distinguished home of actor/manager Sir George Alexander (both *The Second Mrs Tanqueray* and *The Importance of Being Earnest* premiered there), a beautiful, intimate (800 seats) theatre but one which required either capacity houses or plays cheap to run in order to break even. Aiming to recreate its glory days Olivier spent lavishly on redecoration, decking it with extravagant banks of flowers and suggesting white-tie for opening nights, a somewhat backward-looking notion soon abandoned. Opening in early 1950 his first production, one of Christopher Fry's more arcane verse dramas, *Venus Observed*, was given lavish Roger Furse designs and a glittering cast (Olivier starred with Denholm Elliott and Rachel Kempson) but barely broke even. Over the next two years there was the occasional *succès d'estime* but more expensive flops including an Irish-set Anouilh, *Fading Mansions*, unwisely given to Tony Bushell to direct. Money became a problem again very soon and then, providentially, Vivien was offered the film version of *Streetcar*. Originally William Wyler had wanted to direct it starring Bette Davis but was beaten to the post by agent/producer Charles Feldman, who made a distribution deal with Warner Brothers and helped bring Kazan on board (he had then directed five films, recently winning an Oscar for *Gentleman's Agreement*). It was Olivier who worked for Wyler – their first film together since *Wuthering Heights* – when he signed to film *Carrie*, based on Theodore Dreiser's novel *Sister Carrie*, to be shot in Hollywood coincidentally with *Streetcar*. Their combined fees would go a long way towards restoring LOP's by now alarmingly slender bank balance.

Kazan swore that initially he did not want to direct *Streetcar* on screen, saying (politely) that it would be like marrying the same woman twice or (less politely) that he just "couldn't get it up again for *Streetcar*." He also had genuine worries about the extent of compromise which might be required to appease the Breen Office within the restrictions of the Production Code; with rape, homosexuality and promiscuity featuring heavily in a long list of problem areas, the film might have some difficulty in being made at all. Warners, as part of their deal, insisted on some star-casting for such a risky venture; Kazan professed himself saddened by having to inform Jessica Tandy that she would not play Blanche in the film but before long he was convinced that a new actress might galvanise him into reassessing the material for the screen ("I needed a high-voltage shot to get my motor going again"). Vivien's casting gave him the leverage to use virtually all the rest of the Broadway cast in Hollywood. Karl Malden, the Mitch on stage and screen, remarked of this situation:

> Jessica was no star and neither was Brando. But Vivien – she could carry us all ...
> Gadge (Kazan) told me something ... he said the first impression the public gets of
> the woman who's on the screen is fifty per cent of the battle. If Jessica had played it

she would have had to work because she wasn't glamorous. Vivien was Hollywood glamour.

Kazan kept Vivien informed of progress on the film once she was cast. There had been an attempt by Lillian Hellman to develop a "cleaned up" script, quickly jettisoned, and both Kazan and Vivien agreed that a script by Oscar Saul, an experienced Hollywood screenwriter which included "opening out" scenes in Belle Reve, was unsatisfactory. Williams came up with some rather wild suggestions for his own version – a scene with Allan singing in drag, an episode with Blanche in an eerie garden setting amid broken statuary and a sign, This Property is Condemned (later used as a title for another play) – but these were also scrapped as were Kazan's own early thoughts of "opening-out" sequences, although the scene in which Blanche talks to Mitch of Allan was relocated effectively to a foggy lakeside restaurant (studio-shot). The only location work was the opening episode of Blanche's arrival at the railway station in New Orleans, filmed at the end of the whole shoot; just as in her last film Vivien's black-clad Anna Karenina vanished into the steam and smoke of her suicide train, so her Blanche first appears emerging in fluttering white through the hissing locomotive steam, like "a butterfly in a jungle" as Kazan described her. Finally Kazan realised, to Vivien's relief, that although *Streetcar* was dialogue-heavy, it was such rhythmic and vibrant dialogue that all involved should simply trust it.

Vivien and Kazan wrote several times to each other while she was still playing at the Aldwych and he was readying the film. He had not seen the London production (possibly, having been told by Selznick that it was "misconceived", he thought it wiser not to), but he was impressed by Vivien's understanding that Blanche's "look" was so important for one whose shaky sense of identity was built on her self-presentation and also by her insistence that she wanted to look right, with no thought of personal vanity. She wanted – Kazan agreed – thin, fine hair for Blanche, prepared to wear wigs or dye her own hair blonde (finally wigs were made by Stanley Hall of Wig Creations, London's foremost stage-hair expert, and flown back regularly from Hollywood for him to re-dress). Agreeing that her London costumes had not been ideal she readily consented to meet Lucinda Ballard to discuss Blanche's screen wardrobe with less stress on tailoring, aiming for "a little more femininity, something more fragile, what Williams calls 'mothlike'". Kazan also calmed her anxieties about the script, insisting that he would not countenance cutting the rape ("Stanley's final act is to destroy her") or what he and Vivien both agreed was the key scene of Blanche gently teasing a young newspaper-boy:

All this contains is the longing every woman has, in fact, every person has during
moments of great loneliness and despair, for love and closeness and romance ...
Blanche's taste for him is not degenerate but romantic and wistful.

Vivien was as perplexed – and eventually as cross – as Kazan in light of the
seeming inability of Joe Breen (a devout Catholic) to comprehend that
Williams's play involved compassion and the Christian virtue of charity. The
Production Code rivalled the Lord Chamberlain for crassness in suggesting that
"the older man" discovered with Allan should simply be changed to "an older
woman". Both Kazan and Williams fought hard to keep as much of the rape
scene as possible; Williams even wrote to Breen to stress that Stanley's violent
act was a pivotal and integral element in his script without which it would lose
its meaning "which is the ravishment of the tender, the sensitive, the delicate
by the savage and brutal forces in modern society" adding that Vivien ("a great
visiting artist") was "dominating the picture and giving it a stature which
surpasses that of the play". In the end the Breen Office yielded more than
might have been anticipated. Throughout, Kazan played an adroit hand;
conceding on what he felt were relatively minor issues (but pretending to care
deeply) in order to win bigger battles and eventually negotiating a balance
between artistic integrity and the concerns of what the shrewd commercial side
of Kazan described to Jack Warner as "the moist seat department". He would
have further skirmishes with the Legion of Decency but the outcome from the
Breen negotiations marked a decided shift in Hollywood's censorship methods
(Geoffrey Shurlock, a later Production Code head, said "*Streetcar* broke the
barrier – it made us think things through").

    Vivien realised how hard Kazan had fought their corner over the script. And
she was instantly captivated when meeting his choice of Lucinda Ballard when
Warners sent her to London. They met first at an Ivor Novello party which
Ballard entered to find Vivien sitting laughing with Danny Kaye; as Novello
introduced them Vivien at once rose to shake hands and Ballard was
immediately as struck by her "exquisite manners and joyous nature" as by her
flawless beauty. A red-headed independent Southern woman, a descendant of
Confederate President Jefferson Davis, Ballard hit it off at once with Vivien,
who later at the party had the room in a roar recounting the occasion when she
and Bobby Helpmann, presented in their *Midsummer Night's Dream* fairy finery
to the royal family in an Old Vic box during intermission, bowed and curtseyed
so low that their elaborate headdresses locked together, forcing them to leave
the box backwards, still intertwined, still bent double. At Notley the following
weekend, which Ballard found like something out of a vanished Edwardian era,

Vivien liked all the revised costume suggestions, which suggested the bleached, pale delicacy of this fraying woman in an alien world. Especially successful was Ballard's realisation of the old ball gown Blanche wears in her tipsily deluded state prior to the rape, described by Williams as "a worn-out, somewhat soiled, crumpled white satin evening gown", to which the designer added a faded corsage and a dime-store tiara, evocative suggestions of lost grandeur and decay. Always "Cindy" from then on to Vivien, the two women became lifelong friends.

Kazan suggested that Vivien and Olivier fly first to New York to visit him and his wife Molly at their Connecticut house for a weekend to discuss *Streetcar* before flying on to California but Olivier was opening his production of *Captain Carvallo* with Peter Finch at the St James's and planned to follow Vivien to Los Angeles a week later, so Vivien flew alone. Whether Molly Kazan was present in Connecticut is not recorded but according to Kazan's biographer Richard Schickel, Kazan "had an affair with Vivien, about which he later boasted in an ungentlemanly way". Kazan's autobiography makes no mention of this although other affairs are referred to; he may have been deliberately obfuscatory or, given his age when he wrote *A Life*, possibly he misremembered, claiming as he does that Olivier was present that weekend. A brief affair is certainly a possibility – Kazan may have been no Greek god but he was fused by a seemingly inexhaustible energy (like Vivien), understood the potent aphrodisiacs of humour and power and had many affairs throughout his lifetime.

They travelled together by train to Los Angeles where Vivien moved into Feldman's house in Cedarwood Drive – it contained one of Hollywood's finest art collections – which he made available for the Oliviers. Vivien responded to the intense commitment of Kazan at work, delighted to be consulted on deciding what items Blanche might have beside her makeshift bed (an old dance-card, a photograph of Belle Reve she suggested), a level of involvement never countenanced at the Aldwych. She remained deeply fond of him – "I think he sends his clothes out to be rumpled" she said of his famously dishevelled rehearsal outfits of creased chinos and casual shirts, a marked contrast to a contemporary West End where men wore suits and ties and women hats and gloves to rehearsals.

The Oliviers had been absent for almost a decade from a Hollywood which now regarded them as visiting royalty, returning to a strikingly different film colony. Movies had moved on from the world of Dorothy in Oz or Andy Hardy on Main Street, changed irrevocably along with America by a cataclysmic war,

Congressional Investigations into supposed subversion (soon to engulf Kazan), plus the threat of television, and the country in 1950 was facing up to a rescrutiny of The American Dream, probing behind the apparently blandly reassuring Eisenhower era as it shifted into an Age of Anxiety. Kazan sensed this; he was one of the American directors battling hardest for Hollywood to realise a truly adult potential as he scrapped over *Streetcar*, a tussle which charged the film with a commitment which energised everyone involved.

Vivien was still an iconic Hollywood name although she was at pains in the interviews she gave at this time to indicate the differences between the two Southern belles she played. Sisters Blanche and Scarlett may have been under the skin but, as Vivien stressed, one was blonde and the other brunette, one from Mississippi and one from Georgia, one survives like the Tara she saves while the other goes under, lost like Belle Reve with no resources after generations of buccaneering men have squandered her heritage. She and Kazan had had long discussions before filming and seemed to agree on most aspects of Blanche. However, Schickel claims in his biography that Vivien arrived on the Warners' lot "with a desire to teach these Americans something about real acting, English acting" and Kazan said that the enterprise "nearly went blooey" on the first day. Kazan's account described how he insisted on having a mock-up of the set provided to the side of the sound stage with the same dimensions as and similar furniture to the real setting so that he could rehearse while the set-ups were lit (he shot in sequence). Soon during the first rehearsal, in his version, when he suggested something to Vivien she replied "When Larry and I did the play in London...", a testing moment for Kazan with the other actors' eyes on him, sensing a challenge to his authority. He replied ("as gently as I could") that Vivien was not making the film in London with Olivier but in Hollywood with them. He claimed that it took two weeks before she was at ease with him on set, adding ("if you'll forgive the conceit") that those early scenes before she yielded to his authority completely are those in which she appears "most strained". Apart from the fact that they had already spent no little time together discussing the character, the text and the screen evidence go some way to contradict this; those early scenes of Blanche in the Kowalski household are, as in the play, charged with Blanche's theatrics, her attempts to charm and to conceal her dreads and febrile desperation. Vivien is here playing what Williams wrote. Moreover, she was too respectful of other actors – and American actors always commanded her respect – to think that she could condescend to them. Undoubtedly, she was nervous – Jessica Tandy, also British-trained, must initially have felt similarly in a Broadway cast entirely made up of a new American school of dynamic, much less technically based actors. But, like Tandy, Vivien – well before Olivier entered a new theatrical landscape in *The Entertainer* – adapted and adjusted. Kazan went on to admit "Slowly we began to like each other and we became close friends." It developed into a happy set and Vivien was stimulated to be working in such an atmosphere of mutually supportive high-octane energy under Kazan's firecracker personality. Columnists and reporters had predicted tensions, especially between Brando and Vivien, but they got on very well; his wickedly convincing vocal impression of Olivier delighted her and she genuinely found him a thrillingly exciting actor to play opposite, as Kazan noticed, describing them as "two highly charged people exploding off each other". The Blanche/Stella bond was also strong with Kim Hunter finding Vivien a fascinating figure; she had seen *The Skin of Our Teeth* in London ("she was marvellous – a very witty performance") and was surprised by the depth she brought to Blanche, finding her less frail than many often assumed:

> I would say she was a very determined person, was very strong in many respects. The fact that I was totally unaware of any illness during the filming surely says something.

Vivien was certainly happy during *Streetcar* although initially she had longed for Olivier's arrival, bringing Suzanne with him. Olivier too seemed eager to join her, writing before flying "soon OFF to my darling, dear lovely wonderful beloved". Once settled in the house, however, other aspects of a volatile relationship began to surface. Suzanne at 17 was now noticing behind the facade:

> What I remember most was the fights that went on between them – real theatrically pitched arguments behind closed doors. I knew Vivien was naturally high-tempered ... But in spite of the shouting matches it never occurred to me that their marriage was breaking up. It was just too precious to Vivien. I put it down to two overwrought people at the end of long days' work on their separate movies.

There had been suspicions on set that Olivier may have been coaching Vivien in the evenings. Kazan clearly distrusted Olivier's influence over Vivien; in a later letter he suspected she was not totally revealing her true feelings, writing "sounds to me Larry scolded you and said for Chrissake stop being a cunt and be nice to that man. Be your OWN FUCKING PLAIN SELF, WILL YOU?" Possibly, too, it was difficult for Olivier as director of Vivien's stage Blanche to accept how much she seemed to blossom under Kazan while he, although respectful of Wyler, was having a less than joyous experience on *Carrie*. Tensions between married couples, both working, are hardly rare in theatre and film worlds either.

Streetcar remains Vivien's outstanding screen performance, utterly convincing as Williams's emblem of a dying civilisation, totally capturing Blanche's perception of herself as a Southern aristocrat even with her world's trappings gone. She was helped by Ballard's floaty, pale costumes and did not hold back from Blanche's faded appearance. Gordon Bau, the make-up supervisor, gave her all the hollows and lines necessary but kept despairing: "She's just too beautiful, no matter what I do to her" although perceptively he added: "What I can't accomplish with make-up she'll do with acting."

The reviews were remarkable (several finding it even finer than on stage) although Manny Farber, alone among leading contemporary American movie critics, thought Kazan's work flashy while a more recent critic, David Thompson, normally one of the most perceptive around, finds Brando and Vivien performing in different styles. The characters are of course from utterly different worlds but the actor did not find Vivien's work so difficult to adjust to ("one of the great beauties of the screen but she was also vulnerable"). There have been suggestions that Vivien and Brando became lovers – Brando admitted he found her attractive but did not want to invade Olivier's "chicken-coop" – but no scrap of evidence exists to substantiate them. Brando on a few occasions socialised with the Oliviers in Hollywood, especially enjoying a small dinner party they gave shortly before leaving Los Angeles. Later he wrote from New York (dating his letter "Ten years later"... "I always seem to be a trifle tardy with everything, however I eventually arrive") thanking them. He added "Individually you are both extraordinary 'groovy' people and as a marital unit you are in inspiration to all who love." Clearly he had enjoyed his times with them and on *Streetcar*, thanking them for "providing an incentive for my work for which I am, perhaps, the most grateful to you."

Most American actors (Jessica Tandy joined them) agreed with the movie critic Pauline Kael's verdict on the film:

> Vivien Leigh gives one of those rare performances that can truly be said to evoke pity and terror ... you're looking at just about the best feminine performance you're ever going to see.

The movie still grips and shocks today. There have been many subsequent Blanches on stage and television including Bankhead, Uta Hagen, Glenn Close, Claire Bloom, Ann-Margret, Rosemary Harris, Faye Dunaway, Jessica Lange, Cate Blanchett, Rachel Weisz, Natasha Richardson and Gillian Anderson but none has quite matched Vivien's mercurial switches, turning on a dime from elation to frayed desperation, her line readings totally attuned to William's rhythms, capable in the same scene of a delicate lyric grace and a swift, raw rage (as when she turns on an accusatory Mitch to taunt him with her association with the louche Flamingo Hotel which she now renames – "Tarantula! The Tarantula Arms!"). The performance's greatest strength is the way it preserves until a late stage just enough of Blanche's optimism and sense of future possibilities to banish any sense of a preordained solution, making the final scene – Stanley's violent contempt in ripping off her last illusion, the cheap paper shade over a lightbulb, her animal cries and whimpers as the Nurse pins her down before the Doctor prepares her to leave for the Asylum – almost unbearable to watch.

Vivien was tired when filming was over, but exhilarated also from her re-immersion in the modern play she valued above any other and from the experience of working with actors of a different discipline under Kazan, finding the "in the moment" spontaneity of emotion which charges the film with its unusual tension. She knew that despite the cuts (restored later in a remastered version), they had done the author proud (Williams agreed, reported as saying after the New York premiere: "at least one thing I have done has survived with whatever honesty and beauty it had in the beginning, and even more").

Vivien was back at work in London when she began to get word from Feldman of the film's reception, although Kazan had continued to keep her up to date about his negotiations with the Legion of Decency, post-filming (all "toilet water" said Kazan, but "a fucking bore"). A private screening at Warners of a final cut had a starry audience – Cukor, Tracy, Cole Porter, Elizabeth Taylor, Charlie Chaplin, Howard Hawks and Ethel Barrymore included – and Harry Mines of Warners told her "The room was filled with a hushed, emotional silence afterwards" while Feldman wrote "It is a great film. You are absolutely wonderful", adding that Ethel Barrymore had written to him ("I think Vivien Leigh's is the greatest – most moving and varied – performance I've ever seen on the screen").

Vivien had hoped Olivier would have a similarly rewarding experience on *Carrie*, another American classic with a central character on a downward slide, but although Olivier's Hurstwood is often moving, the adaptation diluted Dreiser, and Jennifer Jones, the second Mrs David O. Selznick, was the kind of shallow actress Olivier could not abide (he briskly described her as "a cunt" in a letter to Vivien). But he found Hollywood itself on this occasion rather enjoyable and was able to spend time with friends such as Spencer Tracy (an actor he revered) the Kanins and the Colmans. They were *the* couple to snare for social events and he and Vivien were swamped by invitations although during *Streetcar* and *Carrie* they tended to refuse most, dining out usually just once a week, often *à deux* at the Beachcomber which served the Chinese food they both enjoyed. Danny Kaye and his wife Sylvia Fine had been determined to throw a big function for them, partly in gratitude for the Oliviers' support of Kaye's early London appearances and also thanks for hospitality in London and at Notley, but also an exercise in scalp hunting with the Kayes keen to impress an impressionable town. Eventually Vivien and Olivier accepted and the Kayes went to work to organise what the press called the social event of the season ("People were almost threatening to commit suicide at Vivien's feet if they were not invited" said Cindy). Olivier's friendship with Kaye (there is no concrete evidence, contrary to considerable posthumous speculation born out of baseless gossip, of any gay affair) surprised many, but he enjoyed Kaye's stage act – unpredictable, zany and dangerous (a quality Olivier always found intriguing) – and both men were essentially private people who came most alive before an audience. Vivien also admired Kaye's work (his "Ballin' the Jack" was one of her subsequent radio "Desert Island Discs") and liked Sylvia too. The bash was held in the Crystal Room of the Beverly Hills Hotel, extravagantly decorated, with two orchestras, one to play during supper and the other for dancing. Hollywood was then at its most tribal, a neo-feudal society, and the cost of admission to the A-List was success, represented at the occasion by the Colmans, Kazans, Humphrey Bogart and Lauren Bacall, Errol Flynn, Lana Turner, Ginger Rogers and Spencer Tracy among the great and some less good. Vivien, dazzling in a dark green silk gown, betrayed her unease at what she could not help feeling was a somewhat manufactured occasion only once; Cindy Ballard told the Oliviers that she was engaged to Howard Dietz, news which Vivien greeted by delightedly embracing Cindy in congratulation while Olivier said only "Not that publicity man?", recalling Dietz only as MGM's erstwhile publicity chief from *Gone With the Wind* and not as a leading Broadway talent (his musicals included *The Bandwagon*). Vivien snapped: "Howard Dietz is one of America's finest lyricists" and walked away from her husband, an unusual instance of public disagreement.

Such differences were clearly not the whole story. When Vivien was completing *Streetcar* on location in New Orleans, Olivier, finishing *Carrie* in Hollywood wrote to her: "Oh, my love, I feel like a half-cooked codfish thrown back with the sea when you're not with me." Both had had draining schedules; Vivien, never the happiest flyer, suggested they sail home and so they travelled back (Suzanne had flown home previously) on the *Wyoming*, no luxury liner but a freighter with only a handful of passengers. Olivier in his memoirs describes this as a period when he was at such a low personal ebb that as he stood at the ship's rail he even contemplated suicide (Mark Amory, who recorded interviews with Olivier, believes that feeling was genuine). He certainly had much on his mind, worried about LOP's drooping fortunes at the St James's and, instinctive patriot that he was, he felt that the forthcoming 1951 Festival of Britain demanded some significant contribution from his company. He recalled that for all his depression he and Vivien spent much of the crossing discussing many possible plays. Vivien was also reading a book by a favourite author, F. Scott Fitzgerald, tracing his struggles with alcohol and his mental problems. It was called *The Crack-Up*.

CHAPTER 12

Two on the Nile

The Festival of Britain aimed to celebrate all the positives in a country still marked by the after-effects of a devastating war, to cover achievements and aspirations in science, technology and the arts while slowly, after five years, the nation was beginning to emerge from the grip of austerity. The theatre world was to be included, of course, and LOP's plans would figure strongly.

Plays considered included J.M. Barrie's *Mary Rose*, a tantalising proposition and an eerie, difficult play, several times mooted for LOP but never put into production (there was no challenging part for Olivier), John Ford's Jacobean tragedy *'Tis Pity She's a Whore* and Shaw's *Caesar and Cleopatra*. Vivien had not been satisfied with her screen performance and was drawn to the idea of a stage version although Olivier would have preferred a role more juicy than the Shavian Caesar which he found a touch arid. It was Roger Furse who first suggested the notion of pairing Shaw's play with Shakespeare's *Antony and Cleopatra*; Olivier saw that Vivien looked "quite scared" at the suggestion, initially realising that she would have to span 20 years between the two queens and that Shakespeare's tragedy, overflowing with some of the most challenging, incandescent language of all his plays, would be an awesome venture. Olivier also had qualms; his managerial mind questioned the expense of two large-cast plays, both on an epic scale (although Furse assured him that elements of both sets and costumes could serve both Shaw and Shakespeare) while he too realised the acting challenge. Irving never played Antony, Godfrey Tearle had failed opposite Edith Evans, while later Paul Scofield avoided the part, full of pitfalls. But during a New Year weekend in Paris during which a 'flu-stricken Olivier read through both plays with Vivien he began to respond to the idea of playing two such contrasted roles alternately and persuaded Vivien that Shakespeare as well as Shaw was within her reach. She still had doubts, aware that some thought that possibly she would be over-parted and unable totally to banish a dread that she might let Olivier down. LOP's finances were shaky once more – Notley and LOP gulped down the fat fees from *Streetcar* and *Carrie* ($100,000 and $60,000 respectively) and became even more so when Gian Carlo Menotti's *The Consul*, by which Olivier had been impressed in New York when travelling to Hollywood, presented by LOP, ran up heavy losses despite positive London notices. The firm needed a box-office success, although productions on the scale of the two Cleopatra plays, even at increased prices, would have to play to virtually capacity business throughout the four-month season just to break even.

The box-office telephones rang constantly as soon as the productions were announced, increasing the pressure on the venture and on Vivien; she wrote to Sunny Lash at this time: "I have started to shake all over with fright already so heaven knows what it will be like as the time draws near." She worked even harder than usual, reading extensively on the backgrounds to both plays, covering Plutarch to Thornton Wilder's new novel *The Ides of March* and taking voice lessons from a notable singing coach, George Canelli, who put her through a strict regime of breathing and vocal exercises, often sung, to expand her diaphragm and give her the more expansive resonance which she knew would deepen her portrayals especially of Shakespeare's Cleopatra whose later scenes – full of long, soaring speeches of loss and ecstasy – tax any actor's breath-control.

With two tricky roles to master, Olivier elected not to take charge himself, inviting Michael Benthall to direct, although he was closely involved in all casting and design decisions. Benthall's partner Robert Helpmann was cast as Octavius Caesar (he took enormous pains over his blond wig for this) and, less happily, as Apollodorus in the Shaw, characteristically diverting the company with his acid wit and gossip (Ninette de Valois described him as "cute as a monkey, quick as a squirrel"). A superficially more staid character, a polished old Etonian and Cambridge man, usually at rehearsal impeccably groomed in blazer and crisply pressed trousers, Benthall was just as much a gossip as Helpmann, if less scurrilous. Both were great favourites with Katharine Hepburn (they joined forces for Shaw's *The Millionairess* on stage and on an Australian tour). Benthall could be nervous, evidenced by increased eye-movement (one nickname was "Mick the Blink") and on occasion indecisive although he could stage large-scale scenes efficiently. The company, unusually strong, also included Wilfrid Hyde Whyte (luxury casting as Britannus and

Lepidus), the darkly alluring Maxine Audley and a young Jill Bennett (as Charmian and Iras) along with Peter Cushing, Elspeth March and Dan Cunningham. Roger Furse designed an ingenious set on a revolve, with a dominating Sphinx at the opening of the Shaw which was also used effectively as Cleopatra's Monument at the Shakespeare's close, satisfyingly book-ending the enterprise, with a series of superb costumes by an Old Vic regular, Audrey Cruddas. She came up with sensual, flowing outfits for Shaw's Egypt and a richer, more barbaric look for *Antony and Cleopatra* (with military characters wearing the same uniforms and regalia in both). As Shaw's queen, Vivien went mostly barefoot but to give her more regality and height for the older Cleopatra her costumes were heavier, denser in texture, with thick-soled shoes under long gowns, her wigs dressed and ornamented to suggest imperious command.

Vivien, now as much a master of make-up as Olivier, took special pains to stress the contrasts in her Cleopatras. For the Shaw she used little except a light tanning foundation and rouge to heighten a youthful glow while devising, with the help of an expert from the Max Factor make-up company, an elaborate maquillage for the older Cleopatra, using shading of her jawline, heavier eye make-up and fuller, sensual lips, complementing the weightier jewellery and headdresses Cruddas had designed for that play.

Rehearsals were not always easy. Vivien was popular with the company from the outset, as Maxine Audley recalled ("She took endless trouble with Jill and me particularly, because we went everywhere with her on stage ... It was very tiring but she made it all great fun"). Olivier, of course, had a great deal to concentrate on as actor and LOP's producer, but seemed often remote, even tense, Audley felt: "There were definite undercurrents that she and Larry weren't getting on well", although these undercurrents did not flare up alarmingly in rehearsal. Possibly Olivier was realising that he should have studied both roles in more depth prior to rehearsal; later he admitted that he found neither totally satisfying, mainly because there is comparatively little variety in Caesar while Antony is an elusive tragic hero, often in the play described as a great figure but never actually seen as doing anything especially noble. No actor in recent memory had succeeded in the part. He had also begun to fret over Benthall's ability. There were few qualms about the staging – Benthall was perfectly sound at placing the actors – more ones of interpretation. He seemed to dither over the differences in tone between the plays and was indecisive whenever confronted by any acting problem. Olivier often took against his directors and on this occasion he confided his anxieties to Glen Byam Shaw, who gave him the wise counsel that he had either to let Benthall continue and somehow give him confidence so that the company trusted him or to take over himself at once but not to let the situation drift. Tactfully he elaborated: "You must remember the *enormous* power of your personality, particularly in your own theatre." Finally Olivier opted to retain Benthall but he never felt he had much directorial help. Vivien, gaining confidence daily in the Shakespeare ("like bathing in the sea – one swims where one wants" she said of the verse, while comparing Shaw to boarding a train and just sitting in one's place) was also anxious about Benthall, perhaps made more so by pillow-talk instruction from Olivier. He remained concerned about how the theatre critics ("those bastards") might receive her daring in tackling "the most sacred and exacting of all Shakespeare's female roles", constantly reminding her of technical details, not least yet again the need to lower her vocal register in the Shakespeare.

Although a guaranteed commercial success even prior to opening, Vivien was still trepidatious as she faced two first nights in succession. She was aware that she was on safer ground in the Shaw, knowing the text so well and feeling confident in approaching its ironies and teasing comedy; as on screen, she unerringly traced the growth in Cleopatra from uncertain teenager to a queen seasoned in statecraft.

Olivier always championed Vivien's Shakespearean Cleopatra. To him it was Cleopatra's play (his note for future Antonys was simple – "Cleopatra's got you by the balls"), adding that "Vivien knew how to play the part. She seized it, fashioned it and formed it, then showed us the magic." The only surviving evidence of magic is preserved in some highlights recorded later in the 1950s opposite Peter Finch, then her lover, and perhaps not entirely comparable to the Cleopatra opposite Olivier. But in these extracts it is clear that her voice had a satisfying richness and resonance, most impressively in her speech close to Cleopatra's death as she rhapsodises over the godlike Antony of whom she has dreamed. Even on an old recording with little technical sophistication her handling of these soaring pentameters conveys a voluptuous strength.

Most of the London critics had nothing but praise for the entire undertaking; Ivor Brown, especially focusing on Vivien in his *Observer* notice of both plays, headlined his review "A Lass Unparalleled". Olivier was able to say "So, we were home and dry." Financially that was so. And critically, but for one voice of extreme dissension.

Kenneth Peacock Tynan was then 24. The illegitimate son of Sir Peter Peacock, a pillar of business and civic service in Warrington, and brought up by his mother in Birmingham, a precocious child mad about theatre and cinema from boyhood, he was hungry for fame, success and access to A-List talent, not necessarily in that order. An Oxford undergraduate star, flamboyantly dressed in keeping with his middle name (gold lamé shirts, suits of finest purple doeskin), a mover and shaker in student theatre and journalism deliberately cultivating a provocative persona of languor, even effeteness (although firmly heterosexual) and using his stammer often to effect, he cultivated James Agate, who encouraged his critical ambitions, staged a student First Quarto *Hamlet* and was contracted to write a book of theatre pieces after graduation while directing a repertory theatre at Lichfield. He was sacked – too iconoclastic for its financial backer – from this job but soon, undaunted, was directing at London's then fringe-venues before the *reclame* of the publication of *He That Plays the King* (1950) for which, with characteristic chutzpah, he persuaded one of his heroes, Orson Welles, to write a Preface. In an era which still valued deference, Tynan's lack of any respect was unorthodox to say the least, as he fearlessly laid into contemporary dramatic critics ("H.H." – Agate's successor Harold Hobson on *The Sunday Times* – was not spared) and argued his case for radical change. Personalities which impacted positively on Tynan then included Olivier, Welles, Richardson, Scofield and the director Peter Brook while those who did not included Gielgud, the acting couple of Michael Denison and Dulcie Gray, Eileen Herlie and, attracting particular contumely, Vivien Leigh. Her Lady Anne in *Richard III* was brushed aside as "coldly kittenish" while Sabina was described dismissively as "sweet", adding "when you have said that half a dozen times, you have said everything".

Tynan, of course, like many ambitious young meteors, wanted to make a name for himself in a hurry and he cared not at all if he damaged reputations or bruised egos in doing so. He had continued to direct, although his own ego suffered no small dent when he was sacked again, this time from a production of Cocteau's *Les Parents Terribles* at the Arts Theatre run by actor Alec Clunes, when the star, Fay Compton, felt strongly after opening pep-talks and early rehearsals that while Tynan undeniably could talk the talk, he seemed unable to walk the walk and Clunes fired him. Few theatrical ventures followed for the aspirant *homme du théâtre* although he acted in Alec Guinness's Festival of Britain *Hamlet*, which had a jinxed first night and received poor reviews, one of which, from the *Evening Standard* critic (and Tory MP) Beverley Baxter, whose wife was a friend of Vivien's (their daughters shared parties), singled out Tynan's Player King for special obloquy. Tynan wrote to the *Standard* in reply with a combative letter much enjoyed by the features editor, Charles Curran, who commissioned several profiles from him. They included an ambivalent piece on Charles Laughton using (surprisingly and by no means for the last time) that shopworn critical tactic of quoting the opinion of "a friend" or "as someone said".

His piece on Vivien was the most trenchant, particularly so of her Shakespearean Cleopatra, describing her as "presenting a glibly mown lawn where her author had imagined a jungle", slipping in a reference to her age ("approaching forty ... she had already reached the height of her powers"), and again using the technique of quoting anonymous others ("'She plays it,' as someone said, 'with her little finger crooked'"). He went further, angering Olivier immeasurably, with the implication that he saw Vivien as a handicap to Olivier's talents. His hero, with "curious chivalry", was taming his mighty power on stage to avoid overshadowing her. Olivier considered that this impugned his professional integrity. His Antony had been far from a failure; most critics had found much of it extremely fine, lacking only that sense of a former, world-bestriding magnificence and warrior charisma. Olivier never would reduce his stage amperage for anyone, Vivien included – any possible lack of magnetism in his Antony had nothing to do with conjugal deference. It was more than gallantry which lay behind his opinion of her performance:

> She was brilliant, and in my opinion the best Cleopatra ever. She was radiant and beautiful and shone through the lines as if they had been specially written with her in mind.

It should be stressed that Tynan had a dubious theory about Cleopatra. He asserted on several occasions that the part was beyond the range of Anglo-Saxon actresses, incapable of its mercurial shifts of emotion or of its erotic passion. This lofty kind of *obiter dicta* surfaced again when Peggy Ashcroft received his lash for her Stratford Cleopatra, with Tynan insisting only a European actress was capable of properly inhabiting the role (thank you, Judi Dench, Glenda Jackson, Barbara Jefford, Helen Mirren, Vanessa Redgrave, Janet Suzman, Josette Simon, Maggie Smith *et al* – we'll let you know).

It is more telling, in properly considering Vivien's Cleopatra, *contra* Tynan, to turn to the verdicts of colleagues rather than to other critics. Gielgud, who had harboured doubts in advance, described it as her "finest classical performance". Peggy Ashcroft, never given to facile praise, wrote to Vivien of "how very, *very* much I enjoyed your exquisite Cleopatra". Robert Donat also wrote: "I shall never forget your last scene – its music and its serene yet tragic loneliness", while for Sybil Thorndike, Vivien was "more like what I'd imagined Cleopatra than any other I've ever seen – vicious and noble and exciting".

Antony and Cleopatra drew fashionable London, especially popular with Bloomsbury and with writers and scholars. Raymond Mortimer, the *Sunday Times* literary critic, another not easy to please, did not know Vivien well but was moved to write:

> I came out of the theatre hardly able to speak, I had been so moved … I never expected to see the Cleopatra I imagine whenever I read the play – and there she was. The variety you brought to the part was infinite. Nothing could be more brilliant than your scene with the Messenger, it seemed; then you outdid yourself on the Monument, an incomparably exacting scene.

John Steinbeck, visiting London, enthused "These two evenings are by far the finest thing that has ever happened to me in the theatre." Jamie Hamilton published J.D. Salinger in the UK and brought him to both plays; Salinger wrote to Vivien that the Shakespeare in particular had been "a very special evening", enclosing a copy of *For Esmé with Love and Squalor* as thanks (Vivien was a fervent Salinger fan, converting many friends including Gielgud) and Hamilton added "Jerry Salinger lost his heart to you." Vivien was especially touched by Glen Byam Shaw's opinion; no great Benthall admirer, he found that the performances transcended any production faults and had only one criticism of Vivien's Shakespearean performance, feeling that the early scenes needed more sensuality (Olivier was, he found, too battle-weary too early) although judging her "incandescent" in the closing passages. The writer and biographer Christopher Sykes, who said he had read his favourite play "at least 30 times", also was dazzled by the later scenes in particular:

> As for your last act, the uninitiated can only gasp and goggle and wonder how the deuce it is done.

Sykes was one of many who wrote to protest to the *Evening Standard* after Tynan's piece appeared in July; he said it "disgusted" him – "not only because it was clearly calculated to cause you pain but because it was *bosh*". She had not heard from Tony Guthrie – usually peripatetic – for some time but he too wrote to her, calling her "Dear Girl":

> I feel so insulted by the article by a Mr. Tynan as if … as if … words fail me. No one is on any account to HIT him because that is what he CRAVES.

Newspaper editors like controversy, meat and drink to Tynan. The press was changing as he entered journalism. While, slowly, the country began to inch away from austerity, newspapers became less reverent, less deferential in a predominantly still class-bound Britain, prefiguring changes soon to filter into a theatrical landscape which Tynan viewed as ossified, almost wilfully escapist, ready for demolition and rebuilding. He would rarely directly criticise Olivier, of whom he remained virtually always in unconditional awe. His first wife, the effervescent actress and writer Elaine Dundy (*The Dud Avocado*, her first novel, was a major success), American-born and astute, later suggested that there was a hidden agenda to Tynan's attacks on Vivien, in his eyes an unworthy consort for his hero:

> From the first I saw Ken not as a man surrendering himself body and soul to his idol but as a man cannily campaigning for a big job with his idol.

This was written after Dundy's divorce from Tynan and may be wisdom in hindsight to a degree. But Tynan knew of Olivier's shattered hopes of leading the Old Vic into becoming a National Theatre. He campaigned publicly and with maximum publicity himself on behalf of a National Theatre. And eventually he did work alongside Olivier when at last the National Theatre opened with Olivier as its first Director and Tynan his close ally as Literary Manager. His antipathy to Vivien is surely rooted in his hero-worship (it was nothing less) of Olivier, who summed it up neatly years later. Tynan's second wife and biographer, Kathleen, interviewing Olivier for her book after her husband's death, having read for the first time his earlier assessments of Vivien's work and shocked by their harshness, had Olivier's explanation that for Tynan "Vivien came between me and my fucking genius".

Tynan's power increased when he replaced Baxter as the *Standard*'s theatre critic and the theatre world realised that now there was a hungry big beast in the West End jungle. The iconoclast energetically laid about things, attacking the woefully unadventurous spirit of London producers (he was rarely savage to Beaumont, however) and the dearth of work seriously plugged into contemporary British society. Vivien, beautiful, admired, a fashion icon, mistress of Notley, made a good whipping-girl, emblematic of all that in his eyes stamped British theatre with a surface sheen cloaking no real substance. Soon Coward, Rattigan and Emlyn Williams would suffer under Tynan's scourge in his seductively sizzling prose. A prime sufferer, Gielgud expressed that best ("It's wonderful when it isn't you").

Tynan's dismissal of her Cleopatra hurt Vivien deeply although she seemingly took it on the chin as actors must, continuing to try to improve her Cleopatra in Shakespeare's play particularly. Byam Shaw, seeing it for a second time, assured her that she had fully incorporated his note about the opening, now playing it much more from "below the waist", with more abandoned sexuality. As he said, one of the strongest aspects of her performance was her ability to convey Cleopatra's overwhelming physical appetite for Antony, describing her as "sublime" in the latter part of the play, admitting that he wept:

> What you did for me was to make me realise that the love between a man and a woman can be more important than anything else in the world and this is something far beyond tears.

The "establishment" aura about "The Oliviers" which irked Tynan (Olivier's glorious talent absolved him to a degree) was amply illustrated during the St James's run by a visit to both plays from Churchill and, later, an invitation to a dinner given by him ("By Jove, she's a clinker!" was his verdict on Vivien). Vivien's diary also records a Sunday lunch at Chartwell later in the summer, when he gave her the rare gift of one of his paintings, a study of her favourite roses in a vase, a picture which always thereafter hung in her bedroom. "The Oliviers" also joined Danny Kaye, the trio dressed in Edwardian sailor-suits, to perform the Howard Dietz/Arthur Schwartz number "Triplets", a show-stopper at 1951's charity show *Night of 100 Stars* at the Palladium. Hollywood came calling when Selznick mooted a film of Vivien's favourite F. Scott Fitzgerald novel, *Tender is the Night*; Olivier was drawn to the role of Dick Diver and by the thought of Vivien's ideal casting as his damaged wife Nicole, but his interest evaporated when Selznick explained that much as he would love the idea of Vivien in a David O. Selznick film once again, he loved that of the second Mrs Selznick (Jennifer Jones) more. The film emerged, sadly, a gelidly costly failure.

The two Cleopatras, expensive to run, only just inched into profit at the St James's and so, largely encouraged by Cecil Tennant, a limited New York season was arranged, involving most of the London company. It would be Vivien's first Broadway appearance since *Romeo and Juliet*; she seemed genuinely enthused by the plans, beforehand enjoying a late summer holiday, invited by Korda to join him, his Greek-born third wife Alexa, Graham Greene (who had written in glowing terms of Vivien's *Streetcar* screen performance) and Margot Fonteyn on board his yacht *Elsewhere*, stylish and sleek with a luxurious blue-and-white interior design, on a cruise through the Aegean before sailing through the Mediterranean. Korda's young nephew Michael remembered the trip well in his *Charmed Lives*:

> Charm was Vivien's secret weapon as if the nuns had drummed it into her along with cleanliness and good manners. She went swimming and fishing with me, played gin rummy with Alexa, inspected the engineer and took to the helm at the captain's direction, charming the poor man so effectively that we made our landfall in Corsica at least twenty miles off course.

He remembered his uncle benevolently smiling as the yacht tossed during heavy winds, saying Vivien was "the only person in the world who could be charming while she was throwing up".

The company of *Two on the Nile*, as the Cleopatra plays were dubbed on Broadway, travelled by sea on the *Mauretania*. Everything seemed to promise a golden time in New York; the advance bookings at the Ziegfeld Theatre were encouragingly strong, *Streetcar* was performing well in cinemas and, as a couple, Vivien and Olivier were returning to New York as theatrical royalty. Rather than stay in a hotel they moved into Gertrude Lawrence's East 60s apartment at her invitation (remembering her appearance as the volatile Amanda in *Private Lives* with Olivier as her second, ill-used spouse: "That's the least I can do for the poor husband I walked out on twenty-one years ago" she said).

Their reception in New York was rapturous, the notices highlighting the way that in this presentation Shaw acted as a witty prologue to Shakespeare. *The New York Times*'s Brooks Atkinson admired Vivien's Shakespearean performance in particular, describing her beauty as no surprise but adding:

> It is a pleasure to report that she also has captured the infinite variety of the ruler of the Nile. She is smouldering and sensual, wily and treacherous but she is also audacious and courageous ... she does not go down whimpering but with pride and glory, grave and triumphant.

Colleagues were equally enthusiastic. Robert Sherwood "never dreamt *Antony and Cleopatra* could be so well done" while Lynn Fontanne wrote "Vivien, you knocked me cold with wonder." But none of this seemed to bring Vivien much delight and slowly, to Olivier's dismay, she began to slip into a worryingly depressed state. He had noticed a change "imperceptibly at first" on the voyage on board the *Mauretania* when her behaviour was unexpectedly timid, seeking his protection, to him a new kind of attitude, "like a slightly frightened daughter"; initially Olivier found this pleasing, giving him a kind of paternal feeling of happiness, although he wondered if possibly the prospect of Broadway was making her nervous. The opening nights just before Christmas to an audience like a *Who's Who* of American stage and screen, made them the most celebrated pair in New York, with endless press coverage, reunions with friends (the Lunts, Korda, who retracted his reservations about Vivien in Shakespeare, Sunny Lash) and showers of invitations; Diana Vreeland of *Vogue* described Vivien's arrival at a New Year party: "Only England could have produced her ... she was so terribly good-looking. She had an air of exquisite unreality about her."

But while Vivien seemed in radiant spirits backstage when her *Streetcar* Oscar was presented (Olivier was photographed kissing her in congratulation – his old flame Greer Garson collected the award on Vivien's behalf at the Hollywood ceremony), she was sinking into one of her worst "episodes" of depression, detached from reality, to date. The Lawrence apartment, interior-designed to the nth degree in almost 50 shades of grey (slate, smoke, steel etc.), including walls and carpets, unsurprisingly for one who loved colour seemed to depress her and Olivier, who was then commuting to Philadelphia to oversee the Broadway-bound production of *Venus Observed*, with Rex Harrison and Lilli Palmer, regularly found her sitting on the bed "wringing her hands and sobbing, in a state of great distress". Despite the break on Korda's yacht she had been physically below par; it seemed to be a form of laryngitis, most likely psychosomatic, although possibly it was linked to another flare-up of the patch on her lung caused by her tuberculosis – not helped by heavy smoking – which tended to occur whenever she was run down or unusually stressed. Soon she was, according to Irene Selznick, "in a pitiful state". She had seen a doctor who prescribed antibiotics for her throat (to Suzanne she had written, sounding blithe enough, "my days are spent in bed wondering just what kind of noises are going to emerge at night!") but then refused any further treatment and carried on at the Ziegfeld.

The camera and the photographer's eye can detect signs beneath the surface. That Vivien was seriously ill at this time was confirmed by the photographer Philip Halsman, commissioned by *Life* magazine to take the photographs for a feature on the Oliviers. Halsman had heard that Vivien suffered from tuberculosis but was still taken aback by her frailty when she arrived at his studio although the session, he thought, went well:

> Her features were exquisite, she was full of gentle charm and friendliness and at the end of the sitting I had the feeling that I was photographing something very unusual: an angel-like star.

He saw a startling contrast when looking at his developed film, images not of an ethereal angel but "a tired and sick young woman". He took more photographs with different lighting the next day – Vivien wore more make-up – and although Halsman did not normally show his work to his subjects he took them to the Waldorf Astoria (the Lawrence greys had finally proved too much) where, Halsman was aware, she spent most of each day in bed under doctor's orders ("I felt a pang of sadness seeing her pale and emaciated in the huge hotel bed"). He had been pleased by his work on the second sitting but Vivien disliked them so intensely that she tore the prints up, threatening that she would tell her friend Henry Luce of *Life* if Halsman attempted to have any published. Later the press officer on *The Two Cleos*, Dick Haney, called Halsam to tell him Vivien had not noticed the contact-prints inside the envelope which Olivier had found and thought wonderful, telling Halsman to make new prints and submit them to *Life*. Halsman's images were used on the cover and to run with the feature. Five years later in London he was asked to photograph Vivien for a double-portrait with Olivier. As he entered her dressing-room she rose to greet him, saying what a pleasure it was to see him again, "with an angel-like smile".

Wilfrid Hyde White was also fascinated by Vivien – he was less fond of Olivier whose remoteness unsettled him – admiring her discipline ("never once late for long rehearsals") and her extraordinary resolution:

> She was ill during the New York run – shivering with weakness while waiting for her cue. When it came she shook off all symptoms and even knowing how ill she was one could not detect any deterioration in her performance.

For Broadway a young Alec McCowen had taken over the minor role of the Messenger in Shakespeare's play. For him it was a dream job; he had visited New York briefly once previously, falling in love with the city and being impressed by American acting and by *Streetcar* on Broadway. He too found Olivier somewhat distant but loved acting with Vivien, who gave no indication of resentment at having to rehearse with a new actor:

> She was always in the moment, even when she was physically under par and there were nights when I could see in the wings how weak she was. And I must have done something right – Olivier had cut the play with the Shakespeare expert John Dover Wilson and in London a chunk of the Messenger scene was cut. But Vivien had him put back the lines, which made the scene even better, certainly for me and I think it made Vivien even more mercurial in the scene. To be on stage with her she was frightening in the rage with the Messenger for bringing unwelcome news – she really had a go at me, spitting and scratching. I thought she was lovely in the Shaw. It's not an easy play – I've done it – but she was delightful and funny and cunning. But I thought she was really wonderful in the Shakespeare – I've done that too, a dreadful Antony, but she was easily the best Cleopatra I've seen. Majestic at the end.

Still Vivien seemed to be in distress off stage, worrying Olivier further when she became "abnormally nervous" about the couple's social reputation, in the grip seemingly of "some strange obsession" which she could not articulate. After much persuasion, advised by Irene Selznick, she most reluctantly allowed Olivier to take her to see a psychiatrist, an awful experience for both

("Her hysterical terror of photographers as we entered and as we left the doctor's was distressingly pathetic" remembered Olivier in *Confessions*).

Psychiatry was becoming something of a growth industry in Manhattan, with many fashionable practices opening from the late 1930s onwards. Gertrude Lawrence's most recent musical success had been in the Kurt Weill/ Ira Gershwin/Moss Hart *Lady in the Dark*, which grew out of Hart's experiences of psychoanalysis under Dr Lawrence Kubie whose opening phrase at a session ("I am listening") was the show's original title and remains its opening line. Hart was always deeply grateful to Kubie and claimed he helped him enormously to understand and then deal with his psychological problems but Kubie has had some poor posthumous press. Gore Vidal knew of him through his treatment of Tennessee Williams and had a low opinion of psychiatry in general and of Dr Kubie, describing the former with characteristic patrician disdain as a "peculiar calling" and the latter, in a much-discussed piece in *The New York Review of Books* as "a slick bit of goods on the make among the rich, the famous, the gullible". This was unfair; Kubie had decided views, not least on the training of psychiatrists, and agreed with Freud's belief that hysterical disturbance is rooted in the recollection of childhood suffering, but he was highly respected (his book *Neurotic Disorder of the Creative Process* (1959), was regarded as a key text). John Lahr, Williams's biographer, argued that Kubie was in fact a most impressive figure who helped Williams see and understand the story of his family.

The visit to Kubie frustratingly led nowhere. Vivien did not respond to his gentle approach and questions. When he asked her about her childhood she simply laughed and replied "You tell me about your childhood and I'll tell you about mine", then clammed up although revealing to Kubie as she left her dread of any publicity about her visit. The single session with Kubie yielded no results and Vivien resisted, claiming horror of publicity but more likely dreading the slightest possibility of being institutionalised, any suggestion of a return visit or of consulting another psychiatrist. Kubie, on the other hand, remained seriously worried about what he described as her "explosive" state of mind; when she had a more devastating breakdown two years later he took the trouble to write to Olivier in London and advise on possible doctors and courses of action. Olivier cannot be blamed for Vivien's illness – only then beginning to be described and diagnosed as manic depression – but a problem was that like many of his generation he found psychiatry somehow suspect, smacking of quackery. He said that when in contact with American psychiatrists especially he felt "I might be a creature from another planet".

Possibly his suspicions were connected to his sister Sybille's mental problems, rarely mentioned and passed over in *Confessions*. In 1929, Sybille, then married to Gerald Day and living in Hertfordshire, suffered a breakdown about which Day subsequently published a book, *River of Damascus* (under his own name but changing Sybille's – she is "Sylvia" in his account). He described how his young wife "became suddenly insane", given up as incurable after a period of bizarre behaviour when she would use elaborate hand gestures "like a priestess in a third-rate melodrama". Friends and a local doctor suggested she was either simply hysterical or "putting it on" while a London doctor diagnosed her condition as "delusional depression". Like Olivier subsequently, Day felt helpless and guilty:

> As if she were in a wizard's castle lying under an evil spell – I was the Prince who should have rescued her but I had failed.

Sybille eventually recovered, helped greatly, according to Day, not by "conventional" psychiatry such as existed in England in 1929 but by the Guild of Spiritual Healing. Olivier took no heed of Sybille's advice that he should at least explore such treatment for Vivien (and of course possibly she would have refused to participate) but, like Day, he also remained somewhat wary of "shrinks", a suspicion not then uncommon and born out of a fusion of distrust and Anglo-Saxon embarrassment, itself largely due to the stigma attached to mental illness and the sheer lack of understanding in England of what it involved.

In place of any further treatment for Vivien, Olivier arranged a holiday to follow the Broadway run, staying with Coward at his house in Jamaica. Coward was close to both (according to Graham Payn – "never one to take sides he was more fond of her than of Larry") but he too tended to be uncomfortable with mental illness (despite earlier nervous breakdowns of his own) and at times lost patience with Vivien, ascribing her troubles simply to alcohol or exhaustion. But he was delighted to be their host on this visit and listened attentively as Olivier confided his concerns about Vivien and then, revealing his misunderstanding of the real trouble:

> Had a long talk with Vivien and tried to convince her that nervous exhaustion is the result of physical exhaustion and that she needs a long rest. I love her and can't bear to think of her being unhappy inside.

Unaware of the depth of the problem when she reassured him that she was absolutely fine – the manic-depressive's ability to deflect concern can be akin to the alcoholic's cunning over drink – Coward continued to counsel "a long rest" and then advised Olivier "If anybody's having a nervous breakdown, you are."

In England Olivier had to prepare to film *The Beggar's Opera*, directed by Peter Brook. There were other possibilities in the air; Cukor had suggested a film based on Edith Sitwell's *Fanfare for Elizabeth*, which Olivier assured its author "had a revered place on our bookshelves", in which Vivien would play Anne Boleyn to Olivier's Henry VIII, but despite huge enthusiasm from Sitwell no satisfactory script emerged from her revisions. Finally the film was shelved. Cukor also wanted to tempt Vivien into the screen version of Daphne du Maurier's *My Cousin Rachel* (for which she was excellent casting) but he was never happy with Nunally Johnson's screenplay and that notion fell by the wayside for them. Pascal also crossed Vivien's path again when he bought the American rights to Pirandello's *Six Characters in Search of an Author* and offered Vivien the part of The Stepdaughter opposite Olivier for an American tour prior to Broadway. They passed on that, another venture which never saw the light.

Finally Vivien decided to take Coward's advice and have a long rest. Work on Notley was mostly finished although for Vivien the gardens would always be work in progress. She read a great deal and enjoyed those weekends when the Abbey became alive to guests' enjoyment and when Olivier had time off from filming. Some grand houses seem to exist solely for their owners, unwelcoming to – even resentful of – other guests, but Notley was the polar opposite, as everyone who stayed there seemed to agree. Jamie Hamilton wrote to Vivien then, unaware, like most people, of any cracks in the foundations:

> Your happiness in each other is so perfect that it affects your guests and makes them as happy as yourselves.

Sibyl Colefax found that "more and more Notley is perfection" and Ginette Spanier remembered, as she told Vivien, "the joy of driving up Notley's drive and seeing you – looking 15 – standing in the middle of the lawn."

Olivier was far from always happy then. *The Beggar's Opera* was proving a vexing experience; as actor and co-producer he clashed regularly with Peter Brook, who had aimed for a Hogarthian highwayman Macheath in atmospheric chiaroscuro and was ending up with a bandbox-trim figure in a film of crisp Technicolour clarity. One of Macheath's doxies, Polly Peachum, was played by a relative newcomer, Dorothy Tutin – she had been Cecily in Asquith's film of *The Importance of Being Earnest* the previous year, an enchanting rosebud with a few unexpected thorns – a dark-haired beauty with a seductively husky voice and looks slightly reminiscent of a young Vivien. Olivier began an affair with her which continued – with occasional gaps – over the next five years. Born with a romantic soul, Tutin fell totally in love with Olivier; she was not sexually experienced – one of the attractions for Olivier, whose extramarital dalliances during his marriage to Vivien, and thereafter, tended to be with women considerably younger than himself – but had a tender gravitas beyond her years (she was 22 to his 45) and at that time was happy to be a discreet mistress. It is impossible to say whether this was his first affair since marrying Vivien but he had no thought of divorce in order to marry Tutin, although he was very fond of her and thought her a fine actress. Vivien certainly heard whispers of what was going on ("that Dot Tut" was occasionally referred to) but betrayed no overt jealousy or rage. Towards the end of 1952 a Hollywood film for Paramount was offered to both Vivien and Olivier. *Elephant Walk*, based on a sub-Maugham novel by Robert Standish, was a triangle-drama set in Ceylon (as Sri Lanka was then called), produced by the amiable Irving Asher, an American who had worked in England, but Olivier's post-production work on *The Beggar's Opera* ruled him out (he was dubious about the script in any event).

Accounts vary as to who was responsible for casting Peter Finch. One version has Vivien, mink coat over a ball gown, arriving late at night with the script at Finch's flat and waking up Tamara and him to tell him he must play the part while another (more likely and that told by Finch's fellow Australian actor-friend and biographer, Trader Faulkner) has Asher being taken to the Old Vic by Olivier to see Finch in *An Italian Straw Hat*, soon after which he was offered the part. Finch was still under contract to LOP which would benefit financially from his casting, and from Vivien's; LOP's finances were bumpy once again – the St James's had had no major success for some time and *The Beggar's Opera* did not promise to be a blockbuster – it lost every penny of the £250,000 it cost to make. It may make a better story to portray Vivien's decision to make the film as a tale of passion for Finch and/or planned revenge for Olivier's affair with Tutin but a primary reason was financial (Vivien's fee was a remarkably high one at that time). Olivier's version of events contains no record of taking Asher to the Old Vic to see the actor he regarded still as his protégé. He claimed – although Vivien's affair with Finch had not yet begun – that when he heard Finch would co-star "the penny dropped, and it was dropped with the knell of a high-pitched chapel bell". Nowhere in describing *Elephant Walk* – or indeed anywhere else in his memoirs – does he mention Dorothy Tutin's name. Also if Olivier had any fears for Vivien's health at this time he did not voice them in *Confessions* beyond the vaguest mention of American doctors: "Whether the doctors didn't explain it or I didn't understand it matters not." It mattered for Dr Kubie, who had given clear warnings to Olivier in New York that Vivien was very ill, but Olivier still insisted as she got ready to leave for location in Ceylon: "Vivien's condition seemed to have righted itself."

Elephant Walk was scheduled to be filmed in Hollywood after a month of Ceylon location work. Vivien, accompanied by Finch, was seen off to Colombo by Olivier on the tarmac at London Airport. He charged Finch to "take care" of Vivien and described how:

> as the plane began to move gently forward they both looked back at me through the window, Peter making a gallant effort to look the assuringly protective friend and she, with a little smile of infinite sweetness, blowing me a sad little kiss.

Olivier then returned to complete his work on *The Beggar's Opera* and to Dorothy Tutin's arms. He would find himself on the set of *Elephant Walk* after all only two weeks later.

CHAPTER 13

Crack-Up

There were several reasons for Vivien's acceptance of *Elephant Walk* – a large fee of $175,000 (part of Paramount's largesse on what was its biggest-budget film – $3,000,000 – to date), the kudos of a Hollywood blockbuster with potentially international appeal to follow *Streetcar* after two British-made disappointments, an escape from the Olivier/Tutin affair over which instinct had seemed to counsel her to avoid creating a fuss in the meantime and, possibly over-riding some of these, the desire to return to the East, something she had often mentioned.

Initially the omens were fair. She was aware that the script was efficient at best but found the central story strong – not unlike *Rebecca*, it centred round a new wife, Ruth Wiley, being taken to her husband's estate, a family tea-plantation sited in the path of a traditional elephant route, where she falls for the rugged estate manager (Dana Andrews). She liked Asher and thought that the director William Dieterle, who had impressive Hollywood experience (Laughton's *Hunchback of Notre Dame* included), could bring a narrative vigour to boost the exotic locations. Letters from Olivier, replying to her early enthusiastic reports from the Sinhalese location near Kandy, arrived promptly ("I was very worried you should be having so little sleep ... be careful of your lovely self, my darling. Is the work terrible in this heat?") although a note of rueful nostalgia is sounded in a reference to the 1930s "when we were in our toils of rash passion and uncertain conscience". By 1953, of course, the passion was less rash but with Olivier's propensity to guilt and the continuing involvement with Tutin, some uncertain conscience was resurfacing.

He was anxious to pursue the question of what production LOP, ideally with them co-starring, might offer London for Coronation year. At first he voiced doubts ("All is not well in the Coronation plan garden") when a possible play,

Lesley Storm's *Favonia*, proved unsatisfactory but soon he was elated, having just read Terence Rattigan's *The Sleeping Prince*, set during an earlier Coronation (George V's in 1911) which had "a magical part" for Vivien, which their beloved Alfred Lunt would direct and which Beaumont would co-produce. He admitted that he was tired, longing for his planned solo holiday with the Waltons at their home on Ischia but seemed jubilant that Rattigan had provided "a glorious simplification of all our problems", adding:

> A new Rattigan play written specially for us for the Coronation, and Alfred – Oh blimey O'Reilly it's too good to be true!

He did not know, when he sent that letter, that in Ceylon the set of *Elephant Walk* had disintegrated into near chaos. Vivien had written and cabled several times since her arrival, in one letter pleading with him to try to snatch time to visit her and when that proved impossible urging him to come to California later, possibly with Tennant with whom they could discuss the Coronation production. She signed herself "Elephant Girl" and in another cable described her encounter with a cobra (defanged) for the film, sounding more than slightly edgy. At the same time she wrote to Coward, describing her ride on an elephant, her delight in the beauty of Ceylon, and adding: "Everyone is charming except they treat me as if I were a raving lunatic." Soon afterwards two things happened; she began an affair with Peter Finch and, almost simultaneously, began to show worrying signs of instability, exacerbated by heavy drinking.

The Finch affair began soon after *Elephant Walk* filming was under way. Some saw this as a form of revenge for Olivier's liaison with Tutin, although, equally possibly, she intuited some imminent psychic crack-up and her pleas to Olivier to join her in Ceylon or Hollywood were barely masked calls for protection to save her from looming disaster. The oppressive heat had unsettled her and she had betrayed other signs of unease; she found the Sinhalese delightfully friendly but had on one occasion, surprised by the silent appearance at her side of a Sinhalese member of the crew, reacted in a kind of nervous terror to the man's dark eyes, claiming such eyes had always frightened her (possibly a long-buried reaction from her early Indian years). Her insomnia increased in the humidity and, of course, Finch was a dangerously attractive man with a strong sexual drive. He was also a heavy drinker, an early example of what journalists liked to call "hell-raisers". He had made steady progress in England on stage and on screen after the long run of *Daphne Laureola*, a lucrative earner for LOP. He and Tamara were regular Notley weekend guests but he had been far from a faithful husband (Maxine Audley was one of his lovers and testified to his beguiling charm and sexual energy). Finch knew and was drawn to the East and – a crucial bond with Vivien – had known childhood abandonment. His mother Betty was married to an Army Captain, George Finch, but fell in love with a Black Watch major, Jock Campbell, at which point Finch took his young son (aged two) away before divorcing Betty, later telling Peter that Campbell was his natural father. Betty reappeared in her son's life only years later. As Finch liked to put it: "I changed hands faster than a dud pound note." Much of his boyhood was spent with his flamboyant grandmother Laura, first in Paris – where Isadora Duncan and Nijinsky were regular visitors to the house – and then in India where Laura, a keen Theosophist, was a happy member of a group, a kind of commune, of those who followed the teachings of Ouspensky. Laura packed Peter off to his Aunt Dorothy (another enthusiastic Theosophist) in Australia and in adolescence he drifted into acting, first in vaudeville as a comic's feed, then in radio and theatre. The widow of one of his early directors said of him:

> Every part he played he played so intensely that he kept a portion of it, like a mosaic, within himself ... He was always those pieces of himself, scattered about within his character, till in the end I really don't think Peter knew what he really was as a person.

This echoes Tarquin on his father: "I don't think he ever really knew who he was." Olivier may well have seen something of a kindred spirit in Finch, who – like Olivier – relished danger on the stage and who certainly regarded Olivier as his most important mentor, remaining always grateful for the risk LOP had taken in casting an unknown in a leading role in *Daphne Laureola*. Both Vivien and Olivier had shown Finch and Tamara great kindness and he must have realised the potential damage of a sexual involvement with Vivien, a woman he found blindingly attractive, but it must be stressed that he then had no idea that Vivien was ill. Contrary to various accounts, their affair did not begin in England, but after *Elephant Walk* filming started in Ceylon.

Dana Andrews, himself no mean drinker, began early on in the film to intuit that something was very wrong with Vivien, more than elated high spirits in an exotic location but a near-manic insistence on keeping active without a break, organising post-filming excursions and drinking much more than usual. She made friends with a well-known Sinhalese character, Bevis Bawa, who had been equerry to five successive British governors of the island before turning to the creation of a remarkable garden at his estate, Brief, known as one of the most ravishing gardens in Asia. A lively raconteur with an air of mischief, Bawa was precisely the kind of character Vivien found entertaining when in an "up" phase and he proved a delightful guide to an island she wanted to explore as much as possible within the filming schedule. He in turn found her an entrancing companion and a similarly intrepid spirit. Hearing one night at dinner of Adam's Peak, from which the views at sunrise are breathtaking (did she have a faint memory of Himalayan dawns?) she at once said she wanted to climb it to reach the summit before daybreak ("My heart," said Bawa, "thumped to a halt and Peter swallowed a chicken bone"). The journey and climb would have made work the next day impossible; instead she was taken up the nearer and lower Bible Rock ("She was a bit groggy at the knees next day but looked as fresh as ever").

There were nights when Vivien slept not at all. Finch, it was noticed, seemed to have abandoned his own quarters; on some occasions they disappeared into the cooler hills and remained outdoors all night. Vivien was beguiled by Finch's brand of Eastern mysticism – he liked to talk of "twin souls" and "Karma" – as he spoke of his time in India (his voice she found, as did many women, could exert a hypnotic spell) and also by a vulnerability beneath the macho exterior which so many found devastatingly attractive. They talked of India – her early years the separation from her parents, his essentially orphaned boyhood – and Vivien found the combination of Ceylon's exoticism and Finch's powerful sex-appeal irresistible. But she also felt guilty, drank even more and resorted to the familiar actor's ruse of picking holes in the script when she had not properly mastered her lines (surviving stills from the location show her looking often puffy and strained), altogether alarming Dieterle so much by her behaviour that finally Asher called Tennant in London to ask Olivier to come out. Dieterle, sensing serious trouble, firmly told Finch to behave, insisting he return to his own quarters before Olivier arrived.

When Vivien knew that he was on his way she seemed to pull herself together, at least enough to work coherently, leading to speculation that her wild behaviour had been purely a ruse to lure Olivier to her side, possibly to frighten him enough to end his affair with Tutin and, if she ended her fling with Finch, return to private as well as public lives fully as "The Oliviers".

Dieterle gave Vivien a day off in order to drive to Colombo to meet Olivier at the airport but Bawa later wrote that he accompanied her, originally arranging to meet Olivier at Kandy:

> So we went for a picnic about ten miles from Kandy. Halfway through our sandwiches and beer she said "I think I will go down and meet Larry at the airport after all." It was a drive I'll never forget. At Ambepussa we dropped in for a quick gin and tonic and had another at Galle Face – we arrived at Ratmalama just in time to see Larry getting into a taxi looking very cross indeed.

Ever the professional, Olivier insisted she return to the *Elephant Walk* set. Vivien had a more romantic idea in mind – a stop at a rest house for a drink and sex – which, when Olivier declined, "was met with a blaze of rage that surprised even me". Those who expected pistols at dawn between Finch and Olivier were disappointed; Vivien's maid, Ethel Helmsing (another long-serving and utterly loyal character, deeply concerned for Vivien), told Olivier of Vivien's nocturnal excursions with Finch but, in typically British fashion, nothing was said, no overt challenge made, between the two men. Olivier was on the island for only three days, during which time Bawa took him and Vivien for a mountain jaunt on which he described them performing an improvised sketch for him as two Cockney naval ratings. Clearly grasping the situation and with Vivien back to seeming normality, Olivier – as he so often did – simply detached himself, wished Asher the very best of luck and took off for home, with his Ischia holiday now booked for the period when the *Elephant Walk* unit moved to Hollywood. Later he said – as if playing the role of a *mari complaisant* – that there was little to be done: "Was he (Finch) not simply doing what I had done to her first husband seventeen years ago?" He added, that as he left for Ischia "I managed to insulate my feelings in a soft coat of numbness."

The final days in Ceylon passed without further disturbances although it was noted that Dieterle was occasionally shooting backgrounds – against which another actress might be photographed at a future date – increasing suspicions that Vivien might not after all be able to complete the film. Olivier had said nothing to Finch, Asher or Paramount about Vivien's mental crises in the past and possibly the future as outlined by Kubie. Trouble flared up as soon as *Elephant Walk* left Ceylon. The nightmare of the next few weeks began not long after the flight took off from Colombo; Vivien's fear of flying had never entirely abated and this long journey was disturbed very soon by a major panic attack as she screamed, trying to rip off her clothes (a compulsion to strip naked – to expose the self – is a familiar symptom of a manic Bipolar phase) before Finch could give her a sedative and eventually calm her. In Hollywood Vivien moved into a house in Cukor's grounds, rented by the absent Spencer Tracy, sharing with Finch and Tamara; Finch's nanny-surrogate and agent-colleague of Tennant's, the redoubtable Olive Harding – "Auntie Olive" to Finch – had heard of events in Ceylon and smartly booked Tamara on the *Queen Elizabeth* (and on to Los Angeles), not an easy arrangement as Tamara became aware that she had a battle on her hands.

When she arrived at the house, travel-weary and with her three-year-old daughter Anita, Vivien – wearing a dramatic red sari – greeted her, showed her to what was intended as the Finches' area (the house was rudimentarily divided), and insisted that Tamara also dress in a sari for a welcome party which Vivien had organised for her that evening with "a few people" due to arrive presently when Finch returned from the studio. After changing as told, Tamara found Vivien in a completely altered mood, suddenly ill and unable to face people, leaving Tamara to entertain what transpired to be 70 people including Hollywood *gratin*, none of whom she had met before. Later Tamara, understandably, felt bitter that nobody concerned with Vivien had thought to inform Finch or her about Vivien's illness: "The manifestations of a person who is ill in that way – if you don't know it – are completely unexpected" she said, gradually realising over the next few days as Vivien's mood-swings became more familiar, that something very serious indeed was wrong, as if her psyche was often doing a bizarre series of time shifts, talking ostensibly of Finch although it seemed more that she was talking of Olivier and of the Tristan and Isolde level of love on which their affair had begun. Finch was little help during this period, returning as late as possible from Paramount (where shooting mostly went on around Vivien's scenes) and usually being uncommunicative with Tamara.

There were hopes that the trouble was over when Vivien, with little recollection of recent behaviour and again looking in surprisingly good shape, seemed on set totally professional as before. Fellow actor Edward Ashley was impressed by her work on a key scene, with Vivien as a newly arrived bride at a banquet round an elaborate formal dining-table, with a substrain of divided emotions. Dieterle mapped out a complex slow panning shot, closing in for a close-up of Vivien, and professed himself delighted with the first take. But Vivien asked for another, saying she had been thinking about the scene, suggesting she could bring something more to it and so Dieterle, who respected Vivien's work despite all the problems to date, set up for another take, as Ashley recalled:

> I watched. It was incredible, the nuances she brought … a sense of foreboding, a sense of suspense. And this is where I must say she was a superb actress. Dieterle was thrilled.

Word of trouble on *Elephant Walk* had leaked out, however. Hedda Hopper, for whom Vivien had scant regard ("Me? Afraid of a hat?!" was her reaction to suggestions she should remember the columnist's power) cattily pointed out that an Oscar celebration photocall had brought out over 20 previous Academy Award winners but no Vivien (she was working that day). She agreed to Paramount's request to be interviewed by Hopper's less feline rival, Louella

Parsons, who did not probe into professional or marital problems, but soon after that interview *Elephant Walk* moved into its worst crisis. On set Vivien seemed utterly lost, mumbling and unable to remember her lines, addressing Finch as "Larry", occasionally slipping into dialogue from *Streetcar* and even turning on Sunny Lash, who once again was attempting to help her. The hysteria mounted as her voice spiralled out of control when she began to yell Blanche's lines to an aggressive Mitch: "Get out of here quick before I start screaming fire!", then collapsing to the floor, a huddled and dishevelled figure, make-up ruined, unable to stop her convulsive sobs. Nobody knew what to do until Asher suggested calling David Niven, who came to the Paramount set as quickly as possible, asked to be left alone with Vivien and then, when her weeping had subsided and he had raised her to her feet, slowly walked her through the set and the shaken crew to his car to drive her home.

Varying versions of subsequent events exist but one thing seems consistently clear – Finch, never strong when confronted by volatile emotional situations, took evasive action, moving with Tamara to a new address and leaving others to deal with the situation. According to Asher, who must have been wishing he had never read *Elephant Walk*, Finch was spending a good deal of time away from the fall-out at Oblate, a bar-restaurant across the street from Paramount Studios ("I don't think Finchie was the strongest character who ever lived"). The first edition of Niven's memoirs describe three days of nightmare shot through with a vein of jet-black comedy, with Vivien thinly disguised as "Missee", more than likely with some embellishments (Niven's anecdotes, often hilarious, could become progressively embroidered) but basically giving a credible account of Vivien in one of her extreme manic phases. He described arriving at the house to find the maid, Mae, adding to the drama with her near-hysterical insistences that Vivien was "possessed" and refusing to remain, then after getting Vivien to her room and returning downstairs, he was startled when first she appeared wearing only a transparent nightdress and vamping him heavily and then, after she returned to her room and he had gone downstairs, when she reappeared, totally naked, at the top of the stairs:

> Her hair was hanging down in straggly clumps; the mascara and make-up made a ghastly streaked mask down her chin; one false eyelash was missing; her eyes were staring and wild.

Niven's account made no mention of the later presence of Stewart Granger whose memoirs also give a version of this awful time. According to Granger he had a call from Niven asking for help, with the situation complicated by the presence at the house of that bad penny, Vivien's old flame John Buckmaster, seemingly equally manic, who had turned up in Hollywood after twice in the recent past being committed to a mental hospital. Arriving at the house Granger found Buckmaster on the landing naked except for a towel and insisting that a "higher power" had sent him to take care of Vivien. The impressively tall and well-built Granger squared up to the much slighter Buckmaster to tell him firmly that he had been sent by a higher power still ("If you're a good boy I'll drive you back to your hotel, otherwise you'll go in an ambulance") which immediately had the desired effect. In Granger's version, after he drove Buckmaster to his hotel, The Garden of Allah (apt address for emissaries of higher powers) he and Niven were led a merry dance by Vivien. Granger had called the understanding Paramount doctor who arranged for him to pick up a prescription for sedatives from Schwab's drugstore, promising to come over once a pill had taken effect. Also dressed by now in only a towel, Vivien was sitting as if hypnotised, gazing at the snow on the television as it buzzed loudly (no all-night television then) but becoming suspicious when Granger tried to coax her to eat some scrambled eggs (doped) and drink some coffee (also doped). She insisted that the sleepily unsuspecting Niven drink some of the coffee. Before long Niven was snoring gently and Vivien dropped her towel to slip outside, sitting naked by the pool. Trying to get her to swallow another pill Granger gave it to her to take with a glass of water; Vivien looked intently at the pill in her hand and then threw it into the deep end of the pool. Left with just one pill, Granger resorted to trying to force it down her but Vivien managed to grab it and throw that one into the pool too. Finally, as she returned to watch the flickering television set near the slumbering Niven, Granger called the studio physician again to explain the situation; the doctor seemed unsurprised, warned Granger that patients could be devious in such states but agreed to come immediately with two nurses.

When the doorbell rang Vivien suddenly ran upstairs to stand glaring in hostility on the landing, retreating against the wall as the doctor entered with two stout nurses. As Vivien screamed at them to leave, one of the nurses (the other concealed a hypodermic syringe in her hand) gently called to her: "I know who you are – you're Scarlett O'Hara." Shrinking back further Vivien yelled: "I'm not Scarlett O'Hara! I'm Blanche Du Bois!" Granger managed to put his arms around her, quietly assuring her that everything would be fine, then carefully lifted her up and carried her into the bedroom. Then, becoming firmer, he pinioned her body under his and told the nurse to put the needle in; as Vivien felt the injection she gave him a look of despair ("as if I had betrayed her") whispering "How could you? I thought you were my friend." Granger had no idea that among the few things which held terrors for Vivien were needles, but must have realised how grim a parallel this episode made with *Streetcar's* final scene as doctor, nurse and straitjacket arrive for Blanche.

Olivier had no idea of events in Hollywood until shortly after his arrival in Ischia when he received a call from Asher which made the extent of Vivien's breakdown clear. Calling Tennant to join him in London for the long flight to Los Angeles via New York, Olivier began the journey to Vivien's side. This has been wildly misrepresented. An Olivier biographer, Donald Spoto, asserts (with no supporting evidence) that Danny Kaye met Olivier at Idlewild, disguised in a US Immigration Officer's uniform, dark wig and powdered latex mask (a transformation apparently unnoticed at close quarters by the stage's master of make-up), ordered him into a cubicle to strip naked for a full body-search, after which Kaye removed his disguise and then took Olivier off for a night at the St Regis Hotel in Manhattan. Spoto, who claims that Kaye and Olivier had an intense affair over a ten-year period, makes no mention of Tennant's accompanying presence or of the fact (as Terry Coleman outlined in his Olivier biography) that flight and hotel records prove that Olivier spent less than 24 hours in New York (he and Tennant flew on to Los Angeles shortly after midnight), during which he had a brief sleep and a massage (at the Sherry-Netherland Hotel). Kaye did meet the two men at the airport; he liked to make himself useful to stars, Gielgud, hearing the gossip on publication of Spoto's book ("unexpected news to me") recalled how Kaye liked to treat celebrity friends, once sending a limo to meet him at LAX and providing lavish Hollywood hospitality (but making no pass – "perhaps he thought better of it when he met me!"). The Spoto story is not to be taken seriously. Olivier has stood accused of some indifferent behaviour but it stretches credulity that a man travelling to visit his seriously ill wife, in company with his friend and agent, should take time out for such an escapade. Not to mention the highly unlikely suggested collusion of the US Immigration Dept's in Kaye's scenario as outlined by Spoto.

In Hollywood, Elizabeth Taylor replaced Vivien in *Elephant Walk*. The studio did everything possible to quiet the rumour mill and behaved to Vivien with remarkable generosity. Niven, a loyal friend throughout this whole sad episode, invited Olivier and Tennant to stay with him and then Olivier faced the encounter with Vivien ("more dreaded than any other in my life"). At the house he found her outside on a balcony, her face in her hands, and when she turned to look at him only pin-pricks of pupils were visible in her normally clear, bright eyes. With that characteristic actor's habit of observation in detail he noted that her voice had a tone of the "dream-like amazement that people in the theatre use for mad scenes when they can't think of anything better", so that his initial reaction was to assume "she was putting it on" (shades of reactions to his sister Sybille's first crack-up). He admitted that he was "not able for the life of me to think of anything to ask her beyond did she think perhaps there was something the matter with her", to be told "with the wonderment of a first communion" that she was in love. With Peter Finch. In *Confessions*, writing of that encounter, he reveals the sole instance of any feeling of resentment towards Finch – "where the hell was he by the way, I wondered?"

The next day Olivier and Tennant met the three doctors who had variously attended on and treated Vivien since her breakdown. Dr Fraser McDonald, a physician suggested by Paramount, had been the most regular, along with Drs Greenson and Grotjohn, both psychiatrists with patients among Hollywood's elite. Olivier's wary perspective on mental illness was evidenced again by his reaction to Grotjohn's *mittel*-European accent, like a shrink in a Hollywood movie (he called him "the big maestro") who insisted that Vivien must be taken home ("She wants her mo-o-ther!") at which he had to suppress the impulse to giggle. Tennant had similar Anglo-Saxon attitudes to American psychiatry and subsequently its costs, later arguing for some time over the expense of Hollywood doctors and the psychiatric nurses required for Vivien's transportation home – he settled (reluctantly) when Dr McDonald insisted that the nurse accompanying Vivien home, Doris Cotchefer, had to cope with "three or four occasions" when she was "aware that the life of the patient was at stake." Olivier was the only one who could sign any sectioning or committal papers for Vivien and nobody wanted that to be arranged in California.

For what Olivier called "the escape from Hollywood" she had to be sedated for the plane journey to New York. On the airport tarmac a nurse appeared with what seemed to Olivier an unnecessarily large needle at the sight of which Vivien made a terrified effort to escape ("To my horror I saw the nurse was enjoying it; she was waggling the needle in her hand") before he, Tennant and Niven, who had accompanied them, managed to catch her, forcing her to the ground, biting and kicking as the needle went in, screaming a torrent of abuse at Olivier. Finally, Vivien was stretchered on to the aircraft, leaving Niven to comfort Olivier before he joined Tennant on the plane.

Arriving at La Guardia, Vivien, although tottery, managed to walk off the plane and into Kaye's car waiting to drive the party to discreet friends of the

Kayes on Long Island to spend the hours until their London flight. Travelling with two nurses, again sedated, she was driven to Idlewild lying across Olivier's and Kaye's knees, covered by a blanket in the back of the chauffeured limousine. On the tarmac it was clear that the sedative given on Long Island had worn off; Vivien, possibly suspecting further hypodermics, refused at first to leave the car and finally – in Olivier's version, the sole surviving account – he and Kaye dragged her out and held her for another sedation while nearby flashbulbs exploded and reporters shouted as Tennant did his best to screen what was going on and eventually the nurses manoeuvred her into the reserved first-class cabin. She slept until towards the end of the flight when the sleepless, unshaven Tennant could only be amused when she told him he looked dreadfully tired, asking if he was all right. At London Airport two English nurses came on board to help Vivien; she managed to put on some lipstick and comb her hair before shakily summoning a faint smile for the cameras (word of her illness had reached the London press). She was escorted into a waiting car and driven directly to Netherne Hospital in Coulsdon, Surrey, then a leading establishment for the treatment of mental and nervous disorders, a large, handsome building sitting in extensive tree-studded grounds, where she was committed (sectioned) into the direct charge of its main practitioner, Dr Rudolf Freudenberg. The Oliviers' GP, Dr Armando Child, who had many theatrical and musical patients (the Waltons included) had advised this although Olivier knew of Netherne and of Freudenberg already; his sister Sybille had been a patient there during two further episodes of her nervous condition and thought highly of him. She guessed, rightly, that Freudenberg would administer narcosis treatment to Vivien, involving several weeks of sedative-induced sleep with the patient wrapped in sheets soaked in ice-cold water to reduce body temperature, wakened at regular intervals for light nourishment (milk and eggs featuring heavily), then once again sedated. This was a fairly routine treatment at that time. The single entry, shakily written, in Vivien's diary then was: "Larry and Drs. Freudenberg and Child took me to Coolsden. Heathrow – Larry left me in Coolsden."

Freudenberg had insisted on strictly no visitors during the treatment. Olivier returned to the Waltons' sanctuary on Ischia where his hosts did everything possible to shield him from a pursuing press. He wrote from the island at the end of March, addressing Vivien as "My Wandering precious love" (she could not very well wander far, confined securely at Netherne), assuring her that after he had slept for nearly two days at Notley after their return to London he was now soothed by the peace of Ischia:

I am looking through my window through a dark olive tree onto the shining path
made by the sun sinking onto the sea … the only meaning my whole life has is
that you should get well.

He signed that letter "Your ever adoring Larry boy". There were those at
home – Oswald Frewen most strongly among them – who questioned Olivier's
vanishing act (he told few where he was going and any mail had to be enclosed
inside envelopes addressed to the Waltons). Although Freudenberg wrote to
keep him informed of the narcosis treatment's progress, telling him how
cheered Vivien had been by his letter from Ischia, it was left to Leigh and
Coward to hover protectively over Vivien. In Olivier's absence, with no other
person to sign any necessary papers to continue her committal, Leigh went to
Netherne at Freudenberg's request to persuade her voluntarily to remain there
for longer to gain full benefit from her treatment. Coward could not visit but
often sent some token of reassurance – flowers, a silly postcard, scent – which
she always remembered gratefully ("all I had to hang on to at that dreadful
time"). Indeed the tone of Olivier's letter chimes oddly with a section in
Confessions on this period when, after hearing from Tennant that Vivien's
"Awakening" was imminent, he returned to London.

Olivier wrote that he now noticed "slight but perceptible personality
changes" which he could describe only by saying she was no longer, after
Freudenberg's treatment, "the same girl that I had fallen in love with". She was
not a girl, she was 40 and Olivier does not seem to have taken entirely on board
what doctors had been and were telling him. In New York, Kubie had been so
concerned when hearing of the *Elephant Walk* debacle that he had written to a
fellow psychiatrist in London, detailing her symptoms which for Kubie were
clearly classic symptoms of manic depression (as Bipolar was then termed).
A more resonant term is Tristimania, the old eighteenth-century word for a
mixed condition of what once was called "melancholia" with spells of extreme
elation (the word was used as the title for Jay Griffith's book on her experience
of the illness, one of the most vivid descriptions of what the condition
involves). Kubie had written to Olivier, saying that he was saddened but not
surprised by the news of Vivien's breakdown, suggesting that Olivier contact
his colleague Dr Edward Glover, one of the most respected British psychiatric
doctors, with a Wimpole Street practice, to whom he had outlined Vivien's
symptoms:

I did this because I thought that the situation was so explosive that anyone who
was going to take hold of it on her arrival in England would have to be armed with
this information to use for her benefit.

He added, referring to "our failure", that he deeply regretted that Olivier and he had not persuaded Vivien to understand "the need for intensive treatment to prevent just such a mishap as this".

But just as in New York Olivier had reacted to Kubie with some suspicion, feeling foreign in his presence and listening to diagnoses in psychiatric terms which he could not fully comprehend, so now he did not act on Kubie's advice and did not contact Glover. Child had recommended Netherne (along with Sybille), although whether the narcosis treatment significantly improved Vivien is debatable. Kubie in 1952 had told Olivier what manic depression involved – a cyclical pattern, likely to be permanent, of deep depression alternating with elated mania, mood changes which could vary from intermittent to regular and at that time regarded as at best containable but not curable. Ralph Greenson, the Hollywood doctor whom Olivier seemed to trust most of those who dealt with Vivien there, had also written separately to him and also urged him to consult Dr Glover, describing him as "the most outstanding psychiatrist and psychoanalyst in England". Peter Hiley, whose four years to date with LOP had given him insights into the Oliviers, both of whom he deeply admired despite the awareness of how difficult both could on occasion be, had a view on this: "Larry, I think, afterwards wanted to justify himself by saying, 'Well, she was ill much further back'." Olivier said himself:

> Whether the doctors didn't explain or I didn't understand matters not; the fact is I was quite unprepared for what was in store.

It seems most unlikely that Kubie was unclear about what he called a potentially "explosive" illness and Freudenberg was also unambiguous when he wrote to Ischia to keep Olivier informed about Vivien's Netherne treatment. In outlining her symptoms he stressed the value of psychotherapy, then a comparatively recent concept in England, and Olivier perhaps felt unable totally to trust the opinions of doctors (American ones in particular) who spoke what seemed to him an alien language. And of course Vivien, although now accepting that she suffered from a serious disorder, was never easy to cajole into doing anything she did not want to do. She had a lifelong dread of any possibility that she might be institutionalised or (her special terror) of being abandoned – Olivier's committing her to Netherne in her eyes was tantamount to that – but her illness may well have been better contained by regular psychotherapy had its value been made completely clear to her (later she did find, and trust, an excellent psychotherapist).

As it was, Vivien spent several weeks after leaving Netherne in University College Hospital, still not fully recovered. Coward noted when she called him from her room:

a heart-breaking conversation. She started in floods of tears and then made a gallant effort to be gay and ordinary but the strain showed through and she didn't make sense every now and then.

When Coward visited her he found her calm and "really very sweet". She had a series of Electro-Convulsive Therapy (ECT) treatments in University College Hospital, a form of treatment used widely to treat manic depression then. Just as the causes of the illness, whether genetic or a chemical imbalance in the brain, remain unclear so it was not properly known how or why ECT worked (always controversial since its widespread use from the 1930s onwards, now it is rarely used). Basically an electric current was passed through the anaesthetised patient's brain, triggering a short seizure (the "convulsive" element, not dissimilar to an epileptic fit), one theory being that ECT triggers the release of chemicals in the brain, possibly spurring them into greater effectiveness to assist recovery, even help the growth of new brain cells or neural pathways (certainly, in experiments with placebos, patients who were given no electrical surge did signally less well than those who were fully treated). By no means pleasant, the treatment was something which Vivien, although dreading it, came to believe helped her and which she submitted to voluntarily later when she sensed an "episode" might be looming (warning signs included the urge to tidy and rearrange objects, toying with her jewellery, the impulse to clean – generally increased or agitated movement).

With Vivien seemingly improved, Coward felt able to give her one of the "finger-wags" with which he advised his closest friends, telling her she must solemnly promise "*not* to carry on like a mad adolescent of the twenties", soon afterwards noting that she and Olivier "are now going to start afresh down at Notley which may work or may not", his verdict being "I shall be surprised if it does". Coward, of course, like most of her friends, was not completely aware of the extent of her illness and tended to agree with Olivier that Notley's calm might be of inestimably more an aid to recovery than any therapy, unaware or incapable of totally accepting the insidiously cyclical nature of Vivien's condition. Olivier wrote to their French friend Paul-Louis Weiller:

> She will have 3 or 4 months extreme quietness at Notley and freedom from all distractions, in the country.

For a surprisingly long time the Notley Visitors' Book had fewer entries and the signatures were mostly those of familiar friends like Gielgud, Helpmann, the Byam Shaws, the Relphs and Korda while Ernest, Gertrude, Leigh, Suzanne and Tarquin also spent regular Notley weekends. Vivien was happy with the house, changing little apart from hanging some newly acquired paintings (a charming

Marie Laurencin for the Blue Room included) and, outside, continuing to plant more roses, old Bourbons alongside sturdier modern hybrid teas. Dr Freudenberg – Vivien called him her "Rosenkavalier", as Blanche calls Mitch in *Streetcar* – made several visits in the early summer but then wrote to Olivier to say that his Netherne work prevented future visits, urging him to arrange for a recommended consultant psychiatrist from the closer Warneford Hospital in Oxford to visit, or even better, he suggested (the third doctor to do so), Dr Edward Glover. But this was not pursued.

Gertrude was often at Notley during this period but one of the main problems – and a barrier to convincing Vivien of the gravity of her condition – was that Gertrude was utterly incapable of accepting that Vivien was in any sense mentally ill. In a diary entry then Gertrude describes Vivien as "looking lovely and much better and so very adorable". Her explanation of any "episode" was, always, that her Vivien, her "precious pet" simply was "not herself", a description of Bipolar more accurate than she could comprehend. Whether Gertrude ever knew of her Uncle Gabriel's "mania" in Calcutta cannot be known but she seemed quite unable to face what she – and many of her generation – viewed as a shameful secret, not unlike Gladys Cooper's explanations of John Buckmaster's depressed spells as "the flu". Leigh was more aware of Vivien's deep-rooted troubles and had fewer qualms than Gertrude in facing and accepting them; Vivien always seemed calmer in his presence and she and Suzanne had a holiday with him at Woodlands before Vivien returned to work. Olivier felt "a blessed sense of relief that Vivien's condition seemed to have righted itself" (although he surely had had warnings enough that this might be only a temporary "normality") and was now able to arrange the belated production of *The Sleeping Prince*, no longer coinciding with the Coronation but to open after a brief tour at what he hoped would be an aptly named London theatre, The Phoenix, for their joint West End return.

When Vivien collapsed in Hollywood there had been some talk of continuing with production plans for Rattigan's play as scheduled, largely because Alfred Lunt had a strictly limited availability as director. Various possibles to replace Vivien were considered including Glynis Johns as well as American actresses (the role of Mary Morgan, a chorus-girl in a London musical, is American) such as Julie Harris or Judy Holliday but finally it was decided to wait for Vivien's recovery (which Beaumont especially advocated) with Olivier taking over as director when Lunt was no longer available. The play, written for a major royal event and described by Rattigan as "An Occasional Fairy Tale", was a frivol, a feather-light piece set in the Carpathian

Embassy in London during the 1911 Coronation, allowing Olivier as the Carpathian Prince Regent to wear dashingly braided uniforms and Vivien to shimmer under a strawberry-blonde wig in an alluring Balmain evening gown. The emotionally repressed Prince, who sees women solely as necessary physical relief, is shaken by Mary's impact on his young son, the Crown Prince, and on himself when Mary, spellbound by all the trappings of royalty, falls in love with him. Rattigan was happy with the results; it ran to virtual capacity for nearly 300 performances. He felt that Vivien ("one of nature's grand duchesses") was essentially miscast (although very funny) as his Broadway chorine but most critics found it a deftly witty performance fusing a ditsy naivety with a perceptible streak of shrewdness. Ronald Bryden, later the *Observer*'s critic, thought her comedic flair in *The Sleeping Prince* superb; he always recalled a particularly effective piece of silent comic business (not in the text) when a hungover and barefoot Mary, leaving a room, at the last minute almost automatically reached out for a jug of water and downed it in one as she exited ("without a word it brought the house down"). The play, a frail vessel, needed such comedic legerdemain; never Rattigan's best work, it has some decidedly flat passages and a somewhat patronising attitude towards Americans. Vivien never missed a performance, playing even with a broken wrist (she had a bandage made to match the Balmain); Guthrie wrote of that to Olivier. "In a list of Good Troupers I think her name would come *second* (Dame Sybil first – longer service)."

One voice of strong dissent, not unexpectedly, was that of Kenneth Tynan who dismissed the play as "a quilted cushion" before laying into Vivien ("I found her beautiful without being attractive ... a strangely bloodless display"), again with the strong implication that Olivier was operating on less than full throttle, restrained by his wife's secondary talent. It was around this time that Tynan had interviewed Charles Laughton. Subsequently Laughton wrote to Olivier from Liverpool, anxious to correct what he assured Olivier was Tynan's misreporting of something Laughton had said about heroic acting which emerged in print, Laughton felt, as criticism of Olivier, totally unintended. He added that Tynan had quizzed him about Vivien:

> about whom he tried to trip me into saying something and concerning whom he was vicious in a patchouli and excrement kind of way.

Olivier replied, appreciating the explanation but adding that he was only sorry Laughton had talked at all to "the little fucker" as he often described Tynan then. He also took combative issue with his acolyte over Donald Wolfit, of whom he had no high opinion as an actor (he had been put out when Richardson was knighted before him but was splenetic with fury when Wolfit, who already had a CBE, was knighted – "That gives him precedence over me!") but felt he must defend when Tynan went too far, in his opinion, in a Wolfit/Olivier comparison. He wrote a terse letter to Tynan defending his fellow actor as one who had "given substantial services to the cause of the theatre" and strongly telling Tynan "not to allow your personal tastes to outrun fair criticism"; he sent a copy to Wolfit, explaining that he had only not made the letter public because "it is against my principles to cross swords with bastards".

Michael Redgrave came in for less generous treatment than Wolfit from Olivier, in an episode which seemed to involve Vivien only marginally although it made for a potentially uneasy situation given the closeness of her friendship with Rachel Kempson. A section of the press was suggesting that Redgrave's recent classical successes at Stratford, including his acclaimed Antony, were threatening Olivier's pre-eminence – "Look out Larry, there's a Redgrave on your tail!" was one headline. When a del Giudice-produced film of *Antony and Cleopatra* was announced, scripted by Redgrave and co-starring Margaret Leighton, suddenly a press announcement appeared trumpeting an Olivier version with Vivien, produced by Korda (no mention of this appears in Vivien's surviving correspondence). It is hard not to conclude that Olivier, the sole English actor at that date to direct and star in Shakespeare on screen, simply did not want another possibly to match or even better him in a role which had not been an unalloyed triumph for him on stage.

If sabotage was Olivier's intention he succeeded. The announcement of his film to co-star Vivien, a much bigger cinema name than Leighton, had the effect of making del Giudice's continuing fund-raising impossible. Neither film was made.

Whether or not Vivien was fully aware of Olivier's behaviour or dealings with Redgrave, she could be extremely strong in opposition on occasion. One incident has several different versions: Gielgud was arrested and fined for "importuning male persons" in a Chelsea lavatory just before opening the out-of-town try-out of N.C. Hunter's *A Day By The Sea* for H.M. Tennent in October 1953, a time of deeply prurient homophobia, not least in the tabloid press. A crisis meeting was held that evening at Beaumont's house attended by the Tennent hierarchy and legal advisers. Gielgud offered to drop out of the play but Beaumont refused to release him, concerned that if he now refused to face an audience then he might never do so again. Another version – one included in Gielgud's authorised (if not totally reliable) biography – has the summit meeting (without Gielgud) attended also by the Oliviers, the Richardsons and the Byam Shaws, all friends and Tennent regulars. With one exception, they agreed that Gielgud must continue, the dissenter being Olivier, who argued that the production should, at the least, be postponed, whereupon Vivien turned on him, called him a crisp four-letter word and accused him of having always been jealous of Gielgud. This sounds plausibly characteristic of both. Gielgud did open – to an ovation – in the play which went on to a successful Haymarket run. Vivien's concept of friendship involved unconditional loyalty, believing in what Sibyl Colefax described as "the sanctity of personal friendship".

The Sleeping Prince may have been a bubble of a comedy but its style, involving enormous mental energy and concentration to maintain its buoyancy, can be harder work than playing Greek tragedy and both were tired by the end of the run (extremely profitable for H.M. Tennent, LOP and both stars, each on a percentage of the box-office). There was a period for them both at Notley but Vivien was often then in a "down" cycle – not uncommon when overtired – when she would retreat into herself, staring into space but unfocused, even neglecting basic hygiene, all familiar symptoms of her illness; sufferers including American novelist William Styron, and the poets Robert Lowell and Jay Griffiths have evoked most strikingly the abyss of frightening loneliness into which Bipolar people can feel plunged in such states, like an all-enveloping cloak cutting one off from any normal human interaction. Slowly the cloak fell off and she was in high spirits when she and Olivier had an Italian holiday, first at San Vigilio, a beautiful *locanda* on Lake Garda recommended by Kenneth Clark, which became a favourite retreat; Clark described it as "a dream of beauty" and said that of the many places he and his wife Jane had been to in Italy:

> this is easily the most romantic, with a well-run hotel. It lies in a bay, surrounded by magnificent mountains with vari-coloured peninsulas to the east ... you don't have to see other guests if you don't want to.

Churchill and the Duff Coopers had also stayed there and it lived up to everything Clark had described, so much so that Vivien later bought a plot of land nearby, planning at one stage to build a small villa. They then travelled on to Portofino to stay with Rex Harrison and Lilli Palmer at their villa high above the coast, called San Genesio (after the patron saint of actors). This had been a long-standing invitation; Harrison, distressed by the news of Vivien's collapse in Hollywood, had at once urged Olivier to bring her to San Genesio to recover ("I couldn't be more troubled if it had happened to my own sister") but that was not possible then. Finally there, Vivien was able to relax ("It is heavenly here" she wrote to Leigh) but gradually subterranean tremors became evident; Harrison was in the throes of an affair with Kay Kendall – for whom he would soon leave Palmer – and the rumblings increased when Kendall "by coincidence" turned up in Portofino, rather as Vivien had in Capri. She and Vivien, similar in their zest for life, sense of fun and comedic gift, formed an immediate bond and she and Harrison together later became regular Notley weekenders.

Films waited for them both on their return – Olivier for his third screen Shakespeare (*Richard III*) and Vivien for more Rattigan in the screen version of *The Deep Blue Sea*, one of his finest plays, produced by Korda, directed by her old friend from first Hollywood days, Anatol Litvak and co-starring the newcomer of Kenneth More who had made a major impact in the West End production with Peggy Ashcroft as Rattigan's take on Madam Bovary, Hester Collyer. Much was expected from both films but *Richard III*, while mostly critically hailed at the time, was the least successful of Olivier's film Shakespeares and has not worn well while *The Deep Blue Sea* was a major disappointment.

Korda did not seem to appreciate that the quality above any other which made it so taut on stage was its intense lucidity of focus, set in one room (the sitting-room of a shabby apartment in an unfashionable area of London) and taking place over one day, in scrutinising the relationship of Hester, once married to a High Court judge, and her lover Freddie, an ex-Battle of Britain pilot; Hester has tried and failed to commit suicide at the gas fire just before the action begins, moving through to end with her once more in front of the fire (Freddie now off to begin a new life abroad as a test-pilot) but this time going on with life. Essentially it centres round Rattigan's familiar theme of two kinds of love, unequal and destructive, freighted with a potent sense of understated passion in its examination of what, in another play, he called "the real *vice Anglais*", not flagellation but that very English reluctance to express deep emotion.

Korda wanted Technicolour and "production values" and so Rattigan's own screenplay "opened up" the play (Vivien might have pointed them towards *Streetcar*) with flashbacks to Hester's first meeting with Freddie at an upmarket golf club, a glittering society reception featuring a crowded dance floor with many a glamorous ball gown and Vivien in expensive Balmain and a Klosters ski-ing trip. In the play the sense of the past drip-feeds subtly into the story – Hester's recollection of first meeting Freddie is one of the finest passages in all his plays – but on screen the "opening-out" scenes are less finely tuned, at times jarringly so. Another problem was Kenneth More, bluff and hearty, not unlike Freddie, and fond of women. But not, it seemed, of Vivien. His was the only strongly dissenting voice to join that of Beaton in Alan Dent's collection of posthumous pieces on Vivien. More suspected her "almost overwhelming friendliness". Few others did; from childhood, first with Gertrude in India and then with the Roehampton nuns, Vivien had been schooled to treat everyone, royalty or waiter, in the same way. Initially there may have been an element at the Sacred Heart of charm or friendliness used to acquire the affection, even love, she had been used to so far away in India, but by her teenage years her instinctive good manners and friendliness had stamped her character indelibly, with no artifice. More added that he thought she was "spoilt, overpraised and overloved". Possibly some of this animus had to do with the fact that having played opposite Ashcroft he sensed that the screenplay was inferior to the play and he felt that although he could understand the commercial pressures on Korda to cast a star as Hester, Vivien was basically miscast as Rattigan's "plain woman in her 40s". There was indeed a general feeling that she was just too glamorous, lacking the essential upper-middle-class ordinariness and melancholy for the role, but the main problem was the palpable lack of chemistry between More and Vivien, not helped by the clean, crisp Technicolour demanded by Korda for a film which should be steeped in the muted palatte of drab postwar London (the remake by Terence Davies, also misguidedly tinkering with Rattigan, at least evokes that more satisfyingly). Under the circumstances Vivien does suggest that her new world is unravelling; her performance, often subtly pitched, creates a sense of a woman who has become emotionally drained after a life-altering rejection of a comfortable if passionless marriage and lifestyle, now beginning to comprehend that life with Freddie is fraying and will fall apart.

The carapace of Rattigan's characteristic restraint is present, that very Anglo-Saxon control masking an underlying cauldron of complex emotions (Vivien certainly understood that). But Litvak handled the film poorly according to both Moira Lister (playing a good-time girl, a character not in the play) and Alec McCowen as a straitlaced young husband who discovers Hester before the gas fire at the opening. Inexperienced in films, McCowen was grateful for Vivien's discreet technical hints and encouragement to him on the set, finding her just as welcoming as she had been on Broadway but he sensed:

> She had qualms about the script, but Tolly (Litvak) just wouldn't listen. He was a bit of a martinet and sometimes very harsh to her in front of people although she didn't let it show apart from an occasional tear. She was more concerned that

Kenny More seemed awfully aloof – he was polite enough but you could tell he wasn't really connecting with her. I had very little screen time with him but I didn't think he was anything like as good as he'd been in the play, he just didn't seem the absolutely classic Battle of Britain ex-golden boy.

The film was not helped by an oddly sinister performance from Emlyn Williams as Hester's husband. Intriguingly Vivien's best scenes are those opposite a subtly underplaying Eric Portman, who had his own demons, as a "guardian" figure, the mysterious "Doctor" Miller, another lodger in the house, which have a sense of inner life and urgency too often missing elsewhere. Litvak failed to give the material any genuine cinematic rhythm; in his hands it became an opportunity sadly missed. However, the play's director, Frith Banbury, was generous in congratulating Vivien on her Hester ("all the more remarkable in view of the dissipation of concentration imposed by the changes in the script").

The demands of their films – *Richard III* took Olivier to Spain for location scenes – kept Vivien and Olivier often apart. On *Richard III*, Olivier had a brief affair with Claire Bloom, playing Vivien's old role of Lady Anne. The relationship with Tutin was, for a time, on the back burner although far from over. Bloom was more experienced than Tutin had been – she was also involved with Richard Burton at this time – and she was fully aware that this was no life-changing affair. It was, she said, "the classic situation of the young actress bedazzled by the attentions of her mature co-star, ended without rancour on either side". She was taken to Notley while Vivien was away ("I'm certain I wasn't the first young woman Larry had brought down to Notley for a weekend nor would I be the last"). Dickie and Hester would join them for dinner and everything seemed most civilised ("Vivien, according to Olivier, was quite understanding of the idea").

During that time on the Klosters location Vivien must have been reminded of a previous affair of her own – more of a fling, very brief – while alone in Switzerland on a short holiday before filming on *Streetcar*. Staying in the same Klosters hotel then was Robert Capa, the most brilliant of a legendary roster of photographers attached to the Magnum Agency (his images of the Omaha Beach landings were among the most striking images of World War II). A fascinating character – short, sturdy, an inveterate gambler – Capa reinvented himself from his Hungarian-Jewish origins and had a busy amatory career, usually short-lived romances including affairs with Ingrid Bergman whom he met in Paris just after the liberation and with Hedy Lamarr. According to Bettina Graziani, the elegant Givenchy model, previously Capa's girlfriend for a time, Vivien met Capa one evening at the hotel:

She was alone and fragile. We were all having a drink in the bar. She came down and Capa started to drink with her and then they danced – Russian dances. He was incredible – so much fun. I don't think it lasted long with her. I don't know if he had a life with any woman that lasted very long.

The figures in the carpet became more complex when, on returning to England and back at Notley, Peter Finch reappeared in the Oliviers' lives. *Elephant Walk* had not set the box-office alight and although he was working regularly in British films his life was in some disarray; he had drifted solo in Paris for some time (he believed, "Buddhistically" he said, that life essentially was "flow" – his rationale for avoiding major decisions) before returning to Tamara in London. His experience with Vivien had disturbed him ("After you've been to bed with Vivien, nothing else matters" he told his friend – and Vivien's old Sacred Heart fellow pupil – Bridget Boland) and inevitably shaken his marriage. When finally he returned to London he and Tamara went to *The Sleeping Prince* when Vivien, transformed from the dishevelled, pitiably ill woman Tamara had seen in Hollywood and again dazzlingly composed, acknowledged Tamara's tolerance as she introduced her to other dressing-room guests as "The most courageous girl I know." That courage might well be tested again; although the affair did not then carry on (Vivien and Finch were separated by work), as Tamara acknowledged: "I couldn't fight Vivien. It would have been like trying to fight the Queen." Finch was familiar with Vivien's possessiveness and demanding nature in her manic phases but as well as an almost irresistible mutual physical attraction that bond born out of their absorption in Eastern philosophy (once Vivien, taxed about her religious feelings, described herself as "a Zen-Buddhist-Roman Catholic") and that sense of early abandonment remained strong. Both were damaged people, and such characters tend to respond to others similarly marked by early disturbances to the psyche. But as with Olivier at this time with Tutin and Bloom, so Vivien – as she told Trader Faulkner – "would never have broken her marriage for Peter".

Finch – without Tamara – was a Notley guest for Christmas, 1954 when the guests made up something of a combustible mix of the Waltons (very happy), the Harrisons (very unhappy – appearing nightly in apparent harmony on the London stage in *Bell, Book and Candle* but with Kay Kendall increasingly featuring in Harrison's life), Ernest and Gertrude. And Peter Finch. A keen-eyed observer, Susana Walton later wrote:

I had the distinct feeling that Larry, while setting off the Christmas fireworks, was pointing a rocket directly at Peter, but reluctantly changed his aim at the last minute and shot the rocket up into the evening air.

Over Christmas there was considerable discussion of future plans. Harrison's Hollywood career, following the scandal of his mistress Carole Landis's suicide, was still in the doldrums, about which he regularly moaned, irritated also by the delays in the release of his recent British film *The Constant Husband* (he saw no irony in the title) which co-starred Kay Kendall. Finch had several future British films in the pipeline, including *Simon and Laura*, also with Kendall (with whom he had had a previous fling), but he seemed, that Christmas, as unsettled as Harrison.

Vivien and Olivier professionally remained the theatre's First Couple. For the summer of 1955 they were contracted to lead the company of the Memorial Theatre at Stratford, wooed by their friend and Stratford director Glen Byam Shaw. They would appear together in three Shakespeare plays – *Twelfth Night*, *Macbeth* and, the rarity of the season, *Titus Andronicus*. It was a season offering Vivien three contrasted roles – Viola, Lady Macbeth and the brutalised Lavinia, Titus Andronicus's daughter, in the bloodiest, darkest play in the canon – an undertaking which she knew would present her with the most taxing work she had tackled to date.

CHAPTER 14

Avonside

O nce again before a major undertaking the prospects seemed bright. Olivier was intent on reasserting his classical pre-eminence at Stratford alongside a Vivien who to him seemed equally ready for the months ahead. Suzanne, just out of her teens – she had recently broken up with her first serious boyfriend – wrote to them after a Notley weekend at that time:

> I hope seeing you together and married and in love will teach me a lesson or at least be a pattern of how two people should try to live their lives together.

She could have had no knowledge of the true nature of her mother's illness, her "episodes" invariably explained by her grandmother as nervous "artistic temperament". Manic depression was never mentioned.

Living with a Bipolar person involves tests of patience, of understanding, of love and, vitally, of forgiveness. In either a manic or a depressive phase – the former especially – words, sometimes vile, of accusations and taunts can be uttered by an adored one with no "edit" button who then can seem a total stranger. Perhaps worse are those periods of blank inertia when that person seems oblivious to others, eyes empty, body inert (Vivien said that then she could feel "like an amoeba at the bottom of the sea"). To see Vivien, who when "normal" was so uniquely, intensely alive, in such states must have pierced Olivier's heart. He has stood accused of coldness or indifference; certainly he could be ruthless professionally and should a colleague offend him that person could be cut out of his life. Marriage to Vivien, begun in the wake of such glorious – to him almost mystical – passion inevitably during the worst times of her illness could bring resentment, bitterness, pity, guilt, even hatred at times, a maelstrom of mixed emotions which could insidiously erode that passion.

One way of coping with these often contradictory feelings was to detach himself (his phrase was "self-removing") from the raw feelings involved. Olivier was always an habitual observer, essentially objective. Peter Hiley, a compassionate man who understood Vivien and Olivier better than some of Olivier's intimate circle, once said that although he recognised his boss as a theatrical titan, "as a man he was very light", not in the sense of being inconsequential, but simply "he was not a deep man." He felt that fundamentally Olivier was not really interested in people:

> He would observe someone, thinking that would be a good something for Shylock; but he wasn't wondering what that person was like.

Vivien, thought Hiley, was "not light in that way at all ... a very strong woman, very intelligent, very streetwise, very generous".

Olivier's habit of self-removing put distance between himself and complex situations, such as his firing from the Old Vic and when faced with Vivien's Bipolar symptoms. Their friend Joan Cunliffe asked him after an outburst from Vivien during a bad "episode" why he did not respond, to which his answer (anticipating Archie's song in *The Entertainer* – "Why should I let it touch me?") was "It's better. Better for me, if I don't." By the early 1950s, especially after *Elephant Walk* with Vivien in apparent ruins for so long, his instinct was to retreat more into himself. He did not lack compassion, saddened by Vivien's illness as well as feeling guilty, fearing always in some secret part of himself that his behaviour might have contributed to it but although he too had had low spells ("the black monkey", the equivalent of Churchill's "black dog", was his name for them) he sensed that his own existence, his professional life most crucially, needed his near-exclusive concentration if he was not to endanger his supremacy. In *Confessions* he wrote "Artists must be selfish. It is in fact their duty." He reflected on Vivien: "In so far as she was no longer the person I had loved, I loved her that much less."

He judged that Vivien was in a good state to tackle the 1955 Stratford season. The Memorial Theatre had had a financially disappointing previous year and Glen Byam Shaw needed the Oliviers' star-power to fill the seats but he also greatly admired the work of his two close friends. Their motives for going to Stratford for £60 per week for the major part of the year were not entirely altruistic; Olivier had been stung by suggestions that lightweight vehicles such as *The Sleeping Prince* were unworthy of him and both were aware that the "legend" of the Oliviers, to be maintained, demanded regular joint appearances.

Byam Shaw seemed highly nervous and was grateful when, on the first day of rehearsals with the entire company assembled, Vivien, sensing his jitters, jumped up to give him a big hug. As always on these opening days, the mood was a mixture of tension and elation but there was a strong sense, after the customary opening chats and measurements for costumes and wigs, of a company beginning to come together. The Memorial Theatre had made riverside Avoncliffe, one of the company houses, available for the Oliviers and Vivien soon brightened its somewhat austere interior with some paintings and rugs from Notley. That season had a strong company, familiar faces including Harry Andrews, Maxine Audley, Angela Baddeley and Alan Webb with some promising new talents, among them an Australian trio of Trader Faulkner, Keith Michell and Frank Thring. *Twelfth Night* had Gielgud as director with Byam Shaw for *Macbeth* and Peter Brook for *Titus Andronicus* (he and Olivier had patched up their differences after *The Beggar's Opera*). Olivier, people noticed, seemed in buoyant mood as the season got under way. Unusually, there seemed few financial worries; Hiley and clever accountants had worked out a scheme, approved by the Inland Revenue, whereby Vivien and Olivier became employees of LOP which brought considerable tax advantages. Olivier could still display contradictory meanness, however, bewailing every increase in alimony for Jill (he could be extremely insensitive – "£10,000 a poke" he complained about their sex life, insisting he only had sexual relations with her on seven occasions) and cursing the cost of school fees for Tarquin (although Eton had been at his own choosing). The relationship with his son – helped by Vivien – had improved considerably. Tarquin had had a somewhat surreal conversation two years previously with his father when he accompanied him to see him off at London Airport as Olivier prepared to fly to Colombo during *Elephant Walk*'s first troubles. He talked to his son, all togged up in his Eton suit and feeling rather like a waiter, in the airport's lounge, speaking surprisingly frankly of Vivien, admitting that he could only admire her "gutsiness, her defiance" and adding "and the love-making has never been better", but not attempting to disguise the weight of the problems involved with her psychic disturbances which he told Tarquin he thought had been triggered by her miscarriage nearly eight years before.

The opening elation at the start of Stratford season soon evaporated. From the early *Twelfth Night* rehearsals things started to go awry. Gielgud was not at his happiest; *A Day By the Sea* had been successful but the strain of that period led to a delayed reaction – a minor breakdown in late 1954 – and while he was among many friends and colleagues he had not worked with Olivier on stage for 20 years. With Olivier as director and actor, virtually everything was worked out prior to rehearsal while in both capacities Gielgud was more fluid, instinctively open to experiment (as was Vivien). Gielgud had no pre-planned "concept" of *Twelfth Night*, a favourite play; he loved what he saw as its atmosphere of watered-silk comedy and gravity interwoven and chose a designer just out of the Old Vic School (where Devine and Byam Shaw had been closely associated), Malcolm Pride, to give him a design suggesting a romantic Elizabethan garden somewhat in the pictorial Messel tradition. It was extremely pretty but had unfortunately restricted sightlines which gave Gielgud thorny staging problems.

Olivier had dithered about whether to repeat his Old Vic pickled Sir Toby Belch or to play Malvolio, finally opting for the latter, naturally going against the traditional tight-lipped Puritan and using one of his elaborate transformations of make-up (one of his false noses) and wiggery (coarse, reddish hair) with a speech impediment and a curiously preening gait to suggest a parvenu figure aping his "betters". The whole effect was slightly camp, perhaps not the most tactful notion given Gielgud's sensitivity to the publicity surrounding his arrest. Gielgud's directorial brain was ultra-speedy – thought in an electric blender – and he often spoke before any second thoughts; he blurted out immediately Olivier began his first speech in rehearsal "Oh, no, Larry – that's terribly vulgar!" (a word to which Olivier had taken exception when used by Guthrie to describe his *Henry V* film and to which he took even graver exception now). It developed into an unhappy production, not helped by Gielgud's frequent contradictions in rehearsal ("Come in from the left. Oh, no, no, no – I mean the other left!") or by Olivier's refusal to modify a performance of social realism, with Olivia's household patronising an upstart steward, at odds with the Watteau-esque delicacy for which Gielgud was aiming. Angela Baddeley, playing Maria, thought that a "basic antagonism" between the two men coloured rehearsals:

> I think Larry was a bad boy about it. He was very waspish and overbearing and Johnny became intimidated ... I felt very sorry for him.

Vivien was in an awkward position caught between her director and Olivier ("She was enchanting" said Gielgud, "but torn between what I was trying to do and what Olivier thought she should do"). She had prepared extensively; always inclined to create some imagined previous life, a back-story, for her characters, she was struck by reading a nineteenth-century book, *The Girlhood of Shakespeare's Heroines* by Mary Cowden Clarke, suggesting a Viola having seen Orsino at court when she was a girl and so already in love with him prior to her shipwreck on the Illyrian coast, which gave her an opening into her portrayal of Viola disguised as Cesario – most convincingly in tunic and breeches under a short wig as a slim young boy. Her scenes with Michell (Orsino), and Audley (Olivia) were her most successful, touching and lyrically graceful. Olivier's Malvolio was a crowd-pleaser with its broadly comic business (he insisted on retaining a backward fall off a bench although Gielgud tried to persuade him to cut it) which went against the elusive air of gaiety slightly frosted by melancholy which Gielgud was seeking. Finally, a few days prior to opening and with tensions simmering, Olivier asked Gielgud to leave the cast to themselves ("Go for a walk along the river" he suggested) to get on with things, a humiliation for any director although somehow Gielgud rose above it. A newspaper strike delayed the reviews; they were cool towards the production although Vivien's wistful grace found some favour while Olivier's performance divided opinion. Tynan brushed Vivien aside as providing only "dazzling monotony", against which Olivier defended her: "Absolutely untrue ... she rang every vocal change that anybody could", describing Tynan's notice as "blatantly prejudiced".

Twelfth Night unsettled Vivien. A favourite play under a dear friend with her husband beside her, to which she had greatly looked forward, had been made deeply uneasy. As if in some malign parallel to professional disquiet their private lives became yet again unsettled and slowly the rest of the Stratford season, with sold-out houses, slid into a morass of offstage confusions and distress. The reappearance of Finch at Notley over Christmas had been no accident; he was still besotted by Vivien, the more so as his marriage to an extraordinarily tolerant Tamara was seriously fraying. He was drinking very heavily at this time, having rediscovered his mother. Betty Stavely-Hill, after a life crowded with incident and three husbands, was still a spirited Bohemian figure, living with her daughter Flavia in Chelsea (Finch stayed there more than with Tamara). She did nothing to discourage Finch's involvement with Vivien; Betty and Flavia were extremely fond of her.

Finch began to appear in Stratford at this time. Olivier had begun a new affair, the latest in what he called his "tender venturings into the blessed unction of sex"; at some point early in the season he very discreetly began his involvement with Maxine Audley, a warm and experienced *femme du monde*, deeply sympathetic and with no desire for anything other than a summer-season interlude, conducted mostly at the cottage just outside Stratford which she had rented. Finch's presence became more noticeable; he and Vivien were often seen together in the town and they spent some nights in a room which

Finch had rented or in one of Stratford's hotels. Naturally this became a topic of consuming company gossip, although the Olivier/Audley affair was much more discreet. Few, apart from their closest friends in the company, could appreciate the complexity of the Oliviers' relationship, its guilts, its rifts and the freight of its memories, and some were dismayed by the erosion of what had seemed a great romance, "the legend". While Vivien still needed that sense of romance, Olivier retreated progressively into the maintenance of his purely professional legend. He then could see Finch as a kind of safety valve, capable of satisfying Vivien physically ("You can't be more than one kind of athlete at a time" he said, and Stratford's schedule was gruelling). Finch, too, had a romantic vision. His friend Faulkner said: "To Vivien he spoke more intimately of what he really thought and believed" than he did to anyone else. Finch was prone to identify with those like himself, in some sense fractured; he had a definite affinity with those he saw as victims (Vivien's illness made her such for him) and he pictured himself and Vivien as two outsider lovers pitched against a conventional world. Another Finch biographer, Elaine Dundy, excavated considerable amounts of Freudian undertones in her book, suggesting that the Vivien/Olivier/Finch triangle could be seen in Oedipal terms with Olivier as Finch's surrogate father and Finch impelled blindly to destroy that father by usurping his place sexually with his own mother (i.e. Vivien). Much as Olivier had been swayed by studying the Oedipus Complex when preparing for *Hamlet*, it is highly unlikely that he reflected on his 1955 situation in such Freudian terms. Dundy did however note succinctly of the whole business: "The best you could say about them was probably the worst you could say about them; they did nothing behind Olivier's back."

To begin with, Vivien's increased volatility largely took the form of sudden impulses to socialise, to throw impromptu company picnics or parties at Avoncliffe which of course the younger and more impressionable members took to enthusiastically, depriving Olivier when he was there of much-needed sleep (as well as *Macbeth* to come, he had to get on top of *Titus Andronicus* which he was finding unusually difficult – "like trying to learn dry oats" he moaned to Peter Brook). Nobody's mood was lightened by a *Daily Express* article which appeared shortly before *Macbeth* entered the repertoire. John Barber, very much his master Beaverbrook's voice (the magnate believed provocative journalism created controversy and sales) wrote a piece in the Tynan vein but without his brilliant prose, attacking the "cult" of "The Oliviers", urging readers to look behind the gloss of "the titled lions of Mayfair salons", calling Olivier "an ageing matinee idol" while Vivien, although "undeniably a great beauty" as an actress "seldom touches the heart". It predictably created the controversy Beaverbrook wanted, with many column inches devoted to the differences of opinion Barber had provoked. Within the theatre world it was regarded as unfairly biased; Vivien and Olivier received many letters deploring Barber's piece, from Guinness, Quayle, Richardson and even Marlene Dietrich, who wrote to Vivien, her "sweet beautiful love", to describe her "fury against Barber – if only I were a man I would have knocked his teeth in".

It was against that pressure and offstage drama that rehearsals for Shakespeare's traditionally unluckiest play took place. Byam Shaw, as always, had prepared meticulously and had agreed beforehand with Vivien and Olivier that this would be no trail-blazing "concept" production of *Macbeth* but one crucially focused on the central marital relationship. Uncharacteristically Roger Furse's design was uninspired, with somewhat crude, vaguely medieval doorways and heavy furniture, although the costumes, hinting at the barbaric and richly textured with striking jewellery and armour, were another story. But the central performances, helped by strong casting in support (Michell and Audley as the Macduffs, Harry Andrews as Banquo), gave the production lift-off, possibly the best of all the Oliviers' pairings, as they tackled Shakespeare's portrait of a disintegrating marriage.

The 1937 Old Vic production with Olivier and Judith Anderson under Michel St Denis had been heavily stylised, with symbolic sets and mask-like make-up – Vivien had mischievously described Macbeth's entrance: "You hear Macbeth's first line, then Larry's make-up comes on, then Banquo comes on, then Larry comes on" – with the central pair along the conventional lines of weak man and fiendish woman. Now he left most of his make-up box unopened, adding only a trimmed beard to his own features, and he found it "genuinely possible to make every second of Macbeth human". Vivien knew exactly the scale of the production as a domestic tragedy which was aimed at and geared her own performance accordingly. She did a great deal of background reading once more, finding another Mary Cowden Clarke study, *The Thane's Daughter*, initially helpful in its picture of a character innately cruel, the child of a mother disappointed she was not a boy and one who enjoys killing a moth at a young age. Cowden Clarke's work, born out of nineteenth-century fiction with roots in family structures, helped spark off ideas but for *Macbeth* even more useful was her digging into the play's performance history. She became fascinated both by what Irving's Lady Macbeth, Ellen Terry, had written about the character in her *Lectures on Shakespeare's Women* and by what had been written about Terry's performance. She came to realise that a battle-axe in the grand Mrs Siddons tradition had not been Terry's approach, encouraged by noticing that she had been more influenced by the more delicate Helena Faucit (leading lady to William Charles Macready), who created an essentially domestic figure, as did Terry, who dressed like a figure out of a pre-Raphaelite painting and read Macbeth's letter seated by a fire rather than pacing in the familiar declamatory manner, with a kind of realism unusual in high tragedy. Since then convention had reasserted itself but Vivien set out to proceed further down the path Terry had begun to chart. She visited the Terry Museum at Smallhythe which contained many books on *Macbeth*; she discovered an essay on the Macbeths by Joseph Comyns Carr, the remarkably versatile Victorian dramatist/critic/ designer (he designed the costume for Ellen Terry in *Macbeth* in which Sargent painted her) and found it particularly helpful. It portrayed a woman stamped by her femininity but whose concentration of will and imagination complement Macbeth's weaker instincts, creating "a sublime study in sexual contrast", her personality only disintegrating from the Banquet Scene onwards, marking the beginning of her slide into derangement.

Sybil Thorndike, on an Australian tour, had written wishing the Oliviers luck, adding "It needs a husband and wife to play it" and this was an aspect widely noticed at Stratford, by other actors especially. Vivien's performance was notable for its sensuous physicality. The Macbeths' first meeting was a highly passionate embrace, bodies glued together, with a lingering kiss suggesting a searingly hot sexual bond. After Macbeth decides not to proceed with Duncan's murder she took an electrifying run across the stage right up to him and while he turned away to avoid her taunts she played the following section ("I have given suck...") very close to him, pitching her voice quite low and speaking daringly slowly, shocking him with her own capacity for cruelty and brutality. The desolation at the end of the Banquet Scene hushed the house as did her Sleepwalking Scene for which she wore a subtly different wig (less vibrant, more mousy than her first, suggesting life draining away) and in which her voice alternated startlingly between a harsh, aged croak and the radiant innocence of a younger woman.

She and Furse had spent considerable time working out her principal costume – a dress of clinging green velvet, cut to allow her to move quickly and sinuously. Photographs cannot reveal the detail so telling on stage under lights, its bodice shaded with painted rib-bones and lines to heighten her breasts, even with a suggestion of a belly-button, all designed to stress Lady Macbeth's sexual power. Sybil Thorndike was right; this *Macbeth* gained greatly from the Oliviers' own intimacy, their ability to channel all sorts of emotional memories and images. Ellen Terry had an image of Lady Macbeth's first glimpse of a young Macbeth riding up to a castle as she watches from a window; possibly Vivien recalled her first sight of Olivier as the charismatic, athletic leading man of *Theatre Royal*. Much of the tortured journey in *Macbeth* – Olivier described it as "one going up and one going down ... he goes on and she goes down" – was informed by their nearly 20 years of joint experiences, the joyous and the wretched.

The opening performance received an ovation. Even Vivien's most staunch admirers had been surprised by the power of this Lady, one who actually rarely raised her voice but was perfectly audible to the back row throughout. During rehearsals and all the offstage tensions, Vivien had found time to visit Denne Gilkes, a well-known figure in the town ("The Wise Woman of Stratford") for voice lessons, who wrote to her:

> The voice was fine all through – and I thought the sleep scene was fine, the best I have seen. I think you have "got it".

Peggy Ashcroft wrote to "my darling Macbeths" from Wales:

> Where your playing still haunts me ... I was so awed by what I had seen that I could say nothing of what I really felt ... your interplay of intimacy I've never seen so movingly done or realized about both of them, their terrifying loneliness.

Ashcroft never played Lady Macbeth but Fabia Drake, who had, stressed that she only realised how the Banquet Scene should be played after seeing Vivien's performance, adding:

> Beautiful and sinuous, her Lady Macbeth was like a dangerous snake gliding about the stage ... She was the best I have ever seen. I think Vivien's great beauty caused her to be seriously underrated.

In a later letter Drake, mentioning that she had disliked Olivier's Malvolio which she thought unbalanced *Twelfth Night*, added of *Macbeth*: "I believe *you* enabled him to become what he is." The reactions of many fellow actors were similar. One which may have surprised her was contained in a note from Mu Richardson, who had gone with Jill to a concert and reported Jill as saying "you were the finest Lady McB she had ever seen and she's seen a few. I would consider that *praise* from such a source." One of the most touching was from Leigh, who thought her Lady "the finest performance I have ever seen you give", generously saying that "Larry and you can do together what neither can do apart", adding:

> You will be surprised how much you are always in my thoughts. You have evolved into the only wholly disinterested love of my life.

The critical reaction mostly echoed the theatre world's opinion, many mentioning the conviction of the marital relationship, the Banquet Scene after which the strength almost visibly seemed to ooze out of her and Vivien's occasional almost maternal solicitude (as on "sleek o'er your rugged looks"). The writer Robert Henriques on radio's *The Critics* confessed that he had been dubious about Vivien's casting; after describing how for once he had been utterly convinced by the Macbeths' mutual passion he went on to say that the "terrific sleep-walking scene is one of the greatest things I've ever seen on the stage." There were a few die-hard reviews; Beaverbrook's desire for controversy was presumably satisfied by Barber's fatuous comparison of Vivien with comedian Arthur Askey and Patrick Gibbs in the *Daily Telegraph* took the stereotypical view of *Macbeth*, insisting that "physical attraction is no help" for Lady Macbeth and that Vivien lacked the "domination of personality required".

More surprisingly this was echoed by Tynan. He could write prose as dazzling in enthusiasm as in laceration and his notice was mainly a long, soaring paean of praise for Olivier ("he shook hands with greatness"). By contrast he then dismissed Vivien in one throwaway sentence but for unexpectedly conventional reasons: "Vivien Leigh's Lady Macbeth is more niminy-piminy than thundery-blundery, more viper than anaconda, but still quite competent in its small way." At the time his flip verdict was met with general angry disagreement in the theatre world but this judgement from the most influential critic of his era has become almost received opinion. The history of the theatre tends to be that of reports of first nights. Yet why should Lady Macbeth have to be "thundery-blundery" or like some smothering anaconda? The best Lady Macbeth of recent memory – Judi Dench opposite Ian McKellen – was very much along the lines followed by Ellen Terry and Vivien. Later – when editing the text of *Macbeth* for Roman Polanski's film – Tynan admitted to fellow critic John Russell Taylor that his review of Vivien's Lady had been "one of the worst errors of judgement he had ever made" and that her sexual power "made more sense of the play than any other reading" he had witnessed. But was this really an error of judgement? Tynan was never one to kow-tow to received perceptions and he knew his theatre history; he knew quite well surely that Lady Macbeth need not be turbulently stormy in the Siddons manner. Either his review was coloured by an antipathy to Vivien so ingrained that, most unusually, it distorted his view of the play or it was a piece of calculated cruelty. His admission to Russell Taylor also calls into question his other demolitions of Vivien's performances.

Many colleagues – Quayle, Guinness, Byam Shaw – tried to persuade her not to let Tynan's review affect her, but Vivien was by no means alone amongst actors in remembering one bad review even with a whole sheaf of raves. This time his casual dismissal cut deep, sparking another manic spell. Coward, who had found her performance "quite remarkable" was at Notley soon afterwards when he recorded her "talking wildly at supper, obsessed by press 'persecution'", noting sadly in his diary that in his opinion the main trouble between the Oliviers was fundamentally sexual with Vivien, exacerbated by incipient tuberculosis, having more needs than Olivier could satisfy:

> Here they are trapped by public acclaim, scrabbling about in the cold ashes of a physical passion that burnt itself out years ago. I am desperately sorry because I love them both and I am truly fearful of what may happen.

He had listened to both Olivier and Tarquin, his godson, express fears about Vivien's mental state but he somewhat modified his concern a few weeks later when he expressed the questionable opinion that had Olivier given Vivien "a clip in the chops" years before, then "he would have been spared a mint of trouble".

Vivien's energy when on a "high" could be awesome. Michael Denison remembered after a typical Notley late night walking the next afternoon with Olivier leaving Vivien resting, apparently stricken by pleurisy, then returning to find every light blazing in a house echoing to sounds "like the Duchess of Richmond's ball on the eve of Waterloo". Vivien had telephoned around inviting Stratford actors and friends for a party which went on until dawn. Olivier remained worried and managed to persuade Vivien to see Dr Freudenberg but with the cunning she had shown with previous doctors she convinced him that she was perfectly fine. Freudenberg told Olivier that no ECT or any other treatment was necessary.

Vivien still had *Titus Andronicus* to rehearse. Brook had turned down the offer to direct *Macbeth* (fearing the play's "cursed" reputation as much as anyone), opting instead for his long-nurtured project of *Titus*, never previously seen at Stratford and often considered an impossible play to bring off with its catalogue of horrors outdoing any Elizabethan revenge-tragedy. He had worked for some time to realise his vision of the play's barbarism in a postwar world, composing the music, a blend of eerie dissonant sound and *musique concrète*, designing the set and supervising (with Michael Northen, a technical wizard) the dramatic lighting. It developed into one of the great Stratford productions, a bridge between the previous generation (Barry Jackson, Byam Shaw and Quayle) and the Royal Shakespeare Company under Peter Hall. Generally regarded as no more than Grand Guignol, a chamber of horrors crowded with murders, rape, mutilation and cannibalism (T.S. Eliot described it as "one of the stupidest and most uninspiring plays ever written"), under Brook it emerged new-minted as an austere Roman tragedy leavened by a jagged streak of unsettling dark comedy, using a strikingly versatile set of pillared columns which could represent palace or forest alike with sharply angled shafts of white light, progressively turning to red as the bloodshed mounted. A keen student of oriental dance, Brook exploited Chinese theatre techniques to stylise some of the cruder violence; Vivien as Lavinia, daughter of the Roman general Titus (Olivier), is raped by his Goth enemies who rip out her tongue and cut off her hands. Brook presented this near-balletically with Lavinia's wounds suggested by bloody ribbons flowing out of her sleeves and mouth, a speechless vision of mutilated desolation (Shakespeare describes it as a "mask of woe"), her movement slowed and gliding, infinitely graceful in its pathos and underscored by eerie harp-like sounds. She had not known the play previously (few did) but at Olivier's suggestion she agreed to play Lavinia rather than the larger role of the vengeful Tamora, Queen of the Goths (possibly he felt that Lady Macbeth provided enough darkness for one summer) although before the season went into rehearsal he owned to Byam Shaw:

> I got into trouble this morning with my wife ... for saying she should play Lavinia when of course she now burns to play Tamora, oh dear, oh dear.

Maxine Audley by then was contracted to play Tamora. Nevertheless, Vivien very much liked Brook's infectious energy; her dance experience was useful for the stylised movement which he wanted for Lavinia after her ravishment. She wrote to Mu Richardson:

> I have never enjoyed or perhaps enjoyed is *not* the word – let's say been so interested in – a part before ... how it means one has to really act with one's thoughts and has taught me more than anything I have ever done.

This chimes oddly with Olivier's recollections of Vivien at this time, claiming that "she seemed unable to enter into, let alone explore, the character or problems of Lavinia", adding "for the next five years it was as if she had just lost touch with her craft". But Brook praised her work, sending her a first-night note of warm congratulations and later writing: "Vivien's grace and talent could transform this play in the way that the Japanese theatre transforms acts of cruelty in Kabuki legends," recalling a personal highlight of the production, when the silenced, mutilated Lavinia writes her rapists' names in the sand using two sticks, noting that she found grace in the degradation ("she turned this piece of Grand Guignol into a haunting moment of poetry"). Philip Hope-Wallace described her Lavinia as resembling "a marvellous grieving Christian

martyr from some morbid Veronese canvas". Also, in the five-year period
mentioned by Olivier she went on to success in London with a Coward comedy
and in the West End and on Broadway with Giraudoux' *Duel of Angels*.

What Olivier described as "the crash" only came after *Titus* had opened. The
reviews reflected the critics' surprise at the revelation of the play in Brook's
hands, full of laurels for Olivier's elevation to genuinely tragic status of the
grief-bowed Titus. Mostly Vivien too was admired. Evelyn Waugh, briefly
turning drama critic for *The Spectator*, instantly recognised "We were in for
something of rare quality" and admired Brook's daring in permitting some
grisly gallows-humour, writing that Vivien "established complete confidence
between the audience and the production, the grain of salt which gave savour
to the whole rich stew". Waugh remained captivated by Vivien, seeing many of
her performances. Touchingly – possibly aware of her Bipolar condition – he
later sent her a copy of his novel of a period of personal psychic disturbance,
The Ordeal of Gilbert Pinfold. Tynan again went against the tide regarding
Vivien's Lavinia. He made no mention of Brook's jet-black comedic vein and
after another of his tsunamis of praise for Olivier once again swept Vivien aside
in a single sentence:

> As Lavinia Miss Vivien Leigh received the news that she is about to be ravished on
> her husband's corpse with little more than the mild annoyance of one who would
> have preferred foam rubber.

It would seem that on this occasion Olivier lost patience with Tynan; he did
not reply personally but among his papers there is a letter from Tennant at this
time answering what seems to have been a request to his agent to explore the
possibility of legal action. However, Tennant's letter makes it clear that he
agrees with "counsel's opinion" ("I fear dignified silence is the only reply").

At the party after *Titus*'s first night there was a marked contrast between an
exhausted Olivier in a corner making desultory conversation with Angela
Baddeley and a dangerously animated Vivien:

> In the other corner of the room Finch had a group of ladies, Vivien included, in fits
> of laughter with an hilarious bawdy pantomime rendering of erotic wallpaper in a
> spinster's bedroom.

The remainder of the Stratford season spiralled into a period when the private
tensions underlying the whole season were as turbulent as anything the public
were seeing on the stage. Olivier's affair with Audley continued while Finch
practically usurped his place during Notley weekends, also regularly turning up
at Stratford. In both places Vivien's manic phases involved ceaseless post-
performance parties and while, extraordinarily, she never missed a performance,

her post-show drinking noticeably increased, worrying all who knew how alcohol could affect her in such states. Upset by this and the turn of events with Finch, Suzanne felt impelled to write to her mother:

> I wouldn't dream of either criticizing or condemning your actions. But I can't for the life of me see what you see in him or really what drives you to him.

She suggested that possibly she and Vivien could holiday together after Stratford was over ("if I could help in any way I should very much love to"). Rachel Kempson, who knew all about the tensions of triangular relationships, was also concerned and wrote on the same day as Suzanne after a Notley weekend that she was praying that this crisis in her friend's marriage might pass or that Vivien, Olivier and Finch might somehow establish a modus vivendi which could bring some sort of peace to all three.

Olivier felt an increasing need for "a condition of detachment" from his marriage then and came to Notley only occasionally. Trader Faulkner recalled a weekend when he was present with the other three. Faulkner was with Vivien late on Saturday night discussing reincarnation over gin in the drawing-room:

> She was convinced Peter was an 'old soul' full of timeless wisdom, tenderness and understanding – all the qualities that every woman looks for in a man. Larry was a brand new soul with a plastic karma and a marital deficit.

Somewhat recalling the *Streetcar* scene of Stanley overhearing Blanche and Stella, Faulkner became aware of Olivier's shadow. He had overheard. Finch, already sensing possible confrontation, had taken his habitual evasive action and disappeared into the garden where Faulkner later found him talking to "a very reluctant flock of white doves", berating himself for deriving a kind of perverse pleasure out of highly charged situations.

There was one such charged situation at the end of the season according to various sources, Faulkner and Finch's old Australian mate Bertie Whiting included. Determined finally to resolve the situation, fearing that eventually the press might write of the tangled triangle, Olivier insisted on dinner *à trois* at Notley. When coffee arrived Vivien left both men to the port in the dining-room to resolve the question. Neither knew quite how to begin and finally Olivier defused the tension by resorting to role-playing, acting the part of a dotty old lord of the manor while Finch, picking up his cue as it were, improvised His Lordship's decrepit ancient retainer. They elaborated their double act, hugely diverting themselves until the early hours before suddenly the door was flung open to reveal Vivien in her nightdress demanding "Which one of you is coming to bed with me?" The men, by now squiffy on port, dissolved into wild laughter, soon joined by Vivien; dawn at Notley saw all three in hysterical mirth, rather like the close of Coward's "three-sided erotic hotch-potch", *Design for Living*. Before long the story was doing the rounds in Finch's regular London haunts such as the Buckstone Club or the Salisbury and other familiar West End actors' pubs.

Finch knew that in real life such a pattern of living was not sustainable but while he fully intended to break with Vivien, well aware of the possibility of scandal, he was not yet strong enough to do so. After all the tempests of the season it ended with a surprisingly happy party at Avoncliffe with Vivien and Olivier together seemingly in joyfully sparkling form, with an impressive buffet and a cabaret with specially written material. To the tune of Irving Berlin's contrapuntal "You're Just in Love" from *Call Me Madam*, Vivien and Olivier sang a *Macbeth*-themed lyric:

I see daggers and there's nothing there,
I see witches in the filthy air;
Someone's ravelled up our sleeve of care,
I wonder why, I wonder why.

It made a sharply contrasted end to a season stamped by a backstage atmosphere described by Quayle as "nightmarish", full of "awful tensions beneath the gaiety".

Tensions tightened towards the end of the year when Vivien and Finch ran off together, initially to Paris. Loyal to both Oliviers, Ginette Spanier had firmly told Vivien that Finch could not stay with her and Paul-Emile at the Seidmann apartment on the Avenue Marceau; Vivien vanished abruptly on her first night but next morning she was back and Finch had joined her there. The couple, meeting up with Alan Webb, then travelled to stay at the house of the Oliviers' friend Paul-Louis Weiller in the south of France. A rich industrialist, cosmopolitan and a connoisseur of beautiful women (he had a major crush on Diana Cooper), his luxurious Provencal villa was set amid pines near a beautiful beach. They had not been there long when Olivier, accompanied by the Seidmanns, turned up – appearances had to be maintained, for all that Vivien used to claim that actresses (Bernhardt was usually cited) had always had lovers – before Olivier took her off, first to San Vigilio for Christmas. There, joined by the Waltons in the peace beside the lake, the *locanda* overseen as always by its owner Leonard Walsh ("Leonardo"), an outsize personality responsible for its unique atmosphere, Vivien became noticeably calmer. The drama involved with Finch – there had been an earlier "elopement" attempt, aborted by fog at London Airport, an episode which Rattigan used as the plot for his screenplay *The VIPs* – seemed to dissolve. Vivien had agreed to appear the following year in Coward's comedy *South Sea Bubble* for Beaumont and the initial press announcements stated that Finch would co-star, but in early 1956 he quietly dropped out, replaced by Ronald Lewis. Tamara finally had had enough; Finch was living at Betty's Bury Street house while "Auntie Olive" sorted out maintenance for Tamara and Anita.

Early 1956 saw the Oliviers travel after San Vigilio to Bavaria – Tarquin was stationed there with the Coldstream Guards – from where Vivien wrote to Maxine Audley "I am being very healthy and restful in the mountains." Audley's affair with Olivier had also come to an end, most amicably, soon after Stratford. There were other changes too, all seeming to mark a new phase in the Oliviers' lives. Durham Cottage was sold (with a cook and a secretary, they needed more space) and they leased the Waltons' house in nearby Lowndes Place while scouting for a new London home. At the same time Alexander Korda died – a sudden heart attack; he had been a key figure in both careers for 20 years. Olivier gave the address – eloquently heartfelt – at his Memorial Service – but although he already had the film of *The Sleeping Prince* (retitled *The Prince and the Showgirl* once Marilyn Monroe was cast) to make, Korda's death put an end, at least temporarily, to his dream of making one more Shakespeare film, this time of *Macbeth* (for which he never considered any other co-star but Vivien) which Korda had agreed to finance.

For the next few years Olivier continued to try to set up the *Macbeth* film, a project very dear to Vivien also. Yet he became curiously taciturn about the venture, perhaps because it ended in disappointment after several false hopes. The film is barely mentioned in *Confessions* and when questioned about it he would insist that nothing but an outline survived. Yet in his papers held by the British Library there are no less than 13 draft versions of Olivier's screenplay together with many technical papers, set plans, even a shooting script. His ideas comprise a prospect as tantalising as Redgrave's similarly stalled work on *Antony and Cleopatra*, as is clear from the studies of the material by Dr Jennifer Barnes, a leading lecturer in Film Studies. Essentially it was conceived along the lines of the Stratford production with only a few major cuts (the "Dagger" speech is trimmed heavily) and alterations, including an arrestingly recast opening with Macbeth gazing down into a deep pool reflecting his battle-scarred body, "his blood colouring the water around him" (blood becomes a recurring motif throughout). Barnes suggests that the script exemplifies Olivier's tendency to interpret periods of personal crisis through his Shakespearean adaptations, his work on *Macbeth* mirroring a turbulent 1950s period (one draft includes Lady Macbeth having suffered a miscarriage), and the slow collapse of "The Oliviers" mystique. To read the shooting script – imaginatively shifting between bleak, mist-shrouded landscapes often bleached of colour and massive castles with colour bleeding in, and having the Macbeths morph on occasion into the Witches – makes even deeper the regret that the film was never made. Gielgud was only one of those who believed that, magnificent as he had found Vivien in the role at Stratford, her Lady Macbeth on screen might have been finer still. But the economics of the cinema had altered; *Richard III* and *Carrie* had not recovered their costs and so after Korda's death Olivier had to search for funding elsewhere in a harsher financial climate.

The pressure on Olivier to deliver a success with *The Prince and the Showgirl* became all the heavier in consequence. Essentially he was an employee of Marilyn Monroe's production company, directing as well as co-starring. The press rather feebly tried to concoct a scenario out of Vivien's stage role being usurped by the biggest female Hollywood star of the 1950s but she made light of it, claiming she accepted that she was too old to play the part on film – indeed it was Vivien, after seeing Monroe in *How to Marry a Millionaire*, who had suggested she play the role – and besides she had Coward's *South Sea Bubble* to occupy her.

The film proved a well-documented ordeal to make. Olivier was used to living with psychological problems, of which Monroe had many, and he had been warned by other directors (Cukor and Joshua Logan included) of her habitual lateness but he was still knocked off-balance by her level of disorganisation which for him, the supreme professional, smacked of rank amateurism (keeping fellow actors, including Sybil Thorndike, waiting for hours) coupled with her dependence on her on-set acting coach, Paula Strasberg (Monroe had become influenced by the Actor's Studio under Lee Strasberg) whose instructions were anathema to Olivier and his focus on technique. He simply could not work out how to direct her, making him peremptory, which of course could only increase her nerves. In retrospect it seems that the recent Monroe/Arthur Miller marriage (Miller accompanied her to England) was already under stress and that her nervous apprehension had roots deeper than immediately apparent, but the miracle – as Olivier had to admit – was that despite the agony of the progress of filming, on screen she was mesmerising, one of those rare performers whom the camera instantly loves. Some books have suggested that Vivien's jealousy brought her often to the set, attempting to unsettle Monroe, who of course knew that Vivien had created the role on stage. This was not the case. Vivien had accompanied Olivier to meet the Millers' flight – the press literally besieged Marilyn at the press conference – happy to pose smiling for the cameras with Olivier and the Millers. She also acted as hostess for Rattigan at his house near Wentworth golf course at a lavish party held to welcome the Millers. Suzanne was present, writing afterwards to Vivien that while Monroe looked "adorable" she still thought her mother was the most beautiful woman there:

> You did look so wonderful – you also had a sort of happy glow about you which some hostesses find so difficult to have.

Colin Clark, working as a lowly "gofer" on the film, later wrote a book on its making, based on the diary he kept at the time. Contrary to Spoto's allegations of "jealous resentment" and "ungenerous visits" by Vivien to Pinewood Studios, Clark noted only a single visit to the set, possibly made at Olivier's request. Continuing to have "communication problems" with his star, constantly frustrated by Strasberg's Method-ist advice, he may have imagined that an appearance from Vivien and some on-set encouragement might assuage at least some of Monroe's jitters. Clark remembered the occasion well:

> Vivien advanced and, to MM's intense surprise, kissed her lightly on both cheeks. "Marilyn", she sighed, "Larry tells me you are quite superb. He never stops singing your praises. I'm getting a little jealous." Very sweet, very sincere, what an actress! ... everyone was impressed, even Paula. Then she vanished in a cloud of expensive perfume.

Quite a performance, considering she had heard Olivier mostly curse Monroe, his opinion of her lower even than Coward's ("She's no Madame de Stael, is she?"), claiming that directing her was like trying to teach Urdu to a marmoset. Vivien had possibly intuited a problem noticed by Clark. He thought, despite the enormity of the Strasberg problem, that Olivier had made a big mistake by allowing Monroe to sense his hostility and that the LOP coterie (Bushell as assistant director, Roger Furse designing, Carmen Dillon as art director, "Bumble" Dawson overseeing costumes) tended to be sycophantic in taking only his side (Sybil Thorndike challenged Olivier one day when he was noticeably impatient – "Are you helping her or bullying her?"). Certainly Vivien's visit had some effect on Monroe's confidence; Clark noted that at least for some time subsequently "she did definitely seem more committed".

Vivien seemed blooming at that time. She and Olivier both liked Lowndes Place and they seemed to delight in each other once again; it was this period that Olivier described as one when he had decided to try "to fuck our love back into existence". Also *South Sea Bubble* had established itself as a solid success at the Lyric, Shaftesbury Avenue. Not even Coward's staunchest admirer could claim this as among his best work (it has had no major revival). Written in the late 1940s as a vehicle for Gertrude Lawrence, it remained unproduced while she starred on Broadway in *The King and I* during the run of which she died. A revised version under the title *Home and Colonial* had a summer-stock production in 1951 in America, starring Claudette Colbert and directed by Jack Wilson, but when the Oliviers first read it they turned it down as not strong enough. Gritting his teeth, Coward restructured and extensively revised the play and now Vivien was considerably more enthused, delighting the author:

> I honestly think it's a wonderful part for you. You've been tearing yourself to shreds too much and this will really give you a chance to be gay and enchanting and free from care.

Coward knew very well from experience that an actor can become gay and enchanting and carefree in a light comedy only after weeks of mostly grinding hard graft in rehearsal, which was certainly the case with *South Sea Bubble*. After 1945 Coward seemed to go into exile both geographically (Jamaica then Switzerland, high above the contemporary fray) and artistically as his comic arteries hardened. Most of his postwar work (the songs excepted) lacks the zest of those plays from the pre-1945 "years of grace". His imaginary tropical island, Samolo, was the setting of *South Sea Bubble*, later revisited for his only novel *Pomp and Circumstance*. Vivien played Lady Alexandra ("Sandra") Shotter, a blithe spirit rather like Diana Cooper or Edwina Mountbatten, married to the island's "progressive" governor. Deeply royalist and basically conservative to the core, Coward set out to write a satirical comedy scrutinising the notion that colonial possessions should automatically be granted independence which, in Samolo, seems not to be the unanimous wish of the population, headed by the island's leader, Hali Alani, who quietly argues against such Shotter schemes as the democratisation of Samolo's coin-operated public conveniences. Sandra tries to help her husband by charming Alani to see the value of more advanced ideas but when she visits him at his beach hut he misreads her intentions, causing a potential scandal when she knocks him out with a bottle of the island's hooch. Of course her quick wits and his gallantry (he is, naturally, an old Etonian) avert disaster. It would be stretching a point to describe *South Sea Bubble* as a political play but of course even a light comedy cannot help reflecting Coward's questioning of the shifting tides of the period, inevitably taking a dim view of those politicians at home and abroad whose democratising efforts would, to him, reduce his native country's international standing and influence. Rarely off stage and with a tricky drunk scene involving a dance and a rendition of the Roedean School song, Vivien had to work hard on the play but Coward was slipping out of critical favour in the 1950s in the wake of the English Stage Company's "revolution" at the Royal Court under George Devine since *Look Back in Anger*, although it would be some time before the New Wave began to filter into the mainstream.

Produced by H.M. Tennent (LOP had no co-production arrangement but invested in the venture), Beaumont gave *South Sea Bubble* deluxe casting (Arthur Macrae stealing scenes as a laconic visiting novelist, Joyce Carey as a retrograde colonial wife) and William Chappell's production was played at breakneck speed. Vivien's personal reviews were glowing. Tynan was absent and so did not cover it but his *Sunday Times* counterpart, Harold Hobson, was extremely positive, shrewdly noting that for all the seeming paternalism of the play's attitudes Coward occasionally had a provocative unexpectedness which could still surprise, best illustrated he felt by Vivien, the "splendour" of the production ("Her performance shines like the stars and is as troubling as the inconstant moon").

Coward took his cooler personal reviews philosophically, noting that the play was immediately "a capacity hit", clearly settled in for a lengthy Lyric run. Vivien was radiant, as many remarked; it transpired that there was a reason apart from the play's success for the "happy glow" mentioned by Suzanne. Vivien wrote to Coward in Jamaica to reveal what she called her "tender secret", to date revealed only to close family. At the age of 42 Vivien was pregnant.

The news created considerable fuss. Understandably Tarquin was upset to learn he would have a half-sibling from the tabloid headlines in Germany, for which Olivier wrote apologising for "funking" telling him. Coward was less than thrilled that his biggest success for some while would have to find a new star after only four months of the run. The announcement of Vivien's pregnancy had to be made earlier than planned. The *Daily Mail* somehow got wind of the story and although Olivier tried to put the paper's reporter off the scent they knew that it could not remain secret for long. They held a press conference together on a love-seat at Lowndes Place, smiling in what appeared to be genuine delight for the cameras. They were deluged with letters; Ralph Richardson drew his own card, sending "Love and congratulations on your Great Expectations". There was a good deal of malicious gossip also, suggestions that Vivien had chosen to announce the news to upstage Marilyn Monroe or – more commonly – that she was not pregnant at all. Spoto, citing no reference, claims that it seems to have been "a phantom pregnancy or a deliberate ruse".

Vivien had been socially very quiet during her period in *South Sea Bubble* although she rehearsed intensively for 1956's *Night of a Hundred Stars*, performing a routine with Olivier and John Mills to Irving Berlin's "Top Hat" at the end of June. Also that summer Radie Harris attended a dinner at the Oliviers' when the pregnancy was toasted with champagne. Vivien gave her final performance at the Lyric on 11 August (she had played for five weeks on tour and over three months in London). On the following day, a Sunday, she miscarried. The pregnancy was real. The five days following that Sunday had several engagements in Vivien's diary; "5 a.m." is written against that 12 August Sunday (the time she began to miscarry) and the following days' appointments are faintly scored out in pencil, cancelled or postponed. Also Hester Olivier, then imminently expecting her second child, was at Notley at the time and remembered the arrival of the doctor, who had to inform them that it had been impossible to save the baby. It was a girl. Hester also recalled seeing Vivien, gently weeping, the next day as she handed over to Hester the baby clothes put together to date. Olivier told a reporter that the medical advice given – that Vivien could work until early August – had been followed, adding "We are bitterly disappointed. It is just bad luck. Fate." They received scores of letters of sympathy, one from the Millers "to express our hope that you will soon again feel the joy of life" and signed by "Arthur" and "Marilyn".

Coward was not pleased. He had replied to Vivien's first letter sounding happy enough, admitting he was sad to lose her from *South Sea Bubble* but telling her to take care and to eat marrons glacés at three in the morning if she felt the craving. But his diary recorded his true feelings:

> *South Sea Bubble*, if only they had the sense to see it, was a life saver for Vivien. It gave her a glamorous success on her own, away from Larry's perpetual shadow.

He remained in a huff, cross that the delay in telling him the news lost time to find a strong replacement (Elizabeth Sellars took over and the play continued although business dropped considerably), growing crosser when he discovered that Beaumont had known of the pregnancy before he did. He concluded:

> I'm sick to death of them both at the moment ... as they haven't even bothered to write to me they can bloody well get on with it.

Vivien did write contritely to apologise and Coward, who acknowledged also in his diary that "Friendship is a rare business", kissed and made up with her in Dublin when she went to visit him while he supervised the production of his next play, *Nude with Violin* ("Vivien was really very sweet and I think and hope the air is now cleared").

There were no concrete plans for either Vivien or Olivier until a European tour of *Titus Andronicus* in the summer of 1957. The pregnancy had been another reason for delaying decisions but both seemed to have recovered from the blow of the miscarriage (Olivier had written to Tarquin that "Puss is better and sweeter than for many years ... pray God it can keep like that and life can be heavenly again"). They continued to look at occasional possible London homes, although they lost one property (near Beaumont in Lord North Street) to Harold MacMillan, who offered a higher price. In the meantime Lowndes Place was comfortable enough.

Although Olivier had not been able to find any rapport with Marilyn Monroe he had liked Arthur Miller with whom he probably had some sympathy (although Miller, protective of his wife, uneasy in an unfamiliar country amid English actors, was aware of Olivier's competitive streak and that Monroe came to echo Kazan in thinking that on screen he was trying to outmatch her "like another woman, a coquette drawing the audience's attention away from herself"). It was Miller who inadvertently helped change the course of Olivier's career and of the Oliviers' lives. Vivien and Olivier were loyal to George Devine at the Royal Court and Vivien booked seats for John Osborne's first play to be seen in London, *Look Back in Anger*, which she admired for its muscular dialogue and energy but to which Olivier's response was barely lukewarm ("it's just a travesty on England" he said to Miller). When Miller told Olivier how much he had liked it – recently he had created quite a stir in describing contemporary British theatre as "hermetically sealed off from life" – Olivier joined him on a second visit and had a Damascene conversion. Accounts vary as to whether on that visit Olivier met Osborne and suggested that the young writer might possibly have a play for him in the future, or whether it was Devine to whom he raised the possibility of appearing in Sloane Square. In any event nothing happened immediately but in fact Osborne was at work on a new piece, as yet untitled, which would contain the role which would both galvanise and re-channel Olivier's career.

At 50, his film career apparently becalmed and having to grub around to find *Macbeth* backing (del Giudice appeared providentially but proved sadly a spent force with no access to significant capital), his stage work also now seemed flat and uninspiring ("I was feeling frustrated by the boredom of my own career"). Hiley noticed this professional dissatisfaction then and his sudden change of attitude to the New Wave:

He genuinely wanted a part of it. He saw people taking their ties off, wearing T-shirts, talking politics and he thought "This is wonderful! I can be young again!" Vivien was not so impressed. She could see through a lot of the phoniness in it.

Olivier had worried that the aftermath of her miscarriage might lead to another of Vivien's depressive phases but his fears seemed unfounded. She now had a new psychiatrist, a remarkable Harley Street doctor called Arthur Conachy, both sympathetic and reliable – she came to trust him without too many questions – who was especially careful to warn her of the dangers of alcohol which could trigger symptoms such as heightened libido when on a "high". He also found anti-depressants with few side-effects which he urged her always to have with her when travelling.

After *The Prince and the Showgirl*, apart from some final editing, was completed, Vivien and Olivier left for a Christmas holiday in Spain with the Seidmanns which included a stay with friends of the quartet, Bill and Ann Davis, at their beautiful *finca* just west of Malaga. The Davises recalled another gilded expatriate American couple – Gerald and Sara Murphy on the Riviera in the 1920s with a glittering circle of friends – and their restored house, La Consula, set amongst pines and palms with huge gates leading to the house with its pillared porch and pool, was a haven of tranquillity. Hemingway was just one of the regular visitors to La Consula, simple enough outside but with a stylish interior, the walls hung with works by Jackson Pollock and Mark Rothko. The Davises were undemanding hosts – Vivien and Olivier spent a good deal of time on long walks and they and the Seidmanns returned via Paris well restored to full health. Vivien did not plan any work prior to re-rehearsing *Titus*; she worked on Notley's garden and also visited Leigh, who had moved to a new house (Zeal's), still in Mere, as comfortable as Woodlands but more manageable.

Olivier had also planned, unusually for him, a quiet time but now had a play to tackle before the Stratford company regrouped for the European tour. After rehearsals in mid-March 1957 he would open in April at the Royal Court, playing the role of a clapped-out music-hall performer in the play which John Osborne had now completed and called *The Entertainer*.

CHAPTER 15

At Court

Produced the year after the Suez crisis, *The Entertainer* reflected a shifting post-imperial Britain. The title character Archie Rice, pickled in *accidie*, tours in tacky revues among semi-nude chorus-girls (one clad in Britannia's shield and helmet) playing a crumbling music-hall circuit, those Palaces and Empires closing their doors as the pink on the maps of the globe dwindled. After reading the first act Olivier was at first interested in playing Billy Rice, Archie's father, a retired veteran of the halls reflecting the values of a lost Edwardian England, but of course on receiving the complete play Olivier realised what the more subversive Archie offered. Whether or not he took on board the layer of metaphor in the play he knew a great role when he saw one. Having told Devine that it would be unlikely his plans could fit anything else in that year he became at once available for a limited season at the Royal Court before *Titus*.

Tony Richardson, Devine's associate who had directed *Look Back in Anger* and would direct *The Entertainer*, knew what a coup it would be to land Olivier for Archie, to bring the theatrical establishment's leading actor, once the personification of a mighty England in *Henry V* now to represent a nation in decline at the Royal Court, flagship of the New Drama in the heart of London's upmarket Sloane Square. The timing was right – Olivier was unsettled professionally and he had appeared in only two new plays (mediocre Fry and Rattigan) in the past two decades. But he was, as Richardson spotted, an instinctive showman; he described Olivier as at heart what the French call a *cabotin*, not the *grand seigneur* he presented to the world and not precisely a ham, but a performer who lives and breathes for acting alone. Olivier sensed that Archie, the stalled comic "dead behind the eyes", as well as personifying an altered England and being emblematic of a new theatrical world, seemed to have a hotline into aspects of his own personality which he had never been asked previously to confront on stage. It offered him a kind of rebirth.

There was however no part for Vivien, at least in the Royal Court's view. When Osborne and Richardson met the Oliviers, summoned to the Connaught Hotel suite which became their temporary quarters while Lowndes Place was redecorated, first Olivier asked that George Relph play Billy Rice (Relph always addressed his letters to Olivier as "My Dear Son") and for Archie's daughter Jean, with studied offhandedness, suggested "a little actress you may have come across" – Dorothy Tutin. When the casting of Phoebe, Archie's faded, tippling wife, arose he instantly proposed Vivien, forestalling the obvious objection from dramatist and director that she was just too glamorous by describing how she could be aged up and glammed down by wearing a rubber mask, as Edith Evans had recently done. He did not mean a literal mask, more a complicated make-up of latex, used to age Evans in the film *Queen of Spades*. An Olivier biographer, Anthony Holden, wrote that the notion of Vivien's casting and the latex suggestion came from Devine and Vivien but this is contradicted by both Richardson and Osborne, closely involved of course. Richardson recalled several meetings on this subject before the notion was dropped, guessing (probably correctly) that this was because of Vivien's "innate sense of self-preservation". He felt that "with a convert's zeal" Olivier was determined she should play opposite him even if wrong for the role. Vivien was far too intelligent not to realise that she would be miscast as Phoebe, even covered in latex, and she certainly did not wish to appear inadequate opposite her husband – and his mistress – on the Royal Court stage.

She had no work scheduled until *Titus* re-rehearsals in May. There were some lovely spring weekends at Notley; Gary and Maria Cooper, the Fairbankses and the Richardsons were there on various weekends and Rex Harrison, his career resurgent after *My Fair Lady*, came regularly with Kay Kendall. She and Vivien delighted in each other's company; sometimes after dinner they would perform an informal cabaret, a song-and-dance act reminiscent of the 1920s Dolly Sisters, and on Sundays they would mess about on the river. But when *The Entertainer* began rehearsals she felt excluded. Richardson recalled Olivier "after all these regal years" behaving like a boy let out of school, capering and bucking-and-winging ("he preened as the hoofer he really was"). Vivien also was uncomfortably aware that his affair with Dorothy Tutin, which never had completely ceased, had resumed in earnest.

One witness – a compassionate one – to the offstage events as *The Entertainer* rehearsed was its author. Osborne's treatment of some of his wives (Jill Bennett and Mary Ure not least) and his own admissions of "bad behaviour" have given him a misogynistic reputation and indeed his emotions about women were deeply complex. But he seemed to find a kinship with Vivien, first developing when she accompanied him and Olivier to the few surviving London music-halls such as the Metropolitan or Collins's in Islington:

> She took to it all, laughing at the dog acts filling the stage with flags, the xylophone players with their "popular melodies". Unlike the slumped, morose audience, Vivien joined in.

Vivien became a watchful presence at Royal Court rehearsals. The Rolls would glide from Knightsbridge to Sloane Square, Vivien in mink inside chauffeured by the Oliviers' new driver, a cheerful Cockney ex-Barnardo's boy, Bernard Gilman. He had been a relief driver, taken on permanently on the spot by Vivien on his first probationary day when, driving her down Bond Street, he screeched to a halt, jamming on the brakes outside an exclusive man's shop to point out: "Cor-look! What a lovely waistcoat!" Gilman in his smart brown uniform would escort her into the Royal Court circle to watch rehearsals, an uneasy presence for Olivier and Tutin especially. All at the Royal Court had heard the rumours about Olivier's private life and his visits to Chelsea Reach where Tutin lived on a houseboat as did the nearby Trader Faulkner whose unrequited adoration of her only complicated the emotional tangle. Osborne observed the auditorium as well as the stage:

> It was, of course, impossible to know what she was feeling and I could only guess at the pain ... If Larry was out of his depth now and then, so were we all, but none more so than Vivien, which made her isolation increasingly obvious.

Osborne and Richardson both recalled a Saturday morning run-through towards the end of the rehearsal period. Olivier had been simply marking the devastating scene near the end in which Archie begins to sing the blues before slowly crumpling in despair down the side of the proscenium arch. Suddenly that day he began to act full out, totally inhabiting the scene, the raw, naked emotion spilling out of him. Osborne's is the more vivid description:

> The spring sunshine and the noise of the Sloane Square traffic poured through the open door. A dozen of us watched, astounded. Vivien turned her head towards me. She was weeping. I immediately thought of the chill inflection in Olivier's Archie voice: "I wish women wouldn't cry. I wish they wouldn't."

There was one "episode" which revealed Vivien's pent-up feelings of disappointment and fear of the future, crystallised by witnessing Olivier's committed embrace of a new theatrical world which seemed to have no place for her. Richardson recalled her going to Olivier's dressing-room after the first act of a dress-rehearsal full of praise but at the end, with Richardson, Osborne and Devine also in the room she reappeared ("like a tigress protective of her energy she was word-perfect in her complaints and criticisms"), accusing Olivier of compromising the later part of the play when, thinking that Brenda de Banzie (Phoebe) might steal the show with a powerful near-closing scene, he resorted to cheap tricks to win back the audience's sympathy, before sweeping out with a final complaint about the reek of Devine's pipe ("a knock-out punch" said Richardson). This rather subdued Olivier for a time but he was back to full power for the opening, one of the glorious first nights at the Court. The famously tightwad ESC ran to a few cocktail sausages and some cheap white wine for an onstage party at which Scots-born Mary Ure sang "Bonny Mary of Argyle" and "Vivien sang rather sweetly" in Osborne's recollection. Every seat was immediately sold after the mainly ecstatic notices and a West End transfer after *Titus* was being discussed. All Vivien had to look forward to was to repeat her Lavinia (with Tynan's mockery still impaled in her memory).

The British Council-sponsored European tour of *Titus Andronicus* became a somewhat bizarre mixture of nightmare, black comedy and some contrastingly happy highlights. The play was unfamiliar in Europe and possibly it was a miscalculation to give Vivien top billing – Lavinia has only a few scenes before she is silenced – which rather bewildered audiences expecting some kind of Scarlett O'Hara personal appearance. The opening in Paris was triumphant, packing the vast, ornate Théâtre Sarah Bernhardt before a glittering audience of politicians and diplomats along with the Seidmanns, Jean-Pierre Aumont and Douglas Fairbanks Jr; the company assembled on stage after curtain-calls to see Vivien presented by Roger Seydoux, France's Minister of Culture, with the Légion d'Honneur (Paul-Louis Weiller had smoothed the way to this) for which she thanked him in fluently idiomatic French. Several parties were held in Paris including a lavish affair at an empty Weiller property in the Marais which the millionaire had transformed into a sumptuously decorated eighteenth-century mansion, crowded with Parisian socialites and stars of stage and screen including Maurice Chevalier, Marie Bell, Edwige Feuillère, Charles Boyer and Jean Marais. Jean-Pierre Aumont and his wife Marisa Pavan took the Oliviers on their rest day to Touraine; Aumont knew that they had been to the area years before but was still astounded that Vivien seemed to be able to greet shopkeepers and waiters by name, realising that she had an inveterate curiosity about people besides an incredible memory for names. The Aumonts took them to a Son et Lumière show at Chenonceaux; Olivier sat with his arm around Vivien and as the lights changed "they were illuminated by a red reflection which reminded me of those hellish flames in London thirteen years before".

At Florence they were close enough to I Tatti to visit the aged Berenson, taking with them the flamboyant company member Frank Thring. The Australian-born actor – called "The Many Splendoured Thring" – always dressed in black and wearing dark spectacles with suitably outsize frames – had been subdued when his Stratford marriage (which was something of a surprise) to the svelte actress-model Joan Cunliffe collapsed after only a year. Although Berenson's reaction to the voluble Thring is not recorded, the actor was thrilled by the villa and its exquisite garden which for Vivien was among her favourites, with its beds of luxuriant azaleas and roses. In Venice they were able to meet up briefly with Suzanne, feed the St Mark's Square pigeons again and stroll through canals and squares which they had explored at the height of their affair over 20 years before.

It was too good to last; before moving on behind the Iron Curtain Vivien was inextricably sliding into a manic phase. She became set on partying every night, even after official parties following first nights and, seemingly inexhaustible, during the days she would explore Belgrade, diving into side-street galleries and buying paintings or seeking out little local restaurants. Olivier could not keep up with the pace. In Belgrade the company was entertained by the Coopers' son John Julius Norwich (a Secretary at the Embassy) and his wife Anne, who noticed his weariness. Anne was discussing the drawbacks of Belgrade life when Olivier interrupted her to say: "If you don't like your life, change it." This has been understandably widely seen as Olivier's perspective on his own situation then, although the aperçu (taken from H.G. Wells) was one of his favourites (he used it in his Foreword to Fabia Drake's autobiography).

Amongst the company was a young actor – another Australian – Michael Blakemore. Later an outstanding director, novelist and memoirist he wrote vividly of that 1957 tour. He realised that Vivien was not fully stretched in *Titus* and that "If she couldn't be at the centre of the play she was determined to be at the centre of the company's offstage life". He, like the rest of the company, was unaware of the true nature of Vivien's illness (as Audley had said at Stratford: "The saddest thing is that we didn't realise that she had an illness. We all thought she was just behaving badly"). In Zagreb, the one nightclub (state-run) in the city, its Austro-Hungarian past slightly faded by then, was called the Ritz Bar which Vivien, who had her reserved table, turned into the actors' hangout during their stay (Blakemore watched her one night drink her minder under the table).

There was, Blakemore recalled, a special schoolchildren's matinee one afternoon. At the half-hour Vivien had not appeared while the vast theatre began to fill with hordes of expectant children chirruping in their hundreds ("It seemed appalling to deny them their Scarlett O'Hara"). With ten minutes left before curtain-up she appeared "somnambulistically drunk, not in the least unruly but quite stunned by sleeplessness and alcohol", having eluded her minders. She was put into her costume and then the company, holding its collective breath, watched her walk like an automaton into the wings and on to the stage. In Blakemore's recollections she never dried but there was a dislocating pause before each speech "like one of those international calls when the satellite is playing up". Then Olivier went into Titus's great, soaring speech of lament ("I am the sea") gradually upping the volume like a surfer cresting the waves until the end, a pause followed in Paris and Venice by thunderous applause. On this occasion Vivien spoke:

> Her words were not angry or loud – the tone was almost affectionate – but had the piercing clarity of a child's voice and penetrated every corner of the theatre … About this great moment of theatre she had given her verdict. To him, to the entire cast and to a thousand Croatian children. "Silly cunt", she had said.

The old maxim that farce piddles on tragedy's doorstep could have had no better illustration. The children of course had not understood, but the company bent over double on stage and in the wings to stifle their laughter:

> Olivier, invincible in Paris, had become ridiculous in Zagreb. He would never forgive her, though as a couple they had probably long been doomed.

On the night before the company were to travel to Vienna, Vivien went missing again. It emerged that she had hit a bad "down" patch and sat up all night on a park bench with Bernard Gilman (the British Council had arranged for the chauffeur to travel with the company) who finally persuaded her to walk to the station. That journey became an ordeal. A fierce heatwave made their train into a sauna and Vivien became manic once again, chasing Maxine Audley along the corridors until suddenly she tired and fell asleep on Audley's shoulder. There were no unfortunate incidents in Warsaw where *Titus*'s unflinching portrait of horror and brutality clearly had a grim resonance not long after its time under the German Occupation. The company had a realisation of another life, not least in Warsaw which Hitler had destroyed methodically street by street, brought home to them when they were shown the footage of the devastation.

Titus had a final flourish back home, playing a season in London in another building facing destruction, the cavernous Stoll Theatre in Kingsway. Vivien, still needing activity, became fixated on a mission, a crusade. Their old home of the St James's was now also threatened with demolition which roused her to agitate against what she saw as wanton barbarism for commercial profit (an office-block was the proposed replacement for the St James's). All her bottled frustrations and disappointments went into her campaign, well-intentioned but initially lacking organisation. At short notice a march on Parliament was planned to protest against the London County Council's decision to grant planning permission for the demolition. Her chum Alan Dent and Athene Seyler joined her at the head of her line of campaigners (not all that long, although swelled by some of the *Titus* company). The St James's needed large sums spent on renovations and at the time gathered only limited support for preservation. Olivier had not had much commercial success there and although he felt that publicly he must support Vivien his backing was tepid at best. The march, with Vivien ringing a bell followed by supporters bearing hastily made placards as they processed down the Strand, had some press coverage and Vivien appeared on television to publicise her case but the St James's hardly became a *cause célèbre*.

What did grab major headlines was a House of Lords debate on state assistance for the arts two days later. Olivier accompanied Vivien to the Lords for the occasion, seated in Black Rod's box in places reserved for distinguished visitors. The speeches included one from Lord Esher, Olivier's old nemesis from the Old Vic, which may explain why he discreetly left while the mostly uninspiring debate continued until, during a bottom-numbing oration from Lord Blackford calling for museum charges, Vivien rose dramatically; projecting her voice as if in Drury Lane she made her statement ("My Lords, I wish to protest against the St James's Theatre being demolished") – a frightful breach of protocol resulting in Black Rod, General Sir Brian Horrocks, rapidly ushering her out of the chamber (Vivien told him it was the worst audience she had ever played to). The press seized on the story – and on the fact that Russian newspapers misunderstood the incident and reported that Vivien had been making a protest on behalf of better working conditions for Westminster staff. At the Stoll she told reporters that should the St James's join the Gaiety and the Stoll under the wrecker's ball she might leave the country ("It may interest you to know that I can act in French, German, Italian and even Serbian"). Her blood was up. She arranged another march, this time with proper organisation, from the St James's to St Martin's in the

Fields where theatrical luminaries (Vivien, Olivier, John Clements, Felix Aylmer of Equity) addressed the rally which had a much larger turnout including Edith Evans, Michael Redgrave and Richard Attenborough among the marchers. Olivier's support was cosmetic; he was no longer interested in the St James's and privately had said to Maxine Audley: "This is the most expensive menopause in history." Despite continued campaigning the St James's battle was eventually lost although not before Vivien had secured some eminent support (Churchill, scolding her gently for her methods in the Lords, sent a £500 cheque towards the fighting fund).

The menopause was not the cause of Vivien's activism. She only rarely made direct political statements (she was a natural Liberal), although she and Kay Kendall marched for integration in London schools and against apartheid. The St James's campaign was born out of a genuine love of London's architecture, her emotional involvement with the St James's and her fretting nervous energy at that time. She had grown accustomed over the years to Olivier's "self-removings" and must have intuited another one looming and that this one might lead to a fateful rupture. In *Confessions* Olivier mentioned that at this time "I found myself wishing increasingly strongly to form a union with someone to whom I had been growingly attracted for a few months." This was Dorothy Tutin – never named – and he had begun his affair with her not "a few months" but five years previously. In Olivier's version Vivien asked him one day if he was in love with "this girl" and when he admitted that he was she was sympathetic about it. Then, still in his version, she "exploded" a few days later in Lowndes Place. Determined to punish him by depriving him of sleep, when she noticed he had almost dropped off she got up out of bed "in her manic state", found a wet face-cloth and began to hit him across the face with it. He got up and disappeared into another room, locking the door, but Vivien pursued him and began hammering on the door, clearly intending to keep it up all night. He went on to describe how "something snapped in my brain" – he came out, grabbed Vivien and pulled her along the corridor back into their bedroom, flinging her across the room. As she fell across the bed she struck the corner of her eyebrow on the marble top of the bedside table, opening up a wound near her eye. "I realised with horror", he wrote, "that each of us was quite capable of murdering or causing death to the other." He fled to a furnished room in a mews nearby, his "escape-hatch" as he called it. Gertrude's diary records for that night: "Called to Viv's at 3 a.m. Dreadful tragedy. Spent the night at Lowndes Cottage." When Olivier returned next morning after this

Strindbergian episode he found Mary Mills also there, dressing Vivien's wound. That day they had to head an Equity delegation to the Minister for Housing; they were photographed looking decidedly sombre, Vivien wearing an eye-patch which she explained away as necessitated by a mosquito-bite.

Olivier concluded his description of this scene by adding that "the break must be made". His chronology is wayward and at times contradictory in his memoirs, but at that point he was still not ready for divorce and she was not going to give in without a fight. Her diary for 1957 records two visits from "D. Tutin" to Notley, the first in June when the Hamiltons were present, the other for a "picnic under willows" in early July, and there were two meetings in London in August, one ("Tutin") on 2 August, the other ("Miss Tutin") on 8 August. Dorothy Tutin maintained always the utmost discretion about her involvement with Olivier. She did speak of it in later life to her children and her daughter Amanda Waring remembered her mother saying how deeply she had cared for him. But she was neither a promiscuous woman nor a homewrecker. Possibly Vivien arranged those early meetings to gauge the level of involvement or to warn her off. The final August meeting, after the incident of Vivien's damaged eye, would have been more dramatic; Gertrude was also present, backing up the claim that if Olivier were to leave Vivien then the consequences (suicide was the implication) would be cataclysmic. Also Olivier received a letter from Tutin's mother who was, understandably, tired of what she saw as Olivier's shilly-shallying ("my selfishly narrow way of thinking" were his words). Gradually Dorothy Tutin disappeared from Olivier's life (although he remained fond of her always – he insisted on her casting in his late *King Lear* on television).

The press remained remarkably silent on the subject of any possible end to the Olivier marriage although there was some speculation when they went on separate holidays later that year. Olivier put his Bentley on the train to Scotland, taking Tarquin with him, to scout for *Macbeth* locations while Vivien went with Leigh and Suzanne to San Vigilio (much to the outrage of a Scottish lady Labour MP who thought this set a terrible example and made divorce look far too easy). To all intents and purposes, however, it seemed even to close friends that they were still together. Late in 1957 they had moved into a new home, a Belgravia apartment at 54 Eaton Square; Olivier wrote to Walton in December:

> We have a beautiful new flat which both Vivien and I love. She is exceedingly bonny and better than she has been for ages and all is merry song in the birdcage.

Suzanne definitely noticed that the move seemed to coincide with renewed happiness, writing to Olivier "I hope the impression that you and Mummy are happy again is a right one."

Together at Notley they entertained the American millionaire Huntingdon Hartford, a theatre buff, who was interested in backing the *Macbeth* film (this also frustratingly led nowhere when a *quid pro quo* appeared – Hartford wanted the Oliviers' involvement in a British stage production of a terrible version of *Jane Eyre* which he had written).

Merry birdsong did not last long. Accounts vary considerably of subsequent developments. Alexander Walker's biography of Vivien states that in his dressing-room at the Palace Theatre where *The Entertainer* reopened in September 1957 Olivier, facing his make-up mirror, told Vivien: "I suppose you should know I am in love with Joan Plowright" (who had replaced Dorothy Tutin as Jean). It makes for a vivid story but all the evidence points to Vivien learning of this only several months later. From what both Olivier and Joan have written, it is clear that their love affair began later when *The Entertainer* was on tour in Brighton (Joan was married, although the relationship was fraying, and initially was anxious to avoid entanglement with anyone else). She was in America during the latter part of *The Entertainer*'s Palace run after its short tour (Geraldine McEwan replaced her). Vivien had visited *The Entertainer* on its first touring date in Glasgow; Colin Clark, still working for Olivier, later wrote that he believed she was suspicious, but the Brighton week was still three weeks away then and it was after that when Olivier wrote his "birdcage" letter to Walton.

Olivier claimed that his "constant pusillanimity" was for fear of aggravating Vivien's illness (although he had told Walton she was "better than she has been for ages"). But he had taken time living a double life before finally leaving Jill and Tarquin and there was similar hesitation before he took definitive steps to leave Vivien.

During the second Palace run of *The Entertainer* while Mary Ure (now Mrs Osborne) was in America and Vivien was also alone in the evenings, she and Osborne frequently spent time together. She would call him to suggest possibly catching a film in the West End. There was no question of any affair; although Osborne reminded himself of St Augustine's maxim "A stiff prick hath no conscience" he had no wish to be cast as "the spare prick at the demise of a very public marriage". Gilman would take them off into central London and after the film to upmarket restaurants such as Fitzrovia's White Tower ("she had witnessed my untutored tussle with an alien artichoke" and was always tactful in guiding him through hefty menus and wine lists). Apart from the outburst in Olivier's dressing-room he never witnessed any "moods of manic caprice". What he relished about her, Osborne found, was a quality which amplified John Betjeman's claim that he possessed only one virtue, hope:

Vivien's virtue, always a prized one in my book, was enthusiasm, the physical expression of hope, the antidote to despair and that most deadly of sins, sloth.

Osborne had heard whispers about Olivier and Joan Plowright but relayed none of that gossip to Vivien. She was kept busy with final details on the Eaton Square apartment; John Fowler, much in demand, would drop everything for favourite clients such as Vivien (he took special care over the apartment's entrance-hall, using a beautiful Chinese wallpaper). There were also plans for Suzanne's wedding to a young stockbroker, Robin Farrington, at Holy Trinity, Brompton in December. Vivien liked Robin very much; she wrote to Suzanne on the eve of her wedding to tell her how much she loved her, hoping "with all my heart that today will be the beginning of a most wonderful and happy life" (it became an enduringly happy marriage). Olivier attended the wedding and the Hyde Park Hotel reception hosted by Leigh and Vivien, somewhat conspicuously inconspicuous ("I feel like the Uninvited Guest" he told the *Daily Express* reporter, comparing himself to Harcourt Reilly in *The Cocktail Party*, as he lurked beside a pillar).

A geographical "self-removing" by Olivier came with the new year when early in 1958 he left for America – much of the next two years would be spent there – initially to New York for *The Entertainer* (Joan Plowright rejoined the cast). Before leaving he saw Vivien begin rehearsals for a new production involving LOP, Jean Giraudoux' *Pour Lucrèce*, adapted by Christopher Fry as *Duel of Angels*. This was Beaumont's brainchild. He had seen the Paris production directed by Jean-Louis Barrault with a lustrous cast including Edwige Feuillère, Madeleine Renaud and Jean Desailly and realised how strong the Feuillère role of Paola, the "bad angel", would be for Vivien. He sent her the French text and she was at once captivated – the part of a woman seeing herself as wronged and seeking revenge must have struck some chords then ("I telephoned Binkie Beaumont the next morning saying 'I want to do it. I just think it is the most marvellous play'"). She reacted similarly positively to Fry's English version (he had previously translated Giraudoux' Trojan war play *Tiger at the Gates*).

This was the posthumously-produced final play from Giraudoux, an extraordinarily versatile man (Quai d'Orsay diplomat, novelist, essayist and dramatist) and a unique stylist – he wrote a study of Racine – but difficult to translate with his fusion of prose, fantasy and a weaving of tragic (often classical) themes with ironic comedy. Fry preserved the acrid atmosphere of this elegant *totentanz*, a variation on the legend of the virtuous Roman wife Lucretia, violated by Tarquin, who kills herself afterwards, urging her family to avenge her. Vivien played the sophisticated Paola whose adultery has been betrayed to her husband by the "pure" Lucille, wife of a self-righteous judge. When she is "cut" by Lucille in public, Paola retaliates, using her lover as her accomplice, by drugging Lucille so that she wakes in a brothel. Ensuing events develop into a revenge which is taken out of Paola's hands, ending in Lucille's suicide.

Beaumont ensured that the West End production was of the highest quality, bringing Barrault over to direct and upping the budget to allow Roger Furse to design some of his finest work, particularly a ravishing first-act setting of a mid-nineteenth-century Aix-en-Provence square with its outside café and a delicate vista of lime trees. For the Paris production, Feuillère, no slouch when it came to costumes, had been dressed by Christian Dior. Beaumont was happy enough to use Dior's designs (supervised by Yves St Laurent after his death) to be made in London by the Berman's costume firm but Vivien insisted that hers be made by Dior's *atelier*. Movement in Barrault's production was crucial; when a character moved it was with a purpose, often sharply angled, and Vivien wanted no rucking-up when rising from a seated position (Elaine Dundy was among those who noticed how Vivien's costume remained pristine while the other women in the company often had to readjust their outfits). Dior gave Vivien's costume the details of the period but they were subtly adapted with no confining whalebone while still supporting breathing and posture by devising a jacket shaped to give the impression of corsetry without its restrictions. It was a stunningly elegant design – a front-fastening jacket of vivid carmine wool and mohair over a curved matching skirt, giving all her movement an incisive assurance, a classic case of costume illuminating character.

In rehearsal Barrault was astonished by Vivien ("What a person! How well we understood each other") and the way she approached Paola:

> She worked on her part with a hatred for her character. She assailed her. She was constantly on the lookout for reasons for not loving her character. This forced me to plead for Paola. It was only when she had exhausted all the reasons for hating her that she assumed her. In the part she was not merely a cat, she had become a panther.

The supporting cast included Claire Bloom's Lucille and Peter Wyngarde, dark and handsomely charismatic, as Paola's accomplice. He, too, had had an unorthodox and peripatetic upbringing – born to a French mother, educated partly in China – and was a complex bisexual personality. During the run he became Vivien's lover; he relished her fun and spirit of adventure off stage although he had to deal with occasional "episodes", having to rescue her one night in the Eaton Square gardens when she was found running around naked and on another occasion finding her sobbing uncontrollably one dawn at Notley. But he described acting with her as one of his "greatest joys" charged with "the fun of playing on two levels", being simultaneously totally inside the play and also being able to connect "in a language of our own like two ventriloquists. It was telepathic." Their scenes together, two dark souls, were mesmerising.

Claire Bloom, who was aware that Vivien knew of her *Richard III* dalliance with Olivier, was also deeply impressed by Vivien:

> I knew her marriage was not as strong as it had been – she described it as twenty years of Tristan and Isolde and Romeo and Juliet rolled into one.

Bloom felt that Olivier ("a dictatorial man") had both fostered Vivien and held her back and that "I always felt in *Duel of Angels* that she had gone through the role with him ... it was hard for her to present herself under the shadow of this great man." Playing Lucille, dressed in contrasting white, Bloom found acting with Vivien – and her style of living – inspirational. ("She showed me how an actress *could* be a woman... a model of how to join your profession to your whole life".)

Duel of Angels settled in for a successful run, with critics all appreciating Vivien's whiplash control of what Barrault described as "so captivating, so beautiful, so irresistible a creature – like the most diabolical of angels", and her remarkable physical and vocal expertise, her voice suggesting a rich honey laced with prussic acid. Of the many letters she received about this performance, a noteworthy one was from the veteran character actor Ronald Squire whose lengthy career had seen him act opposite many outstanding leading ladies. He did not know her well (it is addressed to "Miss Leigh") but had felt he must write:

> It is a long time since I have seen such distinction, poise, grace of movement and high comedy in the truest sense. Your acting survived nostalgic memories of the Edwardian theatre.

After *The Entertainer* closed in New York Olivier returned to England. He and Joan Plowright had been unobtrusively together at the Algonquin Hotel but still he made no move finally to end his marriage. *Macbeth* had had yet another setback when Mike Todd, the showman producer married to Elizabeth Taylor, who had agreed to finance the film, was killed in a plane crash but there were now hopes that the Rank Organisation might come up trumps. Vivien wrote to Suzanne, then in Switzerland where Robin was working for a time:

> It is absolutely heavenly to have Larry back. He is very well, though looks rather odd as he is in the process of growing his beard for *Macbeth*. It is growing in the strangest colours. We *think* the film is definitely on.

It was not. Rank finally pulled out and then a possible Rothschild interest evaporated. The film was shelved, the draft scripts put away, the beard shaved off. Later Vivien would say that the unravelling of her marriage began when she miscarried in 1956; she once articulated this thought to Tarquin, who quietly disagreed with her (this sadly for a time caused a rift between them). But Tarquin was right; losing her baby was a devastating blow but as well as the strain of living with the "monster", as he called Vivien's Bipolar condition and then falling in love with Joan, another significant trigger for Olivier was the collapse of their joint dream of filming *Macbeth*. It was the last bridge with Vivien for him, also a link to his past. *Macbeth* on stage was born out of old alliances (Byam Shaw and Stratford) but he had moved on and *The Entertainer*, while also involving his past (Devine and George Relph) introduced him to a whole new breed of younger actors, Joan included, and a different theatrical landscape (there was indeed a world elsewhere).

Nevertheless, they seemed still a couple. They had dined together earlier in the year with Peter Brook and his actress-wife Natasha Parry when the other guests were Tynan and Elaine Dundy, whose marriage was also under strain. It could have been an awkward situation but Tynan's most recent biographer described it as "a surprisingly harmonious evening with Elaine impressed by the vivacity and beauty of Leigh". The two women thereafter had some jolly lunches – Elaine introduced Vivien to some of London's ethnic restaurants, very different from her regular haunts like Prunier's or The Connaught, which she responded to enthusiastically – and the Tynans jointly had dinner at the Oliviers (Dundy remembered an enjoyable evening with just the four of them and that "Vivien impressed me with her formidable intellect and her knowledge of art, literature and philosophy"). Then Dundy was invited for a Notley weekend. Vivien had been charming to Tynan previously, betraying nothing of what she may have felt about his reviews, but this invitation was for Elaine alone. Tynan badgered her into asking Vivien if he could also come; although reluctant (she was aware that Vivien had psychological problems and she had strongly disagreed with her husband's verdict on Vivien's Lady Macbeth) Dundy called Notley and Vivien agreed.

They found their hostess in high good humour (Olivier was on his way back from Spain visiting Dickie, who had been ill); she had arranged a delicious picnic lunch by the river. Ernest and Gertrude were also at Notley that weekend; Dundy, who had an uncomfortable relationship with her own mother, did not greatly take to Gertrude, "a great disapprover", especially when they took tea together while Gertrude pronounced on Vivien's "illness":

> There is nothing the matter with Vivien. She does not need all those psychiatrists. They just try to make trouble. Why, as a little child at the convent, the nuns told me she loved me so much she used to cover up my photograph with her blanket at night so my picture wouldn't get cold.

Gertrude was clearly trying to warm Dundy's heart by this instance of a child's devotion, instead of which it chilled her to the bone as an illustration of a six-year-old's desolating loneliness.

Both Tynans wrote later of that weekend of what Dundy called "clashing social forces, trigger points and power bases spinning about". Tynan's account was written nearly 20 years later and, like Dundy's, published in 2001. She described how she and Tynan took an afternoon nap, interrupted by Vivien persuading Tynan to don the chain-mail of Sybil Thorndike's *Saint Joan* armour to amuse Olivier on his return. It failed to do so in Dundy's description of a strained dinner with a taciturn host although the evening improved as the women, "like happy, tipsy schoolgirls", danced to records while Olivier and Tynan talked ("Ken was listening as if to the music of the spheres"). Afterwards Tynan told Elaine they had been discussing Olivier's National Theatre dreams but she went on to write that on a post-breakfast walk on Sunday morning Olivier told Tynan that the couple should leave ("He says I'm having a bad effect on Vivien – ever since that piece I wrote in the *Evening Standard* the cycles have been more frequent").

Dundy continued to lunch with Vivien on occasion and her name appears again in the Notley Visitors' Book. Without Tynan's – it would seem he was not invited again.

His account differs; it includes a mention of Vivien's appearance in the bedroom during the Saturday afternoon, describing her hand teasing his Y-fronted genitals until his rebuff while Dundy slept. There is no mention of the dinner's strains or of any conversation with Olivier and in his version it was Vivien who first put on the chain-mail to recite some of Joan's speeches before he is dressed in it. Whose account is the more accurate cannot be ascertained, although Tynan's reads as the vaguer and has several factual errors (Ernest is described as "a petty-bourgeois former colonial administrator").

During a short *Duel of Angels* break Vivien and Gertrude went for an Italian holiday, which developed into a see-saw time of mood-swings. All seemed initially as happy as always at San Vigilio until Vivien suddenly flew at Gertrude in Leonardo's kitchen. He became further alarmed a few days later; when Vivien and Gertrude's car broke down they were rescued by a passing local fisherman and when Vivien invited him into the *locanda* for a thank-you drink Leonardo objected, causing a scene from Vivien leading to the police being called at 2 a.m. whereupon Vivien bit one of them on the finger. Vivien and Gertrude were asked to leave; Gertrude took Vivien off to Florence and then they flew home from Rome. However, when she reopened in Giraudoux' play soon afterwards with Bumble, Kay Kendall and Cecil and Irina Tennant among the audience, she gave an outstanding performance.

The swings continued with what seemed to Vivien a run of misfortunes personal and professional. Olivier had finished filming Shaw's *The Devil's Disciple* with Kirk Douglas and Burt Lancaster which he had not much enjoyed (although he seemed initially attracted to plans for directing and co-starring with Vivien in a film of Rattigan's *Separate Tables* for Lancaster's company) but promptly took himself off first to the Waltons on Ischia and then to stay with the Seidmanns in Paris. From there he wrote to Vivien saying that they should definitely part (divorce went unmentioned) which resulted in a rift of some years between Vivien and Ginette Spanier. On 5 November, her birthday, she had dinner in London with Olivier (his present was a Rolls-Royce, an expensive sweetener), who again expressed his wish for a separation, although nobody could have guessed this two nights later when they threw a lavish dinner-dance at Les Ambassadeurs ("The Party of the Year" in the press), ostensibly to welcome their friend Lauren Bacall to London. They seemed to dazzle as "The Oliviers" again – he in black tie, she in aquamarine silk – greeting the stellar guests, with the women presented by Olivier with a red rose each, Vivien giving each man a red carnation (shades of the torrid love-tokens of their 1939 letters). In retrospect, it was in effect their last joint public appearance as that fabled pair. A few days later Olivier flew to America, deliberately again distancing himself, first to New York for American television and then to California for *Spartacus* under Stanley Kubrick.

Alone in London Vivien wrote a long, anguished letter to Coward, explaining that she wanted him to know before anyone else (she had told only Tennant, Gertrude and Sybil Thorndike, Olivier's surrogate mother):

> Larry has asked for a legal separation ... It is a very acute and terrible shock and I am, and have been, acutely miserable. I always thought that whatever happened

between us – eventually we would be completely together as we used to be. It has always seemed that with a sense of humour and *innate* loyalty and respect and *love*, one would pull through anything. I shall never love anyone as I love him ... Ever since *The Entertainer* I have watched Larry change. It has not altered my love but the change is apparent. *Of course* I am not putting all the blame on him but the fact is that when it came to the point in my life when I had to choose between him and Peter (Finch) there was no question in my mind.

Nowhere does she mention Joan Plowright. She insisted that there were "months of very great happiness" prior to *The Entertainer* before and after her 1956 miscarriage (Hester stressed this too) but then, as she saw it:

Little Miss T., I believe deliberately, stamped back into his life ... and managed in that short space of time to wreck our lives. The fact that he says now she means absolutely *nothing* to him makes it even more dreadful.

Vivien is too hard here on Dorothy Tutin (it was Olivier who suggested her for *The Entertainer*'s first run). This letter also contradicts Olivier's *Confessions* statement that after the miscarriage of 1956 "Vivien was quietly but firmly resistant to the idea of trying again ... Perhaps it was for the best." Vivien's letter to Coward says that ever since losing that baby "I have implored him to let us have another child but he has refused." Once again it is impossible to say which version is true. But it is plain that Olivier still had not told Vivien about Joan and still had not raised the question of divorce. Vivien asked for Coward's discretion (she dreaded "those charming newspapers"), ending with: "I do not know quite how I shall manage. It seems like the end of life to me."

Professionally there was trouble too. Claire Bloom's commitments meant she had to leave the cast at the Apollo, much to Vivien's regret (she always wanted to act with her again) and Ann Todd was cast to take over as Lucille. A somewhat glacial blonde beauty, whose Hollywood career never quite took off (although *The Seventh Veil* had been a huge domestic hit), she and her first husband Nigel Tangye had been Chelsea friends of the Oliviers although Olivier was none too fond of her second, film director David Lean. The outcome at the Apollo was wretched. The circumstances were unfortunate; Barrault was unavailable and so the stage manager supervised re-rehearsals which Vivien attended conscientiously (which is more than many stars do, leaving the majority of the work with replacements to understudies). Todd had been busy on a television play prior to rehearsals and struggled with the text (a challenging one with its heightened language and syntax), often prone to paraphrase. The backstage atmosphere became chilly. Todd in her memoirs wrote that she felt Vivien was in some way jealous of her. There had always been rumours of a 1930s fling between her and Olivier although Vivien normally did not seem much bothered by such old news, and it was evidently not because of Todd's ability in *Duel of Angels* (when told that Todd had been mugged one weekend in Brighton, Vivien rapidly retorted: "Perhaps it was someone who had seen her performance"). Not long after Todd joined the cast Vivien asked for a brief rehearsal to work on a passage in the play which she felt had gone slack and Todd replied by complaining to Vivien in a note about the backstage atmosphere, to which Vivien responded, pointing out that she had rehearsed:

> as many times as you wished me to ... so you must believe me when I say that I found it hard to credit you are too exhausted to give me ten minutes to perfect something which is vitally important to the meaning of the play ... I will not, if I can help it, see things less than perfectly done as possible.

The production continued, with only a marginal backstage thaw, until late November. Vivien wrote to Coward of Todd's frequent mangling of the text ("Miss T. says some very queer things – however, it is all good experience!") and was not sorry when the play closed (this mutual dislike between two leading ladies was most unusual in Vivien's career).

As *Duel of Angels* ended, Olivier had briefly to return to England when Dickie died. Although the brothers had not been especially close during most of Dickie's adult life – Olivier could be dismissive, even mocking, of him at times – they had become closer during Dickie's last illness (he had Leukaemia) and Olivier flew home for the burial which Hiley had organised to be held at sea off Portsmouth. Vivien attended the ceremony, on a minesweeper, and then returned with Olivier, Hester and Olivier's sister Sybille to Notley. In the published *Confessions* Olivier wrote that he left the women in the main house and then went to sleep in Dickie and Hester's neighbouring cottage. However, an earlier draft records a less comfortable version with Vivien coming into his room at Notley wanting them to make love which he refused ("I suffered grievously for her being made to feel so horribly undignified") before he left to go to the cottage. Hester's recollection matches Olivier's draft; she remembered hearing raised voices in the main house ("And he then rushed out and slammed the door and went to the cottage"). Olivier left very early for London next morning with no goodbyes, and then soon afterwards flew back to New York to complete television's *The Moon and Sixpence* in which he played Maugham's fugitive artist. Hester was convinced that at this stage Vivien still knew nothing of Joan Plowright. For the meantime Hester remained at Notley still working the dairy farm but clearly Olivier's thoughts were on the future and the disposal of the house in which he had dreamed of a tranquil old age, the effective end of the "baronial" era, when he told Hester that the dairy herd should be sold.

After receiving Olivier's Paris letter Vivien had visited Leigh at Zeal's, always a quiet haven. There she wrote to Olivier seeming to agree with the notion of a legal separation but taking it further and, for the first time, mentioning the word 'divorce':

> I intend to divorce you on the grounds of desertion – mental and physical – as soon as our present chores in the theatre and television are over – we are in any case separated. I did not want to do this until you had finished your work here but our telephone conversation tonight led me to think I was talking to a complete stranger – which is what you have chosen to become ... Our lives will lie in quite different directions. I feel confident I should make my own life – and you have *always* made yours.

Olivier, whose scruples about the stigma of divorce and guilt of his first one had never entirely left him and who to that date had still not articulated the thought to Vivien – was probably relieved to receive that. But as she had suggested to Coward, Vivien faced an uncertain future – she had never really lived alone and her lives with Leigh and then Olivier covered 25 years – and the Notley scene following Dickie's burial left her feeling not only bereft but humiliated. A new Rolls-Royce was no substitute for the sense of living with and being a part of another person.

Like Olivier, Peter Finch had moved on. Vivien had stayed close to Betty and Flavia who still adored her, with Betty hoping always that Finch and Vivien would get back together. By 1958 Finch was living mostly with his actress-girlfriend Yolande Turner (soon his second wife) in her Beauchamp Place bedsit although still prone to wanderlust and still drinking heavily. According to Yolande in the only account available, Betty asked Finch and Yolande (whom she disliked) to call at her mews house; when they arrived Betty told them that Vivien was there. She barely glanced at Yolande, giving Finch all her attention as she sat on a sofa in a pastel silk dress "smiling that lethal pussycat smile" before telling Finch that she wanted him back, that she would happily live in an attic with him, an uncomfortable scene for Yolande to witness and then to hear her lover tell Vivien that it was too late and that he now loved Yolande:

> I felt terribly sorry for Vivien. She looked frightened and very fragile. There was something terribly wrong.

Yolande understandably resented Betty and Finch for subjecting her to this episode, and felt even more sad on Vivien's behalf when Finch led her to the car outside where Gilman was waiting. Finch was back in the house after just one minute and when Yolande (who knew something of his tangled history with Vivien) asked him if the farewell had been painful Finch simply replied: "No, not really." Like his mentor, Finch had done another act of self-removing (he would do one more some years later when walking out on Yolande and their two children).

At every turn then Vivien must have sensed gloom everywhere. Oswald Frewen was very ill (he died not long afterwards): "It has been a dreadful year, hasn't it?" Vivien wrote to Leigh, although she added that "Suzie has certainly done a lot to brighten it." Suzanne gave birth to her first child, Neville, in early December (giving rise to the predictable headlines: "Scarlett O'Hara is a Grannie"). She did not join Ernest and Gertrude for Christmas with Leigh at Zeal's that year but went to spend it with Hester at Notley (it would be her final Notley Christmas – soon it was advertised "For Sale" in *Country Life*). Inevitably Hester too was melancholy that Christmas; she wrote not long afterwards to Vivien: "Please don't let the things that have happened to us alter anything between us, I couldn't bear it, you know how much I've always loved you."

Vivien had not totally abandoned hope of some kind of reconciliation with Olivier. Suzanne and close friends including Victor Stiebel and Rachel Kempson wrote urging him not to take the final step to divorce. Stiebel resorted to self-confessed moral blackmail, suggesting that Vivien might cease her visits to Dr Conachy if Olivier refused a rapprochement. Rachel Kempson wrote along the same lines while Suzanne tried to impress upon him how much Vivien truly loved and needed him. He replied to Suzanne, confessing that even if Vivien were miraculously restored to the woman she used to be, they had grown apart, while of Stiebel's appeal he wrote to Joan Plowright (in England while he was in America then) that it did not make him feel a shred of guilt but only confirmed "a complete and solid cold determination" to set himself against any reconciliation. He then wrote to Vivien to state clearly that it would be better for both if they did not meet when he returned from Hollywood after *Spartacus* and that he planned to go directly to Stratford for his next commitment, *Coriolanus* under the young Peter Hall. From Hollywood he wrote again, initially friendly with congratulations for surviving the ordeal of recreating Sabina in *The Skin of Our Teeth* on British television (with George Devine – rather caught in the middle between two of his oldest friends, well aware of the current situation – as Antrobus again), although she had not enjoyed it (the tape survives – it was poorly re-imagined for a different medium and Vivien was not tempted by television again). He added "I still tremble when I think of my last effort", although *The Moon and Sixpence* had been well received. Then he adopted a different unusually formal, quasi-legal tone, with many erasures and revisions:

> I think it best to reaffirm at this point my decision of last Sept-Oct. which I have reiterated each time we have communicated since then.

Urging Vivien that she should "feel firm and resigned in the acceptance of this state of affairs" he argued that they had ten weeks before his return for Stratford rehearsals in which to prepare an announcement for the press. The facade must no longer be maintained. "I think," wrote Olivier "it is time now to drop the legend."

CHAPTER 16

Ending a Legend

S elf-imposed absence in America only confirmed Olivier's feelings for Joan Plowright, feelings very different from those he had felt for Vivien back in the 1930s, just as she was a very different as well as a younger and less sophisticated woman (he described his new love as "like a fresh moon ... a communion that is transcendent"). The separation strengthened what she felt too, as their transatlantic letters confirm; she was now separated from her husband, Roger Gage, and extremely busy professionally. When Vivien changed her mind after seeming initially to agree with Olivier's request for a legal separation and suggesting divorce Joan accepted his decision not to bring her name into the equation until a separation (at least) or divorce (at best) was agreed, although she admitted that the situation made her "feel sometimes that I was living in a Charlotte Bronte novel". Olivier dreaded any "visitation" from Vivien to Joan similar to the dealings with Dorothy Tutin.

Vivien in London was not working but socially was extremely active. Coward thought that Olivier's leaving for America "may have done her a power of good" and occasionally accompanied her to the theatre while she also saw a good deal of Kay Kendall and Lauren Bacall. The press regularly featured these three glamorously entertaining women who enjoyed regular lunches and theatregoing together ("The Gay Trio who are the Talk of the Town" was one headline in those more innocent days) while Bacall gave good quote ("When they made the three of us they sure broke the moulds and threw them away. They don't come like us any more"). Both provided sympathetic shoulders for Vivien then, a time when many friends were "taking sides" as happens in most marital crises, although it soon became evident that she did not welcome direct criticism of Olivier. Leigh, always understanding, was clear-eyed about the situation, writing to Gertrude that in his opinion Vivien would find no peace of mind until she recognised that the break was irrevocable:

> Let Vivien accept that what she did to me Larry is doing to her. It must be faced. She owes it to her relations, her friends and herself not to let this destroy that lovely and exquisite personality that we adore and cherish.

Olivier changed his mind about not meeting Vivien on his return from America; she met his flight at London Airport where photographers were around to picture their embrace, seemingly yet again a happy couple, although he went on directly to Stratford. He could easily have commuted from Notley but that now represented his past and he stayed instead in a Stratford hotel during *Coriolanus*; fit and bronzed after *Spartacus* he triumphed in a performance outstanding for its electrifying vocal and physical athleticism. Vivien was at the opening, sitting with him and Bacall at the after-show party thrown by Olivier for the company at the country-house Welcombe Hotel on Stratford's outskirts. Michael Blakemore, also in the 1958 Stratford company, noted the change in Olivier, now contemplating seismic changes in his life both personally and, with the film of *The Entertainer* and a National Theatre on the horizon at last, professionally. In his sober dinner jacket and with dark-framed spectacles "this pleasant, greying man" thought Blakemore, "might have been a successful solicitor celebrating a wedding anniversary." This was only one view of Olivier's metamorphosis as he moved from one act of his life to another; many remarked when he was running the Chichester Festival Theatre and the National Theatre soon afterwards, that off stage he now resembled a civil servant or a bank manager, worlds away from the glittering life of Notley or Eaton Square. That party was the last occasion at which most of the guests would see Vivien and Olivier together.

During the run of *Coriolanus* Olivier commuted to the Morecambe location for *The Entertainer* while Vivien prepared to follow him to the Royal Court. Not, however, in a trail-blazing new British play. Occasionally the ESC tackled revivals (*Rosmersholm*, *The Country Wife* in the latter of which both Olivier and Vivien had seen Joan Plowright act for the first time) but the decision to stage Georges Feydeau's 1908 farce *Occupe-toi d'Amélie*, adapted by Coward as *Look After Lulu* and co-produced with H.M. Tennent, even with Richardson directing and the Francophile Devine in the cast, raised many eyebrows. Osborne is reported to have dropped into the theatre during rehearsals to see Vivien and Tony Quayle on stage with Beaumont in the stalls and assumed that he was hallucinating; the Court was supposed to conquer Shaftesbury Avenue, not the other way round. Vivien had been indirectly responsible for the production;

when travelling to Newcastle to open *Duel of Angels* Barrault, who had directed a famous Paris production of Feydeau's play, suggested Vivien should play the central role of a vivacious cocotte in a sparkling new English version, a notion she mentioned to Beaumont, who passed it on to Coward. The marriage-broking did not lead to a heaven-made match; Coward, who had considerable input from his secretary Cole Lesley, worried that Feydeau's essence is primarily that of situation and visual comedy and in compensation inserted rather too many sub-Cowardisms, forced epigrams and puns, all bloating the running time of a piece which should be cumulatively fleet. It had been produced on Broadway with a plucky but strenuous performance from a then little-known Tammy Grimes, over-designed by Beaton at his most frou-frou and was a rapid flop. Unwisely, little revision was done prior to London; all concerned seemed to think that the New York failure was due to Cyril Ritchard's frenetic musical-beds production and that with Vivien, the supposed *wunderkind* Richardson (Barrault unfortunately was not available) and Roger Furse's less stressful designs everything would come together.

Richardson's comedic sense was hefty and he made the same mistakes as Ritchard on Broadway, pumping up the frantic physical high-jinks with a too knowing ooh-la-la naughtiness in a production which confused mental pace with sheer speed. He also miscast some crucial roles; Devine and Quayle were not natural farçeurs while Robert Stephens was less than ideally cast (as he miserably realised) as Lulu's lover Philippe. By far the best performances came from Max Adrian as a panting princeling in hot pursuit of Lulu and from Vivien (both had revue experience, ideal discipline for the rapid-fire insouciance required).

Stephens, just back from appearing in Osborne's *Epitaph for George Dillon* on Broadway, became as fascinated by Vivien as Osborne. Again, there was no physical affair ("the chance of any carnal intimacy was about as likely a prospect as being struck by lightning – she was like royalty") but although he disliked Richardson and the play he had the consolation ("a very big consolation") of a friendship with "the utterly adorable Vivien". He was aware, like most associated with the ESC, of Olivier's relationship with Joan and, indeed, that Olivier possibly trusted him to shield Vivien from that affair which at times had been conducted in the house in Glebe Place (near Sloane Square) where Stephens, no stranger to extramarital dalliance himself, was living with his wife. He would escort Vivien to theatres when they were rehearsing and to matinees after they had opened as well as to various restaurants. A favourite place then, appropriate for a French farce, was the exuberantly Gallic La Popote d'Argent in Marylebone where the younger waiters had a flourishing sideline in selling pornography to customers. Vivien's Rolls would purr to a halt and Gilman would leap out to open the door for her to sweep in with Stephens, who came to admire her as well as to enjoy her company ("To walk along the street with Vivien Leigh on your arm was like walking on air"):

> Vivien must have known that something was amiss but she never once revealed the source of her desperate unhappiness ... she had the most extraordinary, powerful personality I have ever encountered. She had the most exquisite taste and the most impeccable manner, as well as a dazzling beauty and flirtatious wit. She was also keenly intelligent, much more intelligent than Larry. I have never known anyone more perfect.

Lulu began, none too auspiciously, in Nottingham. Osborne described the unlikely mix of Shaftesbury Avenue and Sloane Square: "as doomed an attempt to contradict the enmity of history as an allegiance between France and Albion." The Nottingham atmosphere was divisive, exacerbated by everyone's worries about the play and about Vivien's anxieties. Osborne, summoned to support Richardson, found Coward the most sensible, realising "his cold eye saw quite correctly that Vivien must somehow reconcile herself to the divorce Olivier was set upon" and that although Coward had a vested interest in her capacity to handle a potentially long run in *Lulu*, his concern was prompted "also by his loyalty and affection for them both". Like Osborne, the dramatist "appears not to stoop to the silliness of 'taking sides'".

Despite having friends around her (Mu Richardson was also in the cast) it was for Vivien a lonely time. One Notley weekend before Nottingham her friend Godfrey Winn joined her. They strolled after dinner in the garden but Vivien wanted to stay close to the house in case the telephone should ring – Olivier had arranged to call her after *Coriolanus*. In his autobiography Winn wrote of them "like two ghosts surrounded by a *corps de ballet*" of the white roses which Vivien liked so much, luminous in moonlight. Inside again Winn outlined the plot of a novel which he thought would make a good film but realised that Vivien's thoughts were elsewhere and that she was not really listening. The telephone never rang.

Moving to London with *Lulu*, Vivien was caught in the crossfire between Virginia Fairweather, the production's publicist, and the press photographers. Vivien had never done a "free-for-all", with all newspapers' photographers present for a special onstage call; previously Angus McBean's photographs had been used for press as well as production shots, but she willingly agreed to the Royal Court system. The stalls were packed with photographers, eager for saucy shots of Vivien in either corsets or pantaloons – some Nottingham informal snaps had somehow found their way into some papers – and they turned on Fairweather, even threatening to report her to their editors, when Vivien came on stage in an extravagant but not especially revealing gown. From that point, to Fairweather's mind, "Fleet Street turned hostile to the production." There had already been some carping at such a commercial package occupying the Court stage and the first-night audience gave the evening a cool reception, reflected in notices tepid in the main. Vivien and Max Adrian survived the reviews' tone; the general reaction was that their comparative deft expertise just about kept the production afloat.

Mu Richardson, cast as a randy Countess, witnessed the contrast between Vivien in the dressing-room (the same one inhabited by Olivier for *The Entertainer*) and on stage. On matinee days they would spend the time between the shows together. By this time Olivier had finished in *Coriolanus* and *The Entertainer* had been shot (he quarrelled several times with Richardson and seemed often querulous) and finally he had told Vivien that he loved Joan and wanted to marry her. Then he and Joan went off on a French holiday. Mu Richardson recalled Vivien often in tears:

> And then would come the voice, on the tannoy saying 'Half an hour'. She opened the play – and I came on very soon after. She was as if nothing had touched her at all … Her stance was very rare. You would never know that half an hour before she had been weeping.

Osborne was often around the theatre during *Lulu*'s Court run:

> It must have seemed to Vivien that we – George, Tony, even myself – were the instruments of her present misery and Larry's disapproval of the whole courtly legend surrounding their love and lives. However much one sympathised with Olivier's desperation to escape the destruction of her magic alchemy, it was impossible not to be affected, like Coward, by the pain cascading over both of them.

Coward had been right, however, in remarking that Vivien remained a major star ("the biggest draw in the business"). Business at the Royal Court was strong enough for Beaumont to move *Lulu* to the New (which for Vivien was haunted by memories) for another three months.

That period, in marked contrast to the onstage frolics, was stamped by more bad news. First Kay Kendall and then Ernest died, Kendall in early December from leukaemia aged only 33 and Ernest at 76 just before Christmas. Vivien and Coward went together to Kendall's quiet Hampstead funeral and then she read the words written by Rattigan – many present remembered them later when Vivien died – at the St Martin-in-the-Fields memorial service:

It was as if she had a premonition that the gift of life which she relished so greatly would not be hers for very long – with such intensity and gaiety and fervour did she pack every minute of her stay on earth.

Her father's death was not unexpected. Ernest had been in failing health for some time, his exuberance subdued and his old wayward ways in the past. Vivien and Gertrude attended Mass at the Brompton Oratory one Sunday before visiting him in hospital where he was very ill but conscious. His condition deteriorated during that week and he died early on the Friday morning. They saw his body laid out at the undertakers ("very beautiful and so peaceful" said Gertrude) before the cremation at Golder's Green. Olivier was just leaving for another "self-removing", back to New York to direct Charlton Heston in *The Tumbler* by the Oliviers' old Chelsea friend Benn Levy, and did not attend although he wrote to Gertrude, fondly recalling Ernest and how, despite the many vicissitudes, his long marriage to Gertrude had been essentially strong:

> I wish to God I could support that strength with the confident assurance of alrightness between V and me but terrible shame it is, I do not honestly feel I can do that.

The thought of a second divorce for Vivien made Gertrude's sadness at this time even more acute and Vivien was often with her in the days after Ernest's funeral. Her diary records a call from Olivier from New York on 23 December but Vivien too felt bereft just as Christmas loomed. For all his occasional huffs and impatience with her, Coward in a crisis was rarely anything other than a genuinely loving and loyal friend. He invited Vivien to join him and the Coward "family" (Graham Payn, Cole Lesley) for Christmas at his new Swiss home, Les Avants, in the canton of Vaud, high up in the mountains with stunning views ("It overlooks a beautiful tax advantage" he said once) although he wrote beforehand: "bring plenty of scent, the builders have just moved out and I am terrified of catching painter's colic."

Perched on a mountainside over Lac Leman, Les Avants (often known as Chalet Coward or, to friends, as Silly Chalet) was comfortable rather than luxurious, furnished mainly with pieces from Coward's London flat or from his Kent home. Cecil Beaton, a later visitor, had been led to expect something resembling an Eastbourne boarding-house and pronounced that Les Avants "has no real character, is ugly, is decorated in the typical theatre-folk style" although he conceded that "it is warm and comfortable and it works".

Coward drove to Geneva to meet Vivien, his first house-guest ("She is desolate and missing Larry every minute but is behaving beautifully and her outward manner is gay and charming") and described that Christmas as a happy one with a Christmas Day of bright winter sun and snow so thick the household could not slide down the slopes on their luges, drinks with Swiss neighbours, parlour games and quantities of vodka. To the pursuing press he blithely pretended to assume they had come to see him, entertained them to drinks, regaled them with his future plans and then ushered them out into the snow while Vivien remained in her room until they disappeared. He reported only one "break-down", to him alone on Christmas night. Olivier, her diary noted, called her on New Year's Eve and again on New Year's Day. Before she left, Coward reflected in his diary:

> Whether or not Larry will ever come back to her there is no knowing but if only she would face up to the fact that he probably won't and get on with her life it would be *much* better.

It would be some time still before that could become possible. *The Tumbler*, after a troubled try-out, flopped quickly on Broadway, which was where Vivien was next headed, to star (with Mary Ure replacing an unavailable Claire Bloom) in *Duel of Angels* with Helpmann re-staging Barrault's production, rehearsing in March. Before leaving there was more sadness, another step in what was becoming Blanche Du Bois' "long parade to the graveyard" when she made many visits to the dying George Relph in hospital. She flew out shortly before he died and she wrote at once to Mercia, remembering "the way you and Georgie took me for your friend at the very beginning of Larry and my life together" and insisting Mercia stay at Eaton Square if she wanted to. She had also several times noted for weekends in her diary: "Alone at Notley."

So although she knew that while she was in New York Olivier would be back in England in some ways she was not sorry to leave after such a run of sad events. Besides, there was unfinished business with *Duel of Angels* which she felt she had just begun to master when Claire Bloom had to leave the cast. She liked Mary Ure, although she was aware that her marriage to Osborne was rocky, and although they were no longer lovers, she was delighted when Peter Wyngarde, excellent as Paola's accomplice Marcellus, with his seductive voice and aristocratic bearing, finally decided to come to America too. Vivien had some apprehension that a sophisticated play, requiring immense precision of playing and attentive listening from audiences, might be too rarefied for the 1960s Broadway marketplace and she wanted to give the piece every chance. She was also still very lonely.

That changed during New York rehearsals. For the role of Paola's husband Armand, a crucial supporting character requiring an actor of stylish bearing and ideally not sounding overtly American among the other three principals, Cecil Tennant's clever suggestion was Jack Merivale. Vivien had not worked with him since *Romeo and Juliet* 20 years previously; they had bumped into each other occasionally and she had heard from friends how well he had looked after his half-brother John Buckmaster in times of crisis. Tall, intelligent – schooled at Rugby and Oxford – good-looking in a clean-cut English way, his career had covered Broadway and West End theatre and he was a familiar face in British films, usually cast as reliable, stiff-upper-lip professional or military men with, off stage, a laid-back charm and laconic humour similar to that of his actor-father Philip Merivale (Gladys Cooper's second husband). With dual Canadian and British citizenship he had the bonus of American Equity membership and so was snapped up rapidly for the part. At that time his private life was becalmed after a wartime marriage to the striking blonde actress Jan Sterling ended in divorce.

The mutual attraction – possibly reviving some long-buried feelings from 1939 – between Vivien and Merivale began in rehearsal when he would often join Vivien and Helpmann for meals and when he escorted Vivien to the theatre; it was a plus that he already knew many of her American friends (together they saw Bacall in *Goodbye, Charlie* and Cornell in *Dear Liar*, usually dining together afterwards). She met up with other friends – the Dietzes, the Kanins, Irene Selznick, Thornton and Isabel Wilder – all of whom seemed to think she was in excellent spirits despite all the recent *Sturm und Drang* and clearly exhilarated by re-examining her Paola.

The affair proper began in New Haven where *Duel* played before Broadway. In her diary she noted simply "Jack" after a dress-rehearsal; she had made the first direct move, sensing Jack's qualms about taking things beyond the platonic stage. He had made it a fixed rule not to come between married couples and also, as he said, it was difficult to fall in love with one of the most famous women in the world, not least because of the difference in status and income. From New Haven onwards, however, he would be a devoted lover for a woman who came increasingly to rely on him knowing he would never judge her. It could not have been always easy; he was initially unaware of the full implications of Vivien's Bipolar condition and also he had to accept that in her dressing-room and on her bedside table there would always be Olivier's framed photograph. Merivale was a rare actor without ego; he knew that he would never be a star but was not ambitious to be one although he certainly did not want to live off Vivien or to work exclusively with her.

Duel of Angels needed only fine-tuning in New Haven while Helpmann polished the elegant precision of Barrault's staging and the playing between Vivien and Mary Ure, a more delicate Lucille than Claire Bloom but equally strong in her moral certitude, gradually grew in subtlety. The Broadway opening at the Helen Hayes theatre, an intimate house suited to the play's special style, was a gala occasion with an audience of celebrities and acting royalty from the Lunts to Ethel Merman. Paola enters after only a page of dialogue, on Armand's arm; Merivale realised Vivien was trembling as he led her on to the town-square set to be met by an enormous entrance-round and cheers ("I disengaged from her grip, stepped back and half turned away, leaving her to acknowledge the ovation alone").

Wyngarde told a different story of that opening, stating that before the curtain Vivien received a cable from Olivier asking for a divorce and that she became so upset that he had to persuade her to go on, leading to what he judged the best performance in the play she ever gave ("It was as if she realised she was on her own from now on"). It makes for a more dramatic backstage story – a play, *Letter from Larry*, was based on it – but is contradicted by the facts; Vivien kept every scrap of correspondence and cables from Olivier and there is no such telegram amongst her papers. In fact the question of divorce first arose some weeks later in a letter from Olivier (which Vivien did keep).

For that period she had been mostly level and happy, although clearly still hoping for a possible reconciliation. *Duel* had superb notices – Walter Kerr hailed her Paola as "Miss Leigh's most controlled and captivating performance" – and the crush outside the stage door after each performance was reminiscent of the glory days of Broadway. But Merivale was aware there was still unfinished business. A diary entry says simply "Oh, Notley!" on the day it was sold when she also cabled Olivier ("THANK YOU FOR LOVELY, LOVELY NOTLEY MY DARLING"). She had heard from Hiley who had accompanied Olivier on a last visit to the house he had loved so much, on an April day with great drifts of daffodils all out ("I think L. was very disturbed by it all and greatly saddened"). She had written to Tarquin before she left England:

> It really seems as if Notley is sold. I can hardly write the words … I walk from place to precious place and gaze at beloved views with tears pouring down my face … Oh, Tarkie darling, I just cannot live without him and it is an unbearable pain to be parted from him.

Although Merivale brought her solace then, she still – with some extra pressure now – tried to send her troops into action on her behalf. She persuaded Garson Kanin and Ruth Gordon to write separately to Olivier persuading him not to break irrevocably with her (he replied to Gordon, according to Kanin, with "a hysterical, furious blister of a letter") and her most loyal champion, Rachel Kempson, also entered the lists again. She had suffered decidedly rocky periods in her marriage to Redgrave, although managing to accept his male affairs and somehow largely avoiding bitterness (something she entreated Vivien also to shun), eventually finding an equilibrium in a long relationship with Byam Shaw. She had advised Vivien to consult the eminent psychiatrist Charlotte Wolf, who had helped her, but Vivien remained loyal to Conachy. After their friend Victor Stiebel had interceded with Olivier, Rachel also wrote, stressing that Vivien was sorely aware of the suffering she had caused him but had learnt her lesson and now would accept any terms at all. Olivier ignored Stiebel but Rachel was an old friend and colleague and he agreed to meet her. She wrote a long and loving letter to Vivien detailing this encounter. Olivier, she said, only too evidently remained deeply troubled by the whole divorce issue but despite Rachel voicing – as she had said to Vivien she would – her feeling that he would be haunted always by Vivien should he irrevocably break with her (with which he agreed) he still wanted to continue with plans for a complete split. Rachel felt that she would not be acting as a true friend were she to fail to be totally honest in expressing her sense that any denial of his freedom would only reinforce his resolve.

Touchingly, she tried to give Vivien some comfort by quoting Stiebel's belief that Olivier might return to her at a future stage. Vivien was less sentimental than Stiebel; she used no further personal or epistolary ambassadors.

Merivale was becoming more acquainted with the symptoms of Vivien's illness; Wyngarde, now romantically involved elsewhere, gave him some pointers (he came to admire the commitment of his successor in Vivien's love-life: "He started as her supporting actor and became marvellous with her ... a very rare person"). Gertrude's arrival for a New York visit possibly knocked Vivien off-balance; it was noticed that her post-show life, although never affecting her performance, had become increasingly hectic. She had moved from Hampshire House into an apartment on East 62nd Street from where she decided to write (after quite a gap) to Olivier, now back at the Royal Court in Ionesco's *Rhinoceros*, with Joan in the cast, on which he had given director Orson Welles as tough a time as he had Gielgud in Stratford. This letter, dating from mid-May, was long, written mostly in instalments and partly in pencil, clearly spurred by her new romantic life:

> The smiling photograph of you taken during *Spartacus* is in front of me as I write ...
> your happiness is what I wish *really* more than anything. *Now* – I think that you

and I should meet to discuss just what should happen to us, for time is running out and we have our lives to live and the sooner we put them in some sort of order the better – Don't you think?

She suggested that it would be best if he could fly over after *Rhinoceros* ("neither of us are at our best on the telephone, are we?"), towards the close adding she had found "someone kind and dear who takes good care of me and I shall try to take care of him – and start a different life, I hope a more sensible and quiet one". This letter must have gladdened Olivier's heart – the only sour note was a reference to Joan as his "wretched girl" – and he replied almost immediately, agreeing with her words about time running out and, in reply to her question about whether he agreed they should put their lives in order:

> Yes, my darling I jolly well do is my answer ... We must get our allegiances squared up, one just has to *bend* basic instincts sometimes for a fruitful conducting of life.

Insisting that while definitely wanting a divorce her happiness was what he wished for too, he added a sentence which must have stung:

> My ("wretched") girl is better equipped than you could possibly suppose and looks after me with what seems a special gift for the things in life I really need. Forgive me, love.

This letter reached Vivien on 21 May. There are varying accounts of subsequent events. Alexander Walker's biography asserts that after reading it she telephoned Cindy Dietz, who came to her apartment immediately ("I'm going to do what he wants, of course" Vivien said to her) and accompanied her to her Manhattan physician, Dr Brill, who prescribed tranquillisers. She then lunched with Helpmann (although this, unusually, is not noted in her diary) who advised her to issue a statement (Helpmann was none too fond of Olivier calling him "Old Sourpuss" behind his back). Later that evening's television news announced "Lady Olivier wishes to say that Sir Laurence has asked for a divorce in order to marry Miss Joan Plowright. She will naturally do whatever he wishes." Hugo Vickers's book also suggests "the Mephistolean Helpmann" persuaded her into this, which is perfectly possible although another version, backed up by Jack, claims that Vivien that day first went shopping and then talked to a London journalist, David Lewin, then in New York, who had suggested she issue a statement (although few from Fleet Street would forgo such a scoop).

Whatever the circumstances the news created a sensation when splashed over every newspaper front page in Britain the next morning (Olivier's birthday – for a moment he imagined it was a black birthday joke from Vivien). Vivien had cabled him (the Western Union wire is timed 2.45 a.m. New York time, so she may well have had drink on top of Dr Brill's pills) – DARLING, I HAVE GIVEN A STATEMENT TO THE PRESS STATING THE FACTS – although just before receiving it he had been alerted by Virginia Fairweather. In her words "the witch hunt was on"; Joan at once pulled out of *Rhinoceros* and her understudy went on until Maggie Smith had been quickly rehearsed into the role, then was spirited away to her brother's home (this was the first occasion she had been mentioned in connection with Olivier directly in the press) while Olivier was scrupulously polite to reporters but made no comment. Osborne noted his pained reaction: "as if Nelson had been caught with his hand in the Admiralty till." The news caused a royal fuss; Vivien told Jack later that she had no memory of talking to a reporter or of issuing a statement but she had raised an issue which might possibly prove a hurdle for divorce proceedings with her statement's suggestion of collusion between her and Olivier. The press had a field day in the early summer dog-days for news, with headlines including "The Hazard to Love" and "A Legend Crumbles".

After the drama Vivien in New York at first seemed on a relatively even keel, lunching with Cindy, with Leonard Bernstein, with Rex Harrison and others. She spoke at an Equity Meeting, that diary entry adding "No Show". A simmering dispute between the actors' union and the New York League of Theatre Managers erupted finally, with a different show cancelling a performance shortly before curtain-up each evening until an impasse led to the closure of all Broadway theatres, which saw several productions, including *Duel of Angels*, close prematurely. Its producers, rather than later re-mount and advertise again on Broadway, decided to take the play on a tour of major American cities. When this step was taken Vivien noted only "Strike – oh!" and with an unexpected free evening she and Jack went to the movies (although it is questionable whether Dirk Bogarde's romantic agony as Franz Liszt in *Song Without End* provided much cheer). The following day she lunched with Kay Brown, her old ally in her siege of Scarlett, adding in her diary: "No more play."

The cumulative pressure of recent days saw her slowly slip into a manic phase. Irene Selznick spotted the warning signs – Helpmann promptly disappeared from New York for a time – and explained to Jack what needed to be done. She recommended a Manhattan psychiatrist who gave Vivien, unprotesting, an ECT treatment which was badly handled, leaving her with burn marks on her forehead. Conachy said later:

> She had enough insight at the onset of her condition to go to a psychiatrist in New York ... She had one ECT treatment but unfortunately the technique used was not satisfactory and she refused to have further treatment there.

A decision was made. There would be time – at least ten days – before regrouping in New York prior to the *Duel of Angels* tour – for Vivien to fly home for treatment under Conachy. Some friends believed what several reports later claimed – that Vivien used that to divert attention from her true intent which was to have one more personal plea to Olivier not to take this final step although, even if so, after his most recent letter it could have been with no more than a faint hope of success.

Helpmann – who relished his proximity to Vivien and the attendant publicity – accompanied her to England. Olivier had moved out of Eaton Square although Gertrude and Bumble were there to help with the melancholy task of sorting through some Notley contents temporarily stored at the apartment. While in London Vivien had five ECT sessions with Conachy; she was anaesthetised with sodium pentothal and he used a Shotter-Rich electronarcosis machine (to avoid memory loss) and he also had psychotherapy sessions with her. In the report which Vivien always kept with her afterwards in case she needed treatment overseas Conachy described her as "a person of very high intelligence and education, nimble wit and extremely good judgement", detailing the symptoms of manic spells, which could be sudden in onset, when she might lose "her natural restraint, reasoning power and insight". He was careful to stress that, contrary to any mistaken suggestions of schizophrenia, the essence of Vivien's illness was "a cyclic manic-depressive psychosis" (Bipolar in today's parlance). There was one Eaton Square party when she drank too much (a visiting Coward still put her problems down to "the demon alcohol – this is what it has always been"), probably born out of an unwise visit to Notley under its new Canadian owners, but gradually in London she stabilised. She had planned to see *Rhinoceros* but two possible bookings are scratched through in her diary. There is no record of any meeting with Olivier; Walker's book suggests Olivier slipped into Eaton Square through a service entrance, although the day to which he ascribes the visit (18 June) was extremely busy – she saw Jamie Hamilton, Mercia, the Bushells and Bumble and caught Wesker's *Chicken Soup with Barley* that evening – with no diary note of any meeting with Olivier.

Vivien left London two days later, her diary noting "Wrote L and Jack". Both letters were written on the plane and have a new tone, almost serene. Conachy, as she owned, would seem to have helped her greatly – he was a rare psychiatrist who understood that manic depression can involve the soul as much as the brain – even her handwriting seems firmer, less loopy in these letters. To Jack ("Darling Love") she wrote:

I am on my way to you with a beating heart ... This has been a most extraordinary
week. I think the most extraordinary of my life. Alone and yet so infinitely close
to you.

To Olivier she must have sounded a different woman:

Whatever may happen let us be friends my dearest one. Conachy has done a very
marvellous thing for me – and I am feeling as I have not felt for many many years.
Perhaps all the interim mistakes have made just too much difference for our life
together – I do not know.

While she loved Jack she stressed:

I shall love you all my life and with a tenderness and respect that is all-embracing.
I understand very well how difficult – even impossible – it had become.

Olivier's first response was a chilly legal one; Vivien's solicitors were told by his
that to avoid future misunderstanding it should be clear that he had no
intention of returning to her. Then he wrote himself, referring to "your little
press bombshell on my birthday" and to Joan's impending proceedings for her
divorce, wishing her "Bon Voyage" for her tour, and adding:

Conachy did say he hoped you would do a quarterly "standardising check-up – I
do hope you will, darling, please do and take great care of Jack. He loves you and
however saintlike, don't try too hard – keep hold of that, it's infinitely precious.

He ended with "God bless you, Always, L" but then scribbled that he felt now
he was in touch "with such lovely happiness and Oh I do want to keep it.
Forgive me, love."

Jack met Vivien off her flight, delighted she appeared so well and happy.
During Vivien's absence he had talked long-distance with and written to Olivier,
assuring him he would take great care of her while Olivier replied to express "the
purest kind of gratitude I've ever known" saying that he felt released from the
"barbs" which had been tormenting his hopes, thanking God that four people
could now be happy. Now that he was *au fait* with her condition Jack made a
decision to stay with Vivien always (marriage did not matter). He could be firm
with her and was definitely responsible for the noticeable drop in her alcohol
consumption, one factor which made the *Duel* tour such an enjoyable
experience. It coincided with several future plans – a suggested Old Vic
Australian tour, the title role in a film of Tennessee Williams's novella *The Roman
Spring of Mrs. Stone* scheduled to be shot the following year in Rome – while she
also instigated further searches for a possible country property at home.

Duel reopened successfully in Los Angeles where the film colony welcomed
Vivien back as enthusiastically as New York. She always travelled in style,

staying on this occasion at the Chateau Marmont; like her friend Cole Porter whenever out of town with a new musical, she liked on tour to take some treasured objects (on this trip her Renoir flower-painting) to have around her. There were many friends to catch up with and some to meet Jack for the first time – Sunny Lash, Cukor, Tracy – and a reunion with several Royal Court regulars. Tony Richardson had rented a home in Westwood Village while simultaneously filming *Sanctuary* and rehearsing *A Taste of Honey* prior to Broadway with Joan Plowright, with Devine (helping Richardson with the play) and his new partner, designer Jocelyn Herbert also there, joined by Osborne (involved with a new mistress) and Mary Ure, still his wife. It was all very raffish (although Vivien and Joan did not meet) with visits to a gay bar to which Richardson had been introduced by Christopher Isherwood and Don Bachardy and a bizarre evening when a drunk Ure jumped into the pool, ignored by her husband until saved from imminent drowning by Richardson. With only slight understatement Isherwood described that household as "the setting for a Feydeau farce".

Osborne followed the production to San Francisco where he saw more of Vivien. As an actor he had appeared in Giraudoux' one-acter *Apollo de Bellac* at the Royal Court and in *Duel* anticipated another piece of "French puffery" but he found Vivien's Paola a revelation:

> She strode the stage, a reborn Scarlett with the fires of Atlanta and despised love . . .
> It was defiant, desperate and moving as she swathed her way through the fog of
> French bombast . . . She almost redeemed it by naked personal courage.

He found a Vivien also in peak form off stage, organising company fishing and sailing trips, picnics in redwood forests outside the city or to catch the nightclub act of comedian Bob Newhart. After responsive houses in the city's beautiful Alcazar Theatre, to play a vast Denver barn was less pleasurable but Chicago was another happy date as Vivien wrote to Leigh ("My apartment looks straight over the great lake and of course the Art Gallery is one of the finest in the world so I am happy wandering about there"). Washington was also a delight; she fell in love with one particular room – it had Titian, Velasquez, Constable and Ingres on the walls – in the intimate Phillips Gallery. She did not mention Jack in any letters to Leigh from America.

The company returned to New York at the end of the tour – Olivier was on Broadway in Anouilh's *Becket* and Joan in *A Taste of Honey* but contrary to some accounts neither met Vivien and she saw neither play – and she lunched with Tennessee Williams and with the visiting Tennant; he could tell her that the contract for *Mrs. Stone* had been settled. Williams had once harboured hopes that Garbo might play Karen Stone but still, like the film's scriptwriter Gavin Lambert, professed himself delighted with Vivien's casting. She was slightly disappointed to hear that the film would not now be made in Rome where the story is set (the city fathers wanted no further depictions of Roman decadence following Fellini's *La Dolce Vita*) but at Elstree Studios.

Her costumes were to be made by Balmain and so she, Jack and Wyngarde sailed back on the *Queen Elizabeth*, disembarking at Cherbourg to enormous press interest in "The New Man in Vivien's Life" which Jack courteously deflected, before going on to Paris for fittings, sessions which saw the closeness between Vivien and Ginette Spanier happily restored. This was an especially idyllic time for her with Jack, seeing the Barraults and the Norwiches and on a free day driving to the little house near Paris once the home of Marie Duplessis, model for the heroine of Dumas *fils*'s *La Dame aux Camellias*, a possible play for the Old Vic's Australian tour. In Paris Vivien also met the director Caspar Wrede (a Beaumont suggestion as translator for Dumas's play) and Jose Quintero, confirmed as the director for *Mrs. Stone*. At the end of the Paris visit the Olivier divorce papers were served on Vivien which caused some tears but this was assuaged somewhat by a brief tour with Gilman at the wheel of the new Rolls, taking with them Vivien's art-dealer friend and adviser Willy Peploe, visiting Diana Cooper at Chantilly and then driving through France to Switzerland, ending up at Les Avants for a brief stay with Coward. She had written beforehand for permission to bring Jack and it was a relaxing time, with Coward noting that although he realised Vivien missed Olivier still: "She is putting up a gallant performance and seems very fond of Jack who is constantly fulfilling a long-felt want."

Returning to London involved – finally – the dreaded divorce proceedings in early December just after *Mrs. Stone* went before the cameras. With Olivier and Joan in New York only Vivien and Roger Gage of the parties concerned were present, Gage citing Olivier in his petition while Vivien admitted adultery in London and Ceylon. It took less than 30 minutes to dissolve a marriage of over two decades. Some press reports (and Walker) described Vivien as weeping in court and in the car being driven away afterwards although Hiley, who was present with Tennant, contradicted these. But Jack, Gertrude and Bumble were all waiting for her at Eaton Square. Christmas 1961 was inevitably tinged with sadness although friends made sure she was not too much alone, especially when Jack was working; Beaumont, Rattigan, Dent and Mercia Relph all lunched with her while Christmas dinner was with her friend (an ex-Notley neighbour) Lady Alexandra ("Baba") Metcalfe and on

Boxing Day she dined with Margaret Leighton. On New Year's Eve she threw a small party at Eaton Square – Gertrude, the housekeeper Mrs McCauly ("Mrs Mac"), Bumble, Helpmann and Benthall, Quintero and two principals from *Mrs Stone*, Lotte Lenya and Warren Beatty, who brought his girlfriend, Joan Collins. The latter was less than generous about Vivien in her autobiography; possibly she was mindful of a *Drama* magazine review of her "Q" theatre performance as Sabina in *The Skin of Our Teeth* which compared hers, none too favourably, with Vivien's.

The Roman Spring of Mrs. Stone seemed an ideal project for Vivien at that time. The title character is a famous American actress, recently retired after a failure in Shakespeare ("I lived a long time in a very flattering, very artificial, very insincere world – the world of an actress"). After Karen's wealthy husband's death *en route* for Europe she decides to stay in Rome, beginning a period of what she describes as "the drift", living in an apartment above the Spanish steps, beside the Egyptian sculpture at the bottom of which lurks an unkempt, mysterious young man "who has an appointment with grandeur". Karen is manipulated by a venal Roman Contessa, a procuress who introduces her to Paolo, an attractive young gigolo who similarly exploits her until a richer prospect in films comes along and he moves on, leading to Williams's ending in which Karen throws down her keys to the young man on the steps, revealed as another of Williams's Angels of Death. Karen has "stopped the drift".

The story belongs to the late 1940s when, flush with success (and dollars) after the success of his first two Broadway plays Williams travelled in Europe for a time. On board the *Vulcania* he wrote to his friend Oliver Evans of his delighted discovery of Henry James ("Henrietta James" he called him in the gay gender-changing parlance of the era). Reading *The Aspern Papers* made him eager for more ("I am now looking forward to practically everything the old girl has written"). The influence is heavily evident in *Mrs. Stone* which has a central Jamesian dynamic of the contrast between the New World and an older Europe, together with rather self-conscious echoes of James's lapidary prose style. Set in postwar Rome suggesting something of the neo-realism of movie directors such as Pasolini or Rossellini in which sexual exploitation mirrors economic hardship, the book – like the film – is fascinating but deeply flawed.

The story, informed by subterranean tensions and ambivalent sexuality, needed a better director – a Visconti or a de Sica (who was at one stage interested) – certainly a more experienced one – than Quintero, who had directed a successful production in New York of Williams's *Summer and Smoke* but had never worked on a film. The danger of the material – that so easily it could topple into the traps of becoming a diluted Douglas Sirk-ish "woman's picture" – is not entirely avoided and Quintero had no inkling of how to pace a film. Its movement is pedestrian virtually throughout with the performances stranded too often amid the often impressive production values. Roger Furse's sets evoke a world in which rot has set in, its values decadent like the marketplace it has become; his nightclub setting has a smoky carnality and his apartment for the Contessa, with its slightly worn red velvets and predatory cats, is especially suggestive. The main problem lay in the casting. Most of the vital supporting parts are sharply played, notably Coral Browne, Vivien's near-neighbour in Eaton Square, as Karen's columnist-friend and, stealing the film, Lotte Lenya (incredibly, making her first film since Pabst's *Threepenny Opera* in 1931) as the Contessa, oozing lubricious delight as she fixes up her clients with her string of gigolos.

Vivien is not at her best. Possibly the suggestion of Karen's awareness of her fading beauty affected her although her lack of sentimentality would normally banish such thoughts. Her look was not quite right despite the stylish Balmain clothes; for once Stanley Hall's work was unsatisfactory, with Vivien's wigs (ash-blonde, unflattering) styled so stiffly, allowing next to no movement, that they looked only too often like wigs. Her cool, bleached detachment seems at times mere indifference. But, once again, not for one moment does she ask for the audience's sympathy; she seems, in her best scenes, almost literally thin-skinned with a carapace of cool assurance barely cloaking the solitude, an inner empty despair. It is a performance which needed something to play off – her scenes with Browne or Lenya provide that – but unfortunately Warren Beatty's Paolo is inadequate almost throughout. He was not inexperienced, having played in William Inge's work on Broadway and, in *Splendour in the Grass* (then not released), on screen; his Paolo might have just survived his hopelessly mis-stressed Italian accent but the performance, and a large part of the film, are sunk by his inability to suggest even partly the way the character, as Williams puts it, lives "upon the current of time", instead delivering a Central-Casting gigolo, complacent throughout in a sustained, rather helpless, shrug of a performance. This blank makes Vivien's performance seem chillier, even harder, than the character should be. Williams, however, was enraptured ("I just sat and watched the grace and tragic style of Vivien Leigh") and described the film as "a poem", but then Williams did describe the 1960s as his "stoned age".

On the whole Vivien enjoyed making the film and really liked the gentle Quintero who allowed her a brief break during filming to visit Atlanta to take up an invitation to attend a special gala screening of *Gone With the Wind* coinciding with the centennial of the Civil War, joining de Havilland and Selznick, the other major participants still living. There was probably an ulterior motive; she suggested breaking her journey in New York so that she might meet Olivier. His reply to that notion was speedy, explaining that the press were making life difficult for him already. His attitude was the kind of rejection which Scarlett receives from Ashley Wilkes at Twelve Trees:

> Your projected visit here on the way to Atlanta at this particular time is, I'm afraid, going to heighten all that sort of torment ... I strongly urge that to save more than necessary embarrassment that we didn't, darling, meet at that time.

There are several accounts of a supposed meeting between Vivien, Olivier and Joan in New York (Holden's biography of Olivier even places this in Sardi's restaurant, Walker's of Vivien in a "smart but crowded restaurant"). But no such event took place. Joan Plowright flatly contradicted Holden's Sardi's version ("This is pure invention, like much else that has been written. For the record, there was never any confrontation between us three, in Sardi's or anywhere else"). Vivien's diary has no entry of any such meeting; her friend Radie Harris met her in New York and together they flew to Atlanta. It could have been a depressing occasion – so many participants in the film were dead – but it became a genuinely celebratory affair with almost as much ballyhoo as at 1939's premiere with fans yelling "Scarlett!" all the way down Peachtree Street to Loew's Grand. Aged 47, now Vivien had to stand on the same huge stage of 23 years previously; cleverly, she had had made a gown similar to several from the film, in white satin with a wide skirt covered in blue flowers, still with the same slim waist as the young Scarlett. Jack was working in England but Vivien wrote to him describing the fun of the Atlanta visit, a highlight of which was a slap-up brunch at the delightfully named Aunt Fannie's Cabin followed by copious mint juleps. She was touched by a letter from Selznick ("Your Past and Future Boss") thanking her for the commemorative twenty-one roses she had sent him, in which he acknowledged that *GWTW* owed a great debt to "your magnificent performance... I shall never forget your heroic efforts during these months."

Her return to London coincided with the news which reporters awaiting her arrival gave her, that Olivier's marriage (a very quiet affair, like his wedding to Vivien) to Joan Plowright had taken place in Connecticut. She betrayed no surprise or emotion other than to express her delight for the couple and, attending Bernard Gilman's wedding the following day, continued to look smiling and serene, whatever her inner feelings. *Mrs. Stone* was completed on schedule and without problems.

There was at least the consolation of having found the country house for which she had been searching, a warm-bricked Queen Anne property in Sussex suggested by Dirk Bogarde. When Vivien, Jack and Gertrude drove to visit the house, near Uckfield, she at once fell in love with Tickerage Mill; "We came to a certain point in the drive," said Jack, "and we saw the house and a glimpse of the water beyond it and she let out a sigh." Water – "Ophelia's Brook" had been a favourite Notley feature – was a key factor in Vivien's property specifications and she came to love the changing aspects of the millpond, a small willow-fringed lake, at Tickerage. Hidden in a valley of the River Uck, built of mellow rose-red brick with a large tract of woodland carpeted in bluebells and wood-anemones in spring, it became a haven of a house – and mainly a happy one – for Vivien for the rest of her life. It needed some work; she engaged a clever designer, Paul Anstee, who had worked with Fowler and been close to Gielgud for some time, to supervise the alterations and redecoration necessary while Leigh (with Vivien's ideas in mind plus advice from Stanley Hall and Godfrey Winn, both garden-lovers with houses nearby) would help reclaim and plant the overgrown gardens and the terrace close to the house. During that time Vivien would be at other ends of the world, leading an Old Vic company once more to Australia and New Zealand and then, this time, to South America. Tennessee Williams, now devoted to her, once had hoped she might play Marguerite Gautier in his 1956 play *Camino Real* (Marguerite in *La Dame aux Camellias* was one of her roles on this tour). It is in that strange, bold play that Williams's own credo is trumpeted: "Make voyages! Attempt them!" It might have served as Vivien's too.

CHAPTER 17

Worlds Elsewhere

Vivien's life post-divorce is usually portrayed as a minor-key coda, a personal and professional slow decline stamped by regret and a pining for the past, playing faded heroines and lost beauties. Jean-Pierre Aumont came up with all the clichés in his autobiography: "She died of despair for a love that was gone, for children she couldn't have. She died of sadness." She died of none of those things. Certainly she spent much of that period in a kind of self-imposed exile – in Australia, South America and the United States – but those spells were essentially professional, including an Old Vic tour, two Broadway productions and a Hollywood film, after which she planned to return to the West End in a new play she found almost as exciting as *Streetcar*.

Some well-intentioned friends insisted on treating her as if she were a piece of fragile porcelain; Victor Stiebel, who never forgave Olivier ("I can never feel the same about him again") for insisting on divorce, assumed "my darling is still yearning at shadows", resenting the fact that Vivien still cared for Olivier and always wanted to know what he was up to. Others were more pragmatic. Tony Bushell's old flame Consuelo, who looked after Tickerage while the refurbishments were carried out when Vivien was on tour, appreciated that Vivien was always "hungry for news – any kind of news – from a certain quarter" but was never less than candid, once while detailing an Olivier visit in Vivien's absence to collect some stored Notley items delivering her own perspective on him:

> Larry is not a strong character – he knows *one* thing, all about the theatre – period. He is and has been the centre of adulation attended by as many sycophants as friends. You don't want him to pity you – for that *diminishes* you – the abyss cannot hold you – once down you must come up.

Vivien had been especially touched by a letter from Sybil Thorndike following the divorce, mentioning how much she and Lewis Casson had thought about her:

> and after the first sort of awfulness I felt about the whole split-up I suddenly got it in my head "Perhaps it is the best thing for Vivien – perhaps she'll reach out into a new life and achieve *more*" and I think you will – thro' the misery and unhappiness and beastly publicity you're emerging strong and so *brave* and we both feel you are mounting up into a higher plane somehow.

Although the divorce had been agonising for her she remembered always that Olivier had written to her from New York immediately afterwards to say that it felt "awky to write" but to thank her for going through with it, adding "Oh God, Vivling, how I do pray that you will find happiness and contentment."

There was one grim spell during those years after her life with Olivier ended when her Bipolar condition brought an especially dark period, one of the longest from which she suffered, but that was clearly triggered by sheer exhaustion, the physical and mental strain of starring in (and essentially carrying) a demanding Broadway musical throughout a blistering New York summer rather than by any enveloping clouds of sadness or death-wish regret. Her relationship with Jack – who never tried to exorcise memories of Olivier – only grew in strength and mutual loyalty; he saw her through that long spell of acute distress, realising that while her illness suggested weakness, Vivien was fundamentally a strong character – remarkably so – and agreeing with Conachy who wrote to him of Vivien's condition before they left for Australia, describing her as:

> a most charming, able, intelligent woman afflicted by a manic depressive illness who with courage and marked strength of character has taken a heavy and continuous emotional strain in her stride during the past year.

Conachy again warned Jack that while Vivien was "in no sense an alcoholic" drink was always a danger; Jack had already begun to monitor her alcohol intake and now would always keep a beady eye on her glass at parties. She knew and often acknowledged how lucky she was to have found him.

Vivien had been delighted when Benthall, who planned the Old Vic/British Council tour with all three productions directed by Helpmann, who would be with the company in his native Australia, cast Jack as her leading man although, as he was the first to admit, his box-office power was not remotely equivalent to Olivier's. It was perhaps unfortunate that although the company included some first-rate actors (Frank Middlemass, Mark Kingston, David Dodimead) with promising younger talent (Bruce Montague, Patrick Stewart) in smaller roles it did not include another recognised box-office name. Also the repertoire to many Australians seemed a rum affair of only one British classic alongside two French plays. Moreover *Twelfth Night*, although a set school text, had been produced by all the major companies in an Australian theatre transformed since Vivien toured in 1948, while the "difficult" *Duel of Angels*, critically well-received, was not at all liked by audiences. The most popular was the old warhorse of *The Lady of the Camellias* with Vivien as the consumptive courtesan Marguerite Gautier. "Just as all ballerinas want to dance Giselle" said Helpmann, "all actresses want to play Marguerite", although Vivien's French was good enough for her to realise that Andrew Allen's English version of Dumas, found by her New York lawyer Arnold Weissberger after various possibilities fell through, was decidedly pedestrian. But the play had held the stage for over a century – providing a key vehicle for Bernhardt, Duse and Réjane and on film for Garbo – and the story's durability continues (Baz Luhrmann's *Moulin Rouge* on screen, Pam Gems's *Camille* and the Boublil-Schönberg stage musical *Marguerite*). Like audiences in Paris and London, Vivien had been captivated by the famous Marguerite of Edwige Feuillère, the great romantic actress of the twentieth-century French stage and the parallels with the all-for-love consumptive Marguerite struck her forcibly too, increasing her desire to tackle the part, which she approached more along the Duse/ Feuillère lines of restraint, elegiac where Bernhardt barnstormed.

Another problem on the Old Vic tour was Helpmann's limitations as a director. All three productions were easy on the eye; Furse's neo-Impressionist designs and Dior's costumes for the Giraudoux again, the Australian-born Loudon Sainthill's beguiling single set and witty Elizabethan *Twelfth Night* costumes, and a ravishing Dumas from Carl Toms, coping with the multi-scene demands by concentrating mainly on rapidly rearranged items of beautiful furniture and splashing out on sumptuous mid-nineteenth-century costumes with Vivien's Marguerite showcased in pale silk gowns and enveloping cloaks of feathers and fur. Helpmann always denied that his choreographic background influenced his work but undoubtedly it did; his London productions of *Camelot* and *Peter Pan* were pantomime writ musically and in his trio of productions for the Old Vic there was little below the surface sheen, especially in a routine and over-busy *Twelfth Night* which skimmed over the play's ambiguities of gender and sexuality.

Rehearsals in London were held in the echoing space of the Finsbury Park Empire; the old variety theatre's seats had been ripped out before its conversion into a scenery store prior to demolition. Bruce Montague recalled a distinctly formal first morning in the draughty building with Vivien introduced to the company assembled on stage like a royal inspection of the troops but the atmosphere quickly became more relaxed. Montague always felt that Vivien was "stronger than the frail flower as which she was often treated". She was witty but rarely made jokes as such although Montague remembered one occasion when, for once wearing "Femme" by Rochas rather than her usual "Joy", she had a mock-disagreement with Jack, ending with her tossing her perfume at him with "'Femme' hits shit".

The company was in high spirits when they left for Australia. Vivien was accompanied by Trudy Flockhart (Gilman had been sent on ahead with the Rolls). Unwisely the play chosen to open the tour was *Duel of Angels*, an unfamiliar piece not helped by the Melbourne first night coinciding with a major social event (the Lord Mayor's ball) which resulted in a late curtain and regular arrivals and departures throughout the evening. Vivien wrote to Gertrude rather acidly: "I thought a pack of huskies had been let into the stalls, there were so many off-white fox stoles" and her subsequent criticism on television of that audience ("I never spent a gloomier night than I did in Melbourne") resulted in resentful headlines although Vivien noticed that audiences began to behave better thereafter.

Off stage she seemed happy and, as always, perpetually active – on one occasion she drove at dawn to a countryside forest to find and hear a lyre bird – especially so in a sun-baked Brisbane with barbecues and beach picnics. David Dodimead made audio-tapes during the tour to send home to his partner and recounted many joyful excursions and informal parties. Vivien was initially aghast when confronted by the company with a surprise parody of *This Is Your Life* for her forty-eighth birthday but ended up in peals of helpless laughter (the script, masterminded by Frank Middlemass, presented her as a slum-child urchin climbing the showbusiness ladder from an early life sold into South American white-slavery). She could be mischievous; Bruce Montague escorted her to a *Gone With the Wind* screening (an occupational hazard for her on tour) but as soon as the lights dimmed Vivien nudged him and they took off, while Dodimead mentioned several post-show receptions at which, should they become lengthily tedious, she would plead exhaustion after an hour or so and then take company members off to the nearest nightclub. In Sydney she met up with two of the Old Vic 1948 company, now based in Australia, John Barnard and Hugh Stewart, who had expected to be given an audience by a gracious world-famous star but found her as warm as in 1948 although Barnard sensed an inner shadow:

I had not seen her on stage since 1948. She moved one utterly. She *was* the Lady of the Camellias. It was *her* tragedy … Yet even as I rejoiced that she had joined the ranks of the great ones, I also felt a sense of foreboding.

Regularly Jack reported to Gertrude that Vivien was thriving, calm and relaxed ("I won't say there haven't been flashes of gunfire … but she's never brought up the big artillery"). The same pattern continued in New Zealand where audience reactions seemed to the actors much sharper, although there continued to be some press snipings that Jack (often referred to as Vivien's "constant companion") was no Olivier. The company especially took to Auckland; Dodimead always remembered one late night when, after a party, a still-alert Vivien suddenly decided they should go together for a swim in the ocean, driving the Rolls to a secluded bay. Keeping the headlights on in the pitch dark they realised that with nobody around they could skinny-dip. Vivien plunged in, swimming straight out – "out and out and out for a long, long way" – while Dodimead after a brief dip returned to the car, gradually growing apprehensive:

I waited and waited … it seemed like three hours. And then she came in, bright as a button … As we got back to the house she said "Bacon and eggs!" It was now fully daylight. But that's a story of the madness of her – the best madness and the joy of being with her. She was so alive.

The fun of New Zealand continued when Vivien encountered the famous local character of Sir Ernest Davis, possibly reminding her of her own father Ernest. Then touching 90, he was wealthy from the family distillery and brewing business, an Anglophile theatre-lover and notable in yachting circles. He became besotted by Vivien, even hopefully proposing to her ("all that physical business" was apparently immaterial) and she accompanied him to the races and threw a party for him on his birthday (they extinguished the vast number of candles together with a pair of bellows), which so increased his ardour that after her departure not only did he write to her but he changed his will to leave her brewery shares worth nearly £20,000, a tidy sum then (in consideration "of the great happiness brought to me"), not altogether to his family's delight on his death later that year.

The tour had always been planned to take in another country. The Far East was ruled out for reasons of cost while Jack swiftly vetoed the suggestion of South Africa, still then under apartheid. Equity – and actors – were divided on the issue of playing there and Jack was well aware that Vivien would inevitably, in the press or in radio or television interviews, say how much she abhorred the regime. Eventually the British Council decided on South America – seven countries altogether – although *Duel of Angels* was dropped, replaced by a Shakespeare anthology in which Helpmann, never backward in coming forward into any spotlight, would partner Vivien ("I do not want to appear for the first time in Latin America unless I can make a very strong impression" he told her). He put together an evening which saw them repeat their Titania and Oberon from nearly 30 years before, with further excerpts from *The Merchant of Venice, Much Ado About Nothing* (Vivien's only ventures in Portia and Beatrice) and, with Helpmann a somewhat unlikely Scottish warrior, *Macbeth*, supported by the company in various roles.

They played their first date in Mexico City's brand new but immediately smoothly functioning Cultural Centre where the Shakespeare evening was wildly popular (as it was throughout their two-month tour), always receiving tumultuous final ovations with flowers raining down from boxes and upper levels. *Twelfth Night* suffered; most of the heavy scenery was left behind in New Zealand and the production looked wan against drapes with token set-dressing. *Lady of the Camellias* had South American handkerchiefs sodden at Vivien's closing scene of Marguerite's death; the Australian and South American reviews indicate that her performance captured something of that atmosphere which Henry James wrote was the story's special quality, even without *La Traviata*'s music ("a charm which nothing can vulgarise – it is all champagne and tears … it carries with it an April air"). Arnold Weissberger flew to Mexico City in order to see it and found himself unexpectedly touched by Vivien's Marguerite, describing it as "beautifully delineated and deeply moving".

Their arrival in Buenos Aires coincided with a particularly aggressive phase in a putsch between rival Argentinian army chiefs and the noise from demonstrations at times distracted during performances in another extravagant new building, the San Martin Municipal Theatre, replacing "The Grand Old Lady of Argentinian Theatre", the lovely Teatro Nacional Cervantes.

Vivien's mood and health remained buoyant throughout this leg of the tour also, apart from one Buenos Aires evening when, on edge from the rowdy protests in the streets around their hotel, she had a brief "episode" during which she hurled a clock out of her fourteenth-floor window. She happily visited dance schools, flower shows and gardens as well as dutifully attending regular British Council functions and local civic receptions. Jack assumed that she would want to fly directly home – they had been away for nearly a year – when the tour ended in Brazil but instead they first visited Cindy and Howard Dietz at Sands Point, their home on Long Island. This had become one of Vivien's favourite places – an informal, relaxed household with attractive gardens and a large pool, usually with grandchildren around (she read *Winnie the Pooh* stories to them on this visit) and two of her truly special friends in the Dietzes.

When they reached England, Vivien found Tickerage almost exactly as she had envisaged it when planning the refurbishments with Paul Anstee, with only a few finishing touches left to do and the gardens transformed from the tangled neglect she had left behind. A bonus was that Mr and Mrs Cook had not been happy at Notley under its new owners and returned to her at Tickerage, living in a nearby cottage and, while the gardens could never match the scale of Notley, under Cook they became an ideal small estate with all Vivien's favourite roses, peonies, hydrangeas and viburnums, hundreds of bulbs in spring, and a flourishing catalpa. While she was away Cook had kept her informed about his work on the lake and notes on the wildlife ("we have got 8 moorhens and now 3 wild duck"). Vivien wrote to Lynn Fontanne: "I am simply bowled over by Tickerage's beauty", only going to London for doctor or hairdressing appointments, preferring to enjoy a balmy summer in her new home with Jack often there along with Mrs Mac, back as housekeeper, her favourite Siamese cat Poo Jones, and dogs Sebastian, a poodle and Jason, a golden Labrador given to her as a puppy by Jack.

There were only a few visitors that first summer – Gertrude, Suzanne, Mercia, Rachel Kempson and Diana Cooper, who described Tickerage as "a dream of beauty – your masterpiece" – and there was a happy reunion with Coward who drove down for lunch, delighted to see her so well and happy ("she was at her tiptop best, calm and wise and pretty and *off* the bottle"). Hiley also visited and noticed a change, partly due to her sense now of an extended family (Suzanne, who found her mother "wiser, gentler" had now given Vivien three grandsons) and felt too that she had become even more conscious of the value of friends ("she became less other-worldly and began to show some sense of consequence").

Her return to America towards the end of 1962, however, was born out of her old sense of adventure sometimes heedless of consequence. While in Australia she had been approached by a putative Broadway producer about a new musical based on the play *Tovarich* by Jacques Deval, a success in the 1930s in Robert E. Sherwood's adaptation on Broadway and in London (Vivien's diary records seeing the 1935 West End production with Cedric Hardwicke and the sparkling Eugenie Leontovich – plus John Buckmaster). Set in Paris among the world of post-Revolution Russian aristocrat émigrés, its central pair, a Grand Duke and Duchess reduced to working incognito for a living as butler and maid to a rich family (American in the musical), are also involved in a plot to guard Tsarist millions from suspicious Bolsheviks. Vivien had never imagined herself in a musical but she had always liked the story and agreed to meet and sing for the producer Abel Farbman, who flew to New Zealand to talk to her and hear her sing in the vast Wellington Opera House where she tentatively warbled through Irving Berlin's "Always" (a happy choice – Farbman had worked for Berlin's music-publishing company). She made no decision then but Farbman promised to send the finished script and a tape of the songs when ready. Although it would mean a separation from Jack – he had John Huston's *List of Adrian Messenger* to film – she seriously considered the project, mindful that Rex Harrison had succeeded with no real singing voice in *My Fair Lady* and a plus (as she thought) was that the Oliviers' old friend Jean-Pierre Aumont was the suggested casting for Mikhail opposite her Tatiana. After listening to a tape of most of the songs and reading the script she decided to take on the challenge, rather too blithely telling Aumont on the telephone that "it would be fun". A new musical is many things in rehearsal but only very rarely is it fun. She described her relish of challenges to Barry Norman, then a showbusiness journalist, stressing that she only wanted to do things which interested her:

> The musical *Tovarich*, which I shall be doing in New York next year, comes into that category. It may be a terrible disaster. Who knows? Who cares? The only thing that matters to me is that it's worth doing.

As she discovered, *Tovarich* proved to be an almost text-book example of that fearsome beast, A Broadway Musical In Trouble On The Road. Farbman was inexperienced, as was director Delbert Mann, skilled in television and film (*Marty*) but with no Broadway work to his name. Composer Lee Pockriss and lyricist Anne Croswell had written a musical of *The Importance of Being Earnest* off-Broadway although Pockriss was best known for "novelty songs" (including "Itsy Bitsy Teeny-Weeny Yellow Polka-Dot Bikini") and the bookwriter David Shaw's only significant credit was the Gwen Verdon musical *Redhead*. And neither star had ever sung previously on the musical stage. All the predictable panics, hirings, firings, rewrites, re-rehearsals, rearrangements, rows and endless late-night discussions in hotel rooms went on and at times during the frenzy Vivien wondered what she had got herself into.

The problem with *Tovarich* essentially was that it was what Stephen Sondheim described as a "Why?" musical, meaning why musicalise something that gains little from the transformation? The play is no masterpiece but has a certain delicate charm which, with the right casting (as when the ballerina

Natalia Makarova played Tatiana in a West End revival), just about sees it home. Its plot was not much changed for the musical; the teenage son and daughter of the household still fall for Tatiana and Mikhail respectively but Shaw worked in some "opening out" including a Russian-set prologue and some scenes in a Parisian émigré café. The score is eclectic – ballads, point numbers and waltz-time love songs, some heavily Russian in tone, others with a 1920s-jazz influence – but, like the book, rarely rises above the routine. Vivien had one or two wistful songs which she made effective and an "eleven o'clock number" with her infatuated teenager in which she is taught the Charleston which the choreography managed to elevate into a show-stopper. The letters which Vivien sent to Jack during rehearsals and the touring dates before New York reflect the problems, exacerbated by Jean-Pierre Aumont's inexperience and trouble performing in a foreign language. After a distinguished war career he had acted on stage with Cornell and in Hollywood but although his aristocratic looks were perfect for the part his singing voice was tuneless and the language problem made him slow on stage, a difficulty compounded whenever he was presented with rewrites or new lyrics.

The piecemeal method of shaping a musical – book scenes, dance numbers and songs rehearsed separately before their assembly into the overall production – proved difficult for newcomers to the genre and Delbert Mann was not always sufficiently organised or in control. Although Vivien had been met on arrival by what amounted to a protective delegation – Farbman, Mann, Radie Harris, Kathy Jones (acting as her secretary) and Byron Mitchell (he had played a small part in the Broadway *Duel of Angels* and was to play the teenage son in *Tovarich*) – who saw her established with Trudy Flockhart at Dorset House she began to fret almost immediately. After early rehearsals she wrote to Jack that she wondered "how anything *ever* gets settled" on a musical:

> It is enough to haunt me ... I feel so alien in this medium and not at all sure of what is right and what is not, everyone seems to have a good argument in favour of what they believe is right.

She found some comfort in working with those on the production who really knew what they were doing, most crucially choreographer Herbert Ross and his assistant (and wife) the ex-American Ballet Theatre dancer Norah Kaye (known fondly as "The Duse of the Dance"). They spotted that Vivien, although not a trained dancer, had innate rhythm and that subliminally she intuited that musical comedy was essentially kinetic; they developed this by keeping her in almost continuous movement (except during her soulful ballads) – the prop of a feather duster (recalling Sabina), almost part of her costume of maid's black outfit with frilly white apron, became paramount – and managed to make her dances seem always charged with an authentic musical-comedy energy. The second-act number in which Mitchell, using the name of the family's home town in Pennsylvania ("Wilkes-Barre, PA"), teaches Tatiana the Charleston, is musically and lyrically no classic but Ross and Kaye turned it into an exhilarating five minutes of invention – Vivien and Mitchell (an excellent dancer) inevitably had the audience cheering for a reprise.

As Vivien now grasped, a musical requires immense resources of stamina and concentration. She socialised little apart from always finding time on Sundays during rehearsals to visit "the entrancing household" of Sands Point with the Dietzes and attending a ball for Menotti's Spoleto Festival ("would have been entirely dire had Tennessee not been beside me"). There was no time for much else as she told Jack ("I haven't been near Bloomingdale's or indeed anywhere you will be surprised and happy to know") and she continued anxious ("I am going to have to sing at the theatre next week which is already frightening me to death") but rather unexpectedly seemed to be less trepidatious when rehearsals moved to the Broadway Theatre where they would play in New York ("so *ugly* but really it does not seem much bigger than the Opera House, Manchester") and as Christmas approached, despite the arctic weather and long days' rehearsals, she was able to write:

> Do you know, my darling, I am beginning to enjoy the singing – whether another living soul will or not is quite another question.

She missed Jack very much and her anxieties returned as the out-of-town dates loomed early in 1963 – "They keep saying Philadelphia and Boston do not matter but they *do* to me." Technical rehearsals in Philadelphia were poorly organised although hearing Philip Lang's inventive arrangements with the full orchestra raised spirits and the show's first performance "went surprisingly well". But Vivien was well aware that an enormous amount of work – on book, score and staging – was necessary prior to New York. Try-outs – especially of musicals – always attract "the wrecking crew", so-called friends, colleagues and supporters eager to catch an early performance and, hopefully, to bear news of trouble back to New York. On *Tovarich* in Philadelphia Coward behaved rather naughtily, not exactly boosting morale by giving Vivien a "finger-wag" to deliver his verdict that although she was fine the show was so poor she should not open in it on Broadway (he still smarted from the recent failure there of his own show *Sail Away*). In his diary, while lambasting the "wretched" Aumont and pointing out, with some justification, that the casting of two leading roles with non-singers was not perhaps the brightest of ideas, he added that Vivien was quite remarkable. She looked ravishing, had wonderful star authority and when she did attempt to sing, she got away with it brilliantly.

The cleansing of the stables began in Philadelphia; two supporting actors were fired, scenes and songs scheduled for rewriting and, as is fairly standard practice, the director was sacked too (Vivien's colleague from *The Doctor's Dilemma* Peter Glenville, who had at least directed on Broadway, although with scant success in musicals, took over from Mann to supervise the changes on the road). The work was exhausting – daytime rehearsals, eight performances weekly – and she told Jack: "You would not approve of how thin I am. Even I don't." She was fond of Aumont but found him "nightmarish to act with … he must be the slowest actor on earth."

By the time it reached Boston's Colonial Theatre *Tovarich* had improved although Vivien found some scenes still poorly written; Glenville was keen to inject a vein of seriousness into the froth and Vivien considered some of the back-story (including a speech in which Tatiana recalls her rape in prison) both melodramatic and clumsily written. The Boston reviews were then seen as some indication of likely Broadway receptions and although those for *Tovarich* had definite reservations about the material Vivien was very well received. The senior Boston critic Elliot Norton saw that the show was still in a ragged state but wrote of Vivien:

> You are apt to describe her as naturally graceful. But what she achieves represents something more than grace; she has obviously learned with care the techniques of the dances … Miss Leigh is a first-rater, one of the most gifted comediennes on the English-speaking stage.

Audiences were fighting for tickets in Boston but Vivien was not convinced by all the new material including a totally new opening:

> I knew it would be chaotic because if one alters the whole beginning the whole structure changes.

Most of the creative personnel on the production, cheered by strong business and enthusiastic responses, began to display an optimism anticipating New York success with seemingly only Vivien unconvinced ("a great deal of warmth has been removed") by changes which made for a slicker but somewhat soulless show. She worried also about Jack, plagued by back trouble in London and about Leigh, ailing with pleurisy. Jack became worried enough about her state of mind ("I am so mentally tired I don't know – there have been so many dramas in the theatre this week") that he organised tranquillisers from Conachy to be sent to Boston. An affectionate letter from Coward, atoning for his excess of candour in Philadelphia and written as a "play doctor" might suggest improvements on *Tovarich*, cheered her up:

> Start with the Finale. Work it somehow that you can do the *last* part of 'Vissi d'Arte' somewhere in the second act. Failing that there is always the Bell Song from *Lakmé* ... change the title to Cuir de Russie or Russian Homosexual.

She was touched, too, that Olivier had written, although he had just opened in a London flop (*Semi-Detached*) – his valedictory West End appearance before the National Theatre – to wish her luck; he had heard reports of the show's progress from Broadway producer David Merrick saying "that you are *divine*" and he was impressed by the takings:

> Oh, you are a clever girl! I have come to believe there is no satisfaction to a real artist *quite* like the Box Office!

Tennant and Vivien's New York agent Milton Goldman had obtained an excellent deal for their client ($3,000 per week against 6 per cent of the gross plus expenses and Trudy Flockhart's wages). On Broadway *Tovarich* opened during a brief newspaper strike, a mixed blessing; without press advertising business on most shows slumped but also the criticisms of the show and the production did not appear all at once (the reviews were very mixed). Vivien's personal notices were among the best of her career, most of them marvelling at the thistledown grace of her dancing, the touching simplicity of her ballad remembering first love ("I Know The Feeling") sung in a husky blend of Dietrich and Lenya and the vitality of "Wilkes-Barre, PA" which nightly stopped the show. When the strike ended and advertising resumed, business at the Broadway Theatre climbed steadily – Vivien was still a major draw – and the first months of the run remained upbeat although, rarely off stage, she found it gruelling work (Trudy was permanently in the wings to towel her, drenched in sweat, between scenes). Gertrude flew over for the opening and Jack, having been cast in an off-Broadway *Importance* with a teenage Mia Farrow, also was now in New York to join her in the East 52nd Street apartment into which she moved once it was clear that *Tovarich* would run. Visiting friends found her in ebullient form; David Webster, supremo at the Royal Opera House, wrote:

> I've never known an audience so completely at her feet ... She has a marvellous and quite electrical animation all through. And even *she* can never have looked more strikingly beautiful than she did in the last scene when she came on regally dressed in white and silver ... The poise, dignity and charm were breathtaking.

Against the odds – Georgia Brown seemed a clear favourite for *Oliver!* – Vivien won the 1963 Tony Award for Best Leading Actress in a Musical, sparking a hike to capacity business at the box-office but, as the late summer heat hit Manhattan, gradually, to Jack's alarm, the signs of an imminent collapse, even after a week's holiday spent at Cornell's house, began to appear. The onset of this phase was rapid, beginning soon after her break during a matinee. The previous evening she had seemed odd at a party after the show when Aumont showed home movies of a company outing to Mamaroneck which he thought seemed to knock Vivien off-balance, beginning to drink, smoke and dance ("hurling herself against the walls like a poor, maddened bird"). His version of the Saturday matinee next day gives an account of a disastrous performance with Vivien singing wildly out of tempo, rarely communicating with her fellow performers and then, in the second act as she reached the scene in which Tatiana recounts her assault, suddenly going alarmingly out of control, clawing and kicking at Aumont who managed to improvise (it was basically a quarrel scene) his way to the end of the sequence. For the final scene, dressed in her imperial finery, she simply stood mute as the company Polonaise swirled around her. Back at the apartment Jack had managed to make Vivien rest briefly and tried to prevent her from returning to the theatre for the evening performance but she insisted. Finally doctors called by Jack arrived to sedate her and her excellent and sympathetic standby Joan Copeland (Arthur Miller's sister) played that performance while Trudy and Jack, helpless, watched Vivien locked in her dressing-room mouth all her lines and lyrics. The Hamiltons were out front, sorry to miss Vivien and even more upset when, back at the apartment, she began to clean, obsessively picking up flecks of imagined dust from the carpet ("Poor Jack said 'It's hopeless now. You had better leave me to it'").

In a scenario reminiscent of the Hollywood crisis of 1953 it was decided to return Vivien, accompanied by a nurse, to London for treatment under Conachy. At Eaton Square, Gertrude, Bumble and her secretary Cal Darnell would all be on hand and Jack had no reason not to expect her back and on stage in New York within a week. The flight was uneasy – Vivien woke before expected, even under heavy sedation; the press had got wind of her arrival and photographers pictured her on a stretcher, covered in blankets, at Heathrow where she was met by Laurence Evans from Tennant's office (a former Old Vic General Manager; now a leading agent) and taken to Eaton Square. It was soon clear that this bout of her illness was troublingly serious and she was moved to the Avenue Nursing Home in St John's Wood.

This would be one of Vivien's longest spells of her illness at its most acute, when she felt both at her loneliest (in Bipolar's nightmare landscape there are no friends or companions and depression absorbs life, sucking it into its emptiness) and at her most desperate (sufferers often describe it as a feeling that the self has been kidnapped). Rilke found that his worst spells were like "hurricanes of the spirit" and Vivien, when she similarly felt herself caught in such a tempest, would break the windows of her room or try to escape. The press camped permanently outside (one photographer managed to catch her looking distressed on the balcony) before she was allowed to return (with nurses for day and night) to Eaton Square. Both Gertrude and Bumble watched over her too and she was allowed a few visitors for brief periods – Suzanne, Leigh, Rachel Kempson, Diana Cooper, the latter describing her as "looking 28, dressed like a little powder-blue velvet pussy cat toy, slim as a sugar plum" but she was still far from well. In November she had the shock of Conachy's sudden death; she wrote and sent flowers to his widow, who replied to thank her, adding that she hoped Vivien would take care of herself "which it was his dearest wish that you should do". Her new psychiatrist, Dr Michael Linnett, was *au fait* with her case and took over her treatment smoothly (he was knowledgeable about developments in antipsychotic drugs, which helped adjust the balance of neuro-transmitters) and these seemed to benefit Vivien. There was no question of her return to *Tovarich*; Eva Gabor had replaced her but the box-office collapsed and the production soon closed.

A move to Tickerage gave her even more peaceful days, still with Anne Tovey, her nurse (an Australian – Vivien called her Adelaide) and occasionally receiving ECT treatments there. One day Olivier called; Anne Tovey remembered Vivien suddenly becoming shy, almost afraid to go downstairs until "she just took off like a little schoolgirl meeting her boyfriend. Oh, it was beautiful and they walked by the lake together" and Hester, also at Tickerage then, remembered the two of them talking together until a call from Joan Plowright saw him quickly depart. Jack in New York had had occasional transatlantic conversations with Vivien but when Bumble called him to say nobody was at Tickerage to look after her he quickly arranged to fly back only to find Tickerage fully staffed with Anne and Bumble also present, while Vivien seemed unusually distant. Only later did he discover that Bumble had given her the impression that she had practically to force him to return, rather confirming his feeling that Bumble did not take too kindly to his permanent place in Vivien's life. He felt excluded for a while; Vivien went to join Leigh at Zeal's for a short time during which Jack, always patient, wrote a card to accompany a small birthday present:

This comes at a poor time – in every way. It is given with my love in which you seem not to believe although I promise you it's there ... I am here when you want me.

He waited through that long and cheerless winter until Vivien began perceptibly to recover, Jack one spring day noticing that what he called "the curtain" had lifted, that her eyes were, once again, astonishingly clear. When back to her best form she began to contemplate work, for which there were many offers on the table – *Separate Tables* on screen had vanished as a possibility for her and Olivier (script problems, real or imagined, saw Olivier withdraw from the project) but stage suggestions included a London production of Williams's *Night of the Iguana*, Beaumont's idea of Mrs Cheveley in *An Ideal Husband* (both he and Vivien quietly forgot about any possibility of *Lady of the Camellias* after the disaster of Franco Zeffirelli's overblown and short-lived Broadway production which opened during *Tovarich*), a Wolf Mankowitz musical on Mata Hari and Martha in Albee's *Who's Afraid of Virginia Woolf?* in Paris (in French). She passed on all of them and then producer/director Stanley Kramer offered her a leading role in an "all-star cast" film of Katharine Anne Porter's novel *Ship of Fools* to be made in Hollywood. She rather agreed with Coward ("It *sounds* a good idea – but I couldn't end the book") but Californian friends including Spencer Tracy (a Kramer regular) urged her to consider it and finally she agreed to play Mary Treadwell, something of a kissing cousin to Karen Stone (American, middle-aged and alone, if rather more caustic).

She should have heeded her first instincts. Porter's short stories and the three novellas comprising *Pale Horse, Pale Rider* are all first-rate but her more than full-length *Ship of Fools* (1962), her only novel – although a bestseller and championed by Robert Lowell among others – is bloatedly portentous, based on a translation of the medieval Latin allegory, Sebastian Brant's *Das Narrenschiff* and groaning under its layers of metaphor. Kramer had produced some excellent films but as a director his work tended to be flat-footed affairs announcing Important Themes and often based on fat bestsellers. Before *Ship of Fools* he had directed another "all-star cast" (Tracy, Dietrich, Lancaster, Garland) affair, *Judgement at Nuremberg* (cynically but accurately described by one critic as "An All-Star Concentration Camp Drama with Special Guest Appearances"), scripted by Abby Mann, who also adapted Porter's novel for the screen, heavily underlining the book's signposts in its parable of the rise of fascism. Everything about Kramer's film was on a large scale – grandiose score, complex title-sequence, inflated dialogue – glossing its excessive length. Vivien might have enjoyed meeting Porter, an elegant and sophisticated woman (who had also suffered from tuberculosis), but she did not appear in Hollywood for the filming of her allegorical story. Set on board a liner travelling from Vera Cruz to Germany in 1933, its cross-section of passengers (Jewish, German, American, young and old) is intended as a microcosm of society against the background of nascent Nazism and the brand of anti-semitism peddled by the film's rabidly prejudiced Reiber (a very loud José Ferrer). With Simone Signoret as a world-weary Contessa ("I'm just a woman") in a doomed love affair with the ship's doctor (Oscar Werner) emblematic of old-style Teutonic civilised courtesy and Lee Marvin an over-the-hill baseball player, the whole package is bookended by the philosophy of Glocken, a dwarf (Mankind, Misshapen But Wise). Vivien's role as a much-divorced ex-beauty, disillusioned and wry, had a few decent scenes (fending off a drunk Marvin, with whom she got on well although at some of his lines – "Behind those old eyes you hide a sixteen-year-old heart" – she found it difficult to suppress giggles) and her solo tipsy Charleston, briefly recalling *Tovarich*, was picked out in most reviews but the part was no real stretch for her. Surprisingly many of the notices, especially in America, were respectfully positive although audiences seemed to find it more of a protracted soap-opera, widely dubbed as "*Grand Hotel* at Sea".

Vivien had been nervous. Returning to Los Angeles had initially unsettled her. Her friend Peter Feibleman, the American novelist, visited her soon after she arrived, to find her rather disoriented on the terrace of the house, overlooking the city, which had been found for her and to brighten which Cukor and Katharine Hepburn had brought some paintings and bibelots. Looking down on the illuminated highways and the city she said: "I suppose I'm here ... It's hard to tell in Hollywood whether you're here or not." Her air of abstraction worried Feibleman more when she asked him to bring out a plastic bucket; then she vanished into the profusion of camellia bushes beside the terrace, emerging with the flower-heads all cut off. They were plastic, taped on to the shrub's stems. "I *know* I'm here now" she told him, "It takes a while to be able to see in a place like this."

When filming started, Kramer proved courteous and sympathetic. Her first day on call was daunting; virtually the entire cast were on set for a dinner scene which Vivien had to join before her first lines. Spencer Tracy was "sitting in" at the side observing his friend Kramer at work and when Vivien completed her scene without a hitch in one take he muttered, encouragingly, "Nice to see a professional." Vivien and Signoret struck up a friendship which flourished after some initial differences; Signoret's marriage to Yves Montand was going through a rough patch and Vivien often invited her to join her and Jack (who had flown to join her once filming was under way) for dinner which the French actress, unhappy in Hollywood and understanding of Vivien's own troubles, never forgot. ("I will always be enormously grateful to you and Jack for having let me share your home, your laughs, your friends, your life" she wrote). Elizabeth Ashley, for whom *Ship of Fools* was an early film, was fascinated by Vivien:

> You could see the stains and strains of life in that face but there was still something child-like in it. There are people who age but others who retain something of the child and I think that was true of Vivien – someone once told me the way she put a room together, the way she had a table laid, turned life into a work of art.

Jack was conscious that Vivien's long period of illness was still comparatively recent and grew concerned when her socialising increased. Cukor gave her a party in his beautiful garden, a fully catered affair with a small orchestra for dancing and he also took her to see an ailing, reclusive Cole Porter, knowing how Vivien's company cheered him (he was moved by the contrast between Vivien with Porter, vibrant and full of fun, and Vivien back in the car, very quiet until he noticed her eyes were filled with tears). When Gielgud joined them as a house-guest in Hollywood (in another "all-star" cast) in Waugh's *The Loved One* they were deluged with even more invitations to dinners and parties and Vivien became very tired indeed. At the studio one day she broke down in her dressing-room, telling Kramer as he looked at her drawn face in her mirror that she simply could not work that day. He understood:

> I knew from the best friend she ever had for a limited period, Katharine Hepburn, that she was ill and she couldn't do it. She was ill, and the courage to go ahead, to make the film – was almost unbelievable.

Like their friend Irene Selznick in New York, Hepburn came to Vivien's aid in California, taking her to a respected psychiatrist, Dr Karl Van Hagan for a session of ECT, subsequently organising two further sessions during the rest of the filming which she finished with no further problems. Jack wrote to Gertrude that she seemed "so much better that I don't believe any further treatment will be necessary".

Most of a glorious autumn was spent back at Tickerage which Vivien came to love more with each stay, keenly swapping cuttings with garden-minded friends such as Bogarde, Winn or Stanley Hall. Her former lover Peter Wyngarde visited one day for lunch, later writing: "I don't think I've ever been anywhere else except perhaps George Sand's retreat in Valldemossa where a feeling of the present was so mixed with the past without any sombreness." When *Ship of Fools* opened in the UK the reception for the film was markedly cooler than in America but again Vivien emerged with honour; the doyenne of

British film critics, Dilys Powell of *The Sunday Times*, felt that her Mary Treadwell was "a demonstration of true acting". Possibly more surprising was the *Observer*'s film column the same day, with none other than Tynan panning the film but describing Vivien as giving "a glittering and not over-glamourised performance". She was delighted to hear from Tony Guthrie, who had caught the film at his "local fleapit" in Ireland and thought her performance redeemed the film's sentimentality.

Professionally what Vivien sought was a good role in a challenging new play. Edward Albee's *Tiny Alice*, a baffling puzzle-box of a piece, came her way but did not attract her, even with Gielgud as a Broadway co-star. Soon Jack would be filming in Hollywood (*King Rat*) and so Vivien took the opportunity of joining Jamie and Yvonne Hamilton, inveterate travellers both, on a holiday for a trip lasting several weeks and returning her – finally – to the India of her birth.

CHAPTER 18

Last Acts

O ver the years Vivien, for whom travel never lost its allure and despite the clouded experience of *Elephant Walk*, had at times contemplated a return to the East and when the Hamiltons invited her to join them on their visit to India she accepted promptly. For part of the time they would also travel with their friend "Baba" Metcalfe, a fitting companion – she was the daughter of Lord Curzon, the last Viceroy of India. There were endless arrangements involved – visas, currency, inoculations – but they were lucky that many of the bureaucratic details were speeded through by the Hamiltons' friend Henry Stebbins, the American Ambassador to Nepal (they would stay at the Embassy in Kathmandu).

Linnett gave her a letter outlining her medical history should she need attention while away (it was not required) along with sufficient supplies of her regular medication. Walker's biography states that Vivien's behaviour was often wayward on this six-week long trip but according to Hamilton there was one instance only of real edginess – in Mahabalipuram when she was besieged by clamouring young fans – and he stressed that "V's manners throughout the Indian trip were excellent".

Vivien could recall little of her early life in Darjeeling and Calcutta beyond a blurred kaleidoscope of colours and faintly remembered views. There were not many elements from her early background at Notley or Tickerage – a good deal of Chinese Chippendale but only a few Indian or Persian carpets – although she would occasionally wear saris in hot weather and in both gardens a carefully tended feature was a catalpa, the Indian bean tree which was a special favourite. On this holiday her senses were dazzled; it took in Nepal, Gwalior, Delhi, Madras and Bombay; there was no return to her birthplace although as their plane flew towards Nepal they passed over the mountains, including the majestic Kanchenjunga at which Gertrude had gazed while carrying her daughter. Vivien wrote to Jack, wishing he could have been with her to see the unforgettable view of the Himalayas ("Peaks of blue white you think *must* be clouds"). Stebbins and his vivacious wife proved to be "enchanting hosts", discreetly fending off expats and members of the local Dramatic Society agog to see or meet Scarlett O'Hara. She had a room with a breathtaking view at the Embassy, describing their time in Kathmandu as "a truly marvellous experience", a busy period of expeditions to temples, shrines and villages, occasionally witnessing Buddhist ceremonies which she found surprisingly moving. At the village of Pokra she thought they might hire horses to go down the hillside to a beautiful lake but no horses or mules were available:

> So I said 'There are two bullocks. Please can you attach them to a cart and we shall get in?' This we did sitting on straw and sacking, a most peaceful way of travelling! The lake was the colour of pale jade and very warm.

She was enchanted by the vibrant colours around her:

> Temples everywhere – little markets – *beautiful* faces – Tibetan and Nepalese – all dust roads, every colour of cattle and dogs, people lying down in their tiny shops just pondering. A funeral city along the river – alcoves where the dead are burnt and then go into the river. Above – lines of small temples, heavily carved windows and in the centre the worshipped Penis, sometimes surrounded by flowers and offerings.

In Gwalior they were lodged in a somewhat eccentric Maharanee's palace ("where *nothing* worked!") and where they travelled to a market in a rickety and wheezing bus labelled "Pubic Transport". The group split up in Delhi where the Hamiltons stayed with friends while Vivien was in some comfort in a house belonging to friends of the Stebbins, although they met up most days, once visiting Karajaho and seeing "the most wonderful temples of erotica – *what* pictures you would be taking!", riding on elephants and then on to what she described to Jack as the most stunning bird sanctuary she had ever seen, "near a river full of tropical fish, such colours and strange shapes".

With flights already arranged to Athens before going on to Corfu to spend Christmas with the Furses who had retired there, Vivien could not extend her stay although there was still time for brief visits to Madras where she watched a Buddhist priest bless and feed a whole flock of birds, to Madurai with its imposing temple haunting in the moonlight and to spend a glorious day with the Hamiltons at Kuvalim, swimming in the ocean followed by a seafood beach picnic before leaving in a magnificent sunset for Bombay where she was able to enjoy one last excursion by car into the heart of India. She had slept, she told

Jack, extraordinarily well throughout the whole trip, feeling relaxed even before her time on Corfu.

Christmas that year was in the welcoming house, built to his own design by Furse on a Corfu promontory with splendid views out to sea, quiet and peaceful. It was a somewhat unorthodox Christmas Day – "we stayed in bed all day" – before a similarly unusual dinner ("soup, carrots and leeks") at a neighbour's house in the evening. She read a good deal during that stay, met up with Emlyn and Molly Williams, who had a house nearby and also studied the script of a new play to be co-presented in London by Beaumont, directed by Helpmann, scheduled to rehearse in the early spring.

Glowing with health as all her family remarked, she began 1965 at Zeal's with Leigh. As always with Leigh there were no emotional peaks and troughs; some perceived this as a reflection of Vivien's unconscious – that the marriage to Olivier, given its origins in emotional turmoil and betrayals, was essentially a sin while Leigh remained always a rock of stability. He was now possibly her most constant loving friend. She also saw Suzanne, Robin and the grandchildren, before a busy time of theatregoing (Olivier's *Othello*, his production of Miller's *The Crucible* and Shaffer's *Royal Hunt of the Sun*, all part of a memorable National Theatre repertoire at the Old Vic), parties given by the Millses and lunches or dinners with Beaumont, Dent, McBean, Tarquin, Stiebel, Rachel Kempson and a reunion with Barrault and Renaud, about to play in a London World Theatre season.

During rehearsals for her new play, scheduled as her return to the West End, her diary is blank. It was not an easy time. The play, *La Contessa*, was adapted by American playwright Paul Osborn from a 1954 novel (*La Volupté d'Etre*) by Maurice Druon, translated by Moura Budberg as *The Film of Memory*; Budberg, a voluble, colourful character (ex-mistress of both Maxim Gorky and H.G. Wells), who often invited the Oliviers to her *salon*, had first suggested it as a play. On paper it seemed a fascinating project. Druon was a Renaissance man – Vivien had met him briefly during the war when he was with the Free French and worked at the BBC (he co-wrote the great Resistance anthem "Chant des Partisans") – whose sequence of novels, *Les Rois Maudits* took on a second lease of life when G.R.R. Martin, author of *Game of Thrones*, claimed Druon and these novels as a major influence. But Paul Osborn, who had had Broadway successes including *Mornings at Seven*, never solved the basic problems involved in transferring a novel to the stage, despite what all involved seemed to think was the trump card of a magnetic central role for a mature star actress. The eponymous Contessa is La Sanziani, a once-fabled legend in her own era, an international figure of beauty and fabulous wealth, lover of the Kaiser and famous artists and writers including Gabriele d'Annunzio, now living in penury in a faded Rome hotel, reliving her glorious past with memories of her heyday, projected on to a naive young chambermaid:

> Adolescence is not alone in seeking reassurance from history. A human being on the edge of the abyss likes to be reminded that at eighty Goethe wrote masterpieces and Ninon de Laclos still made love.

La Sanziani was modelled on the extraordinary Luisa de Casati ("La Casati"), who ran through several fortunes and many lovers (painted by Boldoni and John, photographed by Man Ray), projecting herself as a living work of art (years before Performance Art was invented), slim and angular with an aureole of vivid red hair, eyes lined with lavishly applied kohl and who, after living in Venice – where she would walk at night with two cheetahs on diamond-encrusted leashes – and Paris, ended up living in a Knightsbridge room rifling at night through dustbins for scraps of material with which to adorn faded finery by Fortuny or Schiaparelli. Budberg and Gielgud had told Vivien of this unique woman; Gielgud knew Lord Berners, who had been kind to her, not at all fazed when she arrived at his mother's house with luggage including a large python in a glass-fronted suitcase, casually reassuring her hostess when asked about the snake's dietary needs: "Oh, it had a goat for breakfast." This was exactly the kind of intrepid risk-taker Vivien admired and she was further intrigued by hearing of a Paris production of Druon's own version, starring the Romanian-French star Elvire Popesco (the original 1934 *Tovarich* Tatiana).

The material had attracted the interest of various producers and directors; Hollywood's Vincente Minelli had always been fascinated by La Casati but had been beaten to the rights to Druon's novel by Broadway producer Leland Hayward (Minelli did later direct a jinxed movie version – *Time After Time* with Ingrid Bergman and his daughter Liza Minelli – a sad end to his career). Hayward originally thought of both Vivien and a Broadway production but she turned him down, partly because of doubts about the play in Osborn's original version and also because she did not want to play in New York for more than six months (costs had rocketed on Broadway where plays took longer to repay their investment). Hayward then proposed a London production (cheaper to mount) co-produced by Beaumont for which they would accept a six-month West End commitment.

Vivien had some bright ideas for the production, suggesting Brook, Barrault and John Dexter as possible directors (none was available) and for the set the inspired notion of the great exponent of romantic *verismo* design, Lila de Nobili (she owned two lovely watercolours of Paris by de Nobili), but although the designer was drawn to the idea, other commitments could not make her available enough to take it on. The eventual designer, Desmond Heeley, turned out to be an excellent choice; he described himself as "an alchemist of the theatre" (he had assisted Brook with *Titus* costumes) and his main setting, the mirrored decaying grandeur of La Sanziani's room, was perfect for the play's evocation of misted memories. Bumble was also at her best, recreating La Casati's dramatically trimmed outfits (panther fur was a favourite) for Vivien, who was transformed by her red wig, chalk-white skin and dark-rimmed eyes, suggesting both the faded beauty and the often still-alight mind of La Contessa.

Early in rehearsals it was evident that the play had major problems; with so much retrospective material as La Contessa relives her past, it fatally lacked any genuinely dramatic impetus. Supporting characters – the wide-eyed chambermaid Carmela (an early performance from Nicola Pagett whose dark beauty suggested a young Vivien – later she too was diagnosed as Bipolar) or hotel residents including an ambitious screenwriter and a film producer – never became fleshed-out enough to match her.

Helpmann had been appointed as a safe directorial pair of hands only late in preparations and was clueless as to how to fix the problems. The production often looked stunning – Heeley's sets were lit by Tennent's in-house lighting wizard Joe Davis who created a powerfully atmospheric world of contrasting light and shadow – but there was no play on stage. Vivien had worried about the static quality of the action, such as it was, but – again – those involved seemed to have thought her casting and the production values would mask the script's faults. After an uneasy Newcastle opening and poor local reviews, Beaumont went into action, fired by Alfred Lunt, who loyally had travelled to catch Vivien in the play, thought her performance very fine and that it would seem magnificent in a better play. Stiebel had read the script and wrote to Vivien after hearing of the Newcastle woes:

> God! The trials and tribulations of what is laughingly known as Show Business ... it is a difficult play to stage and restage ... Thank goodness Binkie and Hayward have taken action and have brought Mr. Osborn to Newcastle.

It was too late. Osborn was not an unwilling worker but a slow one. The opening scene, once set in a hotel corridor and involving two maids before La Sanziani's entrance from her room, was reworked, finally set in a street café with the film-world's characters arrested by La Sanziani's spectral appearance (behind a scrim, magically lit by Davis). Osborn felt it gave Vivien "an infinitely more exciting, proactive and mysterious entrance". It was not Vivien's entrance that was the problem but the obstinately continuing trouble with what Osborn could see was a basic flaw – he called it "the monologue effect" – but could never solve. *La Contessa* was essentially also out of kilter with mid-1960s theatre – Vivien did have the humour to correct Leigh's misunderstanding that John Osborne rather than Paul Osborn had adapted Druon's novel ("I think J.O. would be very surprised if this particular play were attributed to him"). The play closed after it played out its six weeks on the road. It was the only failure in a leading stage role of Vivien's British career.

She had another stage prospect in view very soon, to rehearse at the end of the year, when Gielgud – who had always wanted to act with her again – asked her to join him in Chekhov's *Ivanov* in America for a limited Broadway season after a tour of Eastern-seaboard cities. Vivien had yearned to play in Chekhov – Beaumont had mentioned *The Seagull* for the future – and it mattered not at all to her that the role of Anna Petrovna, the title character's wife, appears only in *Ivanov*'s first half. Beforehand, with time unexpectedly on her hands after the collapse of *La Contessa*, she enjoyed a fairly quiet summer, mostly at Tickerage. Michael Redgrave had been appointed first director of Guildford's new Yvonne Arnaud Theatre; Vivien joined him and Diana Wynyard on a stage cantilevered over the River Wye outside the building while swans glided upstream, for a pre-opening recital of Shakespeare speeches and sonnets. Redgrave had pitched heavy woo for her to star in his opening season; Natalya in Turgenev's *A Month in the Country*, a favourite play, was offered (Ingrid Bergman played it) but then she had been committed to *La Contessa*.

Otherwise, Tickerage satisfied her, and she visited London only for appointments; Dr Linnett has only a single mention in her diary between June and December 1965 – no ECT treatments, although she was put on a new drug – "Vallium" (sic) as well as remaining on Largactil (Lithium, which could have been of immense help to Vivien, was still a few years away from widespread prescription). Occasionally she would see a play, including *The Homecoming* (she had been a Pinter fan since *The Caretaker*) and Joe Orton's *Loot* (in which she invested – over the years she did rather well out of backing plays). She saw Olivier backstage briefly after his National Theatre performances but heard news of him from others. Bumble had worked in Ireland on his film *Term of Trial*, reporting to Vivien that he seemed settled and that he and "the girl" were giving good performances: clearly she was then unaware that Olivier and "the girl" – a much younger Sarah Miles – had begun a very secret affair (he regularly used his old "Kerr" pseudonym to arrange trysts as "Lionel Kerr") which continued in

London for some time. Bumble knew both Vivien and Olivier well, remaining friends of both. She wrote from Ireland to Vivien:

> His sense of guilt makes him nervous about the past and I think he has to live through life with someone who is the exact opposite of you as a kind of catharsis.

At Tickerage Vivien had several weekend guests and lunch parties, including reunions with American friends such as Irene Selznick, Alexander Cohen (*Ivanov*'s Broadway producer), Radie Harris and others including Diana Cooper, Coward and Dent. She also saw Hester, now remarried, who remained deeply fond of her sister-in-law always.

Ivanov began rehearsals in London – her diary recorded "Tickers under snow" at the start of the year as she left for work (the diary – as always after the divorce – has the name "Vivien Leigh Olivier" written inside and, also as always, the first name and telephone number in the list following belong to Olivier). The company included Jack as the idealistic doctor Lvov in a strong ensemble which flew to America in early February for further rehearsals to include a few American actors; among them the redoubtable Ethel Griffies, reunited with Vivien (she had played her landlady in *Waterloo Bridge* – now 88, she had been already acting in London when *Ivanov* was first seen there).

It was hardly surprising that Gielgud, with his part-Slav ancestry, should have been such an ardent Chekhov admirer from early days (he appeared in all the major plays and directed several). As a young actor, he had appeared in pioneering productions when Chekhov was still unfamiliar on the British stage for the émigré director Theodore Komisarjevsky (a nomad talent and busy womaniser – the pun-loving Gielgud called him "Come-And-Seduce-Me") at the little Barnes Theatre where Beaumont was then general manager, the beginning of their lifelong friendship. For years he had carried a torch for *Ivanov*, the first produced Chekhov play, written when a young doctor, rarely seen in the UK since the Barnes production, and in 1965 he had directed a new version (his own) in the West End for Beaumont when Yvonne Mitchell had played Anna Petrovna, Ivanov's ailing Jewish wife (Mitchell was not available for Broadway). Gielgud was actually somewhat too old for Ivanov but made considerable effort, taking infinite pains over a luxuriantly youthful wig from Stanley Hall (like Vivien he trusted "The Wigs" to take care with his wigs and hairpieces), to shed some years. Gielgud's view of Chekhov generally was very much coloured by Komisarjevsky's approach which softened the dramatist's toughness and ironies to make his work more palatable to British audiences, an approach which tended to lead to far too many productions presenting Chekhov's Russian provincial world as ersatz English country-house drama, missing in earlier plays like *Ivanov* that sense of a young man's impatience, even anger. Gielgud's translation was uninspired for an altogether "veddy English" production which only occasionally fused the mingled yarn of the play as written. Vivien was well cast as the neglected and dying (from tuberculosis) Anna opposite Gielgud, although he never quite faced up to the unpleasant aspects of the character (Chekhov set out to write a play "without villains or angels"), who at one point bluntly informs his wife that she is dying and at another is cruelly anti-semitic.

On this occasion, probably because he had already staged the play, Gielgud was less prone than usual to vacillations or contradictions in rehearsal. It was a happy company; Vivien and Jack made a new friend, the young American actor Miller Lide, who played a small role and understudied Jack. The notices on tour were virtually unanimously enthusiastic (the *Boston Globe* described the company as "a wonderful vivid ensemble of comic and character invention"). The box-office was busy throughout and for once Gielgud called only a few re-rehearsal sessions and so there was time for drives into the country and enjoyable lunches with Gielgud and his later-life partner Martin Hensler (prone to gloom but always relaxed with Vivien) and with Beaumont who flew to join the company in Philadelphia. Even playing the vault of Toronto's O'Keefe Center and bouts of "flu" (Vivien developed an extremely troublesome cough) could not deflate the company's spirits; all seemed to have recovered by the time of their final date in Washington where Vivien spent several afternoons at her favourite Phillips Gallery and helped organise a company party for Gielgud's birthday.

Washington also saw her meet up again with Elaine Dundy, based back in America after her divorce from Tynan. Dundy was commissioned by *The Village Voice* to interview Vivien but it was an awkward dressing-room encounter because of Dundy's issues then with drink and prescription drugs; her questions were unfocused, even banal, decidedly uncharacteristic of the effervescent, acutely intelligent woman Vivien had known in London. Later she steered her life back on course but the two women never had a chance to meet again.

Everyone involved was aware that *Ivanov* might prove a hard sell on Broadway, where musicals had begun their inexorable rise to domination. It opened in early April at the Shubert Theatre where previews went well enough but although the first-night house included friends including the Dietzes, Kay Brown and the Kanins it was a decidedly fidgety audience, many clearly finding the play's panorama of late-nineteenth-century rural Russian life alien and uninvolving. The notices were far from unkind but together mostly suggested that the play was worthy, providing an evening to be respected rather than enjoyed. They were not what Broadway called "selling notices". A perceptive review by the director/critic Harold Clurman saw that Gielgud had overlooked the Gogol-ish element in an insufficiently layered production, and as actor was only at his considerable best in episodes of inner distress. Despite some voiced disappointment that Anna featured only in the play's first half, Vivien received mostly warmly appreciative notices. Tom Prideaux in *Life* owned he had anticipated a soporific evening but instead was held totally and deeply moved by Vivien's suggestion of the buried anguish behind her cloak of apparent calm, like most critics picking out a moment when, without pulling focus, she stopped time for an instant on stage with her understated reaction to Ivanov's news of her impending death. Richard Watts in the *New York Post* found her then "nothing short of magnificent".

Ivanov on Broadway never built to become more than a *succès d'estime*; after packed houses on the road it was disappointing to play to half-empty theatres most week nights (older playgoers filled the matinees) after only a few weeks. With his Anglophile partiality for prestige British work Cohen kept it running through its limited season (he had imported a ready-made physical production and had done extremely well on tour so was not out of pocket), closing finally in mid-June. Vivien and Jack stayed on in New York for a short time, fairly quietly (only two visits to Sybil Burton's achingly "in" nightspot, Arthur's) with a few dinners (Leland and Pamela Hayward, Kay Brown, the Kanins) and a Sunday at Sands Point where she cheered Howard Dietz, now stoically suffering from Parkinson's Disease. The *Ivanov* experience had been tiring and they decided to treat themselves and to join Gielgud and Hensler on a Barbados holiday on Young Island which they all adored at once; Gielgud described it as a paradise "more remote and Robinson Crusoe-ish than Jamaica. No telephones or newspapers." They swam every day (once Gielgud, never the strongest swimmer, got into difficulties – Vivien's diary records "Saved J.G. from drowning!", prolonging a great career by four decades). They returned to New York for a brief visit during which the Leland Haywards introduced her to Truman Capote. They got on splendidly – later he invited her to his famous Plaza Hotel black-and-white masked ball to celebrate *In Cold Blood*'s success but Vivien chose not to fly from England to attend – and he delighted her more when he introduced her to his friend from childhood, Harper Lee, author of one of Vivien's favourite modern American novels, *To Kill a Mockingbird*. Later Lee described Vivien in a letter to her friend Felice Itzkoff as "a character, and I loved her".

Tickerage once again was where she mainly remained when home although she always caught Olivier's stage or film performances (*Khartoum* in August).

One appointment with Linnett that summer and autumn is recorded but no others and no "treatment". She met several times with Toby Rowland, an always cheerfully eupeptic Montana-born American producer who had worked at Tennent's with Beaumont for a time, had produced Williams's *Camino Real* in London and who wanted her for a new Albee play in the West End on which she delayed making a final decision. Feeling the urge to travel later in the year she visited Paris for fittings at Balmain with Ginette Spanier; of the great French couturiers she remained most loyal to the House of Balmain while in England reliant still on Stiebel and Hardy Amies as well as the younger John Cavanagh. She stayed with Jack and Doreen Hawkins at their villa near Nice and before going on to Greece. First she spent time on Spetsos and then sailed to Corfu to the Furses; she found their house a genuine haven, spurring her to say more than once that when she was 60 she and Jack might retire there, although she had said to Finch on his one visit to Tickerage when he had expressed a wish to sail off to a desert island (he had just divorced his second wife): "Well, I shall be working until I drop!" In Corfu she was joined by brothers Alan and Adrian Pryce-Jones, the former the distinguished editor of *The Times Literary Supplement*, the latter something of a loose cannon who had worked in movies (assistant director on *The Devil's Disciple* with Olivier) and in the art world, at times advising Vivien on paintings. They made an entertaining pair although Alan, according to Vivien, was "badly-behaved – foul language" one night, recording next day "Alan in bed". The peace of Corfu, the beauty of the views over the sea and the relaxed atmosphere at the Furse house were matched for her only by the calm of San Vigilio where she and Leonard Walsh ("Leonardo") had made up the quarrel of her previous visit and where she went on for a stay in late August.

Still she havered about work. Composer Dimitri Tiomkin had planned for some time to produce a film based on the epistolary relationship between Tchaikovsky and Nadezhda von Meck in which the great Innokenty Smoktunovsky would play the troubled composer. Vivien was drawn to the subject but the submitted script was far too long and she postponed making any final decision until a new version was ready. She felt surprisingly tired despite the weeks of rest in Greece and Italy: it had taken time finally to shake off the cough developed on the Eastern-state *Ivanov* tour and a large part of September that year was spent in bed. Her diary records her cancellation of two planned Chichester visits to see Olivier, and a couple of visits to Linnett are noted (one mentions "Treatment" – likely to have been ECT which would have been the only one for a considerable time). She saw Mercia, Coward and

Gielgud in London and had a handful of Tickerage guests – the Hawkinses, Enid Bagnold, Hester, Leigh and Bumble – and she spent Christmas that year, when Jack was working, with Leigh at Zeal's.

By then she had signed with Rowland to appear in the British premiere of Albee's *A Delicate Balance*; as in *Streetcar* Jessica Tandy had led the Broadway cast (with her husband Hume Cronyn) and the prospect of Michael Redgrave for London triggered Vivien's final acceptance. She had puzzled over the play – less obliquely elusive than *Tiny Alice* but fused with enigma – and had not been greatly helped by a visit from the author, casually clad with his unusually large feet in pristine white sneakers, who un-obligingly remained enigmatic ("All my symbols are cymbals" was one gnomic reply to Vivien's quest for enlightenment). She had responded to some quality in the play which she (and Albee) could not easily articulate but which she sensed could be theatrically potent and in fact she was ideal casting for Agnes, the matriarch at the centre of what many rate as Albee's best play. It is a somewhat Eliot-ish piece, outwardly urbane, often produced as a sophisticated comedy of manners but in fact a diamond-sharp play, set over a single weekend during which the placid surface of the well-heeled WASP household of a middle-aged couple, Agnes and Tobias, living with the apparently permanent house-guest of Agnes's tippling sister Clare, gradually becomes fractured. From the outset, *A Delicate Balance* is shot through with disquiet; Agnes touches on the possibility of losing her mind near the opening and the household's equipoise is rocked by first the arrival of the couple's neurotic daughter, heading for a fourth divorce, then the sudden appearance of friends Harry and Edna, seeking shelter after fleeing their own home, panicked by some unvoiceable dread. At the close the play returns to Agnes's fears, musing on why we sleep:

> They say we sleep to let the demons out – to let the mind go raving mad ... And when the daylight comes again, comes order with it.

Vivien responded to much of this play – a recurring pattern in a good deal of her work is a balance between outward control and inner turmoil – and she and Redgrave both admired Albee's respect for language, his slightly heightened dialogue. Plans proceeded – Carl Toms was fixed to design and Bumble for costumes while Stanley Hall would supervise Vivien's wig; she knew that Agnes should be conventionally restrained in appearance and asked for some grey in her hair. (Agnes is described as in her early fifties in the text. Vivien was 53.) She had new photographs taken by McBean, some the full glamour works, her face framed in white fur, the others without make-up, unretouched as she imagined Agnes. The intriguing choice of director was John

Dexter, associated primarily with grittier Royal Court work including Arnold Wesker's plays and who had steered Olivier's *Othello*, much admired by Vivien. They had met before; when Beaumont was still considering *Lady of the Camellias* for Vivien he suggested Dexter as director (Beaumont shrewdly saw that Dexter could inject some grit to nudge the pearl inside the oyster of what could seem an overly sentimental play) and Dexter was interested enough to meet Vivien, finding her a natural choice to play Dumas's consumptive beauty:

> A strange, beautiful woman. Stretched tight, almost transparent, pink and white, she seemed ethereal – no other word.

Now Dexter responded positively to Albee's play and agreed to direct. The role of Edna was offered to Vivien's friend Leueen McGrath in New York who was keen to join the venture. Other casting was being discussed before the sudden discovery that Vivien was ill. This had nothing to do with her Bipolar condition; her old enemy of tuberculosis had malevolently returned, explaining the coughs and the exhaustion of much of the previous year. Unusually there are no entries in her diary for 1967 until late April and then only a sporadic few – some meetings with Redgrave, discussing the play with McGrath in London, seeing Margaret Leighton in *Cactus Flower*, lunching quietly with Rachel, Suzanne, Cukor, Stiebel and Coward. The last recorded theatre visit was in late May to see – and enjoy – Alan Ayckbourn's first West End success *Relatively Speaking*.

Work on her lines with Redgrave, who came over on many afternoons to Eaton Square, continued, but she noted "In Bed" in early June, then "In Bed – X-Ray" a few days later followed by "News of Chest" on 8 June. Her secretary Rosemary Geddes had asked on several occasions when Vivien's cough remained persistent if it might be her old trouble, always brushed away with denials ("she was terrified of illness … Until she literally collapsed they thought it was the 'flu'").

Linnett gave her the news. X-rays had revealed a large patch on her lung. She rejected the idea of hospitalisation; she had beaten tuberculosis before and would do so again, although she had to agree to the postponement of *A Delicate Balance* (Rowland promised not to recast but to put plans on hold until she had recovered). She wrote to Miller Lide complaining that "the drugs they fill me with make me feel very peculiar" but added "they say the blasted thing will last 3 months but I'm praying for less and cannot wait for the play".

Apart from one Tickerage weekend she did not leave Eaton Square, occasionally disobeying orders by getting out of bed to water her plants and tend the flowers which poured in when the postponement was announced.

Visitors, Linnett advised, should be kept to a minimum; Coral Browne and Alan Webb, with apartments nearby, occasionally called as did Coward (he gave her a "finger-wag" about her smoking), while Gertrude, Suzanne, Mercia, Tennant and Beaumont also came by. Jack tried to limit their visiting time but when he was cast in a revival of Frederick Lonsdale's *The Last of Mrs Cheyney* he was absent during rehearsals and then in the evenings when it began a pre-London run at Guildford. Towards the end of June the American-based actor Brian Aherne (originally cast as Tony Cavendish in *Theatre Royal* before yielding the part to Olivier) and his wife Eleanor called on her; Aherne was reminded of *La Dame aux Camellias* by Vivien sitting up in bed "in a ravishing nightgown, more beautiful than I can remember, her skin pink and white, her eyes large and lustrous". She seemed practically her old self until suddenly she wilted and her guests quickly left. A journalist friend, Robin Douglas-Home, visited her then, subsequently writing of the flower-filled room and that although pale "there was no trace of surrender in her mood – her throaty laugh, crackling with all the old appeal, rang out again and again."

When Jack had opened in Guildford and became freer during most days he would stay with Vivien until leaving to drive for the performance. The previous month had seen the seventh "anniversary" of their time together; she wrote one of her little notes (like text-messages today), simply saying "My love for all our years together and all our years to come." He was with her when Beaumont telephoned – at Joan Plowright's considerate request, to avoid Vivien learning the news from the press – to tell her that Olivier had been admitted to hospital with prostate cancer, beginning his epic battles with illness over several years. She seemed more concerned about him – immediately writing and ordering white flowers for his room at St Thomas's – than about herself. She seemed to improve gradually with his improvement and on 6 July was able to have "The Wigs" over. Hall brought a 16mm movie, the James Ivory-Ismael Merchant *Shakespeare Wallah* film of the Kendal family's Shakespeare company touring India, evocative of childhood memories. She and Jack watched coverage of Wimbledon on Friday afternoon; she had signed the letters Rosemary Geddes had typed, and settled down in bed with Poo Jones beside her on the bed as Jack left for Guildford. He called her, as usual, after the performance and thought her voice rather faint, assuming she was tired and dropping off to sleep. When he reached Eaton Square around 11 p.m. he looked into the bedroom to see Vivien asleep with the cat curled up beside her. Shortly afterwards he returned to the bedroom to see her on the floor with blood around her on the carpet. Failing to wake her he tried mouth-to-mouth resuscitation, gradually realising that she was dead. He gently lifted her body and laid her on the bed. Then he called Linnett, Bumble and Alan Webb, the last arriving quickly from just around the corner, moved to see Vivien looking so beautiful as if she had just fallen asleep. Gertrude was on holiday in St Andrews but they finally reached her just before midnight before calling Suzanne and then Leigh. Lastly – by now past three in the morning – Jack called Peter Hiley ("He said he'd be there at nine o'clock. And, being Peter Hiley, he was there at nine o'clock").

Donald Spoto wrote that Douglas Fairbanks Jr. was in Olivier's hospital room on the Saturday evening when news of Vivien's death reached him and that Olivier said "Poor, dear little Vivien". But he had heard earlier. Jack's account – verified by Hiley – is that he had waited until 8 a.m. that morning calling Olivier who, by the early hour, guessed the reason for the call before discharging himself from hospital to take a cab to Eaton Square, slipping into the building by the back entrance. Hiley recalled that morning vividly, noticing that Olivier was eager to stay, looking round the apartment and at old familiar objects, photographs (several of him) and paintings ("Absolutely typical. He felt great grief and great responsibility but it didn't stop him going round and being himself, and wondering about pictures on the wall").

His own account in *Confessions* upset many of Vivien's friends and Olivier admirers. According to him, after murmured mutual condolences, Jack, who had done his best to clean up the mess and the blood, showed him into the bedroom and left him alone with Vivien. First the son of the cloth re-emerges, agonising over whether he had somehow been at "the heart of the ulcer", in some way at the root of their problems as he stood:

> alone with one with whom I had shared a life that resembled nothing so much as an express lift skying you upwards and throwing you downwards in an insanely non-stop fashion. I stood and prayed for forgiveness for all the evils that had sprung up between us.

He then continues, also characteristically, to describe what he saw as he looked at Vivien's beautiful dead face, noticing an expression on it which he recognised as one of slight repugnance:

> I had noted that between the bed and the bathroom was a stain, and connecting this with the expression on her face which had caused me to wonder, I now realised what must have happened. What a cruel stroke of fate to deliver that particular little death-blow to one as scrupulously dainty in all such matters as she was.

Many found this in bad taste but Vivien would have understood. She knew always that Olivier's observation of detail, rooted often in the earthy, the elemental, was part of what made him what he was, the actor she admired above all others. The more sentimental accounts then and subsequently often would suggest a tragic figure who died of a broken heart, that she had not wanted to go on living, although her behaviour in her last weeks was entirely typical of the way she had lived most of her life and she still, as she often said, had much to look forward to. What killed Vivien was tuberculosis, a disease described by John Bunyan as long ago as 1690 in *The Life and Death of Mr Badman* as "the Captain of all these men of Death".

A post-mortem established definitely that the cause of death was chronic pulmonary tuberculosis (many could not believe that one could die from tuberculosis in the middle of the twentieth century). A massive haemorrhage suffocated Vivien by flooding her lungs with blood. Montaigne's *Essays*, first encountered in adolescence, were always on Vivien's bookshelves and she would have been familiar with what he wrote of those who battle with recurring illness:

> being so often led to the port, confident that you are still within the accustomed limits, but some day you and your confidence will have crossed the water unawares.

Death would have been virtually instant. No inquest was held.

Gertrude's distress – she was unable at first to comprehend that her daughter was dead – was compounded by her acute shock when she discovered that Vivien's will clearly specified that she should be cremated, contrary to Catholic orthodoxy. She tried to persuade Jack, who had to assume responsibility for all funeral arrangements, to have Vivien buried but he felt he must obey her wishes and so, with only a small gathering of immediate family including Leigh and Jack, she was cremated at Golders Green following a private Catholic service at St Mary's, Cadogan Street. The shock of Vivien's death was magnified by the death of Cecil Tennant in a car crash driving home to Surrey after the funeral.

Letters and cards poured in from around the world to Gertrude and Suzanne, to Jack, Leigh and Olivier. Katharine Hepburn, who had nursed Spencer Tracy before his death earlier that year, was characteristically to the point. She had cared surprisingly little for Olivier ("Great actor. Small man.") but she wrote to Jack: "Devotion is a rare quality … I knew you would stick." Rex Harrison reminded Jack of Vivien's response to *The Cocktail Party*'s notion of guardians in life: "Yours was a guardianship of great worth in the Eliot sense."

On a last visit to Tickerage with Gertrude and Suzanne, Jack saw Vivien's ashes strewn over the lake. She always claimed to be a classic Scorpio, volatile and restless and likely to burn out – she had reacted to Jock Dent's reminder of Rachel, the great French actress who died young having used up too soon all the fuel which lit the lamp of her genius with "How wonderful!" – but possibly she was more of an Aquarian with her love of the sea, of swimming and, with the River Thame at Notley and the willow-fringed Tickerage lake, of always living close to water.

All the requiem Masses, tribute evenings and services in London, New York and California were in their varying ways moving occasions with often eloquent readings and eulogies. The London memorial service held at St Martin-in-the-Fields (where Vivien spoke at Kay Kendall's memorial) had readings from Rachel Kempson and John Clements and an eloquent address by Gielgud (Coward was too grief-stricken to deliver one), those attending including Cicely Courtneidge, star of Vivien's first film, Peggy Ashcroft, Alec Guinness, Kenneth Clark, Dirk Bogarde, Beaumont, Stiebel, Mercia, Lady Diana Cooper and Emlyn Williams. Olivier sat with Ginette Spanier, Leigh with Suzanne, Robin and their three boys. Jack sat alone. Jill Esmond also attended, finding herself after the service with Olivier right behind her. She put her hand on his and he put his on hers, giving it three little squeezes, looking "grey right through". She wrote to Tarquin who was in Dar-es-Salaam working for the Commonwealth Development Corporation:

> You were very fond of her and I thought you would like me to go representing you. Also I wanted to go for myself. I don't quite know why, but I felt an urge. Viv had been part of my life for so long, over 30 years. I wanted to say, I don't quite know what, perhaps good-bye to a great part of my life and with complete sincerity God speed to her soul.

Jill, like Rachel Kempson, had that rare human quality of forgiveness, as indeed did Vivien. Olivier had prayed for forgiveness alone with her body in Eaton Square but she had borne him no ill-will since their divorce; privately she might in its immediate aftermath sometimes have made rude jokes about Joan Plowright but essentially she wished for his happiness. As he did for hers – Terry Coleman is completely wrong in writing that after 1960 Olivier "wanted nothing more to do" with Vivien. He never lost touch with her or ceased to care about whatever she might be doing, as their 1960s letters make clear - in his writing cheerily during *Tovarich*, philosophically in consolation when *La Contessa* failed ("It isn't wasted, you know. It never is"), visiting Tickerage, and always touched by and writing grateful letters of thanks for the flowers or cards she sent for his first nights.

Vivien had seen at least some of the work in his golden early years heading the fledgling National Theatre. There he worked alongside her old adversary

Tynan, appointed literary manager at the encouragement of Joan Plowright, who urged that the National Theatre should be associated with the progressive young. The critic was widely seen as Olivier's hotline to all things new, fashionable and theatrically exciting, although he could be a divisive figure – neither Dexter nor William Gaskill, both of whom crossed the river from the Royal Court in Sloane Square to join Olivier in the Waterloo Road, was comfortable with his influence at the Old Vic. His old ally in LOP, Kenneth Clark, who distrusted Tynan, became worried as a NT Board member by what he described as Olivier's "obsessive fear of being thought old-fashioned." However, Olivier remained obdurately loyal to Tynan, defending him even through the almighty fuss over *Soldiers* (Rolf Hochhuth's play raising the contentious issue of the alleged involvement of Churchill in the death of General Sikorski in 1943), passionately championed by Tynan, and involving him in some economies with the truth. Olivier still backed him in his scraps with the National Theatre Board (his old Hound of Heaven of guilt continued to stalk Olivier over this – he devoted a large chunk of appendices to justifying his stance on the controversy in *Confessions*).

Tynan's later years were clouded, plagued by ill health and stalled projects. His posthumously published *Diaries* of that time only fitfully reveal his magic flair, his ludic subversion; some entries, notably the description of his daughter Tracy's twenty-first birthday party, mostly a long list of celebrities attending, as if validation of his own A-List status, are deeply sad, representative of an overwhelming sense of *accidie*. Olivier's curt refusal – he was not in the giving vein that day – to allow Tynan to write his biography ("I owe Ken a lot but I don't owe him my life") came as a body-blow. Tynan died from emphysema in California in 1980.

Despite the continuing affair with Sarah Miles in the 1960s Olivier remained married to Joan Plowright – they had a son and two daughters – but while Vivien expressed a wish to meet his new family he took her psychiatrist's advice (although Vivien's last few years were free from major Bipolar episodes) and always tactfully deflected any suggestions of a family meeting. After years based in Brighton as well as London (Bedales rather than Eton for Richard Olivier and his sisters) the Oliviers moved to Sussex where Olivier spent most of his later years.

Inevitably that marriage too had its strains, partly because Joan was constantly in demand while acting for him became more difficult and he could become often very unpredictable to deal with. He had promised Jamie Hamilton, a friend for over 40 years, that any Olivier autobiography would be his to publish; he went instead to Weidenfeld and Nicolson and made life difficult for his editors there with stubborn refusals to alter anything. His fierce work ethic saw him through some challenging later ventures even when stage work was no longer viable (*Brideshead Revisited* and *King Lear* on television and some gems among mostly undistinguished but lucrative later films). Only after his eightieth birthday when work became impossible did a real decline set in although even then his old animation and energy would flash through. He could say some unexpectedly venomous things; Gawn Grainger, who acted with him at the National Theatre and was a collaborator on his book *On Acting*, remembered him once recalling "The Oliviers" of the *Cleopatra* 1951 double act adding "We used to fuck three times a day until Peter Finch came along. I'm glad he's dead."

Olivier died in 1989. Jill outlived him, still keeping her counsel about all the tempests in her life, dying in 1990. Leigh Holman, although not without romantic involvements after his divorce from Vivien, never remarried (also never commenting on his private life), dying in 1982. Gertrude Hartley died, aged 84, in 1972. Suzanne's marriage to Robin Farrington endured for over 40 years; he died in 2002, she in 2015. Jack Merivale, after a period of some loneliness following Vivien's death, found happiness again with actress Dinah Sheridan (they married in 1986), who nursed him devotedly through a long final illness (involving regular dialysis) until his death in 1990. Joan Plowright's career continued with distinguished work until increasing blindness forced retirement.

Peter Finch, who seemed to find some equilibrium in later life after his third marriage, died in Los Angeles shortly before the 1977 Academy Awards ceremony (he posthumously won the Best Actor Oscar for *Network*). Olivier may have been happy at the news but Finch left one of the most vivid recollections of Vivien. He was overseas and not present at her memorial service but said:

> I remember her now – walking like an eager boy through temples in Ceylon – walking in the wind near Notley. I always see her hurrying through life. I miss the fact that she is not somewhere in London or Greece or New York, among her friends, talking volumes – with those bright eyes always in laughter.

Epilogue

Vivien died half a century ago but interest in her life and work has never significantly abated. There has been a slew of solo plays based on episodes in her life and also *Orson's Shadow*, a rum affair by Austin Pendleton bringing together Vivien, Olivier, Tynan, Welles and Joan Plowright set during *Rhinoceros* rehearsals, produced in New York and London. Julia Ormond played Vivien to Kenneth Branagh's Olivier in *My Week With Marilyn*, the film of Colin Clark's memoir and there have been several documentaries on her life and on the making of *Gone With the Wind*. The BFI centenary retrospective (2013) of her films drew packed houses while the 2017 Sotheby's sale of many of her possessions attracted an enormous amount of media interest worldwide (and staggering prices).

Biographies of Olivier abound ("an alarmingly high number" according to the author of the latest, Philip Ziegler), decidedly variable in both quality and accuracy, the liveliest being Roger Lewis's *The Real Life of Laurence Olivier*, idiosyncratically combative and not especially kind to Vivien but giving at least a sense of Olivier the actor. Vivien's biographies are fewer but likewise uneven – Alexander Walker's is surprisingly error-strewn, possibly written to a tight deadline – with that of Hugo Vickers easily the best, impeccably researched but dating back to 1988 prior to the availability of much new material. Two predominantly pictorial studies – both excellent – by John Russell Taylor and Kendra Bean – have appeared along with a 2017 collection of essays on aspects of her career, published by Manchester University Press. However, with the exceptions of the earliest – Alan Dent in *A Bouquet* and Felix Barker in *The Oliviers*, the latter tracing their joint careers into the 1950s – it would seem that most biographers did not actually see her work in the theatre.

I managed – by luck rather than judgement initially – to see her on three occasions. In 1963 on a first visit to New York, relatives took me to the theatre, my teenage interest in which was rather earnest – I really wanted to see what sounded an intriguing recently opened American play, *Who's Afraid of Virginia Woolf?* instead of which I was taken to a musical, a genre about which I was then decidedly snooty. The Broadway Theatre was packed but I could not join in the anticipatory buzz and I had not seen *Gone With the Wind* which many around us had been discussing. Then, early in the evening a petite, ineffably graceful creature with bobbed dark hair entered to a burst of applause and fairly soon I was sitting up, taking considerable notice. Even I could tell that *Tovarich* was not a great show and the production little more than workmanlike but for one factor, the quality of Vivien Leigh. Her singing voice was no great shakes but she used what she had with immense finesse, genuinely moving in "I Know the Feeling", she had indifferent comedic material but somehow gave it an insouciant, casual wit and danced with a quicksilver elegance – seemingly at times weightless – which complemented the aristocratic grace of this pretend-Cinderella, even giving the sentimental corn of the ending a curious dignity.

My second visit to Manhattan coincided with the final week of *Ivanov* which I saw with an audience of fidgeting coughers. I had read the play and so could see that Gielgud was inclined to resist the streak of the malign in Ivanov but although Anna Petrovna does not appear in the play's second half she was the character I remembered most vividly. I had expected, I think, something tear-jerking, even sentimental, but what was on stage was a still-loving wife, no wilting flower, literally struck dumb when Ivanov cruelly and crudely tells her she has not long to live, a moment of "stop time", the theatrical equivalent of a movie close-up when Vivien did apparently nothing but stand stock-still, dry-eyed and looking at Ivanov, seemingly making her skull seem as if made of Perspex, giving the audience access to her thoughts as his words percolated into her brain.

The only British occasion was in Liverpool. I had hitched from Scotland to see a girlfriend working in stage management at the Playhouse and when I saw a poster for *La Contessa* at the Empire I decided to catch the matinee and see the Playhouse production in the evening. The theatre was not full and oddly quiet (I knew nothing about the play or that it had received poor notices), an apathy which flickered into attention only momentarily and in the final scene during the afternoon. The piece was inadequate, the production limp, but yet again the attention was held – utterly arrested at points – by Vivien's playing, using a still-seductive deeper voice to give this raddled beauty (she strikingly resembled the Casati of John's portrait) a sense of a mind like Byron's "fiery particle" flickering still, a distinction which blazed belatedly but mesmerisingly in her final scene, dying in the decaying splendour of her hotel room but worlds away in her mind, a scene which nearly redeemed the previous inadequacies. She rightly played the character as Druon had suggested, not as mad but as one who had chosen to live in the richly crowded world of her imagination. Her performance, ceding nothing to a mainly indifferent house, had a spirit which matched that of La Casati. Some years later, reading Coward's story "Star Quality" – about an actress preparing a new play – I was reminded of that Liverpool afternoon. The director in Coward's story concedes that some stars can be monsters of vanity, self-deluded and hell to handle (Coward would not have said that of Vivien) but then goes on:

> Then, my boy, you pay your money at the Box Office and go in and watch her on a matinee day with a dull audience, in a bad play with a fortnight's notice up on the board and the house half-full, and suddenly you are aware that you are in the presence of something very great indeed – something abstract that is beyond definition and beyond praise. Quality – star quality plus!

It was, possibly, that abstract quality, one "beyond definition" which frustrated Tynan – he liked to analyse what he called "High Definition Performance" – who could not understand what it was about Vivien's quality on stage to which he could not respond as others did. And as Korda found, even at the outset of Vivien's career, she was impossible to categorise. Perhaps owing something to those peripatetic early years and her time in France in particular she was never immediately identifiable as a typically English actress – Scarlett, Blanche, Sabina, Antigone, Cleopatra, Paola, Tatiana, Anna Petrovna make a polyglot group – and that quality of mind on both stage and film, allowing an audience access to her characters' inner lives, was unusual in British actresses of her generation. Her theatrical and cinematic worlds were male-centric (she worked only once with a female director and never with a female producer apart from Irene Selznick, co-producer on *Streetcar* in London). Her independence of spirit was unusual in the theatre of her era. Undoubtedly she could be difficult; although never a monster of ego like Lorraine in "Star Quality" she was a perfectionist who often had to fight to make her points in predominantly male worlds as the Hollywood and West End of her time undoubtedly were. Vivien was a star from her mid-twenties but very rarely was she in any sense a diva. Some insist that she deferred too much to Olivier, that she was too compliant a Galatea to his Pygmalion, even although she was discernibly the more intelligent of the two. However, when it seemed necessary, as on *Streetcar*, she had no qualms about speaking her mind. In a different modern era, in a less hierarchically structured and patriarchal theatre with more similarly independent-minded women involved in all capacities, her theatrical career could possibly have been even richer. Her Agnes in *A Delicate Balance* (Peggy Ashcroft played the role in its eventual British premiere for the RSC) would, I suspect, have opened up a rich seam of parts in her later career had she lived (Beaumont suggested Lady Cicely in Shaw's *Captain Brassbound's Conversion*, Hermione in *A Winter's Tale*, Arkadina in *The Seagull* and Becque's *La Parisienne* among possible ventures for her). On screen Scarlett and Blanche ensure there is little chance of her name disappearing into obscurity but others – Libby in *St Martin's Lane*, Emma Hamilton, some of *Anna Karenina* and *Mrs Stone* –are also witness to her extraordinary understanding of screen acting, that rare ability to put up no barrier between the self and the camera which gives her best film performances their particular amperage, their present-tense immediacy.

Her Bipolar condition contributed to that quality. *Touched With Fire*, a fascinating scrutiny by Kay Redfield Jamison, anatomises the link between the artistic temperament and manic depressive illness, instancing an astonishing number of Bipolar people with a special aptitude for the creative arts, for painting, music and performance. In Vivien's case her condition surely informed her understanding of characters often on a nervous cliff-edge (Blanche, Paola, Lady Macbeth, Scarlett). That her marriage to Olivier would have endured had she not been Bipolar, which ultimately he found too much to live with, also seems possible; it was her illness, coinciding with his awareness of another "world elsewhere" in the shifting theatrical landscape of the 1950s which finally destroyed their marriage. That she continued to work so regularly with her condition is testament to an extraordinary will power. And to her courage.

When Alan Dent was preparing *Vivien Leigh, A Bouquet* after her death he asked his contributors to highlight her main qualities. Her beauty of course figured strongly but a remarkable number suggested – contrary to her presentation (not least in most Olivier biographies) as a tragic figure, both fragile and destructive – a stronger and more remarkable character by instancing her courage. Jamie Hamilton, Scottish by background, in a letter to her used the word "gumption", more common north of the Border, echoing the words of – among others – Arthur Conachy, the doctor who understood her best, when he wrote to Jack after her major crisis during *Tovarich*, or of

Osborne watching her on stage in San Francisco or of Sybil Thorndike after her divorce.

Tennessee Williams also admired that quality. After *Streetcar*, she counted him as one of her true friends and he felt the same about her, recognising a psyche not dissimilar to his own ("I have thought about you more times than you would believe" he wrote after her 1953 collapse, adding "I suspect my life is just one long nervous breakdown"). He visited her at Tickerage ("I'll never forget the two views of the lake, the yellow and rose one at sunset and the even lovelier one when it turned silver" – like her he loved the water) and his feelings went beyond the gratitude he expressed for her performances as Blanche and Karen Stone. As another damaged person he understood the crack in her psyche. Vivien and he also made each other laugh; it is often easy to forget that Vivien's life involved an enormous amount of joy. Her eldest grandson Neville was just eight when Vivien died but when later he was asked how he would describe her he immediately replied "funny". John Mills always stressed that what he always recalled about his times with the Oliviers, especially Vivien, was "above all, the laughs" (Coward sometimes added a P.S. injunction to his letters to her: "Don't stop laughing for an instant.")

Williams never forgot Vivien's behaviour to Frank Merlo, the great love of his life, a warm, gentle man whom she had liked from meeting him in 1949. In 1963 Merlo was dying of lung cancer and slowly withdrawing from the world – Williams compared him to a cat, going off at the end to die alone – but often mentioned Vivien. When she came to New York for *Tovarich* Williams called her (from a public telephone, not wanting to be overheard) to suggest Merlo might want to see her. Vivien arranged a small dinner party, treating Merlo unobtrusively as the principal guest, as Williams wrote in his *Memoirs*:

> Vivien centred the whole dinner party around him with an intuitive sympathy that will always endear her memory to me ... She did it without seeming to do it. Having known madness she knew how it was to be drawing close to death.

He added to Alan Dent:

> For the first time he seemed to forget his depression. Another person might have treated him with a concern for his condition. But there was nothing of that, only a delicately exhibited affection for him. He was happy that evening.

It has always seemed to me that Vivien and Williams had similar courage, strikingly so in Williams's case after Merlo's death when his work began to suffer a harsh critical backlash but when he continued, like her, following the collapse of her marriage to Olivier, always to keep working. Williams thought that Marlon Brando never especially liked him but Brando, not without his own troubles, once wrote to Williams in terms which could also apply to Vivien:

> You have been as brave as anybody I've known and it is comforting to think about. You probably don't think of yourself as brave because nobody who really has courage does, but I know you are.

This is echoed in an extract from Robert Louis Stevenson's "We Thank Thee" which Vivien at times quoted and entered in her Commonplace Book. "The quiet mind" mentioned by Stevenson she did not always find but the rest surely applied:

> Give us courage and gaiety and the quiet mind ... strength to encounter that which is to come, that we may be brave in peril, constant in tribulation, temperate in wrath, and in all changes of fortune and, down to the gates of death, loyal and loving, one to the other.

APPENDIX

Facts/False Facts

"**O**h God, why don't they leave the poor darling alone?" Olivier is reported by John Osborne to have groaned as a "gleefully prurient" biography of Vivien appeared. He was in for worse himself. Osborne was writing, not long after Olivier's death, of Donald Spoto's book *Laurence Olivier*, describing it as a "bogus and anile concoction". Spoto's biography claimed that Olivier was bisexual (touched on in Chapter 13), launching a whole extensive and continuing speculative industry. Joan Plowright's remark on *Desert Island Discs* that like many men of genius Olivier had "his demons" was seized on by some to indicate agreement with Spoto although she has pointed out that while Olivier told her of his previous affairs, not one male was mentioned. The response to the suggestions that he had earlier gay affairs would be simply her own robust "If he did, so what?" were it not that if this were the case it would have a significant bearing on any scrutiny of Vivien's life with him.

There is an extensive critical apparatus appended to Spoto's book but – crucially – his assertion that throughout most of the 1950s Olivier had a relationship with Danny Kaye (labelled by Spoto "a dynamically aggressive homosexual") which was "not only physically intimate but also mutually supportive" is given no source or corroboration of any description, but is widely repeated as fact including in subsequent biographies by Michael Munn and Francis Beckett. Also it occurs in a dismissive review of Terry Coleman's authorised biography (2005) by Anthony Holden whose own Olivier biography had appeared before Olivier's death. In his review Holden claimed that British libel laws combined with his "sense of decorum" had persuaded him in 1988 not to publish what he described as evidence in his possession of Olivier's gay affairs "with, among others, Danny Kaye".

The "facts" of this are widely repeated – often wildly exaggerated – on the internet and continue to be cited by other writers; the tirelessly contrarian Julie Burchill squeaked in *The Spectator* that "Brighton's most famous peer was a bisexual married to an insane nymphomaniac" while another journalist, Michael Thornton, who seems to specialise in articles on royalty or stars (usually deceased), has also claimed that Olivier was bisexual, once disconcertingly gazing at Thornton on the Brighton Belle train ("his eyes, dark and hypnotic, trained on my 23-year-old face like a searchlight"). Thornton questioned Emlyn Williams about the possibility of Olivier's bisexuality to which the inveterate gossip reportedly responded with "Is the Pope Catholic?" Covering the 2017 Sothebys sale Thornton wrote that the late actress Phyllis Konstam had told him that Vivien, portrayed as a "raven-haired, green-eyed feline temptress", made "lesbian advances" to Jill as part of her scheme to "snare" Olivier ("their volcanic passion ended in a marriage from hell"). There would seem to be no supporting documentary evidence for such reports.

All this would not be worth space were it not for the fact that it reinforces Spoto's stress that Olivier's alleged bisexuality and "affair" with Kaye seriously affected his marriage to Vivien:

> With Kaye, Olivier was perhaps most himself, vulnerable, relaxed, unconcerned with style and status (as Vivien required him to be) and Kaye therefore gained Olivier's trust and earned his self-disclosure in a way Vivien never had.

This distorts the facts. It was Olivier's own concern with status, utterly without any persuasion from Vivien, which was behind the decision to buy Notley, which marked down Tarquin for Eton and which so enraged him when Wolfit was knighted in addition to his CBE, to give just a few instances. It is not disputed that Vivien and Olivier were friends with the Kayes – and the few surviving letters between them suggest no more than friendship – but there is no convincing evidence to support the showbiz scuttlebutt alleging this supposed affair.

Where and how this kind of gossip initially arose it is hard to pin down. That Olivier was extravagantly theatrical often – greeting male chums with "Dear Boy!" or "Darling Baby!" and often a kiss – is also undisputed but while this may have seemed outrageous and camp to those outside the theatre it was at that time by no means unusual. And, like some other major heterosexual actors (James Mason, Paul Scofield and Peter O'Toole included), there was definitely often a streak of the androgynous, a fusion of the assertively male and the more delicately feminine, in Olivier's acting (an ambivalent scene from *Spartacus* between him and Tony Curtis is regularly cited as an illustration). Similarly, Kaye's occasional flamboyance onstage gave rise to whispers in the wings about his sexuality. His big break from Borscht Belt and club circuits came on Broadway in *Lady in the Dark* as a fashion-photographer (a "swish" in the parlance of the late 1940s), a character built on facets of his act for which his wife Sylvia created much of the material including the persona of an effeminate dress-designer (Anatole of Paris – "he shrieks with chic"). Kaye, too, had an androgynous quality alongside his manic physical and verbal comedy; on occasion he would, in convincing drag, impersonate the sophisticated cabaret singer Kay Thompson. Like Olivier he came most alive in performance, like him he was subject to "the black monkey" of depressed spells, like him he had a forensic interest in medical procedures and like him he was freighted with guilt – about his Jewishness and the complex fusion of gratitude and resentment he felt for the forceful Sylvia; he had various affairs – Eve Arden and Gwen Verdon included – and he and Sylvia had a trial separation but never divorced. Olivier and Kaye certainly were friends for many years (until Kaye abruptly – in Olivier's eyes unprofessionally and unforgivably – reneged on a contract to appear at Chichester under Olivier's successor John Clements) and they admired each other's talent but despite extensive research into this friendship Kaye's scrupulous biographer Martin Gottfried concluded: "There is no evidence of and there are no witnesses to a Kaye-Olivier sexual relationship." Perhaps one of the shrewdest insights came from Sarah Miles, to whom Olivier spoke of many of his friendships. She felt that "those two magicians" possibly craved, even perhaps subconsciously, "some inner nourishment," recognising "a lost soul" in each other, the kind of friendship others could not quite comprehend and about which some were malicious.

Just possibly the whole rigmarole began with the misunderstanding and embroidery of the details of an incident (passed over in previous books) dating from before the alleged 1953 Idlewild episode in which Spoto presents Kaye in heavy disguise and make-up as a US Customs official duping Olivier into a strip-search. In late 1949 Olivier came to New York (literally a flying visit) for a United Nations ceremony at which he read the Declaration of Human Rights on its first anniversary, followed by a formal dinner with General Eisenhower and Eleanor Roosevelt among fellow guests before flying home. Kaye had a penchant for springing surprise practical jokes on his celebrity friends. Once in a San Francisco hotel he borrowed a waiter's jacket to surprise Margot Fonteyn by serving her tea, and in 1949 he borrowed a Pan Am attendant's cap and jacket (no dark wig, no powdered latex mask, no US Immigration Dept.'s uniform), planning at Idlewild Arrivals to stop Olivier, who simply walked on past him, calling over his shoulder: "Your gag didn't work, Danny." This episode was witnessed and reported in New York by columnist Leonard Lyons in "The Lyon's Den" (*New York News*, 12 December 1949) and in London (*Evening News*, 10 December 1949). Possibly – illustrating how such hearsay expands – these details merged with showbiz whispers behind hands, some of it sparked by rumours spread by a dismissed Kaye employee, Robert Steele, to create the Idlewild exaggerated version which Spoto and others accepted as fact. Nevertheless, Spoto easily could have checked the veracity of his claim that Kaye flew on with Olivier to Los Angeles. At the time in question in 1953 Kaye was appearing nightly on the New York stage; he missed no performances.

Spoto's book also mentioned a letter allegedly written to Vivien by Olivier describing his sexual involvement with Kaye as "transitory and unimportant", dating it to 1961, although it seems most peculiar that he should write this after their divorce. According to Spoto, after Vivien's death the letter passed into Jack Merivale's possession although he seems never to have mentioned it even when talking candidly of Vivien to her biographer Hugo Vickers – and it is not amongst his papers at the BFI. Further, Spoto claimed that in *Confessions* Olivier had originally included details of early homosexual experiences but was persuaded to excise them by Joan Plowright. This she has denied; the drafts of the book with their revisions are all in the British Library's Olivier Archive and no such material is amongst the various versions.

Olivier's reaction to what has been alleged in some subsequent books would have been memorably unprintable. Vivien and he have been more recently among the subjects of a new genre – perhaps best called Bioporn – much of it from an American outfit, Blood Moon Productions, specialising in "candid" biographies of deceased stars mostly written in a style which reads like an unlikely marriage between *Confidential* magazine and Barbara Cartland. Among Blood Moon's output is a fat 2011 volume, *Damn You, Scarlett O'Hara*, ostensibly covering "The Private Lives of Vivien Leigh and Laurence Olivier" by Darwin Porter and the British-born Roy Moseley. The latter has been described by Danforth Prince of Blood Moon as "the couple's adopted godson and long-standing friend and personal assistant" while widely on the internet he is described as Vivien's "honorary godson" or "secretary". There is no correspondence between Moseley and Olivier in the latter's Archive while that of Vivien contains only four brief letters from him, all from the 1960s, all formal and addressed to "My Dear Lady Olivier" which – although for a time he worked as a dresser on *Duel of Angels* – suggests no close intimacy.

Any godmother – even an "honorary" one – is due more honour than that paid to Vivien in this joint confection, riddled with errors and stamped throughout by lubricious prurience, presenting both Vivien and Olivier as wildly promiscuous bisexuals. Vivien's lesbian lovers allegedly included Ona Munson, who played Belle Watling in *Gone With the Wind* and, even more implausibly, Isabel Jeans; the males ranging from Oswald Frewen, Gene Kelly, Stewart Granger and Leslie Howard to – predictably – Brando. It is alleged that the latter and Vivien once checked into a Californian motel (unnamed) as "Durango Canyon" and "Petticoat Blossom" (the authors can presumably produce a copy of the register). Olivier's male lovers they claim included Coward, Novello, Byam Shaw, Siegfried Sassoon, George, Duke of Kent, Douglas Fairbanks Jr, Tyrone Power, Cornel Wilde, Kaye, Brando, Tynan, Richard Burton and Peter Finch etc etc. This exercise in what has been described as the literary equivalent of grave-robbing even adds his brother Dickie to the list.

Throughout virtually no sources are given although there are many supposedly "authentic" reported conversations, often unintentionally comic (that between Bette Davis and Olivier is the funniest) while it is hard to credit Vivien, supposedly suspicious of a Jean Simmons/Olivier affair during *Hamlet* filming, addressing her "rival" as "You teenage twat". The book dwells at length on the Olivier/Kaye "affair"; at one point the authors concede that the notion of the pairing "struck some as incredulous" (sic). Indeed. This kind of stuff would be worth barely a mention were it not that much of it is recycled as "fact" on the internet.

Ironically the first to raise the issue of bisexuality had been Olivier himself when in *Confessions* he mentioned "one male for whom some sexual dalliance had not been loathsome to contemplate" although he felt "the homosexual act would be darkly destructive to my soul". There is no suggestion that more than contemplation occurred, although the proximity of this section to a passage on Coward led some erroneously to assume he may have been the "one male" in question. More likely this might have been his contemporary actor-friend Denys Blakelock, best man at his wedding to Jill. They were good friends then; Blakelock was discreetly gay and in adolescence they often stayed at each other's parental home. But, again, there is no evidence of any physical affair.

Terry Coleman suggested that Olivier was briefly the lover of actor Henry Ainley (they both appeared in a 1936 film of *As You Like It*); he based this on some letters written by Ainley to Olivier in the late 1930s, held in the Olivier Archive. The elder (by over 25 years), Ainley does indeed address Olivier in extravagantly affectionate terms ("Larry Darling", "My Pretty" or "Larry Kin

Mine"), signs himself "Henrietta" or "Nancy Ainley" and calls him a "psod" several times, with some mildly saucy *doubles entendres* ("Have you seen my Osric?") but what Coleman fails to comprehend is that these letters (hardly "explicitly homosexual" as Coleman claimed) comprise epistolary role-playing (not at all unusual among actors), heightening in Ainley's case the persona of a floridly jokey "actor-laddie" of the era. Once a strikingly handsome actor with a mellifluous voice (star of James Elroy Flecker's *Hassan*), Ainley's drinking had virtually destroyed his career by the time Olivier knew him. There is no suggestion anywhere of any other gay relationship in Ainley's life; and there would seem to have been no gossip suggesting one with Olivier at the time or later – in a gossipy profession – until Coleman's 2005 book appeared; according to Rosa Ainley, his granddaughter, Coleman's suggestion came as – to say the least – something of a surprise to his surviving family (Ainley had three wives, not a few mistresses and at least six children). A letter from Ainley (not quoted by Coleman) drops the camp persona when in 1938 he wrote to Olivier, clearly aware of Vivien's role in his life:

> Please may I be serious, just for a tick. Allow an old friend just a word. Both of you – be happy. Guard your happiness and shine like the angels you both are.

The over-riding factor in treating the suggestions of Olivier's bisexuality with extreme scepticism is the total absence of any mention of it in Vivien's surviving (extensive) correspondence pre or post divorce or of any report of her reference to it when – certainly in one of her manic phases – she would not have held back. At those times she could often raise Olivier's affairs with Dorothy Tutin or Claire Bloom or accuse him of sexual inadequacies including his self-confessed problem for a time with premature ejaculation. But there is no recorded instance of her citing any gay relationship, either fleeting or (as alleged in the Kaye case) of length. Holden's 1988 biography suggested that the New York airport scene at Idlewild prior to Vivien's transportation home in 1953 was triggered by her jealousy of Kaye's "intense re-union" with Olivier (but he – and Tennant – had been met already by Kaye on arrival at Idlewild from London and again at La Guardia on the stopover from LA on the same day as they returned to London). There are no reports elsewhere of this.

The internet will inevitably keep all the speculation and gossip in circulation. It is of course possible that Spoto may provide sources for his Olivier/Kaye scenario (although he has had over twenty-five years in which to do so). Holden claimed in his 2005 review of Coleman's *Olivier* that he had "evidence" in his possession of Olivier's male affairs, including that with Kaye, material which he had "self-censored" in his own biography of 1988 when

Olivier was still alive, in part because of his authorial "sense of decorum". That seemed markedly less urgent when his book was re-issued, slightly expanded, in 2007 by which time, as he owned, both Kaye and Olivier were "beyond the reach of all but celestial lawyers". However his new material could cause one only to wonder what precisely the "evidence" which he said he possessed but self-censored in 1988 could possibly have been because most of his additions are taken from material published well after that date. The bulk of Holden's "new" material consists of quotes from articles or books by Thornton, Sarah Miles or the Darwin Porter of Blood Moon (which boasts of applying "the tabloid standards of today to the Hollywood scandals of yesterday"). Porter published in 2006 a lurid biography *Brando Unzipped*, from which Holden cites the actor's alleged affairs with both Vivien and Olivier. He also quotes Thornton's 2003 account of Olivier on the Brighton Belle and the assertion that Princess Marina, Duchess of Kent had told Thornton ("most emphatically" in the journalist's words) that Olivier and Kaye had been "épris". Also quoted (to whom and when is not completely clear) is Vivien's old dancing-partner Jack Wilson, claiming that Olivier and Coward had been lovers (by the 1950s Wilson had declined into hopeless alcoholism, cut out of Coward's professional life). Holden also joined those suggesting that Joan Plowright's *Desert Island Discs* mention of Olivier's "demons" was reinforcement of his sexual schism and he quotes her, irked by suggestions that she was responsible for the collapse of the Vivien/Olivier marriage, as saying: "Danny Kaye was attached to Larry far earlier than I" a remark she has refuted, giving in her 2001 memoir the shortest of shrifts to such rumours: "reports by careless biographers that Larry had admitted to relationships of that kind are equally untrue."

Holden's 1988 edition had a critical apparatus reflecting the depth of his research. It remains puzzling that his revised 2007 section on Olivier's alleged gay affairs should cite so much that is less verifiable. In his "evidence" taken from Porter and Thornton every person cited as a source – Kazan, Niven, Williams, Konstam, Charles Feldman, Jack Warner, actress Mildred Natwick, the Duchess of Kent – is dead and none would seem to have left any surviving documentary evidence. Holden wrote that an Olivier/Kaye affair was "common knowledge" in the theatrical profession (although Gielgud – who knew Olivier for half a century and relished "shop" gossip – was only one of those surprised by and sceptical of Spoto's original allegation). It certainly has become a matter of common speculation but that is not quite the same thing.

Sarah Miles is a different case. In her 1994 memoir (*Serves Me Right*) she wrote better and with more compassionate insight than some Olivier biographers.

Holden quotes her saying that Olivier "also loved both men and women" although this was not something Olivier told Miles, only what she surmised when she and her "Lionel Kerr" talked of her early bisexual experience. Although she felt that Coward had been sexually jealous of her liaison with Olivier – speculating that "Noël was after a wee bit of hanky-panky during *Private Lives* back in 1930" – she does not state that Olivier had physical gay affairs while understanding that some need in him sought a close tie with both Coward – a lifelong mentor – and Kaye. A problem with such pervasive gossip is that to question it leads often to furious accusations of homophobia and/or attempted cover-ups. More crucially it compounds the tendency in many Olivier biographies to portray Vivien as a player in some dark, Gothic romantic tragedy. Michael Korda in fiction (his novel *Curtain* is a torrid *roman à clef* with a famous English acting couple and an American entertainer as central figures) and rather too many biographers take this perspective, echoing that of Anthony Quayle, fascinated by Vivien always:

> In the days of the matriarchy she would have been one of those goddess-priestesses, capable of making men great and equally capable of destroying them.

Maxine Audley was struck by Quayle's angle on the Vivien/Olivier relationship:

> He had this wonderful theory that they had made a pact with the devil. He said "You can have everything, all the riches and you will be King and Queen of the theatre but there's only one condition: You must stay together for the rest of your lives."

In this version, bound together irrevocably in *the* great love affair, they seem like a theatrical equivalent of the Duke and Duchess of Windsor. And others paint Vivien and Olivier in similar colours, reflecting a description of them by Eileen Beldon, a member of the 1948/50 Old Vic company who was reminded of Miles and Flora, the beguiling but diabolical children of James's *The Turn of the Screw*. But talk of satanic pacts only glosses the familiar tabloid depiction of "The Oliviers'" relationship as "the marriage from hell" and of her life as a continuing melodrama. Certainly it had its share of heightened drama and the spell cast by "The Oliviers" endured for years, but at its heart was essentially a very human story, its protagonists supremely gifted, beautiful, complex, ambitious, competitive and flawed but locked into no pact with any devil, with no obvious heroes and villains. To portray Vivien as a doomed romantic heroine with Olivier cast as another dark and riven soul is to blur not only her personality but also a considered focus on a seriously impressive body of work. Distortion of the realities of her life illustrates the disturbing proliferation of a modern phenomenon, what the *New York Times* commentator and long-serving literary *eminence grise* Michiko Kakutani examines in her book, *The Death of Truth*. A kind of "New Untruth" has come insidiously to permeate both political and cultural life as a toxic pall of "truth decay", "fake news" and "alternative facts" mushrooms, described by Kakutani as a process of the displacement of reason by emotion and the corrosion of language "which diminishes the value of the truth".

A carelessness regarding the facts of an actor's life may seem only a minor – to some even trivial – example of this trend towards "Post-Truth" in an age of social media. But it still matters, not least when biography becomes a prurient scatter-gun blitz of unsubstantiated allegations such as those peddled by Blood Moon and others. A prolific modern biographer has stressed the hazards for biography "in a culture of gossip and innuendo" and emphasised that, now more urgently than ever, "the biographer is obliged to tell the truth". That biographer was the same Donald Spoto whose Olivier biography, published soon after the actor's death and giving an often inaccurate portrait of Vivien, launched the whole ongoing saga of Olivier's sexuality which persists although the reliability of Spoto's original allegations has been comprehensively demolished.

To my mind, a careful scrutiny of the "evidence" behind this version of Olivier's supposedly bifurcated nature suggests that the hearsay then and later has come to create a herring of deepest-dyed red in understanding Vivien's relationship with him and a distraction from the truths of her remarkable life and career.

Notes on Sources

ABBREVIATIONS

AW: Alexander Walker, *Vivien*
BFI: The John Merivale Papers, British Film Institute
CA: Laurence Olivier, *Confessions of An Actor*
HV: Hugo Vickers, *Vivien Leigh*
LO: Laurence Olivier
LOA: The Laurence Olivier Archive
MFLO: Tarquin Olivier, *My Father, Laurence Olivier*
VL: Vivien Leigh
VLA: The Vivien Leigh Archive
VLAB: Alan Dent, *Vivien Leigh, A Bouquet*

PROLOGUE

The Selznick memos are printed in *Memo from David O. Selznick* (pp. 281, 173 and 187). Gladys Cooper's comments (p. xiv) are in VLAB (p. 62) and the description of her beauty (p. xiv) is in *The Sunday Dispatch* (19 May 1935).
Garson Kanin's remarks are in VLAB (p. 75), LO on critics (p. xxi) in CA (p. xviii). John Gielgud's letter to VL and Byam Shaw's 1953 letter (p. xv) are in VLA. Tyan on VL (p. xxii) appeared in his introductory piece for *The Daily Sketch* (2 October 1953).

CHAPTER 1   A CHILD OF THE RAJ

Selznick's letter to Ed Sullivan (7 January 1939) is in *Memo from David O. Selznick* (p. 193). The recollections of Florence ("Mills") Martin (p. 2) appear in HV (p. 6).

Gertrude Harley's ancestry (p. 3) is traced online: http://chater-geneology.bl ogspot.co.uk/2015/08armenian-something-vivien-leigh-and-her12.html.

CHAPTER 2   HOURS NEARER DEATH

Ian Thompson's recollections (p. 10) are in HV (p. 12) as are those of Patsy Quinn (HV p. 18). VL's version of early theatrical ambitions appeared in "What Success Has Taught Me", a 1930 newspaper interview. Her letters from the Sacred Heart Convent are reproduced in VLAB (pp. 43–4). The description of her moods (p. 14) appears in Thomas Kiernan's *Sir Larry* (p. 119). The entries from VL's diaries are all from those held in VLA. Her memoirs of Mlle Antoine (p. 16) also come from "What Success Has Taught Me". Betty Harbord's recollections (p. 16) appeared in HV (p. 23) – as did those of Hamish Hamilton (HV p. 30), as well as VL's letter to Leigh Holman (19/8/32). VL's remark to Sir Kenneth Barnes (p. 21) appears in Gwen Robyns *The Light of a Star* (p. 22).

CHAPTER 3   YOUNG WIFE AND MOTHER

Patsy Quinn on VL's wedding (p. 22) is quoted in VLAB (pp. 46–7). The many extracts from VL's diaries are from those held in the VLA, as is Hamilton on early memories (p. 23). VL's letter to Jane Glass (p. 24) is quoted in HV (pp. 37–8). Her remarks on motherhood appear in "What Success Has Taught Me". Anne Wilding and Maud Miller on VL appear in HV (p. 43). Alexander Walker interviewed John Gliddon as did Hugo Vickers (AW pp. 48, 54, HV p. 43). *The Green Sash* was reviewed (26 February 1935) in *The Times*. Basil Dean on VL (p. 31) is from *Mind's Eye* (p. 207). The review of *The Mask of Virtue* (p. 34) appeared in *The Daily Mail* (16 May 1935). John Wilson wrote of VL (p. 35) in *Noël, Tallulah, Cole and Me* (pp. 63–4) and Jean-Pierre Aumont on dining in Soho (p. 37) in *Sun and Shadow* (p. 214). LO's impressions of VL are in CA (p. 77). Gielgud's appreciation of VL (p. 38) appears in *Distinguished Company* (p. 70) and Byam Shaw on *Richard II* (p. 38) in VLAB (pp. 88–9). Novello on *The Happy Hypocrite* and VL's letter to Leigh Holman dated from 26 March 1936. Carl Harbord's reference to VL (p. 39) was related to HV by John Merivale (HV p. 61).

CHAPTER 4   ENTER OLIVIER

LO on his mother (p. 42) appeared in an interview with Tynan, *Great Acting* (Jan 1966). Denys Blakelock on the young LO appeared in *Round the Next Corner* (p. 45). Letters from LO to Eva Moore are all in LOA. The sexuality of acting

(p. 45) was discussed by LO in conversation with his son and is referred to in LOMF (p. 56); his comments to Michael Gambon (p. 46) are in Coleman (*op. cit.*, p. 511). The review of *Fire Over England* (p. 47), by Alex von Tunzelman, appeared in *The Guardian* (27 June 2013). VL to Godfrey Winn (p. 48) is from *The Positive Hour* (p. 397). The reviews of *Dark Journey* (p. 50) are from *Time* and *The New York Times*. VL on Tarquin (p. 50) is in a letter to Leigh Holman (26 August 1936 – VLA). Oswald Frewen's descriptions of Capri (p. 50) are from his diary, quoted in AW (p. 80). Jill Esmond's visits to Vivien (p. 51) are referred to in LOMF (p. 67). Rex Harrison's *Storm in a Teacup* recollections (p. 52) appear in *Rex* (p. 67). J.C. Trewin (p. 56) wrote in *Plays and Players* (September 1967). Basil Dean on *Twenty-One Days* (p. 54) is in *Mind's Eye* (p. 251). Juliet Duff's letter (p. 56) is in LOA. Jill Esmond to her son (p. 56) is in MFLO (p. 67).

CHAPTER 5   ALTERED STATES

Sybil Thorndike's letter (p. 57) is quoted in Jonathan Croall's *Sybil Thorndike: A Star of Life* (p. 289), Frewen's recollections in his diary. Sybille's recollections (p. 58) appear in her unpublished memoir of LO held in LOA. John Gliddon on *A Yank at Oxford* (p. 60) appears in AW (pp. 95–6). Simon Callow on *St Martin's Lane* (p. 63) is in his *Charles Laughton: A Difficult Actor* (p. 127) and Larry Adler on that film in AW (p. 104). Wyler to VL (p. 65) is quoted in Alex Masden's *William Wyler* (p. 185). Helen Spencer's letter (p. 67, 24 November 1938) is in LOA as is Anne Rooney's. Letters from LO to VL from the *Normandie* and in Hollywood are in VLA. Coleman on VL's reason for following LO (p. 68) are in Coleman (*op. cit.*, p113). Filming of *Twenty-One Days* (p. 68) was reported by C.A. Lejeune in *Thank you for Having Me* (p. 84). S.N. Behrman on *Serena Blandish* (p. 66) is in his *Tribulations and Laughter* (p. 203) and Granger's account of *Serena Blandish* (p. 69) in his *Sparks Fly Upwards* (pp. 43–4). Angus McBean's recollections (p. 69) appear in *Face-Maker* (pp. 147–8) and Fabia Drake's recollections (p. 69) appear in *Blind Fortune*, p. 96). Irene Mayer Selznick's *Private View* (p. 215) records her viewpoint on VL and *Gone With the Wind*. Hamilton's description of the *Majestic* voyage (p. 70) is in HV (p. 97).

CHAPTER 6   PRINTING A LEGEND

There are many books on *Gone With the Wind*; Gavin Lambert's *The Making of Gone With the Wind* has proved the most reliable. LO on VL's casting (p. 72) is in CA (p. 83). VL's letters to Leigh Holman and her mother are in VLA. Roger Lewis on *Gone With the Wind* (p. 77) appears in his *The Real Life of Laurence*

Olivier (p. 168). Angela Carter's *Observer* article (p. 77) appeared on 3 January 1982 and that by Lou Lumenick (p. 77) in the *New York Post* (25/6/2015). The many letters from LO to VL during *Gone With the Wind* filming are all in VLA. Sunny Lash's letter to LO (p. 85) is in LOA. The description of the reunion of VL and LO (p. 85) is from *Radie's World* (p. 103). LO on *Rebecca* (p. 86) is reported in *It's Only a Movie* (pp. 126–7). The material concerning Jill Esmond and Tarquin Olivier appears in MFLO. *Waterloo Bridge* (p. 89) is discussed in *Dying Swans and Madmen: Ballet, the Body and Narrative Cinema* (p. 205). The recollections of its director, Mervyn Le Roy are in *Take One* (pp. 46–7).

CHAPTER 7   STAR-CROSSED

"Percy" Harris on *Romeo and Juliet* (p. 93) appears in *Design By Motley* (p. 77). Jill Esmond's letters to Eva Moore are in MFLO (p. 77) and VL's to Leigh Holman are in VLA. R.C. Sherriff on *Lady Hamilton* (p. 98) is in his *No Leading Lady* (p. 168). Molly Haskell's *Frankly, My Dear* contains her descriptions of *Lady Hamilton* while Tim Robey's assessment appeared in *The Daily Telegraph* (16 October 2012).

CHAPTER 8   WARTIME DRAMAS

Leigh Holman's letter (p. 103) is in VLA as is Byam Shaw's while LO's to Fairbanks (p. 104) is in LOA. John Clements on VL (p. 104) appears in VLAB (p. 61). The description of Beaumont (p. 105) is in Sally Phipps's *Molly Keane: A Life* (p. 74). Alan Dent on VL (p. 106) is in VLAB (p. 19) and LO's letters on *The Doctor's Dilemma* (p. 107) are in VLA. Beaton's *Diaries* (24 November 1941) include his account of VL in Edinburgh (p. 107) while Colin Clark's observation (p. 108) appears in HV (p. 1). Kenneth Clark's opinion (p. 108) is from VLAB (p. 38). LO's letter to Trudy Flockhart (p. 109) is in LOA as are VL's letters from her ENSA tour while his from *Henry V* on location are in VLA. J.R. Bradshaw's letter (p. 112) appeared in *The Times* (8 July 1955). Aumont recalled Prestwick Green (p. 113) in *Sun and Shadow* (p. 215). Shaw at Denham (p. 114) is reported in *Meeting at the Sphinx* (p. 28). The *Caesar and Cleopatra* review (p. 115) appears online in *The Nitrate Diva* (November 2013).

CHAPTER 9   FROM SABINA TO ANNA

The letters from Beaumont and Wilder (p. 121) are in LOA. Selznick's memo of 19 February 1945 to O'Shea (p. 119) is in Selznick (*op. cit.*, p. 358). LO's letters to VL from the Old Vic's European tour are all in VLA as is Beaton's letter

(p. 124) and those from Sunny Lash and from Selznick and Jenia Reiser. The second meeting between VL and Tarquin (p. 126) is in MFLO (pp. 135–6) and Lynn Fontanne's letter to VL (p. 126) in VLA. Beaton's letter to Garbo (p. 128) is in HV (*op. cit.*, p. 173). Diana Cooper at the Paris Embassy (p. 128) appears in *Darling Monster: The letters of Lady Diana Cooper to her son John Julius Norwich 1939–1952* (pp. 198–9). The verdict on Korda's costume films (p. 130) appeared in *Picture Post* (16 August 1947). The question of VL's damehood (p. 131) is referred to by Anne Edwards in *Vivien Leigh* (p. 160). The description of the Riviera holiday (p. 131) is in MFLO (p. 159).

CHAPTER 10   DOWN UNDER

Alan Seymour's article (p. 134) "The Old Vic in Australia" appeared in *The Australian*. Elsie Beyer's letters from the Old Vic Australian tour are in LOA and VL's to Beaumont in VLA. The views of Michael Redington and Mercia Swinburne (p. 138) are in HV (p. 181) as are those of Georgina Jumel, Terence Morgan and Floy Bell (HV p. 184). LO's letters to Tennant (p. 139) are in LOA and VL's to Beaumont in VLA. On *Antigone*, letters from Hamilton (p. 142), Sydney Carroll (p. 142) and Clemence Dane (p. 142) are all in VLA. Beaton's letter to Garbo (p. 144) is in HV (*op cit.*, p. 190) and those to and from LO and VL in the LOA. Beaton on VL's beauty (p. 144) is in VLAB (p. 19). LO's account of his conversation with VL (p. 145) is in CA (pp. 131–2).

CHAPTER 11   THE KINDNESS OF STRANGERS

Culiffe's letter (p. 149) and Suzanne's (p. 150) are in VLA. The quotes from Kazan (p. 151) appear in his "Notes on *Streetcar*", reprinted in *The Passionate Playgoer* (p. 342). Williams's letter to Helen Hayes (p. 152) is in *Selected Letters of Tennessee Williams* 1947–8 (p. 190) and that from Hayes to VL (p) in VLA. LO's cable to Irene Selznick and her reply (p. 152) are in LOA. Selznick's comments on the London *Streetcar* are all from *Private View*. LO on directing VL as Blanche (p. 154) is from a tape recording with Mark Amory in LOA, reprinted in Ziegler's *Laurence Olivier* (p. 164). All of Braden's impressions of *Streetcar* rehearsals are from his *The Kindness of Strangers*. On Williams's comedic strain (p. 156), Michael Billington wrote illuminatingly in *The Guardian* ("Tennessee Williams at 100 – Funnier than Ever", 28 March 2011). Walter Matthau on Brando (p. 156) is in Staggs, *When Blanche Met Stanley* (p. 87). Tynan on *Streetcar* (p. 157) is in *He That Plays the King* (p. 142). Letters from Diana Cooper and Athene Seyler (p. 158) are in VLA and that from Dent (p. 158) in LOA.

Dent's description of attending *Streetcar* is in VLAB (pp. 103–4). Joan Cunliffe reports of VL's heightened libido (p. 159) are taken from the television documentary *Scarlett and Beyond*. Karl Malden's *Streetcar* recollections (p. 160) appear in Richard Schickel's *Elia Kazan* (p. 211).

The "butterfly in a jungle" analogy (p. 161) is in Kazan's "Notes" (*op. cit.*, p. 347) and his letter to VL (p. 161) is in VLA. Williams to Breen (29 October 1950) – the letter is in his *Letters* (*op. cit.*, pp. 355–6). Geoffrey Shurlock on *Streetcar* and censorship is quoted in "Film Notes", New York State Writers Institute, home page.

The different versions of early *Streetcar* filming (p. 164) are in Schickel's *Elia Kazan: A Biography* (p. 215) and in Kazan's *Elia Kazan: A Life* (p. 386). Kim Hunter on VL (p. 165) is from the television documentary *Vivien Leigh*. Lucinda Ballard Dietz recalled her meeting with VL to AW (*op. cit.*, pp. 199–200). Suzanne Farrington's recollections (p. 165) are also from AW (*op. cit.*, p. 201). Kazan's letter to VL (p. 165) is in VLA as are letters from Harry Mines and Charles Feldman (p. 167). Pauline Kael's review (p. 166) appears in *Kiss Kiss Bang Bang* (p. 352) and Gordon Bau's remarks in *Staggs* (*op. cit.*, p. 176). Mark Amory's opinion of Olivier's feelings (p. 169) was expressed in a 2018 letter to the author.

CHAPTER 12   TWO ON THE NILE

VL's letter to Sunny Lash (p. 171) is in VLA. Maxine Audley on *Cleopatra* rehearsals (p. 172) appears in HV (*op. cit.*, p. 201), Byam Shaw to LO (p. 173) is in LOA. Tynan on VL's Lady Anne and Sabina (p. 174) are in *A View of the English Stage* (pp. 19, 108) and LO's defence in *On Acting* (p. 110). Peggy Ashcroft to VL (p. 175) is in VLA and Sybil Thorndike on VL (p. 175) is in VLAB (p. 99). Letters from Raymond Mortimer, John Steinbeck, J.D. Salinger, Christopher Sykes and Tyrone Guthrie (p. 176) are all also in VLA. The comment from LO on Tynan's reviews (p. 177) is from a taped interview with Kathleen Tynan in LOA. Byam Shaw's letter (p. 178) is in VLA. Michael Korda's *Charmed Lives* (p. 178) contains his memories of Mediterranean cruising with VL. Brooks Atkinson's review (p. 179) appeared in *The New York Times* (30 December 1951). Letters from Sherwood and Lynn Fontanne (p. 179) are in VLA and LO's recollections of VL (p. 179) in CA (pp. 140–1). Diana Vreeland described VL to HV (*op. cit.*, p. 207) as did Irene Selznick (HV, *op. cit.*, p. 208). Philip Halsman on photographing VL (p. 180) can be found on Dina Zoryan's Blog, "Vivien Leigh Discussion Board" (5 April 2010). Wilfrid Hyde-White's recollections (p. 181) appeared in VLAB (p. 73). Those of Alec McCowen are from a conversation with the author (2017). Gore Vidal on Dr Kubie (p. 182) appeared in *The New York Review of Books* (13 June 1985) and John Lahr (p. 182) wrote in *Mad Pilgrimage of the Flesh*. The descriptions of Sybille (p. 183) appeared in Gerald Day's *River of Damascus* (pp. xii–xiii and p. 17). Graham Payn (p. 183) is from *My Life with Noël Coward* (p. 234) while the Jamaican stay was recorded in Coward's *Diaries* (p. 191). Letters on Notley from Hamilton, Colefax and Spanier (p. 184) are in VLA. LO wrote of VL's departure for Ceylon (p. 186) in CA (p. 152).

CHAPTER 13 CRACK-UP

LO's letters (p. 187) are in VLA and VL's to Coward are in the Coward Archive. The description of Peter Finch (p. 189) appears in Trader Faulkner's biography. Bevis Bawa's memoir *The Sometimes Irreverent Memoir of a Gentleman in 20th Century Sri Lanka* contains his recollections of VL and LO's account of his time in Ceylon is in CA (p. 153). Tamara Finch on VL in Hollywood is in Elaine Dundy's biography of Finch (p. 186). Edward Ashley's recollections of *Elephant Walk* (p. 192) appeared in Lasky and Silver's *Love Scene* (p. 112). David Niven's memoir *Bring on the Empty Horses* (first edition) contains his description of VL during the crisis on *Elephant Walk* (pp. 309–21) and Stewart Granger's version is in *Sparks Fly Upwards* (pp. 289–93). The allegation of a Kaye/LO affair first surfaced in Donald Spoto's *Olivier* (p. 196) in which the supposed Idlewild episode occurred (*op. cit.*, p. 211) and Coleman's rebuttal appeared in *Olivier* (pp. 507–8). Gielgud on Kaye appears in *Gielgud's Letters* (p. 483). LO's account of his Hollywood period (pp. 195–7) is in CA (pp. 155–6). Dr. McDonald's letter (p. 196) to Tennant (7 May 1953) is in LOA. Peter Hiley's perspective (p. 199) is in Coleman (*op. cit.*, p. 262). Coward's *Diaries* (p. 211) record his telephone call from VL in Netherne. LO's letter to Weiller (p. 200) is in LOA as is Guthrie's letter (p. 202). Tynan on *The Sleeping Prince* appeared in *The Observer* (12 November 1953). Laughton's letter to LO (p. 202) is undated, written from the Adelphi Hotel, Liverpool; it is in LOA as is LO's reply and his letters to Wolfit and Tynan. Kenneth Clark's letter (p. 204) and Rex Harrison's (p. 204) are in LOA. Kenneth More on VL (p. 206) appeared in VLAB (p. 82). Alec McCowen (p. 207) spoke in conversation with the author (2017). Banbury's letter (p. 207) is in VLA. Claire Bloom's recollections (p. 207) appear in *Limelight and After* (pp. 149–50) and in the television documentary *Vivien Leigh*. The description of VL in Klosters (p. 208) is contained in Robert Kershaw's *Blood and Champagne* (p. 168). Susana Walton on Christmas at Notley (p. 208) appears in *William Walton* (p. 202).

CHAPTER 14   AVONSIDE

Suzanne's letter (p. 210) is in VLA and Peter Hiley on LO in Coleman (*op. cit.*, p. 331). LO's conversation with Tarquin (p. 212) is in MFLO (p. 172). Angela Baddeley on *Twelfth Night* (p. 213) appears in Ziegler, *Olivier* (p. 196). LO's defence of VL (p. 124) is in CA (p. 165). John Barber wrote (p. 215) in *The Daily Express* (10 June 1955). Dietrich's letter (p. 216) is in VLA. The Lady Macbeth costume (p. 217) is in the Shakespeare Museum at Stratford-upon-Avon. The letters from Denne Gilkes and Peggy Ashcroft (p. 218) are in VLA and Fabia Drake (p. 219) wrote in *Blind Fortune*. Robert Henriques (p. 219) spoke on BBC's *The Critics* (15 June 1955). Tynan's *Macbeth* review (p) is reprinted in *Curtains* (p. 99) and his recantation appears in John Russell Taylor's *Vivien Leigh* (p. 99). Coward's observations on the Oliviers in 1955 (p. 220) are in his *Diaries* (p. 278). LO's letter to Byam Shaw (p. 221) is in LOA and VL's to Meriel Forbes in VLA. Peter Brook on VL's Lavinia (p. 221) appears in *The Quality of Mercy* (Nick Hern Books, 2013). Philip Hope-Wallace (p. 221) was printed in *The Manchester Guardian* (17 August 1955). Tynan on *Titus* is in *Curtains* (p. 184) and the description of the *Titus* party (p. 222) in Faulkner's *Peter Finch*. Letters from Suzanne Farrington and Rachel Kempson (p. 223) are all in VLA. The lyrics for the Stratford cabaret (p. 224) are in LOA. All the projected *Macbeth* film material is in LOA. Spoto's assertions on VL's pregnancy (pp. 228–9) appear in Spoto (*op. cit.*, pp. 230–1) and Colin Clark's diary entry of VL at Pinewood is in *My Week with Marilyn* (p. 141). Coward's letter (p. 228) is in VLA and his remarks on *South Sea Bubble* in his *Diaries* (p. 331). Hiley on LO (p. 232) is in Coleman (*op. cit.*) Arthur Miller on LO (p. 231) appears in his *Timebends* (Methuen, 1987, p. 418).

CHAPTER 15   AT COURT

Tony Richardson's recollections of *The Entertainer* are all from *Long Distance Runner* and John Osborne's from *Almost a Gentleman* (p. 42). The European *Titus* tour is described by Michael Blakemore in *Arguments with England*; the Zagreb episode is recalled on pp. 166–7. LO on his affair with Dorothy Tutin (unnamed) is in CA (p. 183). LO's letter to Walton (p. 241) is in LOA. VL's reaction (p. 243) to *Duel of Angels* appeared in a *Sunday Telegraph* interview (9 July 1961). Jean-Louis Barrault's *Memories for Tomorrow* (p. 180) contains his recollections of *Duel of Angels* (p. 243). Peter Wyngarde (p. 245) recalled acting with VL to HV (*op. cit.*, p. 263). Claire Bloom (p. 245) wrote of working on *Duel of Angels* in *Limelight and After* (p. 150) and spoke of VL in the television documentary *Scarlett and Beyond*. Ronald Squire's letter (p. 245) to VL is in VLA. The Tynans' relationship with LO and VL is touched on in Dominic Shellard's *Kenneth Tynan* (p. 207) and their stay at Notley in Elaine Dundy's *Life Itself* (pp. 199–204) and Tynans' *Diaries* (pp. 133–4). VL's letter to Coward (pp. 248–9) is in the Coward Archive. VL's note to Ann Todd (p. 250) is in VLA. Hester St John Ives recalled the events following her husband's funeral to Coleman (*op.cit.*, p. 317). VL's letter to LO (p. 251) is in LOA. The version of VL's meeting with Finch (p. 251) appears in Yolande Finch's *Finchie* (pp. 61–2). LO's letter to VL (p. 253) is in VLA.

CHAPTER 16   ENDING A LEGEND

Joan Plowright's remark (p. 255) appears in her *And That's Not All* (p. 62). Leigh Holman's letter is in VLA. The description of Olivier after *Coriolanus* (p. 255) is in Blakemore (*op. cit.*, p. 224). Robert Stephens wrote of VL (p. 257) in *Knight Errant* (pp. 47–8) and Osborne also wrote of her in *Look After Lulu* in *Almost a Gentleman* (pp. 133–5). Godfrey Winn's weekend at Notley (p. 257) is written of in *The Positive Hour* (p. 394). Meriel Forbes's recollections were to Hugo Vickers (*op. cit.*, p. 271). Beaton on Les Avants (p. 259) appears in Philip Hoare's *Noël Coward* (p. 515) and Coward's record of VL's visit is in his *Diaries* (pp. 423–4). VL's letter to Tarquin Olivier (p. 262) is in MFLO (p. 235). Rachel Kempson's letter (p. 263) is in VLA as are LO's to VL while hers to him are in VLA. Connachy's words were in a letter to John Merivale (20 June 1961) held among his papers at the BFI. VL's letters to John Merivale and LO are in VLA as are LO's replies. Osborne's view of *Duel of Angels* (p. 268) appeared in *Almost a Gentleman* (p. 166). Coward on VL at Les Avants (p. 269) is in *Diaries* (p. 452). Tennessee Williams on Henry James (p. 270) is in a letter to Oliver Smith (*Selected Letters of Tennessee Williams* 1947–8, p. 222). LO's letter to VL (p. 272) is in VLA as is Selznick's letter to VL (p. 272). Joan Plowright's comments (p. 272) are in Plowright (*op.cit*, p. 55). VL's first sighting of Tickerage Mill (p. 273) was recalled by John Merivale to Hugo Vickers (HV, p. 291).

CHAPTER 17   WORLDS ELSEWHERE

Aumont's view of VL's final years (p. 274) is in *Sun and Shadow* (p. 234). Stiebel's letters (p. 274) are in VLA as are Consuelo Langton-Lockton's. Sybil Thorndike's letter (p. 275) in VLA is undated, sent from the Duke of York's Theatre where she was appearing at this time. Conachy's letter (p. 275) is in

John Merivale's BFI papers. Bruce Montague recollected VL (p. 277) to the author (2017). John Barnard discussed VL (p. 278) with Hugo Vickers (HV, p. 295) as did David Dodimead (*op. cit.*, p. 297). Helpmann's letter (p. 279) is in VLA as is that from Weissberger (p. 279). Coward (p. 280) was writing in his *Diaries* (p. 513). VL's interview with Barry Norman (p. 281) appeared in *The Daily Mail* (19 June 1962). The many letters on the progress of *Tovarich* from VL to John Merivale are all in Merivale's papers held by the BFI. Coward wrote of the production in *Diaries* (p. 526). Elliot Norton wrote of the show in *The Boston Globe*. Coward's letter and that from LO (p. 285) are in the VLA. Sir David Webster on *Tovarich* (p. 285) appears in VLAB (p. 101). The Hamiltons on *Tovarich* (p. 286) appeared in HV (p. 307). Diana Cooper's description of VL (p. 387) is in a letter to Beaton (9 October 1963). Anne Tovey's memories of VL appear in HV (*op. cit.*, p. 310). The critic referred to on (p. 288) was Gavin Lambert. Peter Feibleman's Hollywood encounter with VL appears in VLAB (p. 67). Elizabeth Ashley spoke of VL (p. 290) in the TV documentary *Vivien Leigh* and Stanley Kramer on *Ship of Fools* appeared in *Vivien Leigh, An Appreciation* (p. 36). The reviews of the film (Dilys Powell and Tynan) appeared in *The Sunday Times* and *Observer* respectively (24 October 1965).

CHAPTER 18   LAST ACTS

Hamilton spoke of VL in India (p. 292) to Hugo Vickers (HV, *op. cit.*, p. 317). All the extracts from VL's letters from India come from those held among the Merivale papers at the BFI. La Casati is remembered in various books, especially vividly in Mark Amory's *Lord Berners*. Stiebel's letter to VL (p. 296) is in VLA, as is Paul Osborn's. Tom Prideaux's review of *Ivanov* appeared in *Life* (27 May 1966). Harper Lee's letter appeared in *The Guardian* (24 October 2017). John Dexter's memory of VL (p. 303) was written in *The Honourable Beast* (p. 21). Douglas-Home (p. 304) wrote in the *News of the World* (9 July 1967). Hiley on LO (p. 305) appears in Coleman (*op. cit.*, p. 384) and LO on VL's death in CA (p. 228). Hepburn on LO (p. 306) appeared in *Katharine Hepburn* (Grace May Carter, New Word City, New York, 2016). Letters to Merivale from Katharine Hepburn and Rex Harrison (p. 306) are found in HV (*op. cit.*, p. 328). Jill Esmond's letter to Tarquin Olivier (p. 307) is in MFLO (p. 255). LO's letters to VL (p. 307) are in VLA. Kenneth Clark's opinion of Olivier at the NT (p. 308) appears in a letter of 16 June 1966 to Lord Chandos, Chairman of the NT Board in the Chandos Papers held in the Churchill Archive, Churchill College, Cambridge. Gawn Grainger on LO (p. 309) appears in Coleman (*op. cit.*, p. 481). Finch on VL (p. 309) appears in *Radie's World* (p. 190).

EPILOGUE

The extract from Coward's "Star Quality" (p. 312) is from *Collected Short Stories* (p. 483). Neville Farrington was interviewed (p. 483) for *The Daily Telegraph Magazine* (15 July 2017). Tennessee Williams's letters (p. 314) are in VLA and his recollections of the dinner-party (p. 314) given by VL in his *Memoirs* (p. 226). Brando's letter to Williams (p. 315) is printed in Olivia Laing's *The Trip to Echo Spring* (p. 216).

APPENDIX   FACTS/FALSE FACTS

Osborne's review of Spoto's *Olivier* (p. 316) appears in *Damn You, England* (p. 125). Spoto's allegations of LO's bisexuality are in his *Olivier* (pp. 181, 196, 211, 248). Holden's review of Coleman's biography appeared in *The Observer* (4 September 2005). Burchill's *Spectator* piece (p. 317) appeared on 16 January 2016. Thornton's article, headlined "Larry Gay? Of Course He Was" appeared in *The Daily Mail Online* (1 March 2006) and his piece on the Sotheby's VL sale in *The Daily Mail* (30 August 2017). Sarah Miles on the Olivier/Kaye friendship (p. 318) appeared in *Serves Me Right*, (p. 228). The *Damn You, Scarlett O'Hara* section on an alleged Kaye/Olivier affair appears on p. 320. Rosa Ainley's *22 Ennerdale Drive* refers to the reaction to Coleman's hypothesis (pp. 320–1). All the Ainley letters to LO are in LOA. The relevant section of Holden's revised biography, *Laurence Olivier* (Max Press, 2007) appears on pp. 455–63. Joan Plowright's remarks (p. 322) are in *And That's Not All* (p. 130). Quayle on the "pact with the devil" (p. 323) is in HV (*op.cit.*, p. 182) and Eileen Beldon's observation (p. 323) appears in a letter to Sir Barry Jackson (Lewis, *op.cit.*, p. 182). Spoto on biography (p. 323) appears in an interview available online (on *The Writers Store*). Michiko Kakutani wrote in *The Death of Truth* (Collins, London, 2018, p. 12).

Select Bibliography

Agate, James, *Ego 7*, Harrap, London, 1945.

Aherne, Brian, *A Proper Job*, Houghton Mifflin, Boston, 1969.

Aumont, Jean-Pierre, *Sun and Shadow: An Autobiography*, W.W. Norton, New York, 1977.

Bacall, Lauren, *Myself*, Knopf, New York, 1978.

Barker, Felix, *The Oliviers*, Hamish Hamilton, London, 1953.

Barrault, Jean-Louis, *Memories for Tomorrow*, Thames & Hudson, London, 1974.

Bean, Kendra, *Vivien Leigh: An Intimate Portrait*, Running Press, Philadelphia & London, 2013.

Beaton, Cecil, *The Happy Years*, Weidenfeld & Nicolson, London, 1972.

—— *The Strenuous Years*, Weidenfeld & Nicolson, London, 1973.

Beckett, Francis, *Olivier*, London, Hans Publishing, 2005.

Behlmer, Rudy (Ed.), *Memo from David O. Selznick*, Macmillan, London, 1972.

Behrman, S.N., *Tribulations and Laughter*, Hamish Hamilton, London, 1972.

Billington, Michael, *Peggy Ashcroft*, John Murray, London, 1988.

Blakelock, Denys, *Round the Next Corner*, Gollancz, London, 1967.

Blakemore, Michael, *Arguments with England*, Faber & Faber, London, 2004.

Bloom, Claire, *Limelight and After: the Education of an Actress*, Harper & Row, New York, 1982.

Braden, Bernard, *The Kindness of Strangers*, Hodder & Stoughton, London, 1990.

Callow Simon, *Charles Laughton*, Methuen, London, 1984.

Clark, Colin, *The Prince, the Showgirl and Me*, Harper Collins, London, 1995.

Croall, Jonathan, *John Gielgud: A Theatrical Life*, Methuen, London, 2000.

—— *Sybil Thorndike*, Haus Books, London, 2008.

Cole, Toby & Helen Krich Chinoy, *Actors on Acting*, Crown, New York, 1977.

Coleman, Terry, *Olivier*, Bloomsbury, London, 2005.

Collins, Joan, *Past Imperfect*, Simon & Schuster, New York, 1984.

Cottrell, John, *Laurence Olivier*, Prentice-Hall, New Jersey, 1975.

Day, Barry (Ed.), *Letters of Noël Coward*, Methuen, London, 2007.

Darlow, Michael & Gillian Hodson, *Terence Rattigan: The Man and his Work*, Quartet, London, 1979.

Dean, Basil, *Mind's Eye*, Hutchinson, London, 1973.

Deans, Marjorie, *Meeting at the Sphinx*, Macdonald, London, 1945.

Dent, Alan, *Vivien Leigh, A Bouquet*, Hamish Hamilton, London, 1959.

Dexter, John, *The Honourable Beast*, Nick Hern Books, London, 1992.

Dietz, Howard, *Dancing in the Dark*, Bantam Books, New York, 1976.

Dorney, Kate & Maggie B. Gale (Eds), *Vivien Leigh: Actress and Icon*, Manchester University Press, 2017.

Drake, Fabia, *Blind Fortune*, W.H. Allen, London, 1978.

Dundy, Elaine, *Finch, Bloody Finch*, Michael Joseph, London, 1980.

—— *Life Itself*, Virago, London, 2001.

Edwards, Anne, *Vivien Leigh*, W.H. Allen, London, 1977.

Fairweather, Virginia, *Cry God for Larry*, Calder & Boyars, London, 1981.

Faulkner, Trader, *Peter Finch*, Angus & Robertson, London, 1979.

Finch, Yolande, *Finchy*, Wyndham Books, New York, 1981.

Flamini, Roland, *Scarlett, Rhett and a Cast of Thousands*, Collier Books, New York, 1975.

Gottfried, Martin, *Nobody's Fool: Danny Kaye*, Simon & Schuster, New York, 1994.

Gourlay, Logan (Ed.), *Olivier* Stein & Day, New York, 1974.

Granger, Stewart, *Sparks Fly Upwards*, Granada, London, 1981.

Griffiths, Jay, *Tristimania*, Hamish Hamilton, London, 2016.

Grisson, James, *Follies of God*, Alfred A. Knopf, New York, 2015.

Harper, Sue, *Picturing the Past*, BFI, London, 1994.

Harris, Radie, *Radie's World*, W.H. Allen, London, 1975.

Harrison, Rex, *Rex: An Autobiography*, William Morris & Co, New York, 1975.

Haskell, Molly, *Frankly, My Dear: Gone With the Wind Revisited*, Yale University Press, New Haven and London, 2009.

Heilpern, John, *John Osborne: A Patriot for Us*, Chatto & Windus, London, 2006.

Hirsch, Foster, *Laurence Olivier on Screen*, Twayne Publishers, Boston, 1979.

Hoare, Philip, *Noël Coward*, Sinclair-Stevenson, London, 1995.

Holden, Anthony, *Laurence Olivier*, Weidenfeld & Nicolson, London, 1988.

Jamison, Kay Redfield. *Touched With Fire: Manic-Depressive Illness and the Artistic Temperament*, Simon & Schuster, NY, 1993.

Kakutani, Michiko, *The Death of Truth*, Collins, London, 2018.

Kanfer Stefan, *Somebody: The Reckless Life & Remarkable Career of Marlon Brando*, Faber & Faber, London, 2008.

Kanin, Garson, *Hollywood*, Viking Press, New York, 1974.

Kazan, Elia, *A Life*, André Deutsch, London, 1988.

Kershaw, Robert, *Blood and Champagne: The Life of Robert Capa*, St Martin's Press, New York, 2002.

Kiernan, Thomas, *Sir Larry*, Times Books, New York, 1981.

Korda, Michael, *Charmed Lives: A Family Romance*, Random House, New York, 1979.

—— *Curtain*, Chapmans, London, 1991.

Lahr, John, *Mad Pilgrimage of the Flesh*, Bloomsbury, London, 2015.

Lambert, Gavin, *On Cukor*, W.H. Allen, London, 1973.

Langella, Frank, *Dropped Names*, Harper, New York, 2012.

Lasky, Jesse & Pat Silver, *Love Scene*, Berkeley Books, New York, 1978.

Lejeune, C.A., *Thank You For Having Me*, Hutchinson, London, 1964.

Le Roy, Mervyn, *Take One*, W.H. Allen, London, 1974.

Lesley, Cole, *The Life of Noël Coward*, Jonathan Cape, London, 1976.

Lewis, Roger, *The Real Life of Laurence Olivier*, Century, London, 1996.

Mangan, Richard (Ed.), *Gielgud's Letters*, Weidenfeld & Nicolson, London, 2004.

Mann, William J., *Kate: The Woman Who Was Katharine Hepburn*, Faber & Faber, London, 2006.

Madsen, Axel, *William Wyler*, W.H. Allen, London, 1974.

McGilligan, Patrick, *George Cukor: A Double Life*, St Martin's Press, New York, 1992.

Miles, Sarah, *Serves Me Right*, Macmillan, London, 1994.

Miller, Arthur, *Timebends*, Methuen, London, 1988.

More, Kenneth, *More Or Less*, Hodder & Stoughton, London, 1978.

Morley, Sheridan, *A Talent to Amuse*, Heinemann, London, 1975.

────── *John Gielgud: The Authorised Biography*, Hodder & Stoughton, London, 2001.

Mosel, Tad, *Leading Lady*, Little Brown & Co, Boston, 1978.

Munn, Michael, *Lord Larry*, Robson Books, London, 2007.

Niven, David, *Bring On The Empty Horses*, G.P. Putnam's & Sons, New York, 1975.

O'Connor, Garry, *Darlings of The Gods*, Hodder & Stoughton, London, 1984.

Olivier, Laurence, *Confessions of An Actor*, Weidenfeld & Nicolson, London, 1982.

Olivier, Tarquin, *My Father, Laurence Olivier*, BCA, London, 1992.

Osborne, John, *Almost A Gentleman*, Faber & Faber, London, 1991.

────── *Damn You, England*, Faber & Faber, London, 1994.

Payn, Graham, *My Life With Noël Coward*, Applause Books, New York, 1994.

Peters, Margot, *Design For Living: Alfred Lunt and Lynn Fontanne*, Alfred A. Knopf, New York, 2003.

Phipps, Sally, *Molly Keane: A Life*, Virago, London, 2017.

Plowright, Joan, *And That's Not All*, Weidenfeld & Nicolson, London, 2001.

Porter, Darwin and Moseley, Roy, *Damn You, Scarlett O'Hara*, Blood Moon Productions, New York, 2011.

Quayle, Anthony, *A Time To Speak*, Barrie & Jenkins, London, 1990.

Redgrave, Michael, *In My Mind's Eye*, Weidenfeld & Nicolson, London, 1983.

Richardson, Tony, *Long Distance Runner*, Faber & Faber, London, 1993.

Robyns, Gwen, *Light of a Star*, Leslie Frewin, London, 1968.

Salter, Elizabeth, *Helpmann*, Angus & Robertson, Sussex, 1978.

Schickel, Richard, *Elia Kazan*, Harper Collins, New York, 2005.

Sebba, Anne, *Enid Bagnold*, Weidenfeld & Nicolson, London, 1986.

Selznick, Irene Mayer, *A Private View*, Weidenfeld & Nicolson, London, 1983.

Shellard, Dominic, *Kenneth Tynan: A Life*, Yale University Press, New Haven and London, 2003.

Sherriff, R.C., *No Leading Lady*, Gollancz, London, 1968.

Signoret, Simone, *Nostalgia Isn't What It Used To Be*, Grafton Books, London, 1986.

Spoto, Donald, *Laurence Olivier*, Harper Collins, London, 1991.

Staggs, Sam, *When Blanche Met Stanley*, St Martin's Press, New York, 2005.

Stephens, Robert with Coveney, Michael, *Knight Errant*, Hodder & Stoughton, London, 1996.

Strachan, Alan, *Secret Dreams: A Biography of Michael Redgrave*, Weidenfeld & Nicolson, London, 2004.

Sweet, Matthew *Shepperton, Babylon: The Lost Worlds of British Cinema*, Faber & Faber, London, 2005.

Tabori, Paul, *Alexander Korda*, Living Books, New York, 1966.

Taylor, Helen, *Scarlett's Women*, Virago, London, 1989.

—— *Gone With the Wind*, BFI, London, 2015.

Taylor, John Russell, *Vivien Leigh*, Elm Tree Books, London, 1984.

Todd, Ann, *The Eighth Veil*, G.P. Putnam's Sons, New York, 1981.

Trewin, J.C., *Peter Brook*, Macdonald, London, 1971.

Tynan, Kathleen, *The Life of Kenneth Tynan*, Methuen, London, 1988.

Tynan, Kenneth, *He That Plays the King*, Longmans, London, 1950.

—— *Curtains*, Longmans, London, 1961.

—— *Letters* (Ed. Kathleen Tynan), Weidenfeld & Nicolson, London, 1994.

—— *Diaries* (Ed. John Lahr), Bloomsbury, London, 2001.

Vickers, Hugo, *Cecil Beaton, A Biography*, Weidenfeld & Nicolson, London, 1985.

—— *Vivien Leigh*, Hamish Hamilton, London, 1988.

Walker, Alexander, *Vivien*, Weidenfeld & Nicolson, London, 1987.

—— *Hollywood, UK*, Stein & Day, New York, 1974.

Walton, Susana, *William Walton Behind the Façade*, Oxford University Press, Oxford, 1988.

Williams, Tennessee, *Memoirs*, Doubleday & Co, New York, 1975.

—— *Letters*, 1945–57 (Ed. Albert J. Devlin and Nancy M. Tischler), Oberon Books, London, 2006.

Williamson, Audrey *Old Vic Drama No. 2*, Rockliff, London, 1957.

Wilson, John C., *Noël, Tallulah, Cole and Me*, Rowman & Littlefield, Lanham, 2015.

Winn, Godfrey, *The Positive Hour*, Michael Joseph, London, 1970.

Wood, Alan, *Mr. Rank*, Hodder & Stoughton, London, 1952.

Woodhouse, Adrian, *Angus McBean, Face-Maker*, Alma Books, Richmond, Surrey, 2006.

Ziegler, Philip, *Laurence Olivier*, Maclehose, London, 2013.

An extensive amount of Vivien Leigh-related material is available online, including various documentaries on her life and on the making of *Gone With the Wind*. The many websites devoted to her and to Olivier are of variable quality; the best – informative and reliable – is vivandlarry.com.

Index